ANTHEM

A Light unto My Path:
A Devotion from Luther's Writings for Every Day of the Year

Martin Luther

Trans. John Henry Lenker

With Contributions from the ANTHEM editorial team

ANTHEM PUBLISHING
A Division of re:SOURCE DIGITAL PUBLISHING
Formatted and Printed in the United States of America
Digital edition also available.
ISBN: 9798553381943

TABLE OF CONTENTS

Preface iv

I. January 2

II. February 43

III. March 83

IV. April 126

V. May 167

VI. June 211

VII. July 252

VIII. August 293

IX. September 336

X. October 376

XI. November 419

XII. December 461

PREFACE

The aim of these selections is twofold. In the first place they are intended to furnish a text for every day of the year with comments of Luther on the main thought or thoughts of the text, and thus supply a short devotional reading for every day of the year.

The second aim is to introduce Luther to a larger circle of English readers. Luther and his work are not known in this country as they should be. America does not realize what an inheritance she has received from Luther and the Lutheran Reformation. The best way to understand Luther is to have Luther himself speak. His writings are so extensive that there is no trouble in finding something profitable for almost every occasion and condition in life.

These selections have been made chiefly from Luther's sermons and devotional writings. Most of them have been selected from the English translation of a large portion of Luther's Works by the direction and under the supervision of Rev. John N. Lenker, D. D., Minneapolis, Minnesota, and edited by him. Some of the selections have been translated directly from the German by the writer. This work of Dr. Lenker is a great undertaking and should be encouraged by the Lutheran Church in America. Luther will never be understood from mere quotations and selections. His works must be read and studied in their entirety.

There was no difficulty in finding good selections, but frequently it was no easy matter to decide which was the best among a number of very good ones. We often read and reread many pages before deciding upon a selection.

Luther is original and frequently uses very forcible language. The translator finds it no easy matter to make Luther speak good English. His terse and idiomatic German is very forcible and loses in the translation. Luther was only a man, but in mental power and capacity he towered head and shoulders above ordinary men. His comprehensive and penetrating mind often takes in the whole situation and comes to a conclusion at a bound, when other men need to reason step by step to attain the same result. His words occasionally appear vague and enigmatic, but on reading farther his meaning becomes clear and is found to be forcible and even beautiful.

Because Luther sometimes says things in a way that is grating to our sensitive modern ears, we hastily put him aside as vague, harsh and uncouth. But a little patient Christian thinking will soon find great and important truths most forcibly and beautifully set forth. We should always remember that Luther spoke and wrote in the first half of the sixteenth century, when powerful remedies were necessary to cure existing evils.

With Luther the Word of God, or the Holy Scriptures, is everything. When there is a sure word of Scripture there is no yielding in Luther; he could have no patience with the man who denied or perverted God's Word. With the Word he stands and falls.

"The Word they still shall let remain And not a thank have for it."

That Luther and the Lutheran Reformation may be better understood and appreciated is one of the aims of this book, but not the prime and chiefest. That the Holy Scriptures may be better understood, and that men and women, young and old, may be brought to Christ and find comfort and consolation in their Christian faith, this is the chief aim of these pages. That this object may be attained it will be necessary that the book becomes a daily companion. So much time should be set aside each day as is required for the reading of one of the meditations. The Scripture passage should be carefully and thoughtfully read, then read the comments which follow. After that confess your Christian faith in the words of the Apostles' Creed and pray the Lord's Prayer. The whole exercise will not require much over five minutes, but will be most wholesome for your Christian faith and comfort. Surely every Christian family should be able to devote so much time to the nourishment of their souls and to spiritual communication with their God and Saviour. No man or woman is so busy but that every morning or evening five minutes can be spared for such Christian devotion.

With the earnest wish and prayer that many may be brought to a clearer conception of their Christian faith, walk closer with their God and find comfort and consolation by means of this book, it is earnestly commended to all who are interested in their soul's welfare, and especially to those of the Lutheran Confession of Faith.

JOHN SANDER.

Luther's Birthday, 1914.

Lindstrom, Minn.

ANTHEM PUBLISHING

A Light unto My Path:
A Devotion from Luther's Writings for Every Day of the Year

Martin Luther

Trans. John Henry Lenker

"With Luther the Word of God, or the Holy Scriptures, is everything. With the Word he stands or falls."

—Rev. John Sander

January 1st - Luke 2:21

When eight days were accomplished for the circumcising of the child, his name was called Jesus, which was so named of the angel before he was conceived in the womb.

Circumcision was an external mark of God's people, by which they were distinguished from other nations. God has never left his people without a mark or a sign, by which the world may know where his people are to be found. The Jews were known by circumcision, that was their divine mark. Our mark is baptism and the body of Christ. Where there is baptism, there are Christians, wherever they are in the world.

All this is immeasurably above and contrary to reason. If Abraham had followed reason he would not have believed that it was God who demanded circumcision. To our (natural) eyes it is such a foolish thing that there can scarcely be anything more absurd. The Jews had to endure great infamy and disgrace on account of it. But such are all God's works and commandments, in order that haughty reason, which would be clever and wise, may be put to shame, may surrender its self-conceit and submit to God, and believe that whatever he appoints is most useful, honorable and wise. Thus we have baptism in the New Testament in order that we should cling to it in faith and believe that we are thereby cleansed from sin and saved. So the works and words of God are contrary to reason, and reason, in turn, is contrary to God and recoils at the signs that it speaks against. In all this God seeks to bring man's reason into control and make it subject to divine truth.

It was customary to give the child its name in circumcision, as we see here and in the case of John the Baptist. His name is rightly called Jesus, that is, Saviour, "for he shall save his people from their sins." This comes to pass through faith, so that the naming of children signifies that by faith they have a name and are known to God. We are called Christians because of him, are God's children and have the superabundant riches because of his goodness, so that our hearts may be free, joyous, peaceable and unterrified.

January 2nd - Ephesians 2:8, 9

By grace are you saved through faith; and that not of yourselves: it is the gift of God: not of works, lest any man should boast.

God does not condemn or save any individual on account of his works. This is not the fault of our works, but of our nature. The person, nature and entire existence are corrupt in us because of Adam's fall. Therefore no work can be good in us, until our nature and personal life is changed and renewed. The tree is not good, therefore the fruits are bad. No one can become righteous by works or laws; all works and efforts to become righteous and be saved are in vain as long as the nature and the person are not renewed. God will have us clearly understand that the fault lies entirely in the state of our nature, that its birth and origin are corrupt and sinful. This is original sin, or the sin of the nature, or the sin of the person, the real, chief sin. If this sin did not exist there would be no actual sin. This sin is not committed like other sins; but it exists, lives, and commits all other sins, it is the essential sin, that sins not for an hour or a season, but wherever the person is and as long as he lives.

God looks at this sin of the nature alone. This can be eradicated by no law, by no punishment; the grace of God alone, which makes the nature pure and new, must purge it away. The law only makes it manifest and teaches how to recognize it, but does not save from it; the law only restrains the hand or member, it cannot restrain the person and nature from being sinful. Just as little as it lies in one's power to be born and to receive natural existence, so little does it lie in his power to be without sin or to escape from it. He who created us must take it away. Therefore he first gives the law, by which man recognizes this sin and thirsts for grace; then he also gives the gospel and saves him.

January 3rd - Hebrews 1:5

For unto which of the angels said he at any time, you are my son, this day have I begotten you?

These words are a quotation from the second Psalm. We see that the reference here is plainly to Christ, against whom the Jews raged with Pilate, Herod and the chief priests. To Christ God says, "You are my Son." The Jews endeavor to evade this passage of the apostle. Unable to deny that the Psalm refers to a coming king and an anointed one, they assert that the allusion is to David, who was also a Christ. For they designate all kings "Messiahs" or "Christs," that is, anointed ones. But their interpretation will not hold. David never inherited the heathen, nor did the kingdom extend to the uttermost parts of the earth, as recorded of the king mentioned in the Psalm. To no man is it anywhere said in the Scriptures, "You are my Son."

Even when the Jews admit that the allusion of the Psalm is to the Messiah, they resort to two evasions. They maintain that he is yet to come, that Jesus Christ is not the Messiah; and that although called the son of God, he is not God. How shall we reply to them? In the first place we have the testimony of experience that Jesus is he of whom the Psalm speaks; in Christ the prophecy is fulfilled and has become history. He was persecuted by kings and rulers. They sought to destroy him and only brought derision upon themselves in the attempt. They were themselves destroyed, as the Psalm says. Throughout the world Christ is recognized as Lord. No king, before or since, has ruled or can rule in equal extent. The apostle's reasoning, based on the fact that nowhere is it said to any angel, much less to any man, "You are my Son," sufficiently proves that Christ is God. He must be particularly God's Son, having a relation not shared by men and angels. That God does not include him among other sons but especially distinguishes him, indicates his superiority. He cannot be superior to angels without being true God, for angels are the highest order of beings. The apostle lays so much stress upon Scriptural authority that we are under no obligations to accept anything the Bible does not assert. Be certain you have full Scripture authority for all you accept. In all things not found in the Scriptures, ask as does the apostle here, "When did God ever assert it?"

January 4th - Galatians 3:26

You are all children of God by faith in Christ Jesus.

He who is under the law and works unwillingly is a servant. But whosoever has faith and works cheerfully is a child; for he has received the Spirit of God through Christ. Now, the apostle names Christ, referring to the faith that believes and abides in Jesus Christ. No other faith is effective, no other faith is the right faith, let one believe in God as one will. Some there are, particularly among our modern scholars, who say: Forgiveness of sins and justification depend altogether on the divine imputation of grace; God's imputation is sufficient. He to whom God does not reckon sin, is justified; he to whom God reckons sin, is not justified.

Were their theory true the entire New Testament would be of no significance. Christ would have labored foolishly and to no purpose in suffering for sin. God would have unnecessarily wrought mere mockery and deception; for he might easily without Christ's suffering have forgiven sins. Then, too, a faith other than faith in Christ might have justified and saved—a faith relying on God's gracious mercy not to impute sin. In contrast to this deplorable theory and abominable error, it is the apostles practice to speak always of faith in Jesus Christ, and he makes mention of Jesus Christ with a frequency surprising to one unacquainted with the important doctrine of faith in him. Hence our learned university doctors no longer know Christ. They do not recognize the need of him and his benefits, nor understand the character of the gospel and the New Testament. They imagine Christ to be a mere Moses—a teacher who institutes laws and commandments showing how men may be righteous and lead a faultless life. Then they proceed with free will and the workings of human nature, designing thereby to fit themselves for grace, and basely storm heaven.

Let us guard against the hellish poison of this false doctrine and not lose Christ, the consoling Saviour. Grace is given us gratuitously—without cost to ourselves—and yet the gift to us did cost another much and was obtained with a priceless, an infinite treasure—the Son of God himself. It is supremely essential to possess him who has accomplished the purchase for us. Nor is it possible to obtain grace otherwise than through him.

January 5th - Isaiah 60:1

Arise, shine; for your light is come, and the glory of the Lord is risen upon you.

We have frequently spoken of the little word glory. It means honor, brightness, splendor. The gospel is simply a grand report, a message, having its origin in a glorious reality; it is not a mere empty proclamation. A glorious being is to be compared to a sun or a light. The sun is a fountain of light, and its luster is its glory, the diffusion, the distinction of that light.

The gospel is God's glory and our light. It is our light in that it is the medium whereby his work is proclaimed, extolled, recognized and honored throughout the whole world. The gospel is not the actual brightness of the light, nor is it the light itself. It is the rising of the brightness, the approaching of the light. It is simply a manifestation of the light and brightness which existed from eternity. "In him was life, and the life was the light of men." The light did not arise, nor was it openly manifested, except through the gospel. Therefore the gospel is an expression of divine brightness and glory.

It is called gospel—good message—because it reveals and proclaims divine blessings, divine glory, and divine honor or brightness. What is the brightness but the great and glorious riches of his goodness and grace poured out upon us? How has grace appeared? Through the preaching of the gospel. The light and the glory are God himself. Christ says, "I am the light." It is plain that Isaiah is not here speaking of the rising of Christ in the sense of his coming birth. He refers to the rising of the gospel after Christ's ascension. Through the gospel Christ is spiritually risen and glorified in the hearts of believers, bringing them salvation.

January 6th - Matthew 2:1, 2

There came wise men from the east to Jerusalem, saying, Where is he that is born king of the Jews? for we have seen his star in the east, and are come to worship him.

How these wise men could see in this star a sign that unmistakably signified a new-born king, I do not know. Perhaps they read in their histories and chronicles that before the birth of other kings had been signified in the heavens by a star. They knew very well that the Jews were the chosen people of God, who were and had been especially favored of God above all other people. As this was such a beautiful star they likely thought that God had given this people a new king. Perhaps they knew all by divine revelation.

At first these wise men did not regard this king as God, but took him for a temporal king. They came to Jerusalem, the capital city, hoping to find him amid the splendor of the king's palace. For the star, which they saw over the country of the Jews at their home in the east, must have disappeared as they did not see it on their journey until they proceeded from Jerusalem to Bethlehem. So they also worshiped him after the manner of those eastern countries and not as though they considered him God. They did not concern themselves about what this king would be in the future, or what would happen to him. They only ask where he is to be found.

But, my dear hearer, it does not matter much whether you know all about the arts of nature and the wisdom of the world. Be satisfied with what your experience and common sense teach you. It is enough for you to know that in the summer other work must be done than in the winter; that you know how to attend to your farm, stock, home and children. Beyond this think only how you may know Christ. He will teach you how you may know yourself, who you are, and what power abides in you. Then you will know God and yourself, which the masters of the arts of nature and the wisdom of this world do not learn.

January 7th - Isaiah 60:1

Arise, shine; for your light is come, and the glory of the Lord is risen upon you.

We learn from our text what the gospel is, and what is its message. It is the coming of light, the rising of divine glory. It speaks only of divine glory, divine honor and fame. It exalts only the work of God—his goodness and grace toward us. It teaches the necessity of our receiving God's work for us, his grace and goodness, even God himself, if we would secure salvation. The gospel produces in us a twofold effect. First, it rejects our natural reason, our human light. Had we within ourselves light instead of darkness, it would not be necessary for God to send the light to rise upon us. This text forcibly expels and severely condemns all natural wisdom, all human reason; these are absolute darkness, therefore it is necessary for the light to come. So we should guard against all human doctrines and the conceits of reason as darkness, rejected and condemned of God; we should awake and arise to behold this light, and follow it alone.

The gospel casts down all the glory and pride of our own works. We cannot draw comfort nor derive honor from them. If there were in us anything worthy of honor and glory, the divine honor and glory would rise in us to no purpose. Men may, it is true, have their own nature and their self-righteousness, and from these derive temporal honor, praise and glory before their fellows as though they were no sinners. But before God they are sinful, destitute of glory and unable to boast of possessing him and his blessings.

No one can be saved unless he have within himself the glory of God and be able to comfort himself solely with God and his blessings and to glory in these. So the gospel condemns all our efforts and exalts only the goodness and the grace of God, and therefore God himself. It permits us to console ourselves only with him and to glory in no other.

January 8th - Romans 13:10

Love is the fulfilling of the law.

We must properly distinguish between faith and love. Faith deals with the heart and love with works. Faith removes our sins, renders us acceptable, justifies us. Being accepted and justified in person, we have love imparted to us by the Holy

Spirit, and we delight in doing good. It is the nature of the law to attack our person and demand good works; and it will not cease its demands until it gains its purpose. We cannot do good works without the spirit of love. The law constrains us to know our imperfections, and to recognize the necessity of becoming altogether different individuals, so that we may satisfy the law. The law does not exact so much of the heart as it does of works; in fact, it demands nothing but works and ignores the heart. It causes the individual to see that he must become an entirely different person. But faith, when it comes, creates a nature capable of accomplishing the works which the law demands.

It cannot in every case be said that faith fulfils the law. It, however, prepares the way and enables us to fulfil its demands. The law constrains us—teaches us that we must be changed before we can accomplish its works; it makes us conscious of our inability to fulfil it. On the other hand, love and works do not change or justify us. Our love and our works are evidence of justification and of a change, since these are impossible until the individual is free from sin and made righteous.

This explanation is given to enable us to perceive the true nature of the law, of faith and of love; to ascribe to each its own mission; and rightly to understand the Scripture declarations in their harmonious relations, namely, that while faith justifies, it does not fulfil the law, and that while love does not justify, it does fulfil the law.

January 9th - Romans 13:8

Owe no man anything, but to love one another: for he that loves another has fulfilled the law.

Legal obligations make us debtors to men, as, for example, when one individual has a claim upon another for debt. The duties and tribute, the obedience and honor we owe to political government are also of this legal character. Though personally these things are not essential to the Christian—they do not justify him or make him righteous—yet, because he must live here on earth, he is under obligation, so far as outward conduct is concerned, to put himself on a level with other men in these things, and generally help maintain temporal order and peace. Christ paid tribute money as a debt, notwithstanding he had told Peter he was under no obligation to do so.

Another obligation is love, when a Christian voluntarily makes himself a servant of all men. Paul says: "Though I was free from all men, I made myself servant unto all, that I might gain the more." This is not a requirement of human laws; no one who fails in this duty is censured or punished for neglect of the obligation to submit to and serve a fellow man. This fact is very apparent. Let one have wealth, and as long as he refrains from appropriating his neighbor's goods, sullying his honor or injuring his person, he is, in the eyes of the law, righteous. Laws made for restraint of the outward conduct are directed only against evil works, which they prohibit and punish. Good works are left to voluntary performance. Civil law does not extort them by threats and punishments, but commends and rewards them, as does the Law of Moses.

Paul would teach Christians so to conduct themselves toward men and civil authority as to give no occasion for complaint. He would not have them fail to satisfy the claims of legal obligation, but rather to go beyond its requirements, making themselves debtors voluntarily to those who have no claim on them.

January 10th - Romans 12:1

I beseech you therefore, brethren, by the mercies of God, that you present your bodies a living sacrifice, holy, acceptable unto God, which is your reasonable service.

Paul is preaching to those Christians already godly by faith, who are not to be restrained by commandment, but to be admonished. The object is to secure voluntary renunciation of their sinful nature. A preacher of grace persuades and incites by calling attention to the goodness and mercy of God. The latter does not desire works prompted by an unwilling spirit, nor service that is not the expression of a cheerful heart. He desires that a joyous and willing spirit shall incite to his service.

Paul makes use of three words, "living," "holy," "acceptable," to teach that the sacrifices of the Old Testament are repealed. They consisted of bullocks, sheep and goats. The life of these was not spared. They were slain, burned and consumed. But the New Testament sacrifice is a wonderful offering. Though slain, it still lives.

The word "living" has reference to spiritual and not to temporal life. He who keeps his body in subjection and mortifies its lusts does not live to the world; he does not lead the life of the world. The Christian is bodily in the world, but he does not live after the flesh. Such a life is, before God, eternal and a true, living sacrifice. None of the Old Testament sacrifices were "holy," except in an external and temporal sense, but the living sacrifice is holy before God, is designed for the service of God and employed in his honor. They who render this living, holy sacrifice are happy and assured of their acceptance with God.

This our reasonable service is rightly called a spiritual service of the heart, performed in the faith and knowledge of God. Paul rejects all service not performed in faith as entirely unreasonable, even if it has the appearance of spiritual life and of great holiness.

January 11th - Luke 2:48

His mother said unto him, Son, why have you so dealt with us? behold, your father and I have sought you sorrowing.

The holy Virgin was a real martyr for three days, and these days were harder for her than was the external pain of martyrdom to other saints. She had had such anxiety on her Son's account that she could not have suffered any more bitter pain. For that is the greatest torture and woe, when the heart is attacked and tortured. That is only half-suffering when the body alone is afflicted, but when the heart is compelled to endure suffering, only great and noble spirits, with special grace and strength, are able to endure it. But why does God permit these afflictions to come upon his loved ones?

First, that he may guard his own against presumption; that great saints, who have received special grace and gifts from God, may not presume to depend upon themselves.

For if they should at all times be strong in spirit and experience only joy and pleasure, they might finally fall into the fatal pride of the devil, which despises God and trusts in self. Thus God keeps them in humility, so that they do not become proud and carnally secure in regard to their faith and holiness, as Peter did, when he boasted his willingness to lay down his life for Christ.

Secondly, God permits his saints to suffer these trials as an example to others, to alarm the carnally secure and to comfort the timid and alarmed. The wicked and impenitent may learn from this how to amend their ways, keep themselves from sin, since they can see that God deals even with the saints in a way to produce anxiety. Such examples are intended to serve as a means of comfort to alarmed and anxious consciences, when they see that God has not only attacked them, but also the most exalted saints and permitted them to suffer the same trials and anxieties.

Thirdly, God does this that he may teach his saints to prepare themselves to find Christ and keep him. Mary and Joseph sought the child Jesus for three days without finding him either in Jerusalem or among their friends and acquaintances, until they came to the temple where he sat among the teachers and where the Scriptures and God's Word are studied.

January 12th - Romans 12:14

Bless them which persecute you: bless, and curse not.

The apostle reminds us that we are to conduct ourselves in a Christian manner toward our persecutors, who, to a great extent, are to blame for the distress of the saints. It is well to observe that we are not merely advised, but commanded, to love our enemies, to do them good and to speak well of them; such is the fruit of the Spirit. To "bless" our persecutors means to desire only good for them in body and soul. It is inconsistent for a Christian to curse even his most bitter enemy or an evildoer; for he is commanded to bear the gospel upon his liPsalm The dove did not bring a poisonous branch or a thistle sprig to Noah in the ark; she brought an olive leaf in her mouth. So the gospel is simply a gracious, blessed, glad and healing word. It brings only blessing and grace to the whole world. No curse, only pure lips of blessing and not of cursing. If they curse they are not the lips of a Christian.

It is necessary, however, to distinguish between cursing and censuring or reproving. Reproof and punishment greatly differ from cursing and malediction. To curse means to invoke evil, while censuring carries the thought of displeasure at existing evil, and an effort to remove it. In fact, cursing and censuring are opposed to each other. Christ himself censured, or reproved. He called the Jews a generation of vipers, children of the devil, hypocrites, blind dolts, liars and the like. He did not curse them to perpetuate their evils; he rather desired the evils removed.

But the strong argument is urged that the saints of the Scriptures not only censured, but cursed. Jacob cursed his sons, Reuben, Simeon and Levi. A great part of the Law of Moses is made up of curses. What shall we say to these things? We answer: Without the Spirit's direction, no one can rightly understand and imitate such examples of cursing. When the devil, through his followers, resists and obstructs the Word of God—the channel of blessing—the blessing is impeded, and in God's sight a curse rests upon the blessing. Then it is the office of faith to come out with a curse, desiring the removal of the obstruction that God's blessing may be unhindered.

January 13th - Luke 2:33

Joseph and his mother marvelled at those things which were spoken of him.

What are the marvelous things spoken of him? They are the things of which Simeon had spoken immediately before, when in the temple he took the child Jesus upon his arms, saying: "Lord, now lettest me your servant depart in peace, according to your word; for mine eyes have seen your salvation, which you have prepared before the face of all people; a light to lighten the Gentiles, and the glory of your people Israel." They marveled that this aged and holy man stood there before them in the temple, took the child in his arms and spoke of him so exultingly, calling him the light of the world, a Saviour of all nations, a glory of all the people of Israel.

It must indeed excite wonder that such things were proclaimed openly by Simeon in that public and sacred place with reference to that poor and insignificant child, whose mother was so humble and lowly and whose father Joseph was not wealthy. How could such a child be considered the Saviour of all men, the light of the Gentiles, and the glory and honor of all Israel? At present, after we have had so many proofs of Christ's greatness, these words no longer seem so wonderful; but then, when nothing as yet was known of Jesus, they were indeed marvelous. Joseph and Mary believed them nevertheless, and on that very account they marveled. If they had not believed them, the words of Simeon would have appeared insignificant to them and not at all wonderful.

If Joseph and Mary had judged according to the outward appearances, they would have considered Christ no more than any other poor child. But they disregard the outward appearance and cling to the words of Simeon with a firm faith, therefore they marvel at his speech. Thus we must also disregard all the senses when contemplating the works of God, and only cling to his words, that our eyes and our senses may not offend us. The fact that they marveled at the words of Simeon is also to teach us that the Word of God is never preached in vain. The Word of God must produce results, even if there are only a few who believe it. There are always some who receive it with joy and admiration.

January 4th - 1 Peter 2:5

Ye also, as lively stones, are built up a spiritual house, an holy priesthood, to offer up spiritual sacrifices, acceptable to God by Jesus Christ.

The whole world regards the priest's office—his service and his dignity—as representing the acme of nobility and exaltation; and so it truly is. If anyone would be a priest and exalted before God, let him set about the work of offering up his body to God; in other words, let him be humble, let him be nothing in the eyes of the world.

I will let every man decide for himself the difference between the outward priesthood of dazzling character and the internal, spiritual priesthood. The first is confined to a very few individuals; the second Christians commonly share. One was ordained of men, independently of the Word of God; the other was established through the Word, irrespective of human devices. In that, the skin is besmeared with material oil; in this, the heart is internally anointed with the Holy Spirit. That applauds and extols its works; this proclaims and magnifies the grace of God, and his glory. In fact, the two priesthoods accord about as well as Christ and Barabbas, as light and darkness, as God and the world. The Christian priesthood will not admit of appointment. The priest is not made. He must be born a priest and inherit his office. I refer to the new birth—the birth of water and the spirit. Thus all Christians become priests, children of God and co-heirs with Christ the Most High Priest.

Men generally consider the title of priest glorious and honorable; but the duties and the sacrifices of the office are rarely acceptable. The Christian priesthood costs life, property, honor, friends and all worldly things; all this is to be endured, not for the profit of oneself, but for the benefit of his neighbor and for the honor and glory of God. For so Christ offered up his body. This priesthood is glorious. The suffering and work of Christ is to be viewed as grace bestowed on us, a blessing conferred, requiring the exercise of faith and our acceptance of the salvation offered; then also, as an example for us to follow. We are to offer up ourselves for our neighbor's benefit and for the honor of God. He who so does is a Christian. This is what Peter calls offering sacrifices acceptable to God by Christ.

January 15th - Luke 2:34

And Simeon blessed them.

This blessing means nothing except that he wished them happiness and joy, honor and all prosperity. This blessing seems to be a useless and trivial matter, for people generally do this and wish each other all that is good. But to bless Christ and his parents is a great and exceptional deed, for the reason that Christ and our nature are entirely opposed to each other. Christ condemns all that the world elects, gives us the cross to bear and to suffer all evil, deprives the world of its pleasures, possessions and honors, and teaches that men deal in those things which are altogether foolish and sinful. Then they begin to blaspheme and persecute Christ and his disciples; the whole world is full of those who curse him and wish him all evil, disgrace and misfortune, and there are only a few who really bless him.

There are indeed some who praise him, because he does what they desire and leaves them as they are. When, however, he begins to be Christ to them and they are required to forsake their works and to let him alone dwell within them, they flee and blaspheme. There are also some who believe that, if they were to see the infant Christ with his mother before them, as did Simeon, they would also joyously bless him. But they would certainly stumble at his childhood, poverty and contemptible appearance. They prove it by disregarding, hating and persecuting such poverty and humble appearance in Christ's members, although they might still find Christ, their head, among them daily. If they then shun the cross and hate its contemptible appearance, they would certainly do the same thing if they were to see him with their eyes. But Simeon was of a different mind. Outward appearance did not cause him to stumble, and therefore he does not bless Christ alone, but also his father and mother.

Thus, in blessing the child, Simeon as a preacher and lover of the cross and an enemy of the world, gives a remarkable example of exalting and honoring Christ, who was then despised, cursed and rejected in his own person. He is even now treated in the same manner in his members, who for his sake endure poverty, disgrace, death and ignominy; yet no one will come to their relief, receive and bless them.

January 16th - Romans 12:2

Be not conformed to this world: but be you transformed by the renewing of your mind, that you may prove what is that good, and acceptable, and perfect will of God.

We must be careful to follow neither the customs of the world nor our own reason or plausible theories. We must constantly subdue our disposition and control our will, not obeying the dictates of reason and desire. We are always to conduct ourselves in a manner unlike the way of the world. Thus we shall be daily changed or renewed in our minds. That is, we come each day to place greater value on the things condemned by the world. The mind of the world is altogether unlike the Christian's mind. It not only continues unchanged and unrenewed in its old disposition, but is obdurate and extremely stubborn.

God's will is ever good and perfect, ever gracious; but it is not at all times so regarded of men. Indeed, human reason imagines it to be evil, unfriendly, abominable, because what reason esteems highest, best and holiest, God's will regards as nothing, as worthy of death. Therefore, Christian experience must come to the rescue and decide. It must feel and prove, must test and ascertain, whether he is prompted by a sincere and gracious will. He who perseveres and learns to know himself in this way will go forward in his experience, finding God's will so gracious and pleasing that he would not exchange it for all the world's wealth. He will discover that acceptance of God's will affords him more happiness, even in poverty, disgrace and adversity, than is the lot of any person in the midst of earthly honors and pleasures. He will finally arrive at a degree of perfection making him inclined to exchange life for death, and with Paul to desire to depart that sin may no more live in him, and that the will of God may be done perfectly in himself in every relation. Paul, however, does not consider the Christian absolutely free from sin. Where transformation and renewal are necessary, something of the old and sinful nature ever remains. This is not imputed to Christians, because they daily endeavor to effect transformation and renovation.

January 17th - Luke 2:34

And Simeon blessed them, and said unto Mary his mother, Behold, this child is set for the fall and rising of many in Israel; and for a sign which shall be spoken against.

Why does not Simeon say this to the father also? Because Jesus was her own child, and all that happened to him naturally happened also to her and caused her real pain. Simeon perhaps also addressed Mary alone for the reason that Joseph was not to live until the time of the suffering of Christ, which the mother would experience alone; and in addition to all this sorrow she was to be a poor and lonely widow, and Christ was to suffer as a poor orphan. Mary lived in all the three states of virginity, of matrimony, and of widowhood, the latter being the most pitiable, without any protection or aid. A virgin has her parents, a wife her husband, but the widow is alone.

Simeon declares that Christ is set for the fall and rising again of many in Israel. Christ, however, is not the cause of the fall, but the presumption of the Jews is the cause. Christ came to be a light and Saviour of all the world, so that all might be justified and saved by faith in him. If this is to be brought about, all other righteousness in ourselves, sought outside of Christ with works, must be rejected. The Jews would not hear of this. Thus they take offense at faith, fall deeper into unbelief and become hardened in their own righteousness, so that they even persecuted with all their might all who believed. All who would be saved by their own righteousness do the same thing. They depend upon their works, and when faith in Christ is demanded they stumble and fall.

Christ had been promised only to the people of Israel by the prophets; and these had announced that many among that people would fall away on account of their self-righteousness. This is indeed a terrible example to us Gentiles, to whom nothing has been promised, but out of pure grace we have unexpectedly been brought into the Kingdom and have risen through Christ. The example of Israel's fall should touch our hearts, that we may not also fall, or perhaps fall more grievously than the Jews and Turks, being seduced by Antichrist and bearing the name of Christ to the dishonor of God and to our own injury.

January 18th - Luke 2:44, 45

They sought him among their kinsfolk and acquaintance. And when they found him not, they turned back again to Jerusalem, seeking him.

Here you see what Mary experienced. Although she is the mother of a child in whom she might have gloried before all mothers, yet you perceive how God deprived her of all happiness. She had reason to fear that God was angry with her and would no longer have her to be the mother of his Son. Only those who have passed through similar experiences will understand what she suffered. Therefore we should apply this example to ourselves, for it was not recorded for her sake, but for our benefit. We should profit by her example and be prepared to bear our sorrow, should a like affliction of losing Christ befall us.

When God vouchsafes to us a strong faith and a firm trust in him, so that we are assured that he is our gracious God and we can depend upon him, then we are in paradise. But when God permits our hearts to be discouraged and we believe he takes from us Christ our Lord; when our conscience feels that we have lost him and amidst trembling and despair our confidence is gone, then we are truly in misery and distress. Even if we are not conscious of any special sin, yet in such a condition we tremble and doubt whether God still cares for us; just as Mary here doubts and knows not whether God still deems her worthy to be the mother of his Son. Only strong minds can endure such temptations, and there are not many people whom God tests to this degree.

God does this especially to guard his children against a twofold danger. First, being strong in their own mind and arrogant, they might ultimately depend upon themselves and believe they are able to accomplish everything in their own strength and become presumptuous and overconfident. Secondly, he wants to give us an example. For if we had no examples of saints who passed through the same experiences we should be unable to bear our trials and would imagine that we alone are thus afflicted. But when we see that Mary and other saints have also suffered we are comforted; for their example shows us that we should patiently wait until God strengthens us.

January 19th - Luke 2:36, 37

There was one Anna, ... she was of a great age and had lived with an husband seven years from her virginity; and she was a widow of about forty years, and departed not from the temple, but served God with fasting and prayers night and day.

Anna lived with a husband seven years, and at this time was a widow of eighty-four years. The number seven is commonly taken to signify our temporal life, because all time is measured by the seven days of the week, which is the first and best standard for the measurement of time. God first created days and appointed seven of them as a definite period of time. Of weeks were made months, and of months years, into which our whole life is divided. These seven years therefore signify the whole course of the temporal life and conduct of the saints of old.

Paul explains that a husband signifies the law. As a woman is bound to her husband while he lives, so all are bound to the law who live under it. Now the law has been given to no people on earth except this Anna, the Jewish people, who were entrusted with the oracles of God. Therefore Anna, who lived seven years with her husband, signifies the people of Israel under the law, in their outward conduct and temporal life.

According to Luke the Holy Spirit shows that this saintly Anna, the holy people of old, was not simply under the law and a bond-servant; she also walked in the freedom of faith and the Spirit. This is signified by the many years of her widowhood, meaning the spiritual life of faith led by the saints of old. For the widowhood signifies freedom from the law. Thus the life under the law and the life of faith existed side by side. As to their souls, the believers of old were justified without the works of the law, alone by faith, and in this respect they were truly widows; but as to their bodies and external conduct, they were subject to the law. They did not believe that they were justified by works, but having been justified by faith, they kept the law voluntarily, cheerfully and to the glory of God. He who lives in this manner may also do the works of the law, for Christ and the apostles also have kept the law. These are the people who at the same time live seven years with a husband and about four score years without a husband, who at the same time are free from the law and yet under the law.

January 20th - Proverbs 10:12

Hatred stirs up strife; but love covers all sins.

Where hatred and enmity dwell in the heart, they must inevitably stir up strife and bring misfortune. Animosity cannot restrain itself. It either bursts out in pernicious language, clandestinely uttered against the object of enmity, or it openly demeans itself in a manner indicating its ill will. Hence follow excessive partying, cursing, quarreling and fighting, and, when wholly unrestrained, cruelty and murder. Hatred has but one desire, namely, that everyone be an enemy to his neighbor and speak the worst about him, and if he hears aught in his neighbor's favor, he puts upon it the very worst construction with the result that the other is embittered and in turn comes to hate, curse and revile. Thus the fire burns until only discord and mischief can obtain.

On the other hand love is virtue pure and precious. It neither utters, nor thinks any evil of its neighbor. It rather covers sin; not one sin, nor two, but a "multitude of sins." Love has no desire to reflect itself in a neighbor's sins and maliciously rejoice in them. It conducts itself as having neither seen, nor heard them. If they cannot be overlooked, it readily forgives, and as far as possible mends matters. Where nothing else can be done, it endures the sins of a neighbor without stirring up strife and making a bad matter worse. Where people dwell together there will be mutual transgressions; it cannot be otherwise. No one will always do what is pleasing to others, and each is liable to commit open wrong. Since men must live together in their respective stations of life, he who would live peaceably must so control himself as to be able to bear with others, to overlook their imperfections, to cover their transgressions and thus avert further resulting evil.

Now if you would live as a Christian and enjoy peace in the world, you must make every effort to restrain your anger and not to give way to revenge. You must suppress these passions, subduing your hatred by love, and be able to overlook and bear, even though you have to suffer great pain and injustice. So doing you will develop a noble character fitted to accomplish much good through patience and humility, to allay and abolish enmity and strife, and thereby to reform and convert others.

January 21st - Luke 2:52

Jesus increased in wisdom and stature, and in favour with God and man.

Some inquisitive people who are not satisfied with the information given in the Scriptures have desired to know what Christ did in his childhood, and have received their reward for their curiosity. Some fool or knave has fabricated a legendary book on the childhood of Christ, and has not been afraid to write down his lies and frauds, relating how Christ went to school and a great deal of absurd and blasphemous tomfoolery. Thus with his lies he jests at the expense of the Lord, whom all the angels adore and fear, and before whom all creatures tremble, so that this rascal would have deserved to have a millstone hanged about his neck and to have been sunk in the depths of the sea, because he did not esteem the Lord of all more than to make him an object of his buffoonery.

Christ never went to school, for no schools like ours existed at that time. He did not even have an elementary education. The Jews marveled, saying: "How knoweth this man letters, having never learned?" Yet they were astonished at his wisdom. They thought it strange that a layman and the son of a carpenter should have such great knowledge, having never studied. Therefore they were offended in him and thought that he must be possessed of an evil spirit. Let us then be satisfied with the narrative of the gospel, which tells us enough of his childhood. Luke writes that he "increased in wisdom and stature." Later on he writes that he was subject to his parents. What else should he have related? He was brought up like other children, with the exception that, as some children excel others in ability, Christ was an extraordinary, clever child. Thus no more could be written concerning him than is recorded by Luke. The time for performing miracles had not yet come.

Some are perplexed by the words of Luke according to which Christ, although he was God, "increased in wisdom and stature." We must understand the words of Luke as applying simply to the human nature of Christ, which was an instrument and temple of the Godhead. As he grew in stature his reason developed, and with the development of his reason he became stronger in the Spirit and filled with wisdom before God, in himself and before men.

January 22nd - Romans 12:6

Let us prophesy according to the proportion of faith.

Prophecy is of two kinds: one is the foretelling of future events, a gift or power possessed by all the prophets under the Old Testament dispensation, and by the apostles; the other is the explanation of the Scriptures. Now, the gospel being the last prophetic message to be delivered previous to the time of judgment, and to predict the events of that period, I presume Paul had reference here simply to that form of prophecy which is the explanation of the Scriptures. This form is common, ever prevails, and is profitable to Christians; the other form is rare. When he says prophecy must be according to the proportion of faith, it is plain enough that he does not refer to the foretelling of future events.

Paul does not attach so much importance to the prediction of future events. Such predictions, though they may gratify the curiosity of men concerning the fate of kings, princes and others of prominence in the world, are unnecessary prophecies under the New Testament dispensation. They neither teach the Christian faith, nor contribute to its strength. Hence this form of prophecy may be regarded among the least of God's gifts. Nay, it sometimes proceeds from the devil. But the ability to explain the Scriptures is the noblest, the best prophetic gift. The Old Testament prophets derived their title to the name chiefly from leading the people of their day in the way of faith by explaining the divine Word. These things had much more to do with their title than the fact of their making occasional predictions concerning earthly kings and temporal affairs. The faith whereto their prophecies conformed is perpetual.

It is of much significance that Paul recognizes faith as the controlling judge and rule in all matters of doctrine and prophecy. To faith everything must bow. By faith must all doctrines be judged and held. You see whom Paul would make doctors of the Scriptures—men of faith and no others. These should be the judges of all doctrines. Faith is and must be lord over all teachers. Popes, councils and all the world, with their doctrines, must yield authority to the most insignificant Christian with faith, and his decision of their doctrines and laws is to be accepted. It is inconsistent to reject the judgment of him whom God himself teaches.

January 23rd - Luke 2:49

How is it that you sought me? Did you not that know that I must be about my Father's business?

All things belong to the Father. He gave us the creatures to use in our earthly life according to our best understanding. One thing he reserved for himself, which is called holy and God's own, and which we are to receive from him in a special manner. This is his holy Word, through which he rules the hearts and consciences, and makes holy and saves us. Hence Christ is in his Father's business, when he speaks to us through his Word and by means of it leads us to the Father.

He reproves his parents because they had erred and had sought him among earthly and human affairs, among friends and acquaintances. He will not permit himself to be found in anything outside of his Word. He does not wish to be worldly, nor in that which is worldly, but in that which is his Father's, as he always manifested from his birth through his entire life. He was in the world, but he did not conform to the world. To Pilate he said: "My kingdom is not of this world." He waits alone on that which is his Father's, i. e., the Word. Faith has no other foundation to stand on. Hence, the wisdom, thoughts and hopes of the mother of Christ and of Joseph must fail while they were seeking him in other places. For they did not seek him as they ought, but as flesh and blood do, which always gropes after other comfort than that of the Word; for it always wants what it can see and feel, and acquire by meditation and reason.

God permits them to fail in order that they may learn that all comfort not based on the Word, but on flesh and blood, on men and all other creatures, must inevitably fail. Here everything must be abandoned: friends, acquaintances, the whole city of Jerusalem, and everything belonging to these and to men; for all this neither gives, nor aids comfort, until the Lord is sought in the temple, since he is in that which is his Father's. There he can truly be found and the heart is made to rejoice, otherwise it would have to remain without the least comfort.

January 24th - Romans 12:4, 5

As we have many members in one body, and all members have not the same office: so we, being many, are one body in Christ, and everyone members of one another.

This apt and beautiful simile clearly teaches the equality of all Christians; that one common faith should satisfy all; that gifts are not to be regarded as making one better, happier and more righteous than another, in the eyes of God. All the members perform certain functions of the body because they are members of it; and no member has its place through its own efforts or its own merits. It was born a member, before the exercise of office was possible. It acts by virtue of being a member; it does not become a member by virtue of its action. It derives its existence and all its powers from the body, regardless of its own exertions. The body, however, exercises its members as occasion requires. The eye has not attained its place because of its power of seeing—not because it has merited its office as an organ of sight for the body. In the very beginning it derived its very existence and its peculiar functions of sight from the body. It cannot therefore boast in the slightest degree that by its independent power of seeing it has deserved its place as an eye. It has the honor and right of its position solely through its birth, not because of any effort on its part.

Similarly, no Christian can boast that his own efforts have made him a member of Christ, with other Christians, in the common faith. Nor can he by any work constitute himself a Christian. He performs good works by virtue of having become a Christian, in the new birth, through faith, regardless of any merit of his own. It is evident, then, that good works do not make a Christian, but Christians bring forth good works. The fruit does not make the tree, but the tree produces the fruit. Effect does not produce cause, but cause produces effect. Now, if good works do not make a Christian, do not secure the grace of God and blot out our sins, they do not merit heaven. One cannot secure it by his works, but by being a member of Christ; an experience effected through faith in the Word of God. None but a Christian can enjoy heaven.

January 25th - Matthew 13:20

Let both grow together, until the harvest.

We should not marvel nor be terrified if there spring up among us many different false teachings and false faiths. Satan is constantly among the children of God. These words teach us how we should conduct ourselves toward these heretics and false teachers. We are not to uproot nor destroy them. The servants who are able to distinguish the tares from the wheat must indeed be very spiritual, but even then he says publicly, "Let both grow together." We have to do here with God's Word alone; for in this matter he who errs to-day may find the truth to-morrow. Who knows when the Word of God may touch his heart? But if he be burned at the stake, or otherwise destroyed, it is assured that he can never find the truth; the Word of God is snatched from him and he must be lost, who otherwise might have been saved. Hence the Lord says, the wheat will also be uprooted if we weed out the tares, which is something awful in the eyes of God and never to be justified.

From this observe what furious and raging people we have been these many years, in that we desired to force others to believe; the Turks with the sword, heretics with fire, the Jews with death, and thus root out the tares by our own power, as if we were the ones who could reign over hearts and spirits, and make them pious and right, which God's Word alone must do. By such murder we separate the people from the Word, so that it cannot possibly work upon them, and we thus bring with one stroke a double murder upon ourselves, in that we murder the body for time and the soul for eternity, and afterwards say we did God a service by our actions, and wish to merit something special in heaven.

Therefore this passage should in all reason terrify the grand inquisitors and murderers of the people, even where they are brazen-faced, and should have to deal with true heretics. But at present they burn the true saints and are themselves heretics. What is that but rooting up the wheat, and pretending to exterminate the tares, like insane people? But it is apparent that they are themselves tares and evil seed, having fallen from the faith and trusting in their works.

January 26th - Matthew 5:44

Love your enemies, bless them that curse you, do good to them that hate you, and pray for them which spitefully use you, and persecute you.

You may say, shall evil go unpunished? What would be the result were all evil to be tolerated and covered up? Would it not encourage the wicked in their wickedness until life would not be safe to anyone? It is truly the office of civil government and also of the father of every family to show anger against every evil, and to punish and restrain it. Every pastor and preacher, yes, every good Christian, is commissioned to admonish and censure when he sees a neighbor committing sin, just as one brother in a family should admonish another. But to be angry with evil and to inflict official punishment is a different thing from being filled with hatred and revenge, or holding ill will and be unforgiving.

Is it not inconsistent with the character of love to be angry and to reprove a neighbor when he is observed to sin;

much rather love desires his improvement. Parents correct with a rod a disobedient and obstinate child, but do not cast it out and become enemies to it because of that disobedience. Their object is only to reform the child. So you may censure your brother when he sins, and manifest your displeasure and indignation, that he may perceive and confess his wrongdoing, but his obstinacy does not justify you in becoming his enemy, or in entertaining ill will toward him. He who truly loves will be distressed at a beloved neighbor wickedly trespassing against God and himself, but will not turn pale with hatred and revenge. True, when fervor and admonition fail to effect any reform, the sincere-hearted Christian must separate himself from his obstinate neighbor and regard him as a heathen; but he must not become his neighbor's enemy, nor wish him evil.

Anger and censure prompted by sincere love are very different from the wrath, hatred and vindictiveness of the world, which seeks only its own interests and is unwilling to tolerate any opposition to its pleasure. True love is moved to anger when a neighbor's good demands it. Though not insensible to evil and not approving of it, it is yet able to tolerate, to forgive and cover all wrongs against itself, and it leaves untried no expedient that may make a neighbor better. Sincere love makes a distinction between the evil and the person; it is unfriendly to the former, but kind to the latter.

January 27th - John 2:1, 2

The third day there was a marriage in Cana in Galilee; and the mother of Jesus was there: and both Jesus was called, and his disciples, to the marriage.

It is indeed a high honor paid to married life for Christ himself to attend this marriage, together with his mother and his disciples. His mother is present as the one arranging the wedding, the parties married being apparently her poor relatives or neighbors, and she being compelled to act as the bride's mother; so, of course, it was nothing more than a wedding, and in no way a display.

The second honor is his giving good wine for the humble marriage by means of a great miracle, making himself the bride's chief cup-bearer; it may be too that he had no money or jewel to give as a wedding present. He never did such honor to the life or doings of the Pharisees; for by this miracle he confirms marriage as the work and institution of God. No matter how common or how lowly it appears in the eyes of men, God none the less acknowledges his own work and loves it.

Since then marriage has the foundation and consolation that it is instituted by God and that God loves it, and that Christ himself so honors and comforts it, everyone ought to prize and esteem it; the heart ought to be glad that it is surely the state which God loves, and cheerfully endure every burden in it, even though the burdens be ten times heavier than they are. For this reason there is so much care and unpleasantness in married life to the outward man, because everything that is God's word and work, if it is to be blessed at all, must be distasteful, bitter and burdensome to the outward man.

Marriage is a state that cultivates and exercises faith in God and love to our neighbor by means of manifold cares, labors, unpleasantness, crosses and all kinds of adversities that are to follow everything that is God's word and work.

Christ also shows that he is not displeased with a marriage feast, nor with the things which belong to a wedding, such as adornments, cheerfulness, eating and drinking, according to the usage and custom of the country. God is not concerned about such external things, if it be in moderation, and faith and love reign.

January 28th - Romans 12:16

Be of the same mind one toward another. Mind not high things, but condescend to men of low estate.

Paul speaks of the temporal affairs of men, teaching mutual appreciation of one another's calling and character, offices and works, and that none is to esteem himself better than another because of these. The shoemaker's apprentice has the same Christ as the prince or the king; the woman, the same as the man. While there are various occupations and external distinctions among men, there is but one faith and one Spirit.

But this doctrine of Paul has long been dishonored. Princes, nobles, the rich and the powerful, reflect themselves in themselves, thinking they are the only men on earth. Even among their own ranks one aspires to be more exalted, more noble and upright, than another. Their notions and opinions are almost as diverse as the clouds of heaven. They are not of the same mind in external distinctions. One does not esteem another's condition and occupation as significant and as honorable as his own. True, there must be the various earthly stations, characters and employments; but it is heathenish, unchristian and worldly for one to entertain the absurd idea that God regards a certain individual a better Christian than another upon the contemptible grounds of his temporal station, and not to perceive that in God's sight these conditions make no difference. God treats men alike. He gives his Word and his Spirit to the lowly as well as to the high. "High things" have their place and they are not pernicious. But to "mind" them, to be absorbed in them with the whole heart, to be puffed up with conceit because of our relation to them, enjoying them to the disadvantage of the less favored—that is heathenish.

Where would the wealthy and the powerful be if there were no poor and humble? As the feet support the body, so the low support the high. The higher class, then, should conduct themselves toward the lowly as the body holds itself with relation to the feet; not "minding" or regarding their lofty station, but conforming to and recognizing with favor the station of the lowly. Christ conducted himself with humility. He did not deny his own exaltation, but neither was he haughty toward us by reason of it. He did not despise us, but stooped to our wretched condition and raised us by means of his own exalted condition.

January 29th - 2 Corinthians 11:23

Are they ministers of Christ? (I speak as a fool) I am more; in labours more abundant, in stripes above measure, in prisons more frequent, in deaths oft.

Paul acknowledges that he had to become a fool, something for which he had no desire, by reason of the necessity laid upon him to praise himself. The false apostles, as false spirits habitually do, delivered great, fine, splendid speeches to the multitudes in their vainglorious attempt to raise themselves above Paul, and to make him and his doctrine contemptible and insignificant. Paul was little concerned that he should personally be lightly esteemed and the false apostles highly honored, but he could not bear to have the gospel perish in that way and his Corinthian converts seduced. Therefore he exerts himself to the utmost, at the risk of becoming a fool by his boasting. But in his strong spiritual wisdom, he glories in a masterly way, and skillfully puts to shame the boasts of the false apostles. He shows them that he can glory in the very things in which they glory, and even more. At the same time he declares himself a fool for glorying. He wears the foolscap, that those coarse fools might have a mirror to behold themselves. This is wisely making foolishness minister to the good of the neighbor and to the honor of the gospel. To the just, even folly is wisdom, just as all things are pure and holy unto him.

Paul deals the false apostles a strong blow when he shows them to be ignorant of the grounds in which a true Christian seeks his glory. He teaches them that a Christian glories in the things of which other men are ashamed—in the cross and in his sufferings. The main point of the lesson is that in a preacher or a teacher no vice is more injurious and venomous than vainglory. The ministry is ordained to have as its aim the glory of God and its promotion, and the ministers must, for God's glory, suffer reproach and shame. The world will not endure the Word. For him who seeks his own honor in preaching, it is impossible to remain in the right path and preach the pure gospel. Consequently he avoids striving for God's honor; he must preach what pleases the people, what brings honor to himself and magnifies his skill and wisdom.

January 30th - Matthew 8:10

Verily I say unto you, I have not found so great faith, no, not in Israel.

This saying of Christ has been discussed with solicitude, lest it should imply that Christ did not speak truly, or that the mother of God and the apostles were inferior to this centurion. Although I might say that Christ is speaking of the people of Israel, among whom he had preached and to whom he had come, and therefore his mother and his disciples were excluded, because they traveled with him and came with him to the people of Israel in his preaching, nevertheless I will abide by the words of the Lord and take them as they stand.

First, it is against no article of belief that this faith of the centurion was without a parallel among the apostles or the mother of God. When no article of faith openly contradicts the words of Christ, they are to be taken literally, are not to be adapted and bent by our interpretation, neither for the sake of any saint or angel, nor of God himself. For his Word is the truth above all saints and angels. Such interpretation and adaptation spring from a carnal mind to estimate the saints of God not according to God's grace, but according to their person, and greatness, which is contrary to God, who estimates quite differently, according to his gifts alone. God frequently does through inferior saints what he does not do through great saints. He concealed himself from his mother, when he was twelve years old, and suffered her to be in ignorance and error. On Easter Sunday he showed himself to Mary Magdalene, before he showed himself to his mother and the apostles. He spoke to the Samaritan woman, and to the woman taken in adultery, more kindly than he spoke to his mother. When Peter fell and denied him, the thief on the cross stood firm in his faith.

By these and similar wonders he shows that he will not have his Spirit in his saints limited by us, and that we are not to judge according to the person. He wills to bestow his gifts freely, according to his pleasure, not to our opinion. The purpose of all this is to prevent men from being presumptuous toward others and from elevating one saint above another, thus creating divisions. All are to be equal in the grace of God, however unequal they are in gifts.

January 31st - Luke 2:50

They understood not the saying which he spake unto them.

This should close the mouths of vain babblers who exalt the holy Virgin Mary and other saints, as if these knew everything and could not err; for you can see here how they do err and falter, not only in this that they seek Christ and know not where to find him until they accidentally come to the temple, but also that they could not understand these words with which he censured their ignorance, when he was compelled to say to them: "Wist you not that I must be about my Father's business?" The evangelist has pointed this out with great diligence, in order that men should not give evidence to such falsehoods as ignorant, inexperienced and conceited teachers of work-righteousness present in exalting the saints, even setting them up as idols.

Examples like this are useful and necessary to show us that even the saints, who are the children of God, and highly favored above others, still have weaknesses so that they frequently err and blunder, yea, retain many faults, at times even commit great sins; yet, not intentionally and willfully, but from weakness and ignorance, as we see again and again in the lives of the apostles. This happens in order that we may learn not to trust nor depend on any man, but to cling to the Word of God only; and in order that we may find comfort in such examples and not be led to despair, although we may be weak and ignorant.

In this gospel you have a strong example with which to overthrow the common cry both of the false saints and of the great critics, which they still keep up, and by which, contrary to the Word of God, they continue to reproach us with the writings and teachings of the fathers and the decrees of the Church and the councils. In this they desire to mislead us concerning the Scriptures and the true place to which Christ himself points and where he can surely be found; in order that what happened to Mary and Joseph may happen also to us, namely, that we seek Christ everywhere and yet find him nowhere except where he is to be found, namely, in the Scriptures.

February 1st - 1 Corinthians 9:24

Know you not that they which run in a race run all, but one receiveth the prize? So run, that you may obtain.

Paul here presents a forcible simile in the running of a race, or the strife for the prize. Many run without obtaining the object of their pursuit. But we should not run in vain. To follow Christ faithfully does not simply mean to run. We must run to some purpose. To believe that we are running in Christ's course will not suffice; we must lay hold of eternal life. "He that shall endure unto the end, the same shall be saved." "Let him that thinketh he stands take heed lest he fall."

Running is hindered in two ways. First, by insolence. When our faith is not exercised and we are indolent in good works, our progress is hindered and the prize is not attained. While men sleep the enemy sows tares. Secondly, when individuals pursue their aim at full speed, but are deluded by phantoms, they miss their aim and rush to ruin, or run up against fearful obstacles. Hence the race is hindered when a false goal is set up, or the true one removed.

The goal is removed when the Word of God is falsified and creations of the human mind are preached under the name of God's Word. These things come about when we are not careful to keep the unity of the spirit, and when each one follows his own ideas because he prefers his own conceit. Paul calls love the unity of the spirit, and admonishes to keep the unity of the spirit in the bonds of peace.

He who in the Christian contest seeks his own glory and profit, who finds in the Word and Spirit of God occasion for his own praise and advantage, cannot expect to win. He is wholly entangled, and bound hand and foot. Under such conditions false and indolent Christians run indeed a merry race; but God's Word and ways are merely a pretense, because they subserve their own interests and glory. They never make a serious attempt, nor do they ever hit the mark. So run, that you may obtain.

February 2nd - Matthew 8:2

Behold, there came a leper and worshiped him, saying, Lord, if you will, you can make me clean.

This leper would not have been so bold as to come to the Lord and ask to be cleansed, if he had not trusted and expected with his whole heart that Christ would be kind and gracious, and would cleanse him. Because he was a leper, he had reason to be timid. Moreover the law forbids lepers to mingle with the people. Nevertheless he approaches, regardless of law and people, and of the purity and holiness of Christ.

Here behold the attitude of faith toward Christ: it sets before itself absolutely nothing but the pure goodness and free grace of Christ, without seeking and bringing any merit. Here it certainly cannot be said that the leper merited by his purity to approach Christ, to speak to him and to invoke his help. Nay, just because he feels his impurity and unworthiness, he approaches all the more and looks only upon the goodness of Christ. This is true faith, a living confidence in the goodness of God. The heart that does this has true faith; the heart that does it not has not true faith, as they do who do not keep in sight the goodness of God and that alone, but first look around for their own works, in order to be worthy of God's grace and to merit it. These never make bold to call upon God earnestly or draw near to him.

This confidence of faith, or knowledge of the goodness of Christ, would never have originated in this leper by virtue of his own reason, if he had not first heard a good report about Christ, how kind, gracious and merciful he is, ready to help, comfort and counsel everyone that comes to him. Such a report must undoubtedly have come to his ears, and from this fame he derived courage, and interpreted the report to his own advantage; he applied this goodness to his own need. His faith therefore did not grow out of his reason, but out of the report he heard of Christ, as Paul says: "Faith cometh by hearing, and hearing by the Word of God." This is the gospel that is the beginning, middle, and end of everything good and of all salvation.

February 3rd - 1 Corinthians 13:13

Now abide faith, hope, charity, these three; but the greatest of these is charity (love).

Paul's statement that love is greater than faith and hope is intended as an expression of the permanence, or eternal duration of love. Faith, being limited as to time in comparison with love, ranks beneath it for the reason of this temporary duration. With the same right I might say that the kingdom of Christ is greater upon earth than was Christ. Thereby I do not mean that the Church in itself is better and of higher rank than Christ, but merely that it covers a greater part of the earth than he compassed; for he was here but three years, and those he spent in a limited sphere, whereas his kingdom has been from the beginning and is coextensive with the earth. In this sense, love is longer and broader than either faith or hope.

Faith deals with God merely in the heart and in this life, whereas the relations of love both to God and the whole world are eternal. Nevertheless, as Christ is immeasurably better and higher and more precious than the Christian Church, although we behold him moving within smaller limits and as a mere individual, so is faith better, higher and more precious than love, though its duration is limited and it has God alone for its object.

Paul's purpose in so extolling love is to deal a blow to false teachers and to bring to naught their boasts about faith and other gifts when love is lacking. He means to say: If you possess not love (charity), which abides forever, all else of which you boast being perishable, you will perish with it. While the Word of God and spiritual gifts are eternal, yet the external office and proclamation of the Word, and likewise the employment of gifts in their variety, shall have an end, and thus your glory and pride shall become as ashes. So then faith justifies through the Word and produces love. But while both Word and faith shall pass away, righteousness and love, which they effect, abide forever; just as a building erected by the aid of scaffolding remains after the scaffolding has been removed. Love gives and blesses the neighbor, as a result of faith, and it shall never be done away.

February 4th - Matthew 20:16

So the last shall be first, and the first last; for many be called, but few chosen.

The two words "last" and "first" must be considered from two viewpoints. The first before men are the last before God, and the last in the eyes of men are first in the eyes of God. On the contrary, the first before God are the last before men; and those whom God esteems as the last are considered by men to be the first. This gospel does not speak of first and last in a common, ordinary sense; but it means those who imagine they are the first or the last in the eyes of God; the words ascend very high and apply to the better classes of people; they terrify the greatest of saints. Behold, how Saul fell! How God permitted David to fall! How Peter had to fall! Why is it that so many sects have arisen? No doubt, because they were self-secure and without fear, considering themselves the first. Hence they must become the last.

The substance of this gospel is that no mortal is so high, nor will ever ascend so high, as to have no occasion to fear that he may become the very lowest. On the other hand, no mortal lies so low as not to have the hope extended him that he may become the highest; because here all human merit is abolished and God's goodness alone is praised, and it is decreed as on a festive occasion that the first shall be last and the last first. In that he says, "the first shall be the last," he strips you of all your presumption and forbids you to exalt yourself above the lowest outcast, even if you were like Abraham, David, Peter or Paul. On the other hand, in that he says, "the last shall be first," he checks you against all doubting, and forbids you to humble yourself below any saint, even if you were Pilate, Herod, Sodom and Gomorrah. For just as we have no reason to be presumptuous, so we have no cause to doubt; but the golden mean is here confirmed and fortified by this gospel, so that we look not upon the penny but the goodness of the householder, who is the same and alike to high and low, to the first and the last, to saints and sinners, and no one can boast nor comfort himself nor presume more than another.

February 5th - 1 Corinthians 12:23

Those members of the body, which we think to be less honorable, upon these we bestow more abundant honor; and our uncomely parts have more abundant comeliness.

Thus we see that hand and eye, regardless of their superior office, labor carefully to clothe and adorn the less honorable members. They make the best use of their own distinction to remove the dishonor and shame of the inferior members. However unequal the capacities and distinction of the individual members of the body, they are equal in that they are all parts of the same body. The eye cannot claim any better place in the body than the least distinguished member has. Nor can it boast greater authority over the body than any other member enjoys. And this it does not essay to do. It grants all members equal participation in the body. Likewise, all Christians, whether strong in faith or weak, perfect or defective, share equally in Christ and are equal in Christendom. Each may appropriate the whole Christ to himself. I may boast as much in Christ as Peter. Nor do I envy Peter because he is a more distinguished member of the Christian Church than I. On the other hand, he does not despise me for being a less honored member. I am a part of the same body to which he belongs, and I possess Christ as well as he does.

The self-righteous are unable to concede this equality. They must stir up sects and distinctions among Christians. Priests aspire to be better than laymen; monks better than priests; virgins than wives. The diligent in praying and fasting would be better than the laborer; and they who lead austere lives, more righteous than they of ordinary life. This is the work of the devil, and productive of every form of evil. Under such conditions faith and love are subverted. The unlearned are deluded, and led away from faith to works and orders. Inequality is everywhere. The church leaders desire to sit in high places, to receive all honor, to have their feet kissed, and will honor and respect none but themselves. All this is opposed to Christ's doctrine in our text. In the members we daily bear about with us, God has described the law of love in a forcible manner. The Christian should act in a way to profit not himself but others, and have a sincere interest in them.

February 6th - Luke 8:10

Unto you it is given to know the mysteries of the kingdom of God; but to others in parables; that seeing they might not see, and hearing they might not understand.

A "mystery" is a hidden secret that is not known; and the "mysteries of the kingdom of God" are the things in the kingdom of God, as for example Christ with all his grace, which he manifests to us. He who knows Christ aright understands what God's kingdom is and what is in it. It is called a mystery because it is spiritual and secret, and it remains so where the spirit does not reveal it. For although there are many who see and hear it, yet they do not understand it. There are many who preach and hear Christ, how he offered himself for us; but all that is only upon their tongue and not in their heart; for they themselves do not believe it; they do not experience it.

Therefore Christ says: "Unto you it is given;" the Spirit gives it to you that you not only hear and see it, but acknowledge and hear it with your heart. It is no longer a mystery to you. But others, who hear it as well as you and have no faith in their heart, see and understand it not. To them it is a mystery and will continue to be unknown to them, and all that they hear is only like one hearing a parable or a dark saying. Christ therefore spoke to the people in parables, that they might understand each according to his ability. He spake to them in parables because they did not understand. The parables served to interest and get a hold on coarse and rough people. Although they do not understand them, yet later they may be taught and learn to know. Parables are naturally pleasing to the common people, and they easily remember them, since they are taken from common, everyday affairs, in the midst of which the people live.

But these parables are of the nature that no one can understand them, they may grasp and hear them as often as they will, unless the Spirit makes them known and reveals them. Not that they shall preach that we shall not understand them, but it naturally follows that whenever the Spirit does not reveal them, no one understands them. God conceals and reveals to whom he will and whom he had in mind from eternity.

February 7th - Colossians 3:17

Whatsoever you do in word or deed, do all in the name of the Lord Jesus, giving thanks to God and the Father by him.

The works of Christians are not circumscribed by name, time, or place. Whatever Christians do is good; whenever done it is timely; wherever wrought it is appropriate. So Paul names no work. He makes no distinction, but concludes all works to be good, whether it be eating or drinking, speaking or keeping silence, waking or sleeping, going or staying, being idle or otherwise. All acts are eminently worthy because done in the name of the Lord Jesus. Such is Paul's teaching here. And our works are wrought in the name of the Lord Jesus when we by faith hold fast the fact that Christ is in us and we in him, in the sense that we no longer labor, but he lives and works in us.

The expression "in the name of God" or "Lord Jesus" is frequently uttered falsely and in sheer hypocrisy. Teachers of false doctrine habitually offer their commodities in the name of God. They even come in the name of Christ, as he himself foretells. To speak and work sincerely and earnestly in Jesus' name, the heart must necessarily accord with the utterance of the mouth. As the lips declare in the name of God, so must the heart confidently, with firm faith, hold that God directs and performs the work. No Christian should undertake to do any deed in his own ability and directed by his own judgment. Rather let him be assured that God works with him and through him.

Such an attitude will result in praise and thanks to God as one to whom are due all honor and praise for every good thing. Thus Paul teaches and also Peter. Immediately after declaring that we are to work according to the ability which God gives, Peter adds that "in all things God may be glorified through Jesus Christ." He who undertakes anything in his own ability, however much he may glorify God with his lips, lies and deceives. Thankfulness is the only duty we can perform unto God; and this is not to be rendered of ourselves, but through our Mediator, Jesus. Without him none can come to the Father and none will be accepted.

February 8th - Luke 18:31

Behold, we go up to Jerusalem, and all things that are written by the prophets concerning the Son of man shall be accomplished.

Christ spoke these words on his way to Jerusalem at the time of the Easter festivities before he finished his passion, when his disciples least expected to witness his sufferings, but instead anticipated a joyful occasion at the Feast of the Passover. He spoke them that his disciples might later grow stronger in their faith, when they recalled the fact that he had told them before, that he had voluntarily offered himself as a sacrifice, and that he was not crucified by the power or strategy of his enemies, the Jews. Long before this Isaiah had prophesied that Christ would voluntarily and cheerfully give himself as a sacrifice. The angel also on Easter morning admonishes the women to call to mind what he here says, in order that they might be assured and the more firmly believe that he suffered willingly on our behalf.

The true foundation of a thorough understanding of Christ's passion is when we not only consider his sufferings, but also his heart and will in those sufferings; for all they who view his sufferings so as not to see his will and heart in them are more terrified than they rejoice on account of them. Where one sees Christ's will and heart in his passion, it brings true comfort, assurance and pleasure in Christ. Thus the psalmist praises this will of God and of Christ, when he says: "I delight to do your will, O my God." The apostle in the Epistle to the Hebrews says: "By which will we have been sanctified." It does not say, Through the suffering and blood of Christ, which is also true; but through the will of God and of Christ. They were both of one will to sanctify us through the blood of Christ.

In this gospel he shows us this will to suffer, when he first announced that he would go up to Jerusalem and allow them to crucify him; as if he had said, Look into my heart and see that I do all willingly, freely and cheerfully, in order that it may not terrify nor shock you, when you shall see it, and think that I do it reluctantly, and must do it; that I am forsaken and the power of the Jews forces me to it.

February 9th - Matthew 8:13

Jesus said unto the centurion, Go your way; as you have believed, so be it done unto you And his servant was healed in the selfsame hour.

This heathen is so fully satisfied with Christ's word, that he does not even desire his presence nor deem himself worthy of it. Therefore also his servant was healed in that hour by the power of his faith. Since the occasion is offered, we must say a little about alien faith and its power. Many are interested in this subject on account of the little children who are baptized and are saved not by their own, but by the faith of others; just as this servant was healed not by his own, but by the faith of his master.

First we must let the foundation stand firm and sure that nobody will be saved by the faith or righteousness of another, but only by his own; neither will anybody be condemned for the unbelief and sins of another, but for his own. "He that believeth and is baptized shall be saved; but he that believeth not shall be damned." What then becomes of the young children, seeing they have not reason and are not able to believe for themselves.

We conclude and declare that in baptism the children themselves believe and have their own faith, which God effects in them through the sponsors, when in the faith of the Christian Church they intercede for them and bring them to baptism. This is what we call the power of alien faith, not that anybody can be saved by it, but that through it as an intercession and aid he can obtain from God his own faith, by which he is saved. If I am to live, I myself must be born, and nobody can be born for me to enable me to live; but mother and midwife can by their life aid me in birth and enable me to live. Nobody can go to heaven for me; but he can assist me, can teach, preach, govern, pray and obtain faith from God for me, through which I can go to heaven. The centurion was not healed of the palsy of his servant, but he brought it about that his servant was restored to health. So children are not baptized in the faith of the sponsors or the Church, but the faith of the sponsors gains faith for them, in which they are baptized and believe for themselves.

February 10th - Colossians 3:12, 13

Put on therefore, as the elect of God, holy and beloved, bowels of mercies, kindness, humbleness of mind, meekness, patient; forbearing one another, and forgiving one another.

Observe the tender and sacred style of the apostle's admonition. He does not drive us with the law, but persuades by reminding us of the ineffable grace of God. He calls us the "elect of God," "holy," and "beloved." He desires to call forth in us the fruits of faith, wishing to have them yielded in a willing, cheerful and happy spirit. The individual who truly believes that he is beloved, holy and elect before God, will consider how he may sustain his honor and titles, and how he must conduct himself to be worthy of them. He will love God with a fervor that will enable him to do or omit, or suffer all things, and will ever think that he is not doing enough.

Paul here speaks of that sincere and whole-souled mercy, characteristic of a father or mother who witness the distress of their child for which they would readily expose their lives or give up all their possessions. The Christian heart and mind is constantly devoted to merciful deeds with an ardor so intense as to make him unaware that he is doing good and compassionate acts.

Paul condemns also the works and arbitrary rules of hypocritical saints, whose severity will not permit them to associate with sinners, and who exercise no mercy, but administer perpetual reproach, censure, criticism, blame and bluster. They are unable to endure imperfections in any, though they themselves are sinners and many are infirm.

Christians reject none, and will bear with all. They are as sincerely interested in sinners as they are in themselves. They pray for them, teach, admonish, persuade, do all in their power to reclaim them. The virtues mentioned in the text become us better in the sight of God than pearls, precious stones, silk and gold become us in the eyes of the world. So Christ dealt with the adulteress, brought her to repentance and with gracious words suffered her to depart. So God in Christ has dealt with us and ever deals.

February 11th - 1 Corinthians 5:7

Purge out therefore the old leaven, that you may be a new lump, as you are unleavened.

If we are to be a new, sweet lump, we must purge out the old leaven. A nature renewed by faith and Christianity will not admit of our living as we did when devoid of faith and in sin, under the influence of an evil conscience. Note the apostle's peculiar words. He enjoins purging out the old leaven, assigning as a reason, that you are a new and unleavened lump. By a new unleavened lump he means that faith which clings to Christ and believes in the forgiveness of sin through him; but how shall we explain the fact that he bids them purge out the old leaven that they may be a new lump, when at the same time he admits them to be unleavened and a new lump? How can these Christians be unleavened, when they have yet to purge out the old leaven?

This is an instance of the Pauline and apostolic way of speaking concerning Christians and the kingdom of Christ; it tells us what the condition really is. It is a discipline wherein a new, Christian life is entered upon through faith in Christ, the true Passover; hence, Easter is celebrated with sweet, unleavened bread. But at the same time something of the old life remains, which must be swept out, or purged away. However, this latter is not imputed, because faith and Christ are there, constantly toiling and striving thoroughly to purge out whatever uncleanness remains. Through faith we have Christ and his purity perfectly conferred upon ourselves, and we are thus regarded pure; yet in our own personal nature we are not immediately and wholly pure, without sin and weakness. Much of the old leaven still remains, but it will be forgiven, not be imputed to us, if only we continue in faith and are occupied with purging out that remaining impurity.

This is Christ's thought when he says to his disciples, "Now you are clean through the word which I have spoken unto you," and in the same connection he declares that the branches in him must be purged that they may bring forth fruit. To Peter he says, "He that is washed needeth not save to wash his feet, but is clean every whit; and you are clean, but not all." By faith a Christian lays hold of the purity of Christ; it brings the Holy Spirit, who enables man to withstand and subdue sin.

February 12th - 1 Peter 2:23

(He) committed himself to him that judges righteously.

The apostle had just been saying that Christ reviled not, nor thought of revenge, but rather manifested love and good will toward his virulent enemies. How could Christ approve such malice? Truly he could not endorse it. Nor could he commend his enemies for putting him to death upon the cross without a cause. If I suffer innocently and am unjustly treated, I am not to justify the ill treatment and strengthen the enemy in his sins; for, so doing, I would approve his conduct and assume the guilt attributed. I must not cease to confess the truth and maintain my innocence, both in heart and with my liPsalm But if men will not accept my word, my heart must tell me I have suffered injustice. Rather should I endure ten deaths, could my enemies inflict them, than to condemn myself in violation of conscience.

But what are we to do? If we do not justify our enemies when they make us suffer, they will even do worse things to us; for they desire the name and the credit, in the eyes of the world, of having done right by us; they would have it thought that they do God great service by murdering us. Now, who is to judge and decide the question? Peter declares that Christ committed the matter to him who judges righteously. How should he do otherwise? There was for him no judge on earth. He was compelled to commit the matter to that righteous judge, his heavenly Father. Well he knew that such sins and blasphemies could not go unpunished. The sentence was already passed, the sword sharpened, the angels given orders for the overthrow of Jerusalem. Previous to his sufferings, on his way to Jerusalem, as he beheld the city, he announced its coming doom and wept over it.

As Christ did, so should we conduct ourselves in our sufferings; not approving or assenting to whatever may be heaped upon us, but yet not seeking revenge. We are to commit the matter to God who will judge aright. We cannot maintain our rights before the world; therefore we must commit our cause to God, who judges righteously and who will not allow destruction of his Word and persecution of believers to pass unpunished. Why, then, should I be impatient or desire revenge?

February 13th - 1 Corinthians 13:1

Though I speak with the tongues of men and of angels, and have not charity (love), I am become as sounding brass, or a tinkling cymbal.

Observe how small the word "love" and how easily uttered! Who would have thought to find so much precious virtue and power ascribed by Paul to this one excellence as counterpart of so much that is evil? This is, I imagine, magnifying love, painting love. It is a better discourse on virtue and vice than are the heathen writings. The model the apostle presents should justly shame the false teachers, who talk much of love but in whom not one of the virtues he mentions is found.

Every quality of love mentioned by him means false teachers buffeted and assaulted. Whenever he signifies love and characterizes her powers, he invariably makes a thrust at the same time at those who are deficient in any of them. We may well, then, as he describes the several features, add the comment, "But you do very differently." It is passing strange that the teachers devoid of love should possess such love as Paul mentions here, namely, speaking with tongues, prophesying, understanding mysteries; that they should have faith, should bestow their goods and suffer themselves to be burned. For we have seen what abominations ensue where love is lacking; such individuals are proud, envious, impatient, false, suspicious, malicious, disinclined to service, selfish, ambitious. How can it consistently be claimed that people of this stamp can through faith remove mountains, give their bodies to be burned, prophecy and the like? It is precisely as I have stated. Paul presents an impossible proposition, implying that since they are devoid of love, they do not really possess those gifts, but merely assume the name and appearance. And in order to divest them of those he admits for the sake of argument that they are what in reality they are not.

Paul's purpose is to silence and humble haughty Christians, especially teachers and preachers. The gospel gives much knowledge of God and of Christ, and conveys many wonderful gifts. Some have the gift of speaking, some of teaching, some of Scripture exposition, some of ruling, and so on. But there are to be found few indeed who make the right use of such gifts and knowledge, who humble themselves to serve others, according to the dictates of love.

February 14th - Romans 13:9

If there be any other commandment, it is briefly comprehended in this saying, namely, you shall love your neighbor as thyself.

Love being the chief element of all law, it comprehends all commandments. Its one concern is to be useful and not harmful to man. Love is the chief virtue, the fountain of all virtues. Love gives food and drink; it clothes, comforts, persuades, relieves and rescues. What shall we say of it, for behold, he who loves gives himself, body and soul, property and honor, all his powers internal and external, for his needy neighbor's benefit, whether it be friend or enemy; he withholds nothing wherewith he may serve another. There is no virtue like love; there can be no special work assigned it as in the case of limited virtues, such as chastity, mercy, patience, meekness and the like. Love does all things. It will suffer in life and in death, in every condition, and that even for its enemies. Paul may well say that all other commandments are briefly comprehended in this saying, "You shall love your neighbor as thyself."

This commandment presents the standard by which we are to measure our love. It is an excellent model and holds up a truly living example, "thyself." It is a better model than any example the saints have set. The saints are dead and their deeds are past, but this example ever lives. everyone must admit a consciousness of his own love for himself; of the careful nourishment of his body with food, raiment and all good things; of his fleeing from death and avoiding evil. This is self-love; something we are conscious of in ourselves. What, then, is the teaching of the commandment? To do to another as you do to yourself; to value his body and his life equally with your own body and life. How could God have pointed you to an example dearer, more pleasing, and more to the purpose than this example—the deep instinct of your own nature? The depth of your character is measured by the writing of this commandment in your heart. How will you fare with God if you do not love your neighbor? With this commandment written within your heart, your conscience will condemn you. Your whole conduct will be an example witnessing against you.

February 15th - Romans 13:8

He that loves another has fulfilled the law.

Innumerable are the books and doctrines produced for the direction of man's conduct. There is still no limit to the making of books and laws. These laws and doctrines would be tolerated and received with more favor, if they were founded upon and administered according to the great law of love. Of love's higher authority we find many illustrations in the Scriptures. Christ makes particular mention of this matter when he refers to David and his companions eating the holy show-bread. Though a certain law prohibited all but the priests from partaking of this holy food, Love was empress here, and free. Love was over the Law, subjecting it to herself. The Law had to yield for the time being, had to become invalid, when David suffered hunger.

Had the priest been disposed to refuse David the holy bread, had he blindly insisted on honoring the prohibition of the Law and failed to perceive the authority of Love, had he denied this food to him who hungered, what would have been the result? So far as the priest's assistance went, David would have had to perish with hunger, and the priest would have been guilty of murder for the sake of the Law. Here, indeed, the most strenuous right would have been the most strenuous wrong. Moreover, on examining the heart of the priest, you would find the abomination of making sin where there is no sin, and a matter of conscience where there is no occasion for it. In connection with this same incident, Christ teaches that we are to do good to our neighbor on the Sabbath, to administer as necessity demands, whatever the Sabbath restrictions of the Law. For when a brother's need calls, Love is authority and the Law of the Sabbath is void.

Were laws conceived and administered in love, the number of laws would matter little. Though one might not know all of them, he would learn from the one or two, of which he had knowledge, the principle of love taught in all; and though he were to know all laws, he might not discover the principle of love any more readily than he would in one. No greater wrong, calamity and wretchedness is possible on earth than the teaching and enforcing of laws without love. "Love is the fulfilling of the Law."

February 16th - Luke 18:34

And they understood none of these things: and this saying was hid from them.

The disciples "understood none of these things." That is as much as to say: Reason, flesh and blood, cannot understand, nor grasp that the Scriptures should say how the Son of man must be crucified; much less does reason understand that this is Christ's will and that he does it cheerfully; for it does not believe that it is necessary for him to suffer for us; it will deal directly with God through its own good works. God must reveal it in their hearts by his Spirit more than is proclaimed by words into their ears. Even those to whom the Spirit reveals it in their hearts believe it with difficulty and must struggle with it. Such a great and wonderful thing it is that the Son of man died the death of the cross willingly and cheerfully to fulfil the Scriptures for our welfare; it is a mystery and remains a mystery.

From this it follows how foolish they act who teach that the people should patiently bear their sufferings and death to atone for their sins and obtain grace, and pretend that if they suffer willingly all their sins will be forgiven them. Such persons only mislead the people, for they bury out of sight Christ and his death, upon whom our comfort is founded, and bring the people to a false confidence in their own suffering and death. This is the worst of all things a man can experience at the end of his life, and by it he is led direct into perdition. But learn to say: Whose death! Whose patience! My death is nothing. Christ's suffering is my consolation, upon it I rely for the forgiveness of my sins; but my own death I will suffer to the praise and honor of my God freely and gratuitously, and for the advantage and profit of my neighbor, and in no way whatever depend upon it to avail anything in my own behalf before God.

As Christ now offered himself for us, we should also follow the example of love, and offer ourselves for the welfare of our neighbor, with all we have. We have spoken sufficiently on other occasions that Christ is to be preached in these two ways; but it is talk that no one desires to understand, for "the natural man receiveth not the things of the Spirit."

February 17th - Matthew 4:1

Then was Jesus led up of the spirit into the wilderness to be tempted of the devil.

Jesus was led up of the Spirit into the wilderness, that he might there fast and be tempted; but no one should imitate Christ's example of his own choice and make it a selfish and arbitrary fasting; but instead wait for the Spirit, who will send him enough fasting and temptations. For whoever, without being led by the Spirit, wantonly resorts to the danger of hunger or any other temptation, when it is truly a blessing of God that he can eat and drink and have other comforts, tempts God. We should not seek want and temptation, they will surely come of themselves; we ought to act honestly, and always do our best. The text reads: Jesus was led up of the Spirit into the wilderness; and not: Jesus himself chose to go up into the wilderness. "As many as are led by the Spirit of God, these are the sons of God." God gives his blessings that we may use them with thanksgiving, and not that we let them lie idle, and thus tempt him; for he wishes us to fast by the Spirit or by a need which we cannot avoid.

This narrative is written both for our instruction and admonition. For instruction that we should know how Christ has served and helped us by his fasting, hunger, temptation, and victory; also that whosoever believes on Christ shall never suffer need, and that temptation shall never harm him, but that we shall have enough in the midst of want and be safe in the midst of temptation; because his Lord and Head triumphed over all these in his behalf, and of this he is assured. "Be of good cheer, I have overcome the world."

This is written for our admonition, that we may in the light of his example also cheerfully suffer want and temptation for the service of God and the good of our neighbor, like Christ did for us, as often as necessity requires it, which is surely accomplished if we learn and confess God's Word. But we have practiced fasting as a good work, not to bring our flesh into subjection, but as a meritorious work before God to atone for sins and obtain grace. This has made our fasting a stench, a blasphemy, and a disgrace.

February 18th - 1 Peter 2:23

Who, when he was reviled, reviled not again; when he suffered, he threatened not.

"Did not Christ revile when he called the scribes and Pharisees hypocrites, murderers, serpents, a generation of vipers?" Oh yes, in this we would gladly follow Christ's example. It is much easier than to be patient. We would need no master to help us in this. But a distinction must be made here. Reviling, or pronouncing execrations and threats, is of two kinds. In one case it is official and pronounced by God; in the other without authority and comes from man. It was one of the duties of Christ's office on earth, and one now incumbent upon those called to bear that office after him, to assert the truth and censure the evil. Such a course is essential to the honor of God and the salvation of souls. Official chastisement is a work of divine, Christian love. It is a parental duty imposed of God, who has implanted in the parent nature intense love for the child; at the same time, if parents are godly and have proper affection for their children, they will not connive at, nor let pass unpunished their disobedience. So everyone may and should reprove when official duty or his neighbor's case requires; it serves to reform the subject. "Faithful are the wounds of a friend, but the kisses of an enemy are deceitful."

It was love and sincerity of heart which prompted Christ in his office to censure and reprove. His motive was to turn the transgressors from their blindness and malice, and to rescue them from perdition. But having fulfilled his official duties, and the hour of his suffering having arrived, he suffered patiently, permitting his enemies to heap upon him all possible evil in return for his manifested love and blessing. Instead of angrily reviling and execrating while suspended from the cross, he prayed, "Father, forgive them." It was, indeed, a heart of unfathomable love that, in the midst of extreme suffering, had compassion on its persecutors and blessed them in greater measure than parent can bless child, or one individual bless another. We have here a perfect and inimitable example of patience of the most exalted kind. In it we may behold as in a glass what we have yet to learn of calm endurance.

February 19th - Luke 18:42

Jesus said unto him, Receive your sight: your faith has saved you.

The blind man hears that Christ was passing by; he had also heard of him before, that Jesus of Nazareth was a kind man, and that he helped everyone who called on him. His faith and confidence in Christ grew out of his hearing, so he did not doubt but that Christ would help him. But such faith he could not have possessed had he not heard and known of Christ; for faith does not come except by hearing.

We see here how Christ encourages us, both by his works and words. First by his works in that he sympathizes so strongly with the blind man and makes it clear how pleasing faith is to him, so that Christ is at once absorbed with interest in the man, stops and does what the blind man desires in his faith. In the second place, Christ praises faith in words, and says: "your faith has made you whole;" he casts the honor of the miracle from himself and attributes it to the faith of the blind man. Thus faith is granted what it asks and is besides our great honor before God.

This blind man represents the spiritually blind, the state of every man born of Adam, who neither sees, nor knows the kingdom of God; but it is of grace that he feels and knows his blindness and would gladly be delivered from it. They are saintly sinners who feel their faults and sigh for grace. He sits among the teachers of the law and desires help. The people pass him by and let him sit, that is, the people of the law make a great noise and are heard among the teachers of good works; they go before Christ and Christ follows them. But when he heard Christ, that is, when a heart hears the gospel in faith, it calls and cries, and has no rest until it comes to Christ. Those who would silence and scold him are the teachers of works, who wish to quiet the doctrine and cry of faith; but they stir the heart the more. After he received his sight, all his work and life are only honor and praise to God; he follows Christ with joy, so that the whole world wonders and is thereby made better.

February 20th - Matthew 4:3, 4

If you be the Son of God, command that these stones be made bread. But he answered and said, It is written, Man shall not live by bread alone, but by every word that proceedeth out of the mouth of God.

The tempter attacked Christ with the cares of food for the body and with unbelief in the goodness of God, as if he would say: Trust in God and wait patiently until a roasted fowl flies into your mouth; do you now say that you have a God who cares for you; where is now your heavenly Father, who has charge of you? It seems to me he leaves you in a fine condition; eat now and drink from your faith, let us see how you will satisfy your hunger, when you have stones for bread. What a fine Son of God you are! How fatherly he is disposed toward you in that he fails to send you a slice of bread and permits you to be so poor and needy; do you now continue to believe that you are his son and that he is your father? With like thoughts he truly attacks all the children of God. And Christ surely felt this temptation, for he was no stock, nor stone, although he was and remained pure and without sin, as we cannot.

That Satan attacks with the cares for daily food or with unbelief and avarice, Christ's answer proves in that he says, "Man shall not live by bread alone." As if he said, you wilt direct me to bread alone and do treat me as though I thought of nothing but the sustenance of the body. This temptation is very common also among pious people, and they especially feel it keenly who have children and a family, and have nothing to eat. Here we should consider Christ's work and example, who suffered want forty days and forty nights, and finally was not forsaken, but was ministered to by angels.

Behold how Christ resists this temptation of bread. He sees nothing but stones and what is uneatable, then he clings to the Word of God, strengthens himself by it and strikes the devil to the ground with it. All Christians should lay hold of this saying when they see that there is lack and want, and courage fails. What if the whole world were full of bread; man does not live by bread alone; more than that is needed for life, namely, the Word of God.

February 21st - Matthew 4:6

If you be the Son of God, cast yourself down: for it is written, He shall give his angels charge concerning you: and in their hands they shall bear you up, lest at any time you dash your foot against a stone.

Here Satan held before Christ want and need where there was neither, but where there were already good means by which to descend from the temple without such a newly devised and unnecessary way of descending. Satan here quotes from the Psalter that God commanded the angels to protect the children of God and to carry them on their hands. But Satan like a rogue and cheat fails to quote what follows. The Psalm reads: "For he shall give his angels charge over you, to keep you in all your ways. They shall bear you up in their hands, lest you dash your foot against a stone." The protection of the angels does not reach farther, according to the command of God, than the ways in which God has commanded us to walk. When we walk in these ways of God, his angels take care of us. But the devil omits to quote "the ways of God" and interprets and applies the protection of the angels to all things, also to that which God has not commanded; then we tempt God. That this temptation was for the purpose of tempting and trying God, the answer of Christ clearly proves, when he says, you shall not tempt the Lord your God.

We find many foolhardy people, who risk and endanger the body and life, their property and honor, without any need of doing so, as those who wilfully enter into battle or jump into the water, or gamble for money, or in other ways venture into danger. Good swimmers are likely to drown and good climbers likely to fall. In spiritual matters this temptation is powerful when one has to do with the nourishment, not of the body, but of the soul. Here God holds before us the person and the way, by which the soul can be forever nourished in the richest manner possible, namely, by Christ, the Saviour. But everybody seeks another way to help his soul. The real guilty ones are those who would be saved through their own work; these the devil sets conspicuously on the top of the temple. He persuades them through the Scriptures to believe that the angels will protect them in their way and that their works and faith are pleasing to God. They do not care how falsely they explain the Scriptures.

February 22nd - Galatians 5:14

For all the law is fulfilled in one word, even in this, you shall love your neighbor as thyself.

How can love for our neighbor be the fulfilment of the law when we are required to love God supremely, even above our neighbor? Christ answers the question when he tells us that the second commandment is like unto the first. He makes love to God and love to our neighbor the same love. The reason for this is, first: God, having no need of our works and benefactions for himself, bids us to do for our neighbor what we would do for God. He asks for himself only our faith and our recognition of him as God. The object of proclaiming his honor and rendering him praise and thanks here on earth is that our neighbor may be converted and brought into fellowship with God. Such service is called the love of God, and is performed out of love to God; but it is exercised for the benefit of our neighbor only.

The second reason why God makes love to our neighbor an obligation equal to love to himself is: God has made worldly wisdom foolish, desiring henceforth to be loved amid crosses and afflictions. Paul says: "Seeing that in the wisdom of God the world through its wisdom knew not God, it was God's good pleasure through the foolishness of preaching to save them that believe." Therefore he submitted himself unto death and misery upon the cross, and imposed the same submission upon all his disciples. They who refused to love him before when he bestowed upon them food and drink, blessing and honor, must now love him in hunger and sorrow, in adversity and disgrace. All works of love, then, must be directed to our wretched needy neighbors. In these lowly ones we are to find and love God, in them we are to serve and honor him, and thus only can we do it. The commandment to love God is wholly merged in that to love our neighbors. Christ laid aside his divinity and took upon himself the form of a servant for the very purpose of bringing down and centering upon our neighbor the love we extend to himself. Yet we leave the Lord to lie here in his humiliation while we gaze open-mouthed into heaven and make great pretensions to love and serve God.

February 23rd - Matthew 15:22, 23

Behold, a woman of Canaan came out of the same coasts, and cried unto him, saying, Have mercy on me, O Lord, you Son of David; My daughter is grievously vexed with a devil. But he answered her not a word.

Christ like a hunter exercises and chases faith in his followers in order that it may become strong and firm. When the woman follows him upon hearing of his fame and cries with assured confidence that he would according to his reputation deal mercifully with her, Christ certainly acts as he would let her faith and good confidence be in vain and turn his good reputation into a lie, so that she might have thought: Is this the gracious, friendly man? Are these the good works that I have heard spoken about him? It cannot be true. He might at least speak a word and tell me that he will have nothing to do with me.

Behold, this is a hard rebuff, when God appears so earnest and angry and so utterly conceals his grace, as those know so well, who feel and experience it in their hearts. But what does the poor woman do? She turns her eyes from all this unfriendly treatment of Christ; all this does not lead her astray, neither does she take it to heart, but she continues firmly to cling in her confidence to the good news she had heard and embraced concerning him, and does not give up. We must also do the same and learn firmly to cling to the Word, even though God with all his creatures appears otherwise than his Word teaches. But how painful it is to nature and reason that this woman should strip herself of self and forsake all that she experienced, and cling to God's bare Word, until she experienced the contrary. May God help us in time of need and of death to possess like courage and faith!

This gospel is to us a true example of firm and perfect faith. For this woman endures and overcomes in three great and hard fought battles, and teaches us in a beautiful manner the true way and virtue of faith, namely, that it is a hearty trust in the grace and goodness of God as experienced and revealed through his Word. Without doubt the good news which she had heard about Christ that he was a pious man and cheerfully helped everybody, made her run after him. Such good news about God is a true gospel and a word of grace, out of which sprang the faith of this woman.

February 24th - Matthew 15:25–27

Then came she and worshiped him, saying, Lord, help me. But he answered and said, It is not meet to take the children's bread, and to cast it to dogs. And she said, Truth, Lord, yet the dogs eat of the crumbs which fall from their masters' table.

The woman follows Christ into the home. There she received her last mortal blow. Christ presents her in a bad light; she is a condemned and outcast person, who is not to be reckoned among God's chosen ones. That is an eternally unanswerable reply, to which no one can give a satisfactory answer. Yet she does not despair, but concedes that she is a dog and desires no more than a dog is entitled to, namely, that she may eat the crumbs that fall from the table of the Lord. Is not that a masterly stroke as a reply? She catches Christ with his own words. Where will Christ now take refuge? He is caught. Therefore Christ now completely opens his heart to her and yields to her will, so that she is now no more a dog, but even a child of Israel.

All this is written for our comfort and instruction, that we may know how deeply God conceals his grace before our face, and that we may not estimate him according to our feelings and thinking, but strictly according to his Word. All his answers indeed sound like no, but they are not no, they remain undecided and pending. For he does not say, I will not hear you, but is silent and passive, and says neither yes nor no. He does not say she is not of the house of Israel; but he is sent only to the house of Israel. He does not say, you are a dog, one should not give you of the children's bread; but it is not meet to take the children's bread and cast it to the dogs, leaving it undecided whether she is a dog or not. Yet all those trials of her faith sounded more like no than yes; but there was more yea in them than nay; ay, there is only yes in them, but it is very deep and very concealed, while there appears to be nothing but no. Whoever understands the actions of this poor woman and catches God in his own judgment, says, Lord, it is true I am a sinner and not worthy of your grace; but still you have promised sinners forgiveness, and you are not come to call the righteous, but "to save sinners." Surely, then must God according to his own judgment have mercy upon us.

February 25th - Luke 11:24

When the unclean spirit is gone out of a man, he walks through dry places, seeking rest; and finding none, he said, I will return unto my house whence I came out.

This means as much as to say, "The devil never takes a vacation," and "The devil never sleeps," for he is seeking how he may devour man. Dry places are not the hearts of the ungodly, for in such he rests and dwells like a mighty tyrant; but there are dry and waste places here and there in the country where no people live, as forests and wildernesses. To these he flees in wicked rage because he is driven out. You will remember that the devil found Christ in the wilderness. In Judæa there is not much water, hence we read that it contains many arid wastes. In other countries as our own, which are well watered, the devils stay in rivers and lakes, and there sometimes drowns those who bathe or sail upon them.

That he comes again and finds the house swept and garnished signifies that the man is sanctified and adorned with beautiful spiritual gifts, and that the evil spirit clearly sees that he can do nothing there with his familiar tricks, for he is too well known. Thus when the worship of idols was driven from the heathen, he never attacked the world with that device again. What did he do then? He tried something else, went out, took with him seven spirits, more evil than himself, and entered in with them and dwelt there, and the last state of that man was worse than the first. When Christ had become known in the world and the devil's former kingdom with its idol worship had been destroyed, he adopted another plan and attacked us with heresy and introduced and established the papacy, in which Christ was entirely forgotten, and men became worse heathen under the name of Christ than before he was preached. Such also was the lot of the Jews after the destruction of Jerusalem, and of the Greeks under the Turks. And so all will fare who at first hear the Word of God and afterwards become secure and weary of it. Therefore it is necessary to watch, as the apostle admonishes: "Be sober, be watchful; your adversary the devil, as a roaring lion, walks about, seeking whom he may devour." Wherever he overthrows faith, he easily restores again all former vices.

February 26th - Genesis 8:21

The imagination of man's heart is evil from his youth.

Man without the Holy Spirit and without grace can do nothing but sin, and thus without halting he goes forward from sin to sin. When in addition he will not endure sound doctrine but rejects the word of salvation and resists the Holy Spirit, he becomes an enemy of God, blasphemes the Holy Spirit and simply follows the evil desires of his heart. Witnesses of this are the examples of the prophets, Christ and the apostles, the primeval world under Noah as teacher, and also the examples of our adversaries to-day, who cannot be convinced by anything that they are in error, that they sin, that their worship is ungodly.

But we must distinguish between the theological and the civil standpoints. God approves also the rule of the ungodly; he honors and rewards virtue also among the ungodly, but only in regard to the things of this life and things grasped by a reason which is upright from the civil standpoint; whereas the future life is not embraced in such reward. His approval is not with regard to the future life. We believe that man without the Holy Spirit is altogether corrupt before God, though he may stand adorned with all heathen virtues, as moderation, liberality, love of country, parents and children, courage and humanity. The declarations of the Holy Scriptures prove the same thing. The statement in the fourteenth Psalm is sweeping enough when it says, "The Lord looked down from heaven upon the children of men, to see if there were any that did understand, and seek God. They are all gone aside, they are altogether become filthy; there is none that does good; no, not one. Paul says, "God has concluded them all in unbelief." Christ says, "Without me you can do nothing."

We are therefore to hold fast the doctrine which lays before us our sin and condemnation. This knowledge of our sin is the beginning of salvation; we must absolutely despair of ourselves and give glory for righteousness to God alone. When this has been fixed in our hearts, the foundation of our salvation is largely laid, inasmuch as subsequently clear testimonies are given that God will not cast away the sinner, that is, one who recognizes his sin and desires to come to his senses and thirsts after righteousness and the remission of sin through Christ.

February 27th - 1 Thessalonians 4:1

We beseech you, brethren, and exhort you by the Lord Jesus, that as you have received of us how you ought to walk and to please God, so you would abound more and more.

This text is an earnest admonition enjoining upon us an increasing degree of perfection in the doctrines we have received. It is incumbent upon every evangelical teacher to give this exhortation, and all Christians should render a willing and not a compulsory service. Obedience is due from those who have received the Spirit; but those who are not inclined to render a willing service, we must leave to themselves.

Paul places much value upon the gift of knowing how "to walk and to please God." In the world this gift is as rare as it is great. Though it has been offered to the whole world and has been proclaimed, still there is need of further exhortation with reference to it, and Paul is diligent in administering it. The trouble with us is that we are in danger of becoming indolent and negligent, forgetful and ungrateful.

It was a fact reflecting much credit on the Thessalonians in contrast to the Corinthians and the Galatians that they continued upright in doctrine and true in the knowledge of faith, but they seemed to be deficient in two important features in Christian life, namely, chastity and honesty. Unchastity is a sin against oneself and is destructive of the fruits of faith. Fraud in business is a sin against our neighbor and is likewise destructive of faith and charity.

Though these sins are less pernicious than the gross offenses in error of doctrine and faith, yet God will certainly punish them, if they are not repented of and renounced. Paul threatens such sins with the wrath of God lest anyone imagine the kingdom of Christ one which will tolerate such offenses with impunity. These sins do not come within the limits of Christian liberty and privilege, nor does God treat the offender with indulgence. He will more vigorously punish these sins among Christians than among the heathen. Those who sin through infirmity, suffer themselves to be reproved, and repent at once, the kingdom of Christ treats with pity and forbearance. While God bears with the sinner, he would have us perceive our errors, strive to mend our lives and abound more and more in righteousness.

February 28th - 2 Corinthians 6:1

We then, as workers together with him, beseech you also that you receive not the grace of God in vain.

The apostle's purpose in beseeching his co-laborers is to prevent them from despising the external Word as something inessential or sufficiently well known to them. Though God is able to effect everything without the instrumentality of the external Word, working inwardly by his Spirit, this is not his way of doing. He uses preachers and co-workers to accomplish his purpose through the Word when and where he pleases. Since preachers, therefore, have the office, name and honor of fellow-workers with God, no one must consider himself too learned or too holy to ignore or despise the most inferior preaching, especially as he knows not when the hour may come wherein God will perform his work in him through preachers.

Paul wishes also to show the danger of neglecting the grace of God. He boldly declares here that the preaching of the gospel is not an eternal, continuous and permanent mode of instruction, but rather a passing shower, which hastens on. What it strikes, it strikes; what it misses, it misses. It does not return, nor does it stand still. The sun and heat follow and dry it up. Experience shows that in no part of the world has the gospel remained pure beyond the length of a man's memory. When its pioneers were gone, the light disappeared; factions, spirits, and false teachers immediately followed.

Moses announced that the children of Israel would corrupt themselves after his death, and the book of Judges sufficiently testifies that such was really the case. King Joash did right as long as the high priest Jehoiada lived, but after the latter's death, it was soon ended. Soon after the time of Christ and his apostles the world was filled with seditious preachers and false teachers. Therefore to receive the grace of God in vain is nothing less than to hear the pure Word of God, and yet remain listless and unresponsive. Ungrateful for the Word and unappreciative of it, we merit its loss. Such were the guests bidden to the supper, but who refused to come, and, going about their own business, provoked the master's anger until he swore they should not taste his supper.

February 29th (leap year) - Genesis 6:6

It repented the Lord that he had made man on the earth, and it grieved him at his heart.

If God is wise, how can regret for having created anything befall him? Why did he not see this sin or depraved nature of man from the beginning of the world? Are not the purposes of God eternal and unalterable, incapable of being regretted? The meaning is not that God did not see these things from eternity; he saw everything from eternity; but inasmuch as this wickedness now manifests itself in all its fierceness, God now reveals the same in the hearts of his ministers and prophets. To this passage belong also other similar ones in which God is pictured as having eyes, ears, mouth, nose, hands, and feet. In such passages the Bible speaks of God in the same manner as of a man.

God condescends to the low plane of our understanding and presents himself to us with a childlike simplicity in representations so that he may be made known to us in some way. The Holy Spirit appeared in the form of a dove; not because he was a dove, but in this crude form he desired to be recognized, received and worshiped, for it was really the

Holy Spirit. When the Scriptures thus ascribe to God human form, voice, actions, and state of mind, it is intended as an aid for the uneducated and feeble; we, who have come to greater discernment of Scripture, should likewise lay hold of these representations, because God has put them forth and revealed himself through them. I have constantly followed the rule to avoid, whenever possible, such questions as draw us before the throne of the highest Majesty. It is better and safer to stand at the manger of Christ, the man. To lose oneself in the labyrinths of divinity is fraught with greatest danger.

We cannot define the nature of God; what he is not, we can well define—he is not a voice, dove, water, bread, wine. Yet in these visible forms he presents himself to us and deals with us, that we should not become unsettled spirits which dispute about God, who cannot be apprehended in his unveiled majesty. What we can apprehend and understand he has disclosed. Those abiding in these things will truly lay hold of him, while those following visions, revelations and illuminations will either be overwhelmed by his majesty or remain in densest ignorance about God.

March 1st - Hebrews 9:13, 14

If the blood of bulls and of goats, and the ashes of an heifer sprinkling the unclean, sanctifies to the purifying of the flesh: how much more shall the blood of Christ, who through the eternal Spirit offered himself without spot to God, purge your conscience from dead works to serve the living God?

Christ sacrificed not goats, nor calves, nor birds; not bread, nor blood, nor flesh, as did Aaron and his descendants. He offered his own body and blood, and the manner of the sacrifice was spiritual, for it was offered through the Holy Spirit. Though the body and blood of Christ were visible like any other material object, the fact that he offered them as a sacrifice was not apparent. It was not a visible sacrifice as in the case of those offered at the hands of Aaron. Christ offered himself in heart before God. His sacrifice was perceptible to no mortal. Therefore, his bodily flesh and blood became a spiritual sacrifice.

In the new order, the tabernacle or house is spiritual; for it is heaven, or the presence of God. Christ hung upon a cross; he was not offered in a temple. He was offered before the eyes of God, and there he still abides. The cross is an altar in a spiritual sense. The material cross was indeed visible, but none knew it as Christ's altar. His prayer, his sprinkled blood, were all spiritual, for it was all wrought through his spirit.

The fruit and blessing of his office and sacrifice, the forgiveness of sins and our justification, are likewise spiritual. In the Old Covenant, the priest with his sacrifices and sprinklings of blood effected merely an external absolution, or pardon. It rendered no one inwardly holy and just before God. Something more than that was necessary to secure real forgiveness. With the priesthood of Christ there is true spiritual remission, sanctification and absolution. These avail before God, whether we be outwardly excommunicated or not. Christ's blood has obtained for us pardon forever acceptable to God. He will forgive us our sins for the sake of that blood as long as its power shall last and its intercession for grace in our behalf shall continue, which is forever.

March 2nd - 2 Corinthians 11:19, 20

Ye suffer fools gladly, seeing you yourselves are wise. For you suffer, if a man bring you into bondage, if a man devour you, if a man take of you, if a man exalt himself, if a man smite you on the face.

Paul delivers a masterly stroke when with the same words he praises and rebukes the Corinthians. His commendation of their patience is in reality reproof. He means to say: I have preached the gospel to you at my own expense and jeopardy. By my labor you have attained to its blessing. You have done nothing for me in return, I have been no tax upon you. Now, upon my departure, others come and captivate you, and seek honor and profit from my labor. They boast as though the accomplishments were all theirs. Of these you become the disciples and pupils. Their preaching you accept, while mine becomes odious. My case is that of the bee which labors to gather honey and then come the idle drones and earthworms and consume the sweet which they have not gathered.

You can suffer these false prophets though they be fools and teach you foolishness. In this you display wisdom and patience. But you do not suffer me, who taught you true wisdom. You can permit them to make servants of you, to be your lords and to order you to do their bidding. But I, who have made myself your servant, served you without profit to myself, that you might be lords with Christ, must now be ignored and all my labors lost. You suffer yourselves to be devoured; for you abundantly bestow your property upon them. But I have never enjoyed aught of yours. All my service has been without recompense, that you might become rich in Christ.

You suffer the false teachers to take from you beyond your consent, to exalt themselves above you, to esteem themselves better than you and me, and to exercise their arrogance over you. But you deal not so with me, who have sacrificed my own substance, and have taken from others, that I might bring the gospel to you. They reproach you publicly, smite you in the face, put you to shame and abuse you with insolent words. But my patience with you, my parental tenderness, is remembered no more.

March 3rd - Luke 11:14

He was casting out a devil, and it was dumb. And it came to pass, when the devil was gone out, the dumb spake; and the people wondered.

The dumb, deaf, blind, and demon-possessed man represents all the children of Adam, who through the flesh are possessed of Satan in original sin, so that they must be his slaves and do according to his will. Hence they are also blind, that is, they do not see God. They are deaf, for they do not hear God's Word, and are not obedient or submissive to it. They are also dumb, for they do not give him one word of thanks or praise, nor do they preach and proclaim Christ and the grace of God. But they are all too talkative about the teachings of the devil and the opinions of men. In these things they see only too well and are wiser than the children of light in their undertakings, opinions, and desires. In these things they hear with both ears and readily accept the suggestions of flesh and blood. Therefore whatever we do, in word and deed, as to body and soul, is of the devil, whether it be externally good or bad, and must be redeemed through the work of God. When we are in his kingdom, we acknowledge him, see, hear and follow him, praise and proclaim his name. All this takes place through the Spirit of God in his Word, which casts out the devil and his kingdom.

But when the stronger man, the Gospel, comes, peace flees, and he rages like a madman, for he resents being condemned, unmasked, punished and publicly branded. He gathers up his armor, the powerful, wise, rich and holy people, and sets them all to attacking God's Word, as we see in the persecution of the teachers of the gospel. Such rage and persecution signify that the devil retires very unwillingly and raves in his whole body; as he acts in the body and its members when he must depart, so he also behaves in the whole world, resisting with all his power when he is to give place to the gospel; but it is all in vain, he must be expelled. A stronger one, that is, Christ, comes and overpowers him and takes away his whole armor, that is, he converts some of those same persecutors, and to that extent makes him weaker and his own kingdom stronger. He divides the spoil, too, by using for various offices, graces, and works in Christendom those whom he converts.

March 4th - Ephesians 5:3

Fornication, and all uncleanness, or covetousness, let it not be once named among you, as is proper for saints.

In naming uncleanness in addition to fornication, the reference is to all sensual affections in distinction from wedded love. They are too unsavory for Paul to mention, though in the first chapter of Romans he finds it expedient to speak of them without disguise. However, also wedded love must be characterized by moderation among Christians. While there is a conjugal duty to be required by necessity, it is for the very purpose of avoiding unchastity and uncleanness. The ideal and perfect condition would be cohabitation with the sole view to procreation; however, that is too high for attainment by all.

Paul declares that the sin which he indicates should not even be named of the Ephesians. Unquestionably among Christians there will always be some infirm one to fall; but we must labor diligently, correcting, amending, and restraining. We must not allow the offense to go unchallenged, but curtail and remedy it. An occasional fall among Christians must be borne with as long as right prevails in general and such things are neither tolerated nor taught, but reproved and amended. Paul counsels the Galatians that the brethren restore the fallen in a spirit of meekness; and he blames the Corinthians for not reproving those who sin. I make this point for the sake of those who, as soon as they observe that all Christians are not perfectly holy, imagine there is no such thing as a Christian and think the gospel is impotent and fruitless.

The writer of the epistle assigns the reason why it does not sound well to hear such things about Christians,— because they are saints and it behooves saints to be chaste and moderate, to practice and teach these virtues. He calls

Christians "saints" notwithstanding that in this life they are clothed with sinful flesh and blood. Doubtless the term is not applied in consequence of their good works, but because of the holy blood of Christ. For Paul says, "But you were washed, but you were sanctified, but you were justified in the name of the Lord Jesus Christ, and in the Spirit of our God." Being holy, we should manifest our holiness by our deeds. Though we are still weak, yet we ought duly to strive to become chaste and free from covetousness, to the glory and honor of God and the edifying of unbelievers.

March 5th - John 8:46

Which of you convicts me of sin? And if I say the truth, why do you not believe me?

This gospel teaches how persons become more hardened and furious, the more one teaches them, and lovingly urges them to do their duty. Christ asks them here in a very loving way for a reason why they still disbelieve, since they can find fault neither with his life, nor with his teaching. His life is blameless; for he challenges them with the words, "Which of you convicts me of sin?" His teaching is also blameless; for he adds, "If I say the truth, why do you not believe me?" Thus Christ lives as he teaches.

Every preacher should prove that he possesses, first, a blameless life, by which he can defy his enemies and no one may have occasion to slander his teachings; secondly, that he possesses the pure doctrine, so that he may not mislead those who follow him. Thus he will be right and firm on both sides; with his good life against his enemies, who look much more at his life than at his doctrine, and despise the doctrine for the sake of the life; with his doctrine among his friends, who have much more respect for his doctrine than for the kind of life he leads, and will bear with his life for the sake of his teaching.

It is indeed true that no one lives so perfect a life as to be without sin before God. Therefore it is sufficient that we be blameless in the eyes of the people. But his doctrine must be so good and pure as to stand, not only before man, but also before God. Therefore every pious pastor may well ask, Who among you can find fault with my life? Among you, I say, who are men, but before God I am a sinner. Thus Moses boasts that he took nothing from the people and did them no injustice. Thus Samuel, Jeremiah, and Hezekiah rightly boasted of their blameless life before the people to stop the mouths of blasphemers. But Christ does not thus speak of his doctrine, but says, "If I tell you the truth." For one must be assured that his doctrine is right before God and that it is the truth, and accordingly care not how it is judged by the people. The Jews have no ground for their unbelief; therefore Christ pronounces judgment upon them.

March 6th - John 8:48, 49

Then answered the Jews, and said unto him, Say we not well that you are a Samaritan, and has a devil? Jesus answered, I have not a devil; but I honor my Father, and you do dishonor me.

"You are a Samaritan" sounds worse among the Jews than any crime. In these words Christ teaches us the fate that awaits us Christians and his Word; both our life and doctrine must be condemned and reviled, and that by the foremost, wisest and greatest of earth. Thus one learns to know the corrupt tree by its fruits, as under the pretense of being good, they are so bitter, angry, impatient, cruel and mad as to condemn and pass sentence, when one touches them at their tender spot and rejects their ideas and ways.

Christ here abandons his life to shame and dishonor, is silent and suffers them to call him a Samaritan, while he takes pains to defend his doctrine. For the doctrine is not ours, but God's. I should stake all I have and suffer all they do, that the honor of God and of his Word may not be injured. For if I perish, no great harm is done; but if I let God's Word perish, and remain silent, I do harm to God and the whole world. Although I cannot close their mouths, nor prevent their wickedness, nevertheless I shall not keep silent, nor act as if they were right. Although they do me injustice, yet it remains right before God. Christ says, "I have not a devil," that is, my doctrine is not the devil's lies; but "I honor my Father," that is, I preach in my doctrine the grace of God, through which he is to be praised, loved and honored by believers. For the evangelical office of the ministry is nothing but glorifying God.

When Christ says, "Ye dishonor me," he implies that the Father's and his honor are the same, as he and the Father are one God. Yet along with this he would also teach that if the office of the ministry, which God honors, is to be duly praised, then it must suffer disgrace. Thus we will do to our princes and priests; when they attack our manner of life, we should suffer it and show love for hatred, good for evil; but when they attack our doctrine, God's honor is attacked, then love and patience should cease and we should not keep silent. Although the whole world reviles and dishonors us, we are assured that God will honor us, and will punish and judge the world.

March 7th - 2 Corinthians 6:2

For he said, I have heard you in a time accepted, and in the day of salvation have I succoured you: behold, now is the accepted time; now is the day of salvation.

These words portray the riches of salvation, wherever the gospel abounds; nothing but grace and help; no wrath, no punishment. Indeed, the apostle here employs words of unutterable meaning. He tells us that it is an acceptable time, as the Hebrew expresses it. Our way of putting it would be: This is a gracious time, a time when God turns away his wrath and is moved only by love and benevolence toward us and is pleased to do us good. All our sins are forgotten; he takes no notice of the sins of the past, nor of those of the present. We are in a realm of mercy, where are only forgiveness and reconciliation. The heavens are now open. This is the golden year when man is denied nothing. Whatsoever you shall desire and ask for, you shall surely receive. Be not neglectful: ask while the acceptable time continues.

Paul also declares that it is a day of blessing, "a day of salvation." It is a day of help, wherein we are not only acceptable and assured of God's favor and good will toward us, but we experience, even as we have been assured, that God really does help us. He verifies his assurance, for his beneficence gives testimony that our prayers are heard. We call it a happy day, a blessed day, a day of abundance; for these two truths are inseparably related, namely, that God is favorable toward us, and that his kindness is proof of his favor. God's favor toward us is revealed in the first clause, which speaks of an acceptable time; that he extends help to us is revealed in the second clause, telling of a blessed day of succor. Both these facts are to be apprehended by faith and in good conscience; for a superficial judgment would lead to the view that this period of blessing is rather an accursed period of wrath and disfavor. Words like these, of a spiritual meaning, must be understood in the light of the Holy Spirit; thus shall we find that these two glorious, beautiful expressions refer to the gospel dispensation and are intended to magnify all the treasures and the riches of the kingdom of Christ. May we take heed and accept the gospel with fear and gratitude.

March 8th - Genesis 4:9

The Lord said unto Cain, Where is Abel your brother?

There is clearly pointed out to us here the truth of the resurrection of the dead. This element of doctrine and of hope is found in the fact that the Lord inquiries concerning the dead Abel. God thereby declares himself to be the God of Abel, although now dead. Upon this passage we may establish the incontrovertible principle that, if there were no one to care for us after this life, Abel would not have been inquired for after he was slain. But God inquires after Abel even when he had been taken from this life; he has no desire to forget him; he retains the remembrance of him; God, therefore, is the God of the dead. My meaning is that even the dead, as we see here, still live in the memory of God who cares for them, and saves them in another life beyond and different from this corporal life in which saints suffer affliction.

This passage, therefore, is most worthy of our attention. A towering fact this, that Abel, though dead, was living and canonized in another life, more effectually and truly than those whom the pope ever canonized. The death of Abel was indeed horrible; he did not suffer death without excruciating torment, nor without many tears. Yet it was a blessed death, for now he lives a more blessed life than he did before. This bodily life of ours is lived in sin, and is ever in danger of death. But that other life is eternal and perfectly free from trials and troubles, both of the body and of the soul.

God inquires not after the sheep and oxen that are slain, but he does inquire after the men that are slain. Therefore men possess the hope of a resurrection. They have a God who brings them back from the death of the body unto eternal life, a God who inquires after their blood as a most precious thing. This is the glory of the human race obtained for it by the seed of the woman, which bruises the serpent's head. For God, in answer to Abel's faith in the promised seed, required the blood of the dead, and proved thereby to be his God still.

March 9th - Genesis 4:9

And he said, I know not: am I my brother's keeper?

Cain thinks he has made an effectual excuse for himself by saying that he is not his brother's keeper. But does he not confess by the very word "brother," which he takes upon his lips, that he ought to be his keeper? Is not that equal to accusing himself, and will not the fact that Abel is nowhere in evidence arouse the suspicion in the minds of his parents that he has been murdered? Just so also Adam excuses himself in paradise, and lays the blame on Eve. But the excuse of Cain is far more stupid; for while he excuses his sin he doubles it, whereas the frank confession of sin finds mercy and appeases wrath. All liars and hypocrites imitate Cain their father by either denying their sin or excusing it. Hence they cannot find pardon for their sins.

But let us survey the order in which sins follow each other and increase. First Cain sins by presumption and unbelief, priding himself on the privilege of his birthright. He takes it for granted that he shall be accepted of God on the ground of his own merit. Upon the pride and self-glorification follow envy and hatred of his brother, whom he sees preferred to himself by an unmistakable sign from heaven. Upon this envy and hatred follow hypocrisy and lying. Though he designs to murder his brother, he accosts him in a friendly manner and thereby throws him off his guard. Hypocrisy is followed by murder. Murder is followed by the excusing of his sin. And the last stage is despair, which is the fall from heaven to hell.

Moses took special pains in the preparation of this account to serve as a witness against all hypocrites, and as a chronicle containing a graphic description of their character and ire aroused by Satan against God, his Word and his Church. It was not enough of this murderer that he killed his brother, but he added the further sin of becoming indignant and wrathful when God inquired of him concerning his brother. He is indignant that he should be called to an account concerning the matter at all. His reply is the language of one who resists and hates God.

March 10th - Genesis 4:11

And now are you cursed from the earth, which has opened her mouth to receive your brother's blood from your hand.

We should mark as particularly worthy of note the discrimination exercised by the Holy Spirit. When the penalty for his sin was inflicted upon Adam, a curse was placed, not upon the person of Adam, but only upon the earth; and even this curse was not absolute, but qualified. The expression is: "Cursed is the ground for your sake;" and in Romans 8:20 we read: "The creature was made subject to vanity, not willingly." The earth, inasmuch as it bore guilty man, became involved in the curse as his instrument, just as the sword, gold and other objects are cursed for the reason that men make them the instrument of sin. The Holy Spirit discriminates between the earth and Adam. He diverts the curse to the earth, but saves the person.

In this instance the Holy Spirit curses the person of Cain. Why is this? Is it because the sin of Cain, as a murderer, was greater than the sin of Adam and Eve? Not so. But because Adam was the root from whose flesh and loins Christ, that blessed seed, should be born. It is this seed that was spared. For the sake of this seed, the fruit of the loins of Adam, the curse is transferred from the person of Adam to the earth. Thus, Adam bears the curse of the earth, but his person is not cursed; from his posterity Christ was to be born.

Cain, since he fell by his sin, must suffer the curse being inflicted upon his person. He hears it said to him, "Cursed are thou," that we might understand that he was cut off from the glory of the promised seed, and condemned never to have in his posterity that seed through which the blessing should come. Thus Cain was cast out from the stupendous glory of the promised seed. Abel was slain; therefore there could be no posterity from him. But Adam was ordained to serve God by further procreation. In Adam alone, after Cain's rejection, the hope of the blessed seed rested until Seth was born unto him.

March 11th - Genesis 4:15

Whosoever slays Cain, vengeance shall be taken on him sevenfold.

God deprives Cain of all the divine blessings, both spiritual and civil. He mitigates that sentence by commanding that no one shall slay Cain. But he does not promise that all men shall surely obey his command. Therefore Cain, though possessing this promise in reference to his body, is still a fugitive and wanderer. God left him in a life of uncertainty, doubt and restless wandering, and did no more than protect his life by a command and threat which might restrain the wicked from killing him, on account of the certain awful punishment which would follow such destruction of the murderer. But a promise that he should not be murdered was withheld. The Scriptures are quite silent concerning the number of the years of Cain, and say nothing about the day of his birth or the day of his death. He perished, together with his whole generation. Only a few of his generation are excepted, who were saved by the uncovenanted mercy of God.

The question is here usually asked, to what persons could the words of Cain possibly apply, when he says, "everyone that findeth me shall slay me," when it is evident that besides Adam and Eve and their few daughters, no human beings were in existence. I would reply that they bear witness to the fact that we see the wicked "flee when no man pursueth." They imagine various perils where none really exist. Just as we see it in the case of murderers at the present, who are filled with fears where all is safe, who can remain quiet nowhere, and who imagine death to be present everywhere.

The words of the text cannot be referred exclusively to the fears within Cain, for he had sisters, and perhaps he greatly dreaded that sister whom he married, lest she should take vengeance on him for the murder of her brother. Moreover, Cain had perhaps a vague apprehension of a long life, and he saw that many more sons were born of Adam. He therefore feared the whole posterity of Adam. It greatly increased these fears that Adam had left him nothing more than his stray mercy.

March 12th - Genesis 4:16

And Cain went out from the presence of the Lord, and dwelt in the land of Nod, on the east of Eden.

Moses leaves it to the thoughtful reader to reflect how miserable and full of tears this departure of Cain from his father's house must have been. His godly parents had already lost their son Abel; and now, at the command of God, the other son departs from them into banishment, loaded with divine curses, on account of his sin—the very son whom his parents had hoped to be the only heir of the promise. But they obey the command of God and cast out their son.

Adam and Eve had learned by their own experience in paradise that it was no light sin to depart from the command of God; therefore they thought: Our sin in paradise has been punished with death, and with an infinite number of other calamities into which we have been thrown since we were driven out of paradise. Now that our son has committed so atrocious a sin, it behooves us not to resist the will of God and his righteous judgment, however bitter we feel them to be.

This departure from his home was, I have no doubt, most bitter also to Cain himself. For he was compelled to leave, not only the common home, his dear parents and their protection, but his hereditary right of primogeniture, the prerogative of the kingdom and of the priesthood, and the communion of the Church. Hence we have the expression in the text, that Cain went out from the presence of the Lord. "The presence" or "face of the Lord" are all those things and means by which the Lord makes himself known to us. Thus the face of the Lord, under the Old Testament, was the pillar of fire, the cloud, the mercy seat and the like. Under the New Testament, the face of the Lord is baptism, the Lord's Supper, the ministry of the Word. For by these things, as by visible signs, the Lord makes himself known to us, and shows that he is with us, that he cares for us and favors us. Cain "went out" to where there was no "face of God," no visible sign by which he could derive the consolation that God was present with his favor. A wretched departure full of tears.

March 13th - Genesis 4:24

If Cain shall be avenged sevenfold, truly Lamech seventy and sevenfold.

Here Lamech sets himself above his father Cain, making it appear that he had a more righteous cause for the murder he had committed, and fortifying himself against those inclined to avenge the murder perpetrated by him. For the words of the text are not the words of the Lord, but the words of Lamech himself. It is very probable that the patriarch Adam died about this time; and there is no doubt that Lamech seized this opportunity of transferring the whole government of the world at that time to himself, that he might have all things under his own rule.

Lamech is, therefore, an example of this world, and Moses points to him to show what kind of a heart, will, and wisdom the children of this world have. They gather riches, follow their pleasures, increase their power, and then abuse all these things by their tyranny, making use of them against the true Church, whose members they persecute and slay. In the midst of all these mighty sins, they fear not, but are proud and secure, saying, "What can the righteous do?" "Our lips are our own: who is lord over us?" Thus the true Church has ever Satan as its great enemy, as Christ also says, "that the devil was a murderer from the beginning." The Scriptures declare throughout concerning the true Church, that the wicked are ever shedding its blood.

In this manner the Church was vexed with the cross and persecutions from the very beginning of the world until God, compelled by the wickedness of man, destroyed the whole world by the flood. So also, when the measure of Pharaoh's malice was full, he was drowned with all his host in the Red Sea. So also, when the malice of the Gentile nations was full, they were all uprooted and destroyed by Moses and Joshua. In the same manner later when the Jews raged against the gospel, they were so utterly destroyed that not one stone was left upon another in Jerusalem. Thus also Christ expressly testifies against them "that upon you may come all the righteous blood shed upon the earth, from the blood of righteous Abel unto the blood of Zacharias, son of Barachias."

March 14th - Genesis 4:25

And she bare a son, and called his name Seth: For God, said she, has appointed me another seed instead of Abel.

Seth is derived from a Hebrew verb which signifies, "he placed," or "he established," and was intended to show that this son would be the foundation on which the promise concerning Christ would rest, even though many other sons should be born unto the parents. Eve does not give him an exalted name, such as "Cain," but one signifying that the posterity of Seth should never be suppressed or destroyed. The Cainites are left under a curse without any promise whatever, and they have only so much mercy as they receive from the generation of the righteous as beggars, not as heirs.

Eve is highly to be praised as a most holy woman, full of faith and charity, because in the person of her son Seth she so nobly lauds the true Church, paying no regard whatever to the generation of the Cainites. She does not say, I have gotten another son in the place of Cain. She prefers the slain

Abel to Cain, though Cain was the first-born. Praise is due not only to her faith but to her eminent obedience; for she is not only not offended at the judgment of God concerning righteous Abel, but she also changes her own judgment concerning God. When Abel was born she despised him, and magnified Cain as the first-born, and as the possessor, as she thought, of the promise. Now she acts quite to the contrary. As if she had said: After God's acceptance of him and of his offering, I had placed all my hopes on my son Abel, because he was righteous; but his wicked brother slew him. But now God has appointed me another seed instead of Abel. She does not indulge her maternal affection for Cain. She does not excuse or lessen his sin; but she herself excommunicates him, already excommunicated of God.

In Seth, then, we have a new generation, which arises from and comes to pass in accordance with the great original promise, that the seed of the woman should bruise the serpent's head. Appropriately the name Seth is bestowed, so that Eve may felicitate herself upon the fact that this seed is established, and safe from overthrow.

March 15th - 2 Peter 2:5

And (God) spared not the old world, but saved Noah ..., a preacher of righteousness, bringing in the flood upon the world of the ungodly.

It is appalling that the whole human race except eight persons is destroyed, in view of the fact that this was truly the golden age; for succeeding ages do not equal the old world in glory, greatness, and majesty. And if God visited with destruction his own perfect creation and the very glory of the human race, we have just cause for fear. In inflicting this punishment, God followed his own peculiar way. Whatever is most exalted he particularly overthrows and humiliates. He did not spare the sublimest creatures—the angels—, nor the kings ruling his people, nor the firstborn of all times. But the more highly they were blessed with gifts, the more sternly he punished them when they began to misuse his gifts.

As God, who is by nature most kind, cannot refrain from gracing and showering us with various gifts, so we cannot refrain from priding ourselves upon these gifts and flaunting them. Wretched is our life when we lack the gifts of God, but twice wretched is it when we have them; for they tend to make us doubly wicked. Such is the corruption of original sin, though all but believers are either unaware of its existence or regard it a trivial thing. How property inflates pride, though it occupies relatively the lowest place among blessings! The rich, be they noblemen or peasants, deem other people as flies. To an even greater extent are the higher gifts abused—wisdom and righteousness. This was the sin of the primeval world. Among Cain's descendants were good and wise men, who, nevertheless, were wicked before God, for they prided themselves upon their gifts and despised God, the author.

The old world was guilty, not only of sin against the second table of the commandments, but most of all of sin against the first by making a fine, but deceptive and false show of wisdom, godliness, and religion. As a result of the ungodliness in opposition to the first table there followed that moral corruption of which Moses speaks, that people polluted themselves with all sorts of lusts and afterward filled the world with oppression and bloodshed. Because the ungodly world had trampled both tables under foot, God came to judge it, who is a consuming fire and a jealous God.

March 16th - Ephesians 5:1, 2

Be you therefore followers of God, as dear children; and walk in love, as Christ also has loved us, and has given himself for us an offering and a sacrifice to God for a sweet smelling savor.

Paul admonishes us to be followers of the Father, as beloved children. He employs the most endearing terms—"dear children"—to persuade us with the Father's love to love even as we are loved. What manner of love has God manifested toward us? Not simply that love in which he gives temporal support to us unworthy beings in common with all the wicked on earth; that he permits his sun to rise on the just and the unjust and sends rain on the grateful and the ungrateful. Not only thus did God love us; but he has given his Son for us. In addition to showering upon us both temporal and eternal blessings he has given his own self with all he is, with all he has, with all he does. He who despises such glow of love, which fills all heaven and earth and is beyond all power to comprehend; he who does not permit this love to kindle and incite in him love for his neighbor, whether enemy or friend, is not likely ever to become godly or loving by such measures as laws or commandments, instruction, constraint, or compulsion.

"Walk in love," the apostle counsels. He would have our external life all love. But not the world's love is to be our pattern, which seeks only its own advantage, and loves only so long as it is the gainer thereby; we must love even as Christ loved, who sought neither pleasure, nor gain from us, but gave himself for us—gave himself as a sacrifice and offering to reconcile God unto ourselves, so that he should be our God and we his children. Thus are we to give, or even surrender our goods, whether friends claim them or enemies. We are to be ready to give our lives for both friends and enemies and must be occupied with the thought how we may serve others, and how life and property can be made to minister to them in this life, and this because we know that Christ is ours and has given us all things. All sacrifices are powerless but that of Christ himself; he is the sweet-smelling savor. This sacrifice is pleasing to God. He gladly accepts it and would have us believe that it is an acceptable offering in our stead.

March 17th - John 6:40

This is the will of him that sent me, that everyone which sees the Son, and believeth on him, may have everlasting life: and I will raise him up at the last day.

With these words Christ declares the Father's will, namely, that we come to Christ, see him and believe in him, that we may not be cast out and lost. It is the Father's will that we attain unto eternal life. Therefore the will of the Father is that all who are given to Christ should be saved through Christ in eternity. These are significant words, since faith in Christ is sufficient for the attainment of eternal life. He does not say, you shall fast and pray and do this and that, but, If you wilt believe in the Son, you shall be saved; and this is the Father's will.

But are we not to do any good works? Yes, they are to follow faith, for faith must have good works; but eternal life is not attained by good works, since it is impossible to keep the law. No saint was ever found on earth who has loved God with his whole heart and his fellow man as himself. Therefore God has not said, I should be the one to give life to myself or keep myself. To give life and keep it depends on two things, namely, *seeing* and *believing*. These words are easily said, but no one knows what faith means. It is a grand art and doctrine from which no saint has ever graduated or was able to fathom, unless he was steeped in despair, or cast into throes of external danger and death. The power and effect of faith are especially seen in temptations, when sin, death, devil, and hell are overcome. Nor are these weak enemies; they bring out perspiration, weaken our limbs, and make heaven and earth cramped. When the devil and death come, no one can help except only the person who has said, I am he who shall sustain you Under such conditions we learn what faith is.

He adds, "and I will raise him up at the last day," to refute the foolish understanding of the flesh. That the carnal sense may not here be applied, as though eternal life would be given without physical death, he tells us before that they will indeed die, but will not lose eternal life, as they shall be raised again at the last day.

March 18th - John 8:51

Verily, verily, I say unto you, If a man keep my saying, he shall never see death.

By these words Christ breaks entirely with the Jews in that he ascribes such virtue to his teaching that it becomes a powerful emperor over Satan, death, and sin, to give and sustain eternal life. Here see, how divine wisdom and human reason are in conflict with one another. How can a human being grasp the thought, that a corporeal, an oral word should redeem forever from death? But let blindness run its course. Christ is speaking here not of the word of the law, but of the gospel, which is a discourse about Christ, who died for our sins. For God did not wish to impart Christ to the world in any other way; he had to embody him in the Word and thus distribute him, and present him to everybody; otherwise Christ would have existed for himself alone and remained unknown to us; he would have thus died for himself. But when the Word places Christ before us, it places us before one who has triumphed over death, sin, and Satan. Therefore he who grasps and retains Christ has eternal deliverance from death. Consequently it is a Word of life, and it is true that whosoever keeps the Word shall never see death.

From this we may well understand what Christ meant by the word "keep;" it is not such keeping as one keeps the law by good works; for this word of Christ must be kept in the heart by faith and not by good works. The Jews rage fearfully against Christ, that Abraham and the prophets are dead; they know nothing of what it is to "keep," to "die," or to "live." And to "keep" is not said in vain; for there is a conflict and battle when sin bites, death presses and hell faces us; then we are to be in earnest in holding firmly to the Word and let nothing separate us from it. Thus you see how Christ answers the Jews and praises his own teachings. You say, my Word is of the devil, and wish to sink it to the bottom of perdition; on the contrary I say to you that it has divine power in it, and I exalt it higher than the heaven of heavens, and above all creatures.

March 19th - Isaiah 53:4

Surely he has borne our griefs, and carried our sorrows: yet we did esteem him stricken, smitten of God, and afflicted.

Some reflect upon the sufferings of Christ in such way as to become angry at the Jews, sing and lament about poor Judas, and are then satisfied. Such is not a meditation on the sufferings of Christ, but on the wickedness of Judas and the Jews. Others have pointed out the different fruits springing from a consideration of Christ's passion. The saying is ascribed to Albertus, that to think once, and that only superficially, of the sufferings of Christ is better than to fast a whole year or to pray the Psalter every day. Some people thus blindly follow him and act contrary to the true fruits of Christ's passion; for they seek therein their own selfish interests. A third class so sympathize with Christ as to weep and lament for him because he was so innocent, like the women who followed Christ from Jerusalem, whom he rebuked, telling them they had better weep for themselves and their children.

They meditate rightly on the passion of Christ, who so view Christ as to become terror-stricken in heart at the sight, and their conscience at once sinks in despair. This terror-stricken feeling should spring forth, so that you see the severe wrath and the unchangeable earnestness of God in regard to sin and sinners, in that he was unwilling that his only and dearly beloved Son should set sinners free unless he paid this costly ransom for them. There must be an earnestness here that is inexpressible and unbearable, that a person so immeasurably great goes to meet, and suffers and dies for it. If you reflect that God's Son, the eternal wisdom of the Father, himself suffers, you will indeed be terror-stricken; and the more you reflect, the deeper will be the impression. You must really believe and never doubt in the least that you are the one who thus martyred Christ. For your sins most surely did it. Thus Peter struck and terrified the Jews, when he said to them all in common, "Him have you crucified," so that three thousand were terror-stricken the same day and trembling cried to the apostles: "O beloved brethren, what shall we do?" Where man does not come to this point, the sufferings of Christ have become of no true benefit to him.

March 20th - 2 Corinthians 12:7

Lest I should be exalted above measure through the abundance of the revelations, there was given to me a thorn in the flesh, the messenger of Satan to buffet me.

And must this mighty apostle, O merciful God, be subject to trials lest he exalt himself because of his great revelations? Then how should others, how should such infirm beings as we, be free from self-exaltation? The thorn stands for something painful and afflicting. In "a thorn of the flesh" the thought is not of an instrumentality whereby the flesh stings, but of something that stings the flesh. The Greek text impels us to think of a thorn for the flesh. We may imagine Paul as saying: "As a clog to a dog's neck, as a ring in a bear's nose, a bit in a horse's mouth, or a gag in the mouth of a swine, so is my thorn a clog to my body lest I exalt myself."

Paul himself explains the nature of the clog, or thorn. He calls it "a messenger of Satan," a devil, to "buffet" him, or to jog him. Hence a spiritual trial cannot be meant. The explanation appeals to me that the persecutions and sufferings, which the apostle recounts, constitute the devil's flaying. Thus his meaning would be: I have received great revelations, for which reason the clog is bound to the dog; that is, the many dangers and misfortunes with which the angel of the devil buffets and humiliates my body will make me forget to exalt myself. They are the thorn in my flesh, or upon my body; for God will not permit it to come upon my soul.

The text seems to imply some peculiar work of the devil upon Paul's body, for it says, the thorn, or clog, is the messenger which Satan employs to beat his body; also that the apostle thrice, diligently but unavailingly, besought the Lord to remove it. I do not imagine him praying for the cessation of persecutions in a spirit of unwillingness to suffer them. But since he does not specify the affliction, we must let it remain a secret, a distress only known to himself. It is enough for us to know that while God had given him great revelations, revelations beyond human ken, he also bound the clog to him—gave him a thorn for his body—to prevent the exaltation of himself; and the knowledge of the buffetings and flaying caused by this clog, or devil, are likewise beyond human kin.

March 21st - John 1:4

In him was life; and the life was the light of men.

Just as we interpret the words of Christ, when he says, "I am the life," so also should we interpret these words, and say nothing philosophically of the life of the creatures in God; on the contrary, we should consider how God lives in us and makes us partakers of his life, so that we live through him, of him, and in him. For it cannot be denied that through him natural life also exists, which even unbelievers have from him. Natural life is a part of eternal life, it's beginning, but on account of death it has an end, because it does not acknowledge and honor him from whom it comes; sin cuts it off so that it must die forever. On the other hand, those who believe in him, and acknowledge him from whom they have their being, shall never die; but this natural life of theirs will be extended into eternal life, so that they will never taste death. "He that believeth in me, though he die, yet shall he live." These and similar passages are well understood when we rightly learn to know Christ, how he overcame death and has brought us to life.

When the evangelist says, "In him *was* life," and not, "In him *is* life," as though he spoke of things past, the words must not be taken to mean the time before creation, or the time of the beginning; but they must be referred to the time of Christ's life or sojourn upon earth, when the Word of God appeared to men and among men; for the evangelist proposes to write about Christ and that life in which he accomplished all things necessary for our life.

The words of the evangelist therefore simply refer to the sojourn of Christ on earth. Whoever will disregard the life and sojourn of Christ on earth, and will wish to find him in some other way than as he now sits in heaven, will always fail. He must look for him as he was and sojourned on earth, and he will then find life. Here Christ was made our life, light, and salvation. "In him was life," not that he is not our life now, but that he does not now do that which he then did.

March 22nd - 1 Peter 2:21, 22

Christ also suffered for us, leaving us an example, that you should follow his steps: who did no sin, neither was guile found in his mouth.

The atonement is the chief, the most exalted article of Christian doctrine. Faith alone apprehends it as the highest good, the greatest blessing of our salvation, and recognizes that we cannot, by our works or our sufferings, do or merit anything to atone for sin. The manner in which this subject is Scripturally presented prohibits us from adding to it anything of human origin. But so the accursed popedom has done in the teaching of its pillars and supporters, the monks, who regard the sufferings of Christ merely as an example for us. This is a doctrine not found in the Word of God, but is one of their own trivial, self-selected, self-devised and false human teachings.

They have carried their untruthful, worthless inventions to the extent of claiming for the saints not only sufficient acquired merit for their own salvation, but a large accumulated surplus available for others, which they have bequeathed to the pope, thus furnishing him with an abundant treasury. Through indulgences the pope is to distribute this excess, these superfluous merits, as he feels disposed, at the same time dipping out for himself and his own fat swine the riches of the world; indeed, the church leaders distribute their own merits and works. Oh, shameful abomination, that in the temple of God and in the Christian Church must be taught things which make wholly insignificant the sufferings and death of Christ! Gracious God! what can be said for human merit, for superfluity of human merit, when not one saint on earth has, with all his pains, suffered enough to cancel his own obligations, much less to be entitled to the honor of making his sufferings avail anything before God's judgment seat, by way of remuneration or satisfaction for the mortal sins of others in the face of divine wrath?

The theme of Christ's passion must far outrank every other. His sufferings are like pure and precious gold, compared to which ours is nothing. No one but Christ has suffered for the sins of another. The saint ought to be ashamed to boast of his sufferings in comparison with those of Christ, and ought to rejoice in the privilege of being partaker of the divine plan, of sharing as far as he can, and thus be found in the footsteps of Christ.

March 23rd - Isaiah 53:6

The Lord has laid on him the iniquity of us all.

When man perceives his sins and is completely terror-stricken in his conscience, he must be on his guard that his sins do not remain in his conscience. Just as our sins flow out from a meditation upon the sufferings of Christ and we become conscious of them, so we should pour them again upon him and set our conscience free. Therefore see well to it that you act not like perverted people, who bite and devour themselves with their sins in their hearts, and run here and there with their good works or their own satisfaction, even work themselves out of this condition by means of indulgences, and thus try to rid themselves of their sins, which is impossible. Such false refuge of satisfaction and pilgrimages has spread far and wide.

Cast your sins from yourself upon Christ, believe with a joyful spirit that your sins are his sufferings and wounds, that he carries them and makes satisfaction for them. For if you do not take this course, you will never quiet your heart and secure peace, but you must finally despair in doubt. For if we deal with our sins in our conscience and let them continue within us and cherish them in our hearts, they become much too strong for us to manage and will live forever. But when we see that they are laid on Christ and that he has triumphed over them by his resurrection, and we fearlessly believe it, then they are dead and have become as nothing. In his sufferings Christ made known our sins and crucified them; but by his resurrection he makes us righteous and free from all sin.

Now if you are not able to believe this, you should pray to God for faith. For this is a matter in the hands of God, and is bestowed at times knowingly and at times secretly. Now bestir yourself not to behold Christ's sufferings any longer, but press through all difficulties and behold his friendly heart, how full of love it is toward you, which love constrained him to bear the heavy load of your conscience and of your sin. Thus will your heart be glad and loving toward him, and the assurance of your faith be strengthened.

March 24th - Galatians 5:24

They that are Christ's have crucified the flesh with the affections and lusts.

When your heart is established in Christ, and you are an enemy of sin, out of love and not out of fear of punishment, Christ's suffering should be an example for your whole life, and you should meditate on the same in this way. If a day of sorrow or sickness weighs you down, think how trifling that is compared with the thorns and nails of Christ. If you must do or leave undone what is distasteful to you, think how Christ was led hither and thither, bound a captive. Does pride attack you, think how your Lord was mocked and disgraced with murderers. Do unchastity and lust thrust themselves against you, think how bitter it was for Christ to have his tender flesh torn, pierced and beaten again and again. Do hatred and envy war against you, or do you seek vengeance, remember how Christ, who had more reason to seek revenge, prayed for you and all his enemies with tears and cries. If trouble or whatever adversity of body or soul afflict you, strengthen your heart and say: Ah, why should I not also suffer a little, since my Lord sweat blood in the garden because of anxiety and grief? That would be a lazy, disgraceful servant who would wish to lie in his bed while his lord was compelled to battle with the pangs of death.

One can thus find in Christ strength and comfort against all vice and bad habits. This is the right observance of

Christ's passion and the fruit of his suffering, and he who exercises himself thus in the same does better than by hearing the whole Passion or reading all masses. They are called true Christians who incorporate the life and name of Christ into their own life. For Christ's passion must be dealt with not in words and a show, but in our lives and in truth. Paul admonishes: "Consider him who endured such contradiction of sinners against himself, lest you be wearied and faint in your minds." And Peter says: "Forasmuch as Christ has suffered for us in the flesh, arm yourselves likewise with the same mind; for he that has suffered in the flesh has ceased from sin."

March 25th - Psalm 32:5

I said, I will confess my transgressions unto the Lord; and you forgave the iniquity of my sin.

The first kind of confession is that which is made to God and teaches us that we are all alike wicked sinners. If anyone have special grace, let him thank God and refrain from boasting. Has anyone fallen into sin, it is because of his flesh and blood, nor has any fallen so low but that another who now stands may fall even lower. This kind of confession is so highly necessary that it dare not cease for a moment, but must constitute the entire life of a Christian, so that without ceasing he praises the grace of God and reproaches his own life in his presence.

The second confession is that made to our neighbor, and is called the confession springing from love, as the former is called confession springing from faith. Of this confession we read, "Confess your faults one to another." This kind of confession like the former is necessary and commanded; for God will be merciful to no one, nor forgive his sins, unless he also forgive his neighbor. Besides, faith cannot be true unless it produces this fruit, that you forgive your neighbor, and that you ask for forgiveness; otherwise a man dare not appear before God. If this fruit is absent, faith and the first kind of confession are not honest.

The third kind of confession is that ordered by the pope, which is privately spoken into the ears of the priest when sins are enumerated. This confession is not commanded of God; the pope has forced the people to it and consciences have been troubled and tortured in a manner that is pitiful and distressing. Hence we say of private confession, that no one is compelled to observe it. Still it is a commendable and good thing. When you go to private confession do not give heed so much to what you do, as to what the minister says, that in God's stead he proclaims to you the forgiveness of sins. The word which he speaks is not his, but God's Word; and God will keep it as surely as if he had spoken it himself. This is the way God has placed his Word into every corner of the world. Therefore you ought not to despise it, but receive it with heartfelt desire in true faith.

March 26th - Romans 10:10

With the heart man believeth unto righteousness; and with the mouth confession is made unto salvation.

Let it be said concerning confession that everything ought to be free, so that each person attends without restraint, of his own accord. But what ought one to confess? Here is where our preachers in the past have pounded a great deal into us by means of the five senses, the seven deadly sins, the ten commandments and the like, thereby perplexing our consciences. But it should be that you first of all feel that which weighs you down, and the sins that pain you most and burden your conscience. These you ought to declare and confess to your brother. You need not search long nor seek all kinds of sins; just take the ones that come to your mind, and say, This is how frail I am and how I have fallen; this is where I crave consolation and counsel. For confession ought to be brief. If you recall something that you have forgotten, it is not to trouble you; for you made confession, not as a good work, nor because you were compelled, but in order to be comforted by the word of absolution. Moreover, you can easily confess to God in secret what was forgotten, or you can hear the absolution for it during the communion service.

We are therefore not to worry, even if sins have been forgotten; though forgotten they are still forgiven; for God looks not to the excellence or completeness of your confession, but to his Word and how you believe it. So also the absolution does not state that some sins are forgiven and others not; it is a free proclamation declaring that God is merciful to you. But if God is merciful to you all your sins must be blotted out. Therefore hold fast to the absolution alone and not to your confession; whether or not you have forgotten anything makes no difference; to the extent that you believe you are forgiven. Therefore confession and absolution must be carefully distinguished, that you give attention chiefly to the absolution, and that you attend confession not to do a good work, thinking that because of this good work your sins are forgiven. We are to go only because we there hear God's Word and by it receive consolation. This is confessing in the right way.

March 27th - John 16:16

A little while, and you shall not see me; and again, a little while, and you shall see me, because I go to the Father.

"A little while," Christ says, "and you shall not see me," for I shall be taken prisoner and they shall deliver me to death. But it will not last long, and during this short time you shall be sorrowful, but only remain steadfast in me and follow me. Three days I will be in the grave; the world will rejoice as though it had gained a victory, and you shall be sorrowful and shall weep and lament. Again a little while, and you shall se me," that is, on the third day I will rise again; then you shall rejoice and your joy no man shall take from you; this will not be a joy of only three days, like the joy of the world, but an eternal joy.

An example is here given us which we should diligently take to heart; in suffering, anxiety and distress, we should also remember to be strong and to rejoice because Christ will rise again. We know that this has come to pass; but the disciples did not know what he meant by the resurrection, hence they were so sad and sorrowful. They heard, indeed, that they should see him, but they did not understand what it was, nor how it should come to pass. To such an extent had sadness and sorrow overcome them that they quite despaired.

But since they were unable to understand it, why does Christ relate it or why is it written? In order that we should not despair but hold fast to the Word, assured that it is indeed thus, and not otherwise, even though it seems to be different. We should take to heart and firmly hold fast to these words and keep them in mind when in sorrow and distress; it will not last long, and then we shall also have more constant joy, for as Christ and his elect had their "little while," so you and I and everyone will have his "little while." Pilate and Herod will not crucify you, but in the same manner as the devil used them, so he will also use your persecutors. When your trials come, you must not immediately think how you are to be delivered out of them. God will help you in due time. Only wait. It is only for a little while, he will not delay long.

March 28th - John 16:8, 9

When he (the Comforter) is come, he will reprove the world ... of sin, because they believe not on me.

This is the sin of the world that it does not believe in Christ. Not that there is no sin of the world besides this; but that this is the real chief sin, which condemns the whole world though it could be charged with no other sin. Thus this preaching of conviction is to begin if people are to be brought to a right knowledge and to salvation. The first thing shall be this, that it makes all men sinners, because they do not believe in Christ. Hence God's wrath is declared and the judgment of eternal death is pronounced upon those who in the sight of the world are irreproachable, who even strive with earnestness to live according to the law, or the ten commandments. How is this? Is it sin to live according to the ten commandments? Surely not; but these are not kept. The world recognizes only public, external sins, such as murder, adultery, robbery and what the jurists call and punish as crime. But God's law demands not merely outward form and compliance; it goes to the heart and demands its perfect obedience. Therefore it also judges man not only by his outward walk and conduct, but by the depths of his heart. The world does not know nor see the true offenses, such as contempt of God, impurity of the heart, and disobedience to God's will, which things are and remain in all men who are not sanctified by Christ.

Because no man fulfils the commandments and can be without sin before God, God resolved to send his Son into the world that he might become a sacrifice for us and make satisfaction for our sins by the shedding of his blood in death, and take away from us the wrath of God, which no creature could reconcile, bring forgiveness of sins and bestow upon us the Holy Spirit, so that we might obtain all this, begin to become new men, and come out of sin and death to righteousness and eternal life. This God has now done and has commanded us to preach it through the gospel. He demands of all men repentance and faith. He that believes this preaching has by this faith forgiveness of sins and is in the grace of God. But if they will not accept this Saviour by faith, they are justly condemned in their sins.

March 29th - Acts 10:43

To him give all the prophets witness, that through his name whosoever believeth in him shall receive remission of sins.

This verse constitutes the principal theme of one of Peter's sermons. It is one of the greatest in the writings of the apostles. It contains the vital element of the gospel message, teaching how we may appropriate its blessings, how obtain what it offers, namely, by faith; faith lays hold of what is offered us in the gospel. The message is preached that we may receive and retain it. Through the Word the blessing is pronounced our own—it is offered or given us; but by faith we receive it, make it our own, permit it to work in us.

This power and work in us is called by Peter "remission of sins." This is the blessing conferred through the preaching of the doctrine of Christ, or articles of faith, particularly the article of the resurrection. The meaning of the new message of comfort, the new declaration, is that Christ, through his resurrection, has in himself conquered our sin and death, has turned away the wrath of God and procured grace and salvation; that he has commanded forgiveness to be preached unto us, desiring us to believe that he gives it and confidently to receive it through faith.

Faith must be of such a character as to apprehend and hold fast the truth Peter declares in this verse. It must say, "In his name." That is, it must ascribe to Christ alone the entire agency, merit and power responsible for remission of sins; must believe we have forgiveness, not through our own worthiness, but for Christ's sake alone; must believe that by virtue of Christ's resurrection we obtain remission of sins, every thing not from Christ being completely excluded, and the honor given to him alone. The efficacy of Christ's death and blood alone God would have preached in all the world and accepted by mankind. Therein he rejects the boasting of the Jews and of all who aspire to holiness through their own works, teaching them that they cannot obtain his favor through the law, or by their own efforts. In Christ's name alone is remission of sins received, and that through faith.

We ought to be ashamed to doubt or question the fact of forgiveness of sins and justification before God through Christ alone, to which all Scripture testifies.

March 30th - 2 Corinthians 11:21, 22

Wheresoever any is bold, (I speak foolishly,) I am bold also. Are they Hebrews? so am I. Are they Israelites? so am I. Are they the seed of Abraham? so am I.

In whatever the false apostles can boast, Paul says, I can likewise glory. Here we are shown what is the ground of the false apostles' boasting; their outward respectability—being of Abraham's seed, children of Israel, Christ's preachers. In these they think far to excel the Corinthians, claiming their doctrine and works to be of greater weight because they have Moses and the prophets for their teachers. But they failed to perceive that their boast is in mere externals, that render no one righteous or better before God. Names are of no consequence; they only make a fine show and serve to seduce the simple-minded. Paul boasts of his origin and yet derides his boasting, calling it fool's work. His object is to destroy the boasting of the false prophets, that the people might not be deceived.

Note how, even in Paul's time, great men erred concerning the true sense of the gospel, and many noble preachers would have estimated Christian life by a merely external appearance and name. The true spiritual preachers must have been few. Should it be strange, then, that in our time sincere preachers are not numerous, and that the majority of ministers riot in what they themselves seem and do? It cannot and will not be otherwise.

The thievish drones, which are prone to riot, let them riot! We will resist to the utmost of our power, commending the matter to God, who doubtless will grant us sufficient honor and profit, both temporal and eternal, though we must labor gratuitously, receiving injury and derision as our reward. Our adversaries will not long continue their persecutions, for, as Paul says just preceding our text, they will eventually receive their deserts.

Paul boasts of certain temporal afflictions in which he excels the false apostles, who suffer nothing for the sake either of the Word or of souls, but only boast of name and person. Among the afflictions he names having been a night and a day in the deep. Of other afflictions affecting not his own person, but distressing others, he mentions two: he is weak, if another is weak, and burns, if another is offended. Thereby he plainly portrays the ardor of his heart—the defects and sorrows of others pain him as his own.

March 31st - 1 Corinthians 10:4

They drank of that spiritual Rock that followed them: and that Rock was Christ.

Christ has been typified by various signs and objects in the Old Testament, and the rock is one of them. Note first, that the material rock spoken of had a place independently of man's labors and far from man's domain, in the wilderness. So Christ is a truly insignificant object in the world, disregarded and unnoticed, nor is he indebted to human labor. Water flowing from the rock is contrary to nature; it is purely miraculous. The water typifies the quickening spirit of God, who proceeds from the condemned, crucified and dead Christ. Thus life is drawn from death, and this by the power of God. Christ's death is our life, and if we would live we must die with him.

Moses strikes the rock at the command of God and points to it, thus prefiguring the ministerial office which by word of mouth strikes from the spiritual rock the Spirit. For God will give his Spirit to none without the instrumentality of the Word and the ministerial office instituted by him for this purpose, adding the command that nothing be preached but Christ. Had not Moses obeyed the command of God to smite the rock with his rod, no water would ever have flowed from it. His rod represents the rod of the mouth of which Isaiah speaks: "He shall smite the earth with the rod of his mouth; and with the breath of his lips shall he slay the wicked."

By this statement about the rock the apostle makes all the figures and signs granted to the people of Israel by the Word of God refer to Christ; for where the Word of God is, there Christ is. All the words and promises of God are concerning Christ. Christ himself makes the serpent of Moses refer to himself. We may truly say that the Israelites looked upon the same serpent we behold, for they saw the spiritual serpent that followed them, or Christ on the cross. The beholding was believing in the Word of God, with the serpent for a sign, even as their spiritual drinking was believing in the Word of God with the rock for a sign. We may say the same concerning the cloud. The children of Israel walked under the same cloud that shadows us; they walked under the spiritual cloud that followed them—Christ.

April 1st - Genesis 5:24

And Enoch walked with God: and he was not: for God took him.

For a man to walk with God is not to flee into a desert, or to conceal himself in some corner, but to go forth in his vocation, and to set himself against the iniquity and malice of Satan and the world, and to confess the seed of the woman; to condemn the religion and pursuits of the world, and to preach, through Christ, another life after this. This is the manner of life led for three hundred years by the greatest prophet and high priest of his generation. Moses, therefore, deservedly extols Enoch as a disciple of greatest eminence, taught and trained by many patriarchal masters, and so equipped with the Holy Spirit that he was the prophet of prophets and the saint of saints in that primeval world.

It was the will of God that he should be an example to the whole world in verifying and showing the comfort of the faith in the future life. He is to preach the life beyond this present life; to teach concerning the seed to come, concerning the serpent's head that is to be bruised and the kingdom of Satan that is to be destroyed. Such was the preaching of Enoch, who was, nevertheless, a husband and the father of a family; who had a wife and children, who governed his household, and procured his subsistence by the labor of his own hands. This godly man lived, after the birth of Methuselah, 300 years in the truest religion, in faith, in patience, and in the midst of a thousand crosses, all of which he endured and overcame by faith in the blessed seed.

Enoch's walking with God signifies that he was in this life a faithful witness of eternal life to be gained after this life through the promised seed. Inasmuch as Enoch constantly preached this doctrine, God verified and fulfilled this preaching in the patriarch himself, that we might fully and surely believe it; in that Enoch, a man like ourselves, born of flesh and blood, as we also are, of the seed of Adam, was taken up into heaven by God, and now lives the life of God, that is, an eternal life.

April 2nd - Hebrews 11:5

By faith Enoch was translated that he should not see death; and was not found, because God had translated him: for before his translation he had this testimony, that he pleased God.

As among us we find many to whom such things are considered absurd, and not sufficiently worthy of faith, so there is no doubt that this account was deemed ridiculous by most people. For that reason these things have by divine authority been committed to writing and recorded for the saints and the faithful, that they might read, understand, believe and heed them. They present to our sight a manifest triumph over death and sin, and afford us a sure comfort in Enoch's victory over the law, and the wrath and judgment of God. To the godly nothing can yield more grace and joy than these antediluvian records. What facts could inspire more wonder and admiration than that a man, born of flesh and blood, as we are, and defiled as we are by sin and corruption, so obtained the victory over death as not to die at all! Christ himself is a man, and righteous, yet our sins caused him to suffer the bitterest of all deaths; but he is delivered on the third day, and lifts himself unto life eternal. In Enoch is the singular fact that he died not at all, but was caught up, without death intervening, to the life spiritual and eternal.

This fact makes the narrative under consideration so memorable that God intended to use it for the purpose of setting before the old, primeval world the hope of a better life. Likewise, to the second world, which had the law, God gave the example of Elijah, who also was taken up into heaven and translated by the Lord before the very eyes of his own servant Elisha. We are now in the New Covenant, in a third world, as it were. We have Christ himself, our great deliverer, as our glorious example, who ascended into the heavens, taking with him many of his saints.

It was God's will to establish in every age a testimonial of the resurrection of the dead, that he might allure our minds from this corrupt and in many ways wretched life, in which we gladly serve God as long as it shall please him by the faithful performance of all public and private duties, and especially by instructing others in holiness and in the knowledge of God. Here we have "no certain dwelling place." Christ has gone to prepare a place for us.

April 3rd - Isaiah 55:6

Seek you the Lord while he may be found, call you upon him while he is near.

Think not that you will find the Lord when he has once gone, though you traverse the world. But while he is near, you may seek and find him. For many years, while still in my cloister, I experienced the meaning of such disappointment. I sought God with great toil and with severe mortification of the body, fasting, watching, singing and praying. In this way

I shamefully wasted my time and found not the Lord. No, God does not permit us to find him thus.

To find him, go to the Creed and the Ten Commandments. They will tell you. Regulate your life by them. Be helped by the Lord's Prayer. Begin with yourself; then pray for the Church. Let it be your desire that God's name be everywhere sanctified and that your life conform to his will. For the study and practice of these precepts will leave you no opportunity to do evil. God's Word will soon teach you to sanctify his name, to extend his kingdom, to do your neighbor no injury in mind, body, or estate. Surely we ought supremely to thank God for the great blessings of his nearness to us. We have his presence in our homes. He is with us at our board, by our couch—anywhere we desire him. He offers us all assistance and grants all we may ask. So gracious a guest should indeed receive our high esteem.

There is too much slumbering everywhere in Germany. We cannot perceive how it is possible to preserve the gospel and fill the pulpits for ten years longer. No one for a moment thinks how God has signally, richly and graciously blessed us; how we are in possession of actual paradise, if we only recognized the fact. Yet we shamefully, ungratefully and unreasonably reject the kingdom; as if it were not enough for us to overstep the ten commandments in our disobedience, but must even trample under foot the mercy God offers in the gospel. Then why should we be surprised if he send down wrath upon us? Jerusalem and in fact the entire Jewish nation sinned unceasingly against all God's commandments, and when he proclaimed grace and offered forgiveness of sins, they trampled upon his mercy. Should

Christ not revenge himself when they shamed and mocked his precious blood?

April 4th - Philippians 3:20

Our conversation is in heaven; from whence also we look for the Saviour, the Lord Jesus Christ.

We who are baptized and believe in Christ do not base our works and our hope on the righteousness of this temporal life. Through faith in Christ, we have a righteousness that holds in heaven. It abides in Christ alone; otherwise it would avail naught before God. Our whole concern is to be eternally in Christ; to have our earthly existence culminate in yonder life when Christ shall come and change this life into another, altogether new, pure, holy and like unto his own. Therefore we are no longer citizens on earth. The baptized Christian is born a citizen of heaven through baptism. We should be mindful of this fact and walk here as if native there. We are to console ourselves with the fact that God thus accepts us and will transplant us there. Meanwhile we must await the coming again of the Saviour, who is to bring from heaven to us eternal righteousness, life, honor and glory.

With the believers in Christ, who have their righteousness in him, there should follow in this life on earth the fruits of upright living in obedience to God. These fruits constitute the good works acceptable to God, which being works of faith and wrought in Christ will be rewarded in the life to come. While we walk in the faith of his righteousness, God has patience with the poor, frail righteousness of this earthly life. He honors our human holiness by supporting and protecting it during the time we live on earth; just as we honor our corrupt, filthy bodies, adorning them with beautiful, costly garments and golden ornaments. Because God would confer eternal life upon man, he patiently endures the filthy righteousness of this life until the last day, and until the number is complete. When the time shall be fulfilled, the number completed, God will suddenly bring the world with its governments and conditions of life to an end; he will utterly abolish earthly righteousness, destroying physical appetites and all else. Yet for the sake of Christians, to whom eternal life is appointed, all these must be perpetuated until the last saint is born and has attained life everlasting. For God regards not the world nor has need of it, except for the sake of his Christians.

April 5th - 1 Corinthians 10:3, 4

(They) did all eat the same spiritual meat; and did all drink the same spiritual drink.

Among us one element (bread) alone is not to be offered to the communicant; he who wants the Lord's Supper should receive the whole of it. We have preached and practiced this long enough and cannot assume that there should be anyone unable to understand it; yet if there be one so dense, or claiming to be so weak that he cannot grasp the true meaning of it, we will excuse him; it is just as well that he remain away. For anyone to hear God's Word so long, to have himself coddled like a child, and after all to continue saying, I do not understand, is not a good sign. For it is impossible for you to hear so long and still be unenlightened; since then you remain blind it is better for you not to receive the Lord's Supper. If you cannot grasp the Word that is plain, clear and certain, you cannot grasp the sacrament; for the sacrament would be nothing, if there were no Word.

Moreover this Word has now resounded again and again throughout the world, so that even they who oppose it know it. These, however, are not weak but obdurate and hardened; they set their heads against the doctrine which they hear us prove from the Scriptures with such clearness that they are unable to reply or establish the contrary. Therefore it is out of the question for us any longer to yield or to endure them, since they defy us and maintain as their right what they teach and practice. We wish to receive both elements in the Lord's Supper, just because they wish to prevent us from having them. The thought of causing offense no longer applies to them. The Roman bishops have forbidden both elements as contrary to God's ordinance and command. If now we wish to confess Christ we must receive both elements, so that the people may know that we are Christians and abide by the Word of God. When we go to the Lord's Supper people can see who they are that have heard the gospel; they can observe whether we lead Christian lives. So this is a distinct mark whereby we are recognized, whereby we also confess the name of God and show that we are not ashamed of his Word.

April 6th - 1 Corinthians 5:6

Know you not that a little leaven leavens the whole lump?

Leaven is a common figure with the apostle, one he uses frequently, almost proverbially. Christ also gives us a Scripture parable of the leaven. It is the nature of leaven that a small quantity mixed with a lump of dough will pervade and fill the whole lump until its own acid nature has been imparted to it. This Paul makes a figure of spiritual things in doctrine and life. In the Epistle to the Galatians, he makes it more especially typify false doctrine. For the introduction of an error in an article of faith will soon work injury to the whole and result in the loss of Christ. Such innovation will pursue its course with destructive sweep until even the uncontaminated part becomes worthless; the once pure mass is wholly corrupted.

But in this text he has reference more particularly to an erroneous idea concerning life and conduct. Here it is likewise true that, once the flesh be allowed any license, and liberty be abused, and that under the name of the gospel, there is introduced a leaven which will speedily corrupt faith and conscience, and continue its work until Christ and the gospel are lost. Such would have been the fate of the Corinthians had not Paul saved them from it by this epistle, admonishing and urging them to purge out the leaven of license; for they had begun to practice great wantonness, and had given rise to sects and factions which tended to subvert the one gospel and the one faith.

Nor may we in our works and in our daily life tolerate the yielding to the wantonness of the flesh and at the same time boast the gospel of Christ, as did the Corinthians, who stirred up among themselves divisions and disorder, even to the extent of one marrying his stepmother. In such matters as these, Paul says, a little leaven leavens and ruins the whole lump—the entire Christian life. These two things are not consistent with each other: to hold to the Christian faith and to live after the wantonness of the flesh in sins and vices condemned by conscience. Paul elsewhere warns, "Be not deceived, neither fornicators, nor idolaters, nor adulterers, nor effeminate, nor abusers of themselves with mankind, nor thieves, nor drunkards, shall inherit the kingdom of God."

April 7th - Matthew 26:26–28; Mark 14:22–24 ; Luke 22:19, 20; 1 Corinthians 11:23–25

Take, eat; this is my body which is given for you. Take, drink you all of it; this cup is the New Testament in my blood, which is shed for you for the remission of sins.

These are the words which neither our opponents, nor Satan are able to deny; on them we must stand. Let them make whatever comments they please; we have the clear Word of God, saying, the bread is Christ's body given for us; and the cup is his blood shed for us. This he bids us do in remembrance of him; but the pope commands that it be not done. They say, we are only erring laymen, we do not understand, nor are we able to explain the words. But we reply, It is for us to explain just as much as it is for them; for we are commanded to believe in Christ, to confess our faith, and to keep all the commandments of God, just as well as they are. How then are we to believe without knowing and understanding the Word? I must know the words if I am to believe; for how can I believe without words?

This is how you can stop their mouths and bring them to silence. My faith must be as good as yours, therefore I must have and must know the Word as well as you. These words are certainly clear enough; and there is no one so stupid that he cannot understand what is meant by, "Take, drink you all of it; this cup is the New Testament in my blood." Unless they prove to us that drinking here signifies something different from what all the world understands by the term, we shall adhere to the interpretation that we are all to drink of the cup. Let them bring forward what they please, customs or councils, we reply, God is older and greater than all things.

Thus you see how we are to understand the words of the institution of the Lord's Supper, and firmly hold to them. In them all the virtue is centered, we all must know them, understand them, and cling to them in faith. When you wish to go to the Lord's Supper listen to the words spoken and be assured that they contain the whole treasure on which you are to rely. They are really spoken to you. My body is given, my blood is shed, Christ declares. Why? For the remission of sins. This is what strikes you, that your sins may be forgiven.

April 8th - 1 Peter 2:20

What glory is it, if, when you be buffeted for your faults, you shall take it patiently? but if, when you do well, and suffer for it, you take it patiently, this is acceptable with God.

When the individual accepts Christ and begins to profess his faith in words and life, invariably the world, that eternal enemy of Christ and faithfully obedient servant of the devil, will be dissatisfied. The world regards it contemptible, disgraceful, to live any life but one pleasing to itself, to do and speak aught but as it desires. Its rage is excited toward the Christian and it proceeds to persecute, to torture, even to murder him when possible. We often hear the wiseacres and scoffers say that Christ could have enjoyed peace had he so desired. The same may be said of Christians; they could have peace and pleasure if they would but take advice and conform to the world.

What are we to do? It is a fact that to maintain and obey the truth is to stir up wrath and hatred. Even the heathen assert as much. But the fault lies not with the advocate of truth but with its rejecters. Is the truth not to be preached at all? Must we be silent and permit all mankind to go direct to hell? Who could or would heap upon himself the guilt of such negligence? The godly Christian, who looks for eternal life after the present one and who aims to help others to the same happy goal, assuredly must act the part he professes, must assert his belief and show the world how it travels the broad road to hell and eternal death. But to do so is to antagonize the world and incur the displeasure of the devil.

Since there is no escaping the fact that he who would confess Christ and make the world better must in return for his service and benefactions heap upon himself the enmity of the devil and his adherents, we must remember that it is incumbent upon us to have patience when the world manifests its bitterest, most hateful enmity toward our doctrine and toward our very lives; when it reviles and slanders and persecutes us to the utmost for our principles. Peter here admonishes and persuades Christians unto patience under these circumstances, and at the same time seeks to comfort them with tender and impressive words. If you would be a Christian, then be not so terribly alarmed and so extremely impatient at the torments of the world and the devil.

April 9th - 1 Corinthians 10:17

We being many are one bread, and one body: for we are all partakers of that one bread.

While we live on earth we must bear with one another, as Christ also bore with us, seeing that none of us are perfect. Christ has shown this to us not only by his own example and by his Word, but he has also pictured it to us in the form of the Sacrament of the Altar, namely, by means of the bread and the wine. We believe that the true body and blood of Christ is under the bread and wine. Here we see one thing and believe another, which describes faith. For when we hear the Word and receive the Lord's Supper we have merely a word and an act, yet by it we embrace life and every treasure, even God himself. Likewise love is pictured in these signs and elements. First of all in the bread. As long as the grains of wheat are in a pile before they are ground, each is a body separate for itself, and is not mingled with the others; but when they are ground they all become one body. The same thing takes place with the wine. As long as the berries are not crushed each retains its own form, but when they are crushed they all flow together and become one drink. You cannot say, this is the flour from this grain, or this is a drop from that berry; for each has entered the form of the other, and thus was formed one bread and one drink.

We receive the Lord by the faith of the Word which the soul consumes and enjoys. In this way my neighbor receives me; I give him my goods, body, and life and all that I have, and let him consume and use it in his want. Likewise, I also need my neighbor; I too am poor and afflicted, and suffer him to help and serve me in turn. Thus we are woven one into another, helping one another even as Christ helps us. Therefore when you have received the Lord's Supper, you must be diligent to increase love, aid your neighbor in distress, and lend him a helping hand when he suffers affliction and requires assistance. When you fail to do this, you are not a Christian, or at best only a very weak one.

April 10th - Acts 13:26

Men and brethren, children of the stock of Abraham, and whosoever among you fear God, to you is the word of this salvation sent.

Paul refers to the gospel not simply as the word of peace, as Peter does, but gives it the greater and grander title, "the word of salvation;" in other words, a doctrine calculated to heal and save. No grander name could be found for the gospel; for a message of salvation is an expression of God's grace, forgiveness of sins, abiding peace and life eternal. Moreover these blessings were not to be bestowed upon the Jews alone; they were to be equally shared with the Gentiles, who had no knowledge of God, of the law, or of divine worship. The Gentiles were thus to be made the equals of the Jews, leaving the latter without preference or special merit before God, and without advantage and lordship over the former in the world.

Paul plainly tells the Jews that the law of Moses did not secure them the favor of God in the past and would be equally profitless in the future; that through the gospel message, and only so, they and all Gentiles as well were to be delivered from sin, death and the power of the devil, and to become God's people with power over all. Yet he presents no other tangible token of the great boon he calls salvation and blessedness than his preaching alone. But one may say, The word I hear and Paul I see, a poor human being; but this salvation—grace, life and peace—I behold not. On the contrary, I daily see and experience sin, terror, adversity, suffering and death, until it seems as if in all humanity none are so utterly forsaken by God as the Christians, who hear his message.

This is precisely the precious doctrine to be learned, if we are to be God's children and sensible of his kingdom within us, a doctrine beyond the knowledge and experience of the Jews with their law and the Gentiles with their wisdom drawn from reason. Our salvation stands in the word which Paul here declares of Christ, a word which, in name and reality, is a word of salvation and peace; for salvation and peace are the blessings which it offers and imparts. God has sent this word, Paul says. Its origin and conception is not with man. It is the Word of the God of heaven.

April 11th - 1 Corinthians 11:27

Whosoever shall eat this bread, and drink this cup of the Lord, unworthily, shall be guilty of the body and blood of the Lord.

Let me say in regard to the Lord's Supper that when we have received it we ought to give heed to love, and in this way assure ourselves that we have received the sacrament profitably, and at the same time furnish evidence to others; we should not always continue to come and still be unchanged. Therefore we must turn from our devotions and thoughts to our conduct toward our neighbor, and examine ourselves in this mirror with all seriousness. The sacrament is to act upon us so that we may be transformed and become different people. For God's word and work do not intend to be idle, but are bound to produce great things, to wit, to set us free from sin, death and the devil, and every kind of fear, and make us servants even of the least among men on earth, and this without the slightest complaint on our part, rejoicing rather to find someone in need of our help, and fearing only lest after receiving so much we may not apply it at all.

When the Lord's Supper fails to produce this result there is reason to fear it has wrought injury. Nevertheless, even if the result is not great, we are not to reject those who are imperfect and weak, but those that are indolent and insolent, who imagine that they have done enough when they have partaken of the sacrament. A change must take place in you, and there must be evidence of it, then you will be able to perceive through the symbol that God is with you, and your faith will grow sure and strong. For you can easily feel whether you have grown more joyous and bold than you were before. Formerly the world seemed too narrow for us when we heard of death and thought of sin. If you feel different it is not because of your own strength, for in the past you could not do it. Thus you can discover whether the Lord's Supper is producing any fruit in your own life. If you experience nothing, go to God and tell him of your shortcomings and troubles; we must all do the same thing as long as we live, for not one of us is perfect.

April 12th - Matthew 28:10

Then said Jesus unto them, Be not afraid: go tell my brethren that they go into Galilee, and there shall they see me.

These are the first words they heard from Christ after his resurrection from the dead, by which he confirmed all the former utterances and loving deeds he showed them, namely, that his resurrection avails in our behalf who believe, so that he anticipates and calls Christians his brethren, who believe it, and yet they do not, like the apostles, witness his resurrection. The risen Christ does not wait until we ask or call on him to become his brethren. Can we here speak of merit, by which we deserve anything? What did the apostles merit? Peter denied his Lord three times; the other disciples fled from him; they tarried with him like a rabbit does with her young. He should have called them deserters, betrayers, reprobates, anything but brethren. Therefore this word is sent to them through the women out of pure grace and mercy, as the apostles at the time keenly experienced, and we experience also when we are mired in our sins, temptations and condemnation.

These are words full of comfort that Christ receives desperate villains, as you and I are, and calls us his brethren. Is Christ really our brother, then indeed what more do we need? Brothers according to the flesh enjoy the same possessions, have the same father, the one inheritance; so we enjoy with Christ the same possessions, have in common one Father and one inheritance. He who has a part of this spiritual inheritance has it all.

If I believe on Christ, I become a partaker with him of all his possessions. I obtain eternal righteousness, eternal wisdom, eternal strength, and become a lord and reign over all. The stomach will no longer hunger, sins will not oppress, I will no more fear death, nor be terror-stricken by Satan, but will be like Christ the Lord himself. The title of being Christ's brethren is so high that the heart of man cannot understand it. The Holy Spirit must bestow this grace.

April 13th - 1 Corinthians 15:4

He rose again the third day according to the scriptures.

Here we must remember the custom of the Hebrews, for according to the Jewish reckoning the day began in the evening and lasted until the evening of the next day, as the first chapter of Genesis says: "And there was evening and there was morning, one day," "a second day," "a third day," and so forth. Thus the first and greatest Sabbath began on the evening of the day when Christ was crucified, that is to say, at the time of sunset on Friday. In addition to this the Jews had seven full days which they celebrated, and all of which they called sabbaths. On these days they ate only wafers and unleavened bread, for which reason they are called the days of unleavened bread. Christ rose before sunrise.

How can we say then that he rose on the third day, since he lay in the grave only one day and two nights? According to the Jewish calculation it was only a day and one half; how shall we then persist in believing there were three days? To this we reply that he was in the state of death for at least a part of three days. For he died at about three o'clock on Friday and consequently was dead for about three hours on the first day. After that night he lay in the grave all day, which is the true Sabbath. On the third day, which we commemorate now, he rose from the dead and so remained in the state of death a part of this day, just as when we say that something occurred on Easter day, although it happens in the evening, only a portion of the day. In this sense Paul and the Evangelists say that he rose on the third day.

For this period and no longer Christ was to lie in the grave, so that we might suppose that his body remained naturally uncorrupted and that decomposition had not yet set in. He came forth from the grave so soon that we might presume that corruption had not yet taken place according to the course of nature; for a corpse can lie no longer than three days before it begins to decompose. Therefore Christ was to rise on the third day, before he saw corruption.

April 14th - John 20:16, 17

Jesus said unto her, Mary. She turned herself, and said unto him, ... Master. Jesus said unto her, Touch me not; for I am not yet ascended to my Father.

There are two things concerning the Lord's resurrection that we ought to know and understand. First, the history which relates the events as they occurred, together with the different circumstances under which he revealed himself alive in various manifestations; so that we might have a sure record and testimony of everything as a foundation and support of our faith, inasmuch as this article of faith on the resurrection is the chief one upon which our salvation is finally based, and without which all others would be useless and entirely fruitless.

The second point, that is the more important and necessary, on account of which the narrative has been recorded and preached, is the power, benefit and comfort of the joyous resurrection of the Lord. Concerning this Paul and all the apostles and the entire Scriptures teach and preach richly and gloriously; but most gloriously of all did Christ the Lord himself preach, when he manifested himself first of all to the women. This is the first sermon our Lord delivered after his resurrection, and without doubt also the most comforting one. It was spoken first of all to his beloved Mary Magdalene, and through her also to his disciples after their deep woe, grief and sorrow caused by his departure and death, that he might comfort and gladden them by his resurrection.

But her joy is no higher than the mere bodily pleasure of having her Lord alive again as she had him before; she clung only to the fact of his return and thought that he would again be with them, eat and drink with them, preach and do miracles as he had done before. He does not permit himself to be touched, however, because he wants her to stand still and listen and learn what she does not know, namely: I am not risen to walk and remain with you bodily and temporally, but that I may ascend to my Father. It is not here that I intend to dwell and abide; but I would have you believe that I go to the Father, where I will rule and reign with him eternally, and whither I will also bring you out of your death and sorrow. There you shall have me tangibly, and you shall rejoice forever in eternal communion with me and the Father.

April 15th - John 20:19

Then the same day at evening, being the first day of the week, when the doors were shut where the disciples were assembled for fear of the Jews, came Jesus and stood in the midst, and said unto them, Peace be unto you.

Jesus finds his disciples sitting in fear and terror both from without because of the Jews and from within because of their consciences. They were slow of heart to believe what they had heard from the women and from some of the disciples, that he had risen from the dead. While they were talking about it with sad hearts, Christ appears and hails them with his friendly greeting, "Peace be unto you," which means a wish for everything that is good.

The peace of Christ is hidden from our eyes and senses and is different from that which the world seeks. It is not a visible or tangible peace, consisting of bodily feeling, but an inner and spiritual peace, consisting of faith, which grasps and holds to nothing save what it hears in our text, namely, the gracious words of Christ, which he speaks to all frightened and troubled souls. A Christian, therefore, is contented and satisfied with having Christ as his friend and in him a gracious God who desires his constant welfare, even though, materially speaking, he has no peace in the world, but constant strife and contention. At another place Jesus says, "These things have I spoken unto you, that you might have peace. In the world you have tribulation."

The disciples were not troubled by anyone, yet their hearts were all aflutter, and were neither at rest nor at peace. While they are thus in fear and terror, the Lord brings them peace, not by removing any danger, but by quieting their hearts. The wickedness of the Jews is neither removed nor changed; they are as full of hatred and rage as before. Without there is no change whatever, but the disciples are changed within; they have become courageous and bold, and the hatred of the Jews is now of little concern to them. This is the true peace which is able to calm the heart even in the midst of trouble. It is well called a peace "which passes all understanding;" it is abiding and invincible as long as the heart clings to Christ; for thereby it is certain that it has a merciful God and the forgiveness of sins.

April 16th - John 20:17

Jesus said unto her, ... Go to my brethren, and say unto them, I ascend unto my Father, and your Father; and to my God, and your God.

The apostles were crouching behind barred doors, discouraged and cowed, as sheep without a shepherd, and troubled in conscience. Peter had denied his Lord with an oath, and the others had all fled and proved themselves disloyal. That was, indeed, a fall so deep and terrible that they might well think they would never be forgiven for denying the Son of God, and so shamefully forsaking their dear Lord and faithful Saviour. How could it ever enter their hearts that Christ would send such an affectionate greeting and such a kind good morning to them, and would not only forgive everything, but also call them dear brethren?

Consider what these words contain and offer. Go, my dear sister, and tell the denying and disloyal disciples that they are called and shall be my dear brethren. Is not this placing us with Christ into the complete tenure and inheritance of heaven and of everything Christ has? Rich and blessed indeed must be the brethren and sisters who can boast of this Brother, not now hanging on the cross, nor lying in the grave under the power of death, but a mighty Lord over sin, death, hell and the devil.

But who is he that has instituted this brotherhood? The only Son of God and almighty Lord of all creatures, so that on his own account he did not need to endure suffering and death. I have done all this, he tells us, for your sake as your dear Brother, who could not bear to see you eternally separated from God by the devil, sin and death, and miserably perish; hence I stepped into your place and took your misery upon myself, gave my body and life for you that you might be delivered; I have now risen again to proclaim and impart to you this victory and deliverance, and to receive you into my brotherhood, that you might possess and enjoy with me all that I have and hold. Thus you see, it is not enough for Christ that the historical fact has occurred, and that on his part everything is accomplished; he infuses it into us and creates a brotherhood from it, so that it may become the common possession of us all. He has done this not for himself and his own sake, but as our brother and for our good alone.

April 17th - Luke 24:27

Beginning at Moses and all the prophets, he expounded unto them in all the scriptures the things concerning himself.

The Evangelist states that their heart burned within them while he opened to them the Scriptures, and the gospel following says that Christ opened their minds to understand the Scripture. Here is the point: Moses certainly writes concerning Christ, and Christ is found in the books of Moses; but it is necessary not only to read, but also to understand what is said.

Therefore the Bible is a book that must not only be read and preached, but it also requires the true interpreter, that is, the revelation of the Holy Spirit. Not a single article of faith has ever been preached that was not more than once attacked and denied by heretics, though they read the same Scriptures that we have.

This revelation, therefore, requires pupils of the right kind, who are willing to learn and to be instructed, like these pious and simple-minded disciples, not wise and puffed up minds and self-made masters who reach beyond the very heavens with their knowledge. This is a doctrine that makes our wisdom foolishness and blinds our reason, before it can be believed and understood; for it is not born of man's reason, like other sciences and arts, which have sprung from reason and can be grasped by means of reason. All heresies from the beginning have had their origin here; both Jews and Gentiles, and the Turks at present, grow foolishly violent in regard to our doctrine, because it does not agree with reason and human wisdom. Only pious, simple-minded people can grasp and understand it—they who say: "God has said it, therefore I believe it."

Christ himself thanks the Father with a joyful heart that he hides these things from the wise and understanding and reveals them unto babes.

Thus poor, ignorant women came to the sepulcher without considering that the tomb was covered with a heavy stone; yet these foolish persons are the first to whom Christ reveals his resurrection and calls to be his preachers and witnesses. So he gives these disciples a knowledge of the Scriptures which all the learned scribes did not possess, so that now they view Moses with different eyes, and are forced to confess: I have read and heard this before, but never understood it.

April 18th - Luke 24:36

As they thus spake, Jesus himself stood in the midst of them, and said unto them, Peace be unto you.

The disciples are gathered together in seclusion. They are afraid of the Jews and are in danger of their lives; they are fearful and faint-hearted and afraid of sin and death. Had they been strong and courageous, they would not have thus crept into a corner; later, when the Holy Spirit came, strengthened and comforted them, they were made so courageous that they stepped forth and preached publicly without fear. This is written for us, that we might learn that the gospel of Christ's resurrection comforts only the faint-hearted. They are the poor, conscience-stricken ones, whose sins lie heavily upon them, who feel faint at heart, are loth to die and are well-nigh startled by the sound of a rustling leaf. To these contrite, poor, and needy souls the gospel offers comfort, to them it is a sweet savor.

This is also learned from the nature of the gospel, for the gospel is a message and a testimony, which declares how the Lord Jesus Christ rose from the dead, that he might remove sin, death and all evil from all who believe in him. If I recognize him as such a Saviour, I have heard the gospel aright, and he has in truth revealed himself to me. If now the gospel teaches naught but that Christ has overcome sin and death by his resurrection, then we must indeed confess that it can be of service to none save those who feel sin and death. They who do not feel their sin, and are not dismayed, nor see their infirmities, profit not a whit by it, nor do they delight in it. Though they hear the gospel, it has no effect upon them, except that they learn the words, and speak of what they have heard. They do not treasure them in their hearts, and receive neither comfort nor joy from them.

It were well, if the gospel could be preached only where faint-hearted and conscience-stricken ones are found. But this cannot be, and for this reason it bears so little fruit. The fault is not in the gospel, but in the hearers. They hear it, but they do not feel their own affliction and misery, nor have they ever tried to feel it. Hence none need marvel if the gospel does not everywhere bring forth fruit.

April 19th - 1 Peter 4:11

If any man speak, let him speak as the oracles of God; if any man minister, let him do it as of the ability which God giveth: that God in all things may be glorified through Jesus Christ.

It is necessary that both preachers and hearers take heed to doctrine and have clear, unmistakable evidence that what they embrace is really the true Word of God revealed from heaven; the doctrine given to the holy and primitive fathers, prophets and apostles; the doctrine Christ himself confirmed and commanded to be taught. We are not permitted to employ the teachings dictated by any man's pleasure or fancy. We are not allowed to adapt the Word to mere human knowledge and reason. We are not to trifle with the Scriptures, to juggle with the Word of God, as if it would admit of being explained to suit the people; of being twisted, distended and patched to effect peace and agreement among men. There would then be no sure, permanent foundation whereon the conscience might rely.

Still it is not enough that the office and commandment be God-appointed. We ministers should be conscious—and the people should be taught—that efficacy of office is not of human effort, but is God's power and work. That which the office was designed to accomplish is not effective by virtue of our speech or action, but by virtue of God's commandment and appointment. He it is who orders; and himself will effectively operate through that office which is obedient to his command. In baptism, the Lord's Supper and absolution we are not to be concerned about the person administering the sacraments or pronouncing absolution,— who he is, how righteous, how holy, how worthy. Worthiness or unworthiness of either administering or receiving hand effects nothing; all the virtue lies in God's command and ordinance.

The motive for all Christian effort is named in the words, "that in all things God may be glorified." No one may seek or ascribe to himself power and honor because of his office or gifts. Power and glory belongs only to God. God himself calls his Church, rules, sanctifies and preserves it through his Word and his Spirit. To this end he bestows on us his gifts. All is done purely of grace, wholly for the sake of his beloved Son, Christ the Lord. Therefore, in return for the favor and ineffable goodness bestowed upon us regardless of our merits, we ought to thank and praise God, directing all our efforts to the recognition and glory of his name.

April 20th - Ezekiel 34:2

Woe be to the shepherds of Israel that do feed themselves! should not the shepherds feed the flocks?

To be a shepherd is not to exercise great pomp and glory; but it is a service one is wont to render another, as a servant in a household, who does all in his power to please his master freely and without restraint, and is in all other respects faithful. Thus Christ did all in harmony with his office and his name. When he was here on earth he carefully tended his sheep and provided them with everything needful for body and soul, with good and honest teaching and deeds of mercy. Good shepherds are like the good Shepherd Christ, who tends the sheep, goes before them, cares for those who are sick; who does not flee when the wolves come, but "who giveth his life for the sheep."

It is not enough that we preach correctly, which the hireling can also do; but we must watch over the sheep, that the wolves, the false teachers, may not break in, and we must contend for the sheep against the wolves with the Word of God, even to the sacrifice of our lives. Such are good shepherds, of whom few are found. They are the righteous apostles and preachers, who are but the mouthpieces of Christ, through whom Christ preaches. The hirelings do not care for the sheep, receive temporal wages, riches and honor and feed themselves. They are good to a certain extent, and Christ also preaches through them, but they are not true to the sheep. This may be seen in our shepherds to-day who almost entirely subvert their office. In times past the princes gave the bishops and priests great treasures, besides land and people, so that pious bishops did not want to accept the office, they even fled from it; but that is entirely changed at present and there is a running and racing after the best bishoprics. The greatest rush is for the offices which afford the best livings. They seek their own, not the things of Christ. This is a lamentable and miserable state of things. Thus Paul also warns the elders at Ephesus: Take heed unto yourselves and to all the flock, over the which the Holy Ghost has made you overseers. I know, after my departing shall grievous wolves enter in among you, not sparing the flock.

April 21st - John 16:8–10

When he (the Comforter) is come, he will reprove the world ... of righteousness, because I go to my Father, and you see me no more.

The world is reproved not only because it has sin, but also because it does not know what righteousness is, and how to become pious. The righteousness of which he speaks here does not consist in observing civil or imperial laws and in doing what reason teaches, but the righteousness which is valid before God, or which he regards as righteousness. He says, "Because I go to the Father, and you see me no more." To the world this is strange and ridiculous language. "Because I go to the Father," embraces the whole work of our redemption and salvation, for which God's Son was sent from heaven, and which he performed for us and still performs until the end, namely, his passion, death and resurrection, and his whole reign in the Church. This going to the Father signifies nothing else than that he offers himself as a sacrifice by the shedding of his blood and by his death to pay for sin; afterwards he triumphs in his resurrection and brings sin, death and hell into subjection to himself, and is seated at the right hand of the Father, where he reigns invisibly over all things in heaven and earth, and gathers and extends his Church by the preaching of the gospel; as an external mediator and high priest he intercedes with the Father for those who believe, because they still have weaknesses and sins remaining in them, and gives the power and strength of the Holy Spirit to overcome sin, the devil and death.

This is the righteousness of Christians before God, that Christ goes to the Father, that is, suffers and rises for us, and thereby reconciles us to the Father, so that for his sake we have forgiveness of sin, and grace. This is the righteousness of another, for which we have done nothing and have merited nothing, freely given and appropriated to us to be our righteousness, whereby we please God and are his dear children and heirs. This freely bestowed righteousness comes by faith alone. It cannot be apprehended otherwise than with the heart, which clings to the departure of Christ and firmly believes that for his sake it has forgiveness and redemption from sin and death. This righteousness is not an external thing, but a hidden treasure, not seen with eyes nor comprehended by our senses.

April 22nd - John 16:8–11

When he (the Comforter) is come, he will reprove the world ... of judgment, because the prince of this world is judged.

The word "judgment" means the decision between two parties at variance to decide which is right or wrong. It embraces two elements, aid and punishment, that the innocent party be acquitted and helped to his rights; that the guilty be condemned and punished. The word, however, is generally used for the latter element, the legal sentence of condemnation and its consequence. In this sense Christ uses it here and he intends to indicate that when the Holy Spirit shall pursue the two themes of his preaching and shall reprove the world of sin and righteousness, it will not receive it, nor be willing to be reproved, nor be moved to allow the righteousness of Christ to be offered to it. It will set itself against this teaching and reproving of the Holy Spirit, and condemn and persecute it. Then arises the conflict, and one judgment runs contrary to the other.

But Christ says that the Holy Spirit shall retain the superior judgment and shall prevail in his reproving of the world until the last day. In consequence of this Christians get into straits, the cross and persecution begin. Because the kingdom of Christ is not of this world, but spiritual and invisible, the power and might which the world has are directed against the Church by condemning, persecuting and torturing with sword and fire and other means. The world is also incited by the bitter hatred of the devil against Christ, who seeks to blot out and exterminate the Church. Against this hatred of judgment Christ gives comfort. The devil is already judged and the sentence of condemnation has already been pronounced upon him; the only thing wanting is its execution, that the punishment be inflicted upon him in eternal fire.

This judgment proceeds by power and might of the Lord Christ, sitting at the right hand of the Father; it is publicly proclaimed by the office of preaching, that the prince of the world with all his adherents is already under final condemnation and shall accomplish nothing against Christ. He must let him remain the Lord, under whose feet he shall eternally lie and suffer his head to be trodden upon. Christ makes his enemies his footstool. No one believes this except Christians, who take the Lord's Word for truth and know his power and kingdom.

April 23rd - Isaiah 55:3

I will make an everlasting covenant with you, even the sure mercies of David.

The prophet has reference to the promise made to David in the seventh chapter of second Samuel. In the preceding verses of the chapter, Isaiah most tenderly entreats and invites the whole world to receive the promises of salvation, for thereby shall the poor, the wretched and the afflicted obtain the great treasures of joy and salvation. Immediately following the verse quoted, he speaks of the Messiah, the promised seed of David, as given to the Levites for a "witness,"—a preacher sent by God—and for a "leader and commander to the people." The thought is of a king and ruler differing from Moses and his priests and exponents of the law; a ruler differing from every other lord and king, from David and all worldly rulers whatever, subjecting everything to himself. Not that this leader should set up a new temporal government, or extend Jewish authority among the Gentiles, but that Jews and Gentiles should receive him and believe in him, and obtain the fulfilment of that promise he here terms a covenant of the sure mercies of David. This covenant God enters into and keeps, a divine, sure covenant; through Christ shall be given whatever blessings God's mercy shall bestow, with remission of sins, redemption from death, and life eternal.

Now, if the Christ of this covenant is true man, and, as the promise to David is, of David's flesh and blood; and if he is to bring eternal mercy, he must likewise be God, such gift being in the province and power of God alone. This being true, he cannot remain in death, although he may suffer death by reason of his human nature; he must of his own power rise from the dead. Only so can he raise others and give them everlasting life; only so can he truly be called eternal King of grace, righteousness and life, according to the sure promise of God. Whenever the Scriptures speak of Christ's eternal kingdom, and of everlasting grace, they point out this article of the resurrection of Christ. God has promised to give us Christ, him who was to sit at his right hand—that is, to have the omnipotent, divine power possible only to an eternal Lord and King—and at the same time to have his kingdom on earth.

April 24th - Colossians 3:1

If you then be risen with Christ, seek those things which are above, where Christ sits on the right hand of God.

How is a dead man profited, however much life may be preached to him, if that preaching does not make him alive? Of what use is it to preach righteousness to a sinner, if he remain in sin? or to an erring, factious individual, if he forsake not his error and his darkness? Even so, it is not only useless but detrimental, even pernicious in effect, to listen to the glorious, comforting and saving doctrine of the resurrection, if the heart has no experience of its truth; if it means naught but a sound in the ears, a transitory word upon the tongue, with no more effect upon the hearer than if he had never heard.

According to the text, this nobly wrought and precious resurrection of Christ must essentially be, not an idle tale of fancy, futile as a dead hewn stone, or a painted paper image, but a powerful energy working in us a resurrection through faith—an experience which he calls being risen with Christ; in other words, it is dying unto sin, being snatched from the power of death and hell and having life and happiness in Christ. If you, Paul says, have apprehended by faith the resurrection of Christ and have received its power and consolation, and so are risen with him, that resurrection will surely be manifest in you; you will feel its power, will be conscious of its working within you. The doctrine will be something more than words; it will be truth and life. For those who do not thus apprehend the resurrection, Christ is not yet risen, although his rising is nonetheless a fact; for there is not within them the power represented by the words "being risen with Christ," the power which renders them truly dead and risen men.

The apostle, then, in this text is not referring to the future resurrection of the body, but to the spiritual rising which entails the former. He regards as one fact the resurrection of the Lord Christ, who brought his body again from the grave and entered into life eternal, and the resurrection of ourselves, who, by virtue of his rising, shall likewise be raised: the soul, from a trivial and guilty life shall rise into a true, divine and happy existence; from this sinful and mortal body shall rise out of the grave an immortal, glorious one.

April 25th – 1 John 5:1

Whosoever believeth that Jesus is the Christ is born of God.

Though John's language is plain and simple, yet in the ears of men generally it is unusual and unintelligible. What, according to the world's construction, is implied by the statement, "born of God?" To the world there is no birth but physical. Hence such doctrine as our text sets forth will ever be strange, unintelligible, incomprehensible, to all but Christians. But these speak with new tongues, as Christ says they shall, for they are taught and enlightened by the Holy Spirit.

When the Scriptures speak of being born of God, it is not in a human sense; the reference is not to the conditions of our temporal lives, but to those exalted ones of a future existence. To say we must be born of God is equivalent to saying that if a man is to be redeemed from sin and eternal death, to enter into the kingdom of God and into happiness, his physical birth will not suffice; all that nature, reason, free will and human endeavor may afford is inadequate. Physical, indeed, answers for everything in the way of temporal possession and achievement, every desirable and exalted thing of earth; but all such possession and achievement serves only the physical existence; it is swept away by death, to which event it is ever subject.

Hence there becomes necessary a new and different birth. The demand is for a divine birth, a birth in which parentage is wholly of God; a birth signifying the operation of God's divine power in man, a power achieving something beyond the attainment of his natural capacities and effecting in him new understanding and a new heart. The process is this: when the individual hears the gospel message of Christ—a message revealed and proclaimed, not by the wisdom and will of man, but through the Holy Spirit—and sincerely believes it, he is justly recognized as conceived and born of God. Through that faith, for the sake of his Son, God accepts us as his children, pleasing to him and heirs of eternal life; and the Holy Spirit will be sent into our hearts.

This doctrine condemns those arrogant teachers who presumptuously expect to be justified before God by their own merits and works. The Scriptures clearly teach the very reverse. It is sheer human effort, and not being born of God.

April 26th - John 10:14

I am the good shepherd, and know my sheep, and am known of mine.

Christ here gives us the criterion by which we are to distinguish the true Church, or people of God, from that which has the name and reputation, but in truth is not the Church. The Church neither is, nor ought to be a society which must be organized with an external government, like the Jewish people under the law of Moses. It is not governed and preserved by outward human power; much less is it bound to a succession or government of bishops, as the papacy claims. It is a spiritual assembly, which hears the shepherd and believes in him, and is governed by him through the Holy Spirit. It is outwardly recognized by this alone, that it has his Word, the preaching of the gospel, and his sacraments. Inwardly it is known to him alone, as in turn it also knows him by faith and clings to him when it hears his Word, regardless of the fact that it may neither maintain, nor even know anything of that outward Jewish or papistical government, and may be scattered here and there in the world without any organized external government, as it was in the time of Christ and the apostles, who, apart from and in opposition to the regular power of the whole priesthood, believed in Christ and confessed him.

If you really wish to know what a Christian is you must not look to the law of Moses, the government of the pope, nor the life and sanctity of any man, however holy. A Christian is not one who leads a strict, severe, hermit life; nothing that is in us or can be done by us, makes a Christian. This alone, that one knows this Man, regards him and trusts him as he wishes to be considered, namely, the good Shepherd, who lays down his life for the sheep and knows them. This knowledge is nothing else than faith, which arises from the ministry of the Word, which consists not of our own thoughts, nor does it come from men, but it was brought from heaven and was revealed by Christ himself. In this way and in no other does a man become a Christian. The Word and our faith must always come together. Here we have this comfort, that if anyone knows Christ in this way, he is already known by him and certainly is one of his.

April 27th - Mark 16:14

(He) upbraided them with their unbelief and hardness of heart, because they believed not them which had seen him after he was risen.

Christ upbraids the disciples with their unbelief and hardness of heart. He does not reject them, nor deal too severely with them, but reproves them. It is not an insignificant matter that the Lord rebuked his disciples; for unbelief is the greatest sin that can be named. Christ tells them the cause of their unbelief when he says that their hearts are hardened, still he deals mildly and gently with them. This is told us for our comfort, lest we despair, when, lacking in faith, we doubt, stumble and fall. It is to help us to rise again, to strengthen our faith and lift up our hearts to God, that we may grasp and hold fast the confidence of God, who does not deal severely with us, but can indeed bear with us and overlook much. If we believe him to be a merciful God, he will be found merciful and thus shows himself to us; but a bad conscience and an unbelieving heart have no such trust in God, but flee from him. So should we also deal with our neighbor. If we see him fall from the faith, or err and sin, we should not strengthen him in his wickedness, nor justify his cause, but admonish him and in meekness reprove his faults, yet not hold enmity, nor turn our love from him.

But let no one think that the apostles were altogether unbelieving; they believed what was written in the law and the prophets. There was a faith there, but they did not yet believe all things. Faith is a thing that always grows. Therefore the Lord shows wherein they lacked in faith; it was that they did not believe the resurrection of Christ from the dead. I hold that they believed that they had a gracious God, but this was not enough; they must believe also the resurrection of Christ. Thus the Lord upbraided them with their unbelief and said that in spite of all they had seen, they were not believing, they still lacked a certain article of faith, that on the resurrection. We should therefore expose and reprove what is wrong, but exercise truth and love toward everybody. We see that even the apostles were lacking in the chief things, yet they were cornerstones, the foundation and the very best part of Christendom.

April 28th - Matthew 22:14

Many are called, but few are chosen.

Note what took place in Jerusalem, when the gospel was first heard. It is said, there were in the city at the feast of the Passover eleven hundred thousand men. How many were converted? When Peter stood up and preached, they made a mockery of it and considered the apostles drunken fools. After the apostles had preached the gospel a long time, they gathered together three thousand men and women. But what were they among so many? No one could discern that the gospel had accomplished anything. No change was seen, and scarcely any one knew that there were Christians there. Hence the gospel must not be measured by the multitude that hear, but by the small company that receive it. They appear as nothing, they are despised and persecuted, and yet God secretly works in them.

There is another thing that hinders the free movement of the gospel, namely, the infirmities of the believers. Thus Peter was filled with faith and the Holy Spirit, yet he stumbled and fell—he and all that were with him—when he walked not according to the gospel, so that Paul had to reprove him openly. Mark had journeyed with Paul, but afterward fell away and withdrew from him. Again, Paul and Barnabas strove together, and there arose a sharp contention between them. And before this, we read in the Gospels how often the apostles erred in weighty matters, though they were the best of Christians.

These infirmities of Christians darken the gospel most of all, so that men who deem themselves wise and learned stumble and are offended in them. Few there are who can well reconcile these things so as to take no offense. It was thus even with the disciples. At first when Christ wrought great and excellent works, and gained great honors, they remained steadfast. The common people clung to him, because they saw that with great power he wrought such excellent works, and walked so as to be irreproachable. But when his sufferings began, they all turned away and forsook him. Why was this? Because they considered him not the strong, but a weak Christ. Therefore to bear with the weak Christ is the highest wisdom on earth, which is known to very few men.

April 29th - 1 John 5:4

Whatsoever is born of God overcometh the world.

He who is born of God overcomes the world, John declares. Verily, this is a significant and forcible assertion which the

Holy Spirit makes. It represents a tremendous power, a great work. The child of God must attempt and accomplish great things. The birth effected through the Word and faith makes men true sovereigns, above all earthly rulers. It gives them power even to overcome the world, something impossible to any Roman or Turkish potentate. They effect not their victory by physical force or temporal power, but by the spiritual birth through faith.

In order to understand the nature of the spiritual victory and how it is effected, we must know what John means by the term "world." The reference is not to dominion over territory, to property, or money. He implies the existence of two kingdoms. By the heavenly kingdom we must understand not only spiritual life and godly people, but the Lord and Regent of that kingdom—Christ with his angels, and his saints, both living and dead. The kingdom of the world represents not only the earthly life with its worldly interests, but particularly its lord and regent—the devil and his angels, all unchristian, godless, wicked people on earth. So John means by "world" the devil and his whole earthly dominion.

The workings of these two kingdoms are plainly evident, though the leaders are not visible to mortal eyes. Christ rules effectually in his own power through the Word and the Holy Spirit in the hearts of believers, through the angels who guard his followers, and through his people themselves who exercise authority over one another in loving service, each teaching, comforting and admonishing a noble band of godly, obedient, chaste, benevolent souls. The nature of the devil's kingdom is easily apparent. This kingdom is simply a huge booth filled with faithless, shameless, wicked individuals, impelled by their god to every sort of disobedience and contempt of God and his Word; to false doctrine, the practice of wantonness, vice, and wickedness.

These two kingdoms are opposed. Christians are brought into the conflict to hold the field against God's enemies, whose rule is one of falsehood and murder; they must contend with the enemy's servants, factions, spirits, and wicked individuals, in an effort to restrain evil and promote good. Christians must know how to meet and successfully resist the enemy, how to carry the field unto victory and hold it.

April 30th - Colossians 3:4

When Christ, who is our life, shall appear, then shall you also appear with him in glory.

Here is comfort for Christians in this earthly life, where their resurrection seems untrue to the world and to their own perceptions, though they receive the doctrine of Christ and apprehend him by faith; where they must contend with sin and infirmities and besides are subject to much affliction and adversity; and where consequently they are extremely sensible of death and terror when they should experience joy and life. In this verse Paul comforts them, showing where to seek and surely apprehend their life. Be of good cheer, he would say, for you are dead to the worldly life. This life you must renounce, but in so doing you make a precious exchange. Dying unto the world is a blessed experience, for which you will obtain a life far more glorious. You are now through Christ's death redeemed from sin and from death eternal and are made imperishable. Upon you is conferred everlasting glory. But this risen life you cannot yet perceive in yourselves; you have it in Christ through faith.

Christ is spoken of as "our life." This life is certain, though still unrevealed to you, insured to you beyond the power of any one to deprive you of it. By faith in Christ's life, are you to be preserved and to obtain victory over the terrors and torments of sin, death and the devil, until that life shall be revealed in you and made manifest to men. In Christ you surely possess eternal life. Nothing is lacking to a perfect realization except that the veil whereby it is hidden as long as we are in mortal flesh and blood is yet to be removed. Then will eternal life be revealed. Then all worldly, terrestrial things, all sin and death, will be abolished. In every Christian shall be manifest only glory. Christians, believing in Christ and knowing him risen, should comfort themselves with the expectation of living with him in eternal glory.

Saints must, therefore, by a vigorous and unceasing warfare subdue their sinful lusts if they would not lose God's grace and their faith. To retain the Spirit and the incipient divine life, the Christian must contend with himself. Positive mortification is necessary. And this is the way to mortify sin: it must be perceived with serious displeasure and repented of; and through faith Christ's forgiveness must be sought and found.

May 1st - Galatians 3:24

Wherefore the law was our schoolmaster to bring us unto Christ, that we might be justified by faith.

There are two divine proclamations which came from heaven. One is, "You shall not kill, commit adultery, steal" and the like, and adds the threat that all who transgress these commandments shall die. Though they may compel a man outwardly to appear godly before men, inwardly the heart is left at enmity with the law. The other proclamation is that of the gospel. It tells us how we may meet the demands of the law. It does not drive nor threaten, but kindly invites us, Come, I will show you where you may find what you need to make you godly. Here is the Lord Jesus; he will give it you.

The two proclamations are as opposite to one another as taking and giving, and this distinction must ever be observed. With these two God has ever ruled the world, and still rules it. The law must be declared to coarse and rude persons, who are not influenced by the gospel, until they are driven to acknowledge their imperfections and are humbled. When this has been accomplished, the gospel is to be applied. There are other proclamations besides these two, which have been invented to frighten men's consciences, but they are not from heaven and are mere human prattle. The proclamations of law and gospel are not of men, but of Christ, who sent them forth and put them into the heart of the apostles and their successors so that they understood them, and then into their mouths so that they spake and declared them.

If you believe that Christ died to save you from all evil, and you hold fast to that Word, you will find it so certain and sure that no creature can overthrow it. It is the power of God, and can and will save all who believe it. You will find refuge in the Word and attain everlasting, peace, joy and life. You will be a participant in all the power that is in the Word, which is so deeply hidden that none but they who believe realize that it is so effective and that it accomplishes such great things.

May 2nd - John 10:11

I am the good shepherd: the good shepherd giveth his life for the sheep.

"The good shepherd layeth down his life for the sheep." In this one virtue the Lord comprehends and exemplifies all others in the beautiful parable of the sheep. The sheep has this trait above all other animals, that it soon recognizes the shepherd's voice and will follow no one but him. Though it cannot help and keep and heal itself, nor guard against the wolf, yet it always knows enough to keep close to the shepherd and look to him for help. Christ uses this trait of the animal as an illustration in explaining that he is the good Shepherd. In this manner he shows plainly what his kingdom is and in what it consists. It is to protect the sheep, that is, poor, needy, wretched men who realize that there is no other help or counsel for them. The kingdom of Christ is to be concerned about the weak, the sick, the broken, who need to be helped. This is a comforting declaration.

"A bruised reed shall he not break, and smoking flax shall he not quench." The bruised reeds are the poor, tender consciences, which are easily distracted. But God deals gently with them. The smoking flax (dimly burning wick) he does not wholly quench, but lights it and trims it again and again. When a Christian is not only weak and infirm, but when he falls into such great temptations as to deny the gospel, as Peter when he denied Christ, even then you are not to cast him away, as though he no longer belonged to this kingdom. You must not rob Christ of this characteristic, that in his kingdom abounding grace and mercy alone prevail, and that his kingdom is wholly one of consolation, and that he is a comforting, friendly shepherd, who tenderly invites, and would induce all men to come unto him. All this is effected through the gospel alone, by means of which we are to strengthen the weak and heal the sick. It will give full consolation to all, so that no one, no matter how great a sinner he has been, need despair.

May 3rd - Ecclesiastes 9:15

Now there was found in it a poor wise man, and he by his wisdom delivered the city; yet no man remembered that same poor man.

Wherever we turn our eyes we see, in all conditions of life, a flood of terrible examples of ingratitude for the precious gospel. We see how kings, princes and lords quarrel and fight, envy and hate one another, oppressing their own people and destroying their own countries; they tax themselves with not so much as a single Christian thought about ameliorating the wretchedness of Germany. The noblemen rake and rend, robbing whom they can, prince or otherwise, and especially the poor Church. Townsmen and farmers are extremely avaricious, extortionate and treacherous; they fearlessly perpetrate every sort of insolence and wickedness, and without shame and punishment. The earth cries to heaven, unable longer to tolerate its oppression.

But why multiply words? It is in vain so far as the world is concerned; no admonition will avail. The world remains the devil's own. Notwithstanding the world's refusal to be influenced by the recognition of God's goodness, and in spite of the fact that we are obliged daily to see, hear and suffer the world's increasing ungratefulness the longer it stands, we must not allow ourselves to be led into error; for we will be unable to change it. We must preach against the evil of ingratitude wherever possible, severely censuring it, and faithfully admonish all men to guard against it. Although compelled to live among the ungrateful, we are not for that reason to fall into error, nor to cease from doing good.

But if your good works are wrought with the object of securing the thanks and applause of the world, your reward will justly be that of him who crushes with his teeth the hollow nut only to defile his mouth. If, when you meet with ingratitude, you angrily wish to pull down mountains, and resolve to give up doing good, you are no longer a Christian. You injure yourself and accomplish nothing. Let the God-fearing Christians give evidence of their willingness to hear the Word of God. Let them show by their lives a consciousness of the great blessing conferred by those from whom they received the gospel. Let their hearts and lips ever be ready with the happy declaration: "God be praised." Such manifestation of gratitude assuredly must result when we comprehend what God has given us.

May 4th - Romans 11:33

O' the depth of the riches both of the wisdom and knowledge of God!

Sublime are the thoughts and counsel of God, transcending by far the mind and comprehension of man, yea, of all creatures, when he so richly pours forth his goodness, and out of pure grace and mercy elects, as beneficiaries of that goodness, the poor, and wretched, and unworthy, who are concluded under sin—that is, those who acknowledge themselves guilty before God and deserving of everlasting wrath and perdition; when he does all this that they might know him in his real divine essence, and the sentiment of his heart—that through his Son he will give all who believe everlasting life. And, again, that they might know how he will reject those who, in pride and security, boast of their own gifts, that they are called the people of God in preference to all other nations; who boast that they have special promises; who think that God will acknowledge no nation on earth but themselves as his people and his Church. He will reject them on account of their unbelief, in which they are fettered by the pride and imagination of their own wisdom and holiness.

This is that rich, inexpressible, divine wisdom and knowledge which they possess who believe in Christ, and by which they are enabled to look into the depths and see what the purposes and thoughts of the divine heart are. True, in their weakness they cannot fully reach it; they can only apprehend it in the revealed Word by faith, as in a glass or image. It cannot be apprehended or comprehended otherwise.

Though the world will not do it, we will firmly believe that God is a true God and Lord, wise, just, gracious, whose riches and depth are ineffable. We will glorify him with our whole heart, as he ought justly to be praised and glorified by every creature, for the wonderful government of his Church, through his Word and revelation. He is to be glorified because he manifests such unutterable goodness to all who are in sin and under God's wrath that he translates them, though they are unworthy, from the power of death and hell into the kingdom of eternal grace and life, if they will only seek grace and believe on Christ, his Son.

May 5th - Romans 11:33

How unsearchable are his judgments, and his ways past finding out!

These words show Christians that these sublime and divine mysteries—God's actual divine essence and his will, administration and works—are absolutely beyond all human thought, human understanding or wisdom; that they are and ever will be incomprehensible, inscrutable, and altogether hidden to human reason. When reason presumptuously undertakes to solve, to teach and explain these matters, the result is worthless, yea, utter darkness and deception. If anything is to be ascertained, it must be through revelation alone; that is, the Word of God, which was sent from heaven.

We do not apply these words of Paul to the question of divine predestination—who will be saved and who will not. For into these things God would not have us curiously inquire. He has not given us any special revelation in regard to them, but refers all men here to the words of the gospel. By them they are to be guided. He would have them hear and learn the gospel, and believing in it they shall be saved. Therein have all the saints found comfort and assurance in regard to their election to eternal life; not in any special revelation in regard to their predestination, but in faith in Christ.

Paul speaks here of the marvelous ruling of God in the Church, according to which they who have the name and honor of being the people of God—the people of Israel—are rejected on account of their unbelief. On the other hand, those who formerly were not God's people, but were unbelieving, are now become the true Church in the sight of God and are saved, since they have received the gospel and believe in Christ.

Consequently it was on account of their own unbelief that the former were rejected. Such are God's unsearchable judgments and ways past finding out. By "judgments" is meant that which is right or wrong, what pleases and what does not please him. By "his ways" is meant that which he will manifest unto men and how he will deal with them. These things men cannot and would not search out by their own intellect, and therefore should never oppose their judgments or speculations to God. It is not for them to say what is right or wrong, whether an act or ruling is divine.

May 6th - 1 John 5:4

This is the victory that overcometh the world, even our faith.

It is, indeed, saying very much for the Christian faith to attribute to it such power over the devil and the world—a power transcending all human ability. It requires an agency greater and higher than human strength to triumph over the devil, especially in the perplexing conflicts of conscience, when he vexes and tortures the heart with terror of God's wrath in the attempt to drive us to despair. At such times all our works must immediately sink out of sight, leaving no help or victory except the faith that clings to the word of Christ the Lord, believing that, for the sake of his beloved Son, God will be merciful and will not condemn us for our sins and unworthiness, if we believe in him. Such faith as this stands fast and gains the victory; neither the devil, nor the gates of hell can prevail against it.

The same is true in all temptations. Before we can resist and overcome, we must have faith to believe that through Christ we have remission of sins and the favor of God; that God gives us help and strength to enable us to stand in the conflict and successfully resist the devil, the world, the flesh, and death; that we obtain the victory by the divine power of the Holy Spirit, lacking whose help we all would be far too weak to win. Without faith, we are under the power of the devil and sin, being subject to them by natural birth. We can be liberated in no other way than through faith in Christ.

The faith which believes Jesus is the Son of God is the true, triumphant sort. It is an invincible power wrought in the hearts of Christians by the Holy Spirit. It is a sure knowledge, that does not gaze and vacillate hither and thither according to its own thoughts. It apprehends God in Christ the Son sent from heaven, through whom God reveals his will and his love and transfers us from sin to grace, from death to a new, eternal life; a refuge and trust that relies, not upon its own merit and worthiness, but upon Christ the Son of God, and in his might and power battles against the world and the devil. It is a living, active power, ever followed by victories and other appropriate fruits.

May 7th - James 1:17

Every good gift and every perfect gift is from above, and cometh down from the Father of lights, with whom is no variableness, neither shadow of turning.

We shall designate the "good gifts" the blessings we enjoy here in this life; the "perfect gifts" those awaiting us in the life to come. In the words "good gifts" and "perfect gifts," the apostle comprehends all our blessings, those we have already received in the present life and those to be ours in the life to come. I will not now speak particularly of earthly, transient, and changeable blessings, such as temporal goods, honor, a healthy body, and others. There are many individuals who would give thousands of dollars to have the sight of both eyes. So much do they prize the blessing of sight, they would willingly suffer a year's illness or endure other great inconveniences to obtain it.

But we shall speak now particularly of the blessings we have in Christ's resurrection, a subject appropriate to this Paschal season. God has begun the work of edifying us, of building us up, and will constitute us his own children, his heirs. The great, glorious gifts of the resurrection are these: the gospel, holy Baptism, the power of the Holy Spirit, and comfort in all adversity. What is a slight injury or the loss of some temporal blessing in comparison with these? What reason has any man to murmur and to rage when such divine blessings are his, even here in this life, blessings which none can take away or abridge? If you are called on to renounce money, possessions, honor, and men's favor, remember you have a treasure more precious than all the honors and all the possessions of the world. When you see one living in great splendor, in pleasure and presumption, following his own inclinations, think: I have divine grace enabling me to know God's will and the work he would have me do, and all in heaven and earth is mine.

But these do not represent the consummation of resurrection blessings. We must yet await the real, the perfect gifts. God has only commenced to work in us; he will not leave us in this state. If we continue in faith, God will bring us to the real, the eternal blessings, called "perfect gifts," the possession of which excludes error, stumbling, anger, and any sin whatever. Look to this future life, when assailed by the world and enticed to anger or evil lust.

May 8th - James 1:18

Of his own will he begat us with the word of truth, that we should be a kind of firstfruits of his creatures.

The best thing Christ has sent us from on high is sonship. He brought us forth, made us his children, or heirs. We are truly called children born of God. But how are we born? Through "the word of truth," or the true Word. By this statement James makes a far-reaching thrust at all factions and sects. They also have a word and boast much of their doctrine, but theirs is not the Word of truth whereby men are made children of God. But we have a Word whereby, as we are assured, God makes us his beloved children and justifies us, if we believe in that Word. He justifies us not through works or laws. The Christian must derive his sonship from his birth. The disciples of Moses, and all work-mongers, would effect it by commandments, extorting a work here and a work there, effecting nothing.

The children of God, John tells us, are they who believe on the name of Christ; who sincerely cling to the Word. They are children who cleave to the message that through Christ God forgives their sins and receives them into his favor; who adhere to this promise in all temptations, afflictions, and trouble. The Word here on earth is the jewel which secures sonship. Since God has so greatly blessed you as to make you his own begotten children, shall he not also give you every other good?

Whence do we derive sonship? Not from your own will, not from your own powers or efforts. Were it so, I and other monks surely should have obtained it, independently of the Word; it would have been ours through the numerous works we performed in our monastic life. It is secured, says James, "of his will." It never entered into the thought of man that we should in this way be made children of God. The idea did not grow in our gardens; it did not spring up in our wells. It came down from above, "from the Father of lights," by Word and Spirit revealed to us and given into our hearts through the agency of the apostles and their successors, by whom the Word has been transmitted to us. Hence we did not secure it by our efforts or merits. Of his fatherly will and good pleasure was it conferred upon us; of pure grace and mercy he gave it.

May 9th - Romans 14:1

Him that is weak in the faith receive you, but not to doubtful disputations.

Some are found who know the gospel, but are offended at their own manner of life. They have a desire to walk in godliness, but they feel that they make no progress. They begin to despair and think that with them all is lost because they do not feel the strength they ought to have. They also earnestly desire Christ to be strong in them and manifest himself in mighty deeds. But in this God designs to humble us, that we may see and feel what feeble creatures we are, what wretched, lost, and condemned men, if Christ had not come and helped us.

But thereby we have no furlough to continue for all time in weakness, for we do not preach that any should be weak, but that we should know the weakness of Christians and bear with it. Christ did not hang upon the cross that he might appear as a murderer and evildoer, but that we might learn how deeply strength lies hidden under weakness, and might learn to know God's strength in weakness. Thus our weakness is not to be praised, as though we should abide in it, but rather must we learn not to think that those who are weak are not Christians, nor yet despair when we feel our own weakness. Therefore it behooves us to know our own weaknesses and ever to seek to wax stronger, for Christ must not suffer always, nor remain in the grave, but must come forth again and live.

Hence, let no one say that to remain in ignorance is the true course and condition. It is only a beginning, out of which we must grow day by day, giving heed only that we turn not away and despair when we are weak, as though all were lost. Rather must we continue to exercise ourselves till we wax stronger and stronger, and endure and bear the weakness until God helps and takes it away. Hence, even though you see your neighbor so weak that he stumbles, think not that he is beyond hope. God will not have one judge another and be pleased with himself, inasmuch as we are all sinners, but that one bear the infirmity of the other. Christ also pleased not himself, hence we are to do as he did.

May 10th - Romans 13:1, 2

Let every soul be subject unto the higher powers. For there is no power, but of God: the powers that be are ordained of God. Whosoever resisteth the power, resisteth the ordinance of God: and they that resist shall receive to themselves damnation.

We must understand that we have two kinds of authority: the secular that punishes with the sword, and the spiritual that exercises its office with the Word and by means of preaching. The secular power is ordained of God, as Paul clearly and beautifully declares to the Romans. Since there are few who heed the gospel, and most people remain rogues and knaves, they use the gospel for their own licentious liberty and wantonness; hence it is necessary to have a civil government, which we would not need if all men were Christian and evangelical. God has ordained and designed it, in order that the godly may live in peace; he has established the secular sword to the end that the public peace may be preserved, the wicked punished, and the just protected. On this account we must pay to the government rent and taxes and revenue by which it may be supported and administer its office.

In the gospel we find an entirely different, a spiritual government, one that exists alone in the Word, by which sinners are convicted and the gospel proclaimed to the terrified and alarmed consciences. When the bishops and their officials want to put one under the ban the transgression is published to the whole congregation, otherwise their ban would not be noticed, and the messengers would be shown the door. The secular government should see to it, whenever the clerical authority overreaches its sphere to the injury of souls, that it be restrained, and bishops and their officials be not permitted to excommunicate from the Church any one without his knowledge and will, whenever it pleases them.

It does not concern God very much as to how the secular government uses its power, for he is concerned only about the soul, and with this the secular power has nothing to do. It has received power to rule over the body and over property. Whether we govern well or not does not determine our salvation. But it were a matter of great concern if the spiritual authority were to say, Do this, and you shall be saved; omit this, and you shall be eternally lost, as though at certain times we must not eat eggs and meat and butter, but oil and fish. With Peter we must obey God rather than men.

May 11th - 2 Peter 3:18

But grow in grace and in the knowledge of our Lord and Saviour Jesus Christ.

What is it to know Christ but to look upon him as a gift and as an example? A gift given by God that becomes your own; so that when you see and hear him suffering or doing anything, you may not doubt that Christ himself in such suffering and works is yours, upon which you may depend as though you yourself had done them, and as though you yourself were Christ. This is what it means to know Christ aright: that he with all he has, out of pure divine goodness has been given unto us, that he has rendered satisfaction, obtained salvation and eternal life for us, and that all this is through him and for his sake, bestowed upon us without our merit.

If in this way you have Christ as the foundation and chief treasure of your salvation, then follows the other part of laying hold of him as your example, that you give yourself to the service of your neighbor as he has given himself for you. Then faith and love will be exercised, God's commandment will be fulfilled, and man becomes happy and fearless to do and to suffer any and everything. Christ as a gift nourishes your faith and makes you a Christian; but Christ as an example moves you to do good works; these do not make you a Christian, but they go forth from you who have already become Christians. The pope, however, has changed this entirely; for he commands: If you would be saved, you must pray the rosary, fast, become a Carthusian, buy indulgences, build churches, and do innumerable things, not one of which Christ ever commanded. The worst of all is that when they have practiced such works, which benefit neither God, nor the world, for a time, they boast of them and say: I have fasted so many Fridays with bread and water, I have spent so many years in the cloister, I hope God will not leave me unrewarded for such service, but will on that account give me heaven. That certainly is denying Christ, and a terrible blasphemy of the great and unsurpassable grace of God manifested toward us in his Son, Jesus Christ.

The true knowledge of Christ is to know why he came, and how we may appropriate him to ourselves.

May 12th - Mark 16:15

Go you into all the world, and preach the gospel to every creature.

He that would preach the gospel must cast aside all works supposed to make one just, and allow nothing to remain but faith; I must believe that God, without any merit of mine and regardless of all works, has granted me his grace and eternal life. Therefore we must preach in a way that the glory and praise will be given to God and not to ourselves. Now there is no greater glory and praise that we can give to God than to confess that out of pure grace and mercy he takes away from us sin, death and hell, and that he gives his beloved Son and all his treasures to us.

Faith compels no one to accept the gospel, but leaves its acceptance free to everyone and makes it a personal matter. Thus you see that the pope errs and does the people injustice when he ventures to drive them to faith by force. The Lord commanded the disciples to do nothing more than preach the gospel. This the disciples also did; they preached the gospel and left its acceptance to those who would take it. They did not say: Believe, or I will put you to death.

A question arises as to the words, "Go you into all the world," how it is to be understood, since the apostles certainly did not visit all the world? Their preaching *went out* into all the world, although it has not yet *come into* all the world. This going out has been begun and continues, although it is not yet completed; the gospel will be preached farther and wider until the judgment day. When this preaching shall have reached all parts of the world, and shall have been everywhere heard, then will the message be complete and its mission accomplished; then will the last day also be at hand.

The preaching of this message may be likened to a stone thrown into the water, producing ripples which circle outward from it, the waves rolling on and on, one driving the other, till they come to shore. The preaching was begun by the apostles, and it constantly goes forward, is pushed on farther and farther by the preachers, driven hither and thither into the world, always being made known by those who never heard it before, although it be arrested in the midst of its course and is condemned as heresy.

May 13th - Mark 16:17, 18

In my name shall they cast out devils; they shall speak with new tongues; they shall take up serpents; and if they drink any deadly thing, it shall not hurt them.

How shall we proceed here that we may preserve the truth of this passage? The Lord says all these signs shall accompany them. Now we know that the apostles did not present all the signs, and if the passage shall stand literally, then few believers will be cleared and few saints be entitled to heaven; for these signs, one and all, have not accompanied them, though they have had power to work signs, and have exhibited some of them. These words, therefore, do not refer to the Church as a whole, but to persons separately. If there is a Christian who has faith, he shall have power to do these accompanying miracles, and they shall follow him. Christ says, "He that believeth on me, the works that I shall do, shall he do also." The Lord has given Christians power also against the unclean spirits. There was once a patriarch in the wilderness, who, when he met a serpent, took it in both hands and tore it in two, saying, What a fine thing it is to have a clear and guiltless conscience. So, where there is a Christian, there is still the power to work these signs if it is necessary.

But no one should attempt to exercise this power if it is not necessary. The apostles did not always exercise it, but only made use of it to prove the Word of God, to confirm it by miracles. "They went forth and preached everywhere, the Lord working with them, and confirming the Word with signs following." Since the gospel has now been spread abroad, and made known to all the world, there is no need of working miracles as in the apostles' time. Then let no one without pressing need undertake to work wonders. I know not what I shall say about those who venture to do signs where they are not necessary. I know that it is a dangerous undertaking. The devil, indeed, lets himself be driven out, but he does not intend to suffer for it; he allows it only that he may strengthen the sign-worker in such error. I would not like to trust him. But wherever a Christian dies in Christ with cheerful heart, Satan has been truly cast out and deprived of his power and kingdom.

May 14th - John 16:2

They shall put you out of the synagogues: yea, the time cometh, that whosoever killeth you will think that he does God service.

Christ pointed out clearly enough what would happen to his disciples as a result of their preaching. He mentions two sources of opposition to the gospel, than which none could be stronger: one that the preacher should be excommunicated and put to death; the other that the persecutors would regard this as rendering a service to God. He said that the Holy Spirit should testify of him and that they also should bear witness; and he assures them that their testimony shall not be effaced by this rage and persecution of the world. He gives them this assurance beforehand for the purpose that they may know and be prepared against these same abuses.

It is strange and almost incredible to hear that not only the world shall oppose, with its bitter hatred and rage, Christ, the Son of God and its Saviour, but that also the apostles themselves must be offended at such judgment of the world. Who could ever conceive that Christ and his gospel should be received in this manner among his own people, to whom he had been promised by God, and from whom they were to expect nothing but that which is good, which they also received from him? But here we are told that the gospel is a teaching which, according to human judgment, gives nothing but offense,—a thing unworthy to be heard or tolerated.

The kingdom of Christ on earth shall so come that it must be apparent to all that it is not an earthly kingdom after the manner of men. But the world shall refuse to recognize its nature. It shall not be called the kingdom of Christ or of God, but a destruction and subversion of all good government, both spiritual and temporal. It is well-nigh inconceivable that the Son of God should be so received by those who are called the people of God. For Christ speaks here not of open, malicious, wicked knaves and godless men, but of those who are regarded as the most eminent, the wisest, the most holy, even the servants of God. Who would ever think that God would introduce Christ's kingdom upon earth in this way, establish his Word in all places and gather his Church.

May 15th - John 16:23

Verily, verily, I say unto you, Whatsoever you shall ask the Father in my name, he will give it you.

The Lord points out five things necessary to constitute true prayer. The first is God's promise, which is the chief thing and is the foundation and power of all prayers. He promises that it shall be given if we ask. He promises that we may be sure of being heard in prayer; he even censures the disciples for being lazy and not having prayed. It is truly a great shame to us Christians that God should upbraid us for our slothfulness in prayer.

The second requisite in true prayer is faith. We must believe that the promise is true, and must not doubt that God will give what he promises. The words of promise require faith,—a firm, undoubting confidence that God's promise is true. Such faith and definite assurance the Holy Spirit must impart; without the Holy Spirit surely no prayer will be offered.

The third requisite of true prayer is that one must name something definitely for which he prays, as for strong faith, love, peace, and for the comfort of his neighbor. One must actually set forth petitions as in the Lord's Prayer.

The fourth element in prayer is, that we must earnestly desire that the petition be granted, which is nothing but asking. It is an intercession of the Spirit that cannot be uttered. When Zacchaeus sought to see the Lord, he did not feel how strongly his heart wished that Christ might speak with him and come into his house.

The fifth requisite of prayer is that we ask in the name of Christ. This is nothing more than that we come before God in the faith of Christ and comfort ourselves with the sure confidence that he is our Mediator, through whom all things are given to us and without whom we merit nothing but wrath and disgrace. We pray aright in Christ's name, when we thus trust in him that we will be received and heard for his sake and not for our own.

All these five requisites may be complied with in the heart without any utterance of the mouth. But oral prayer is necessary to kindle and encourage prayer inwardly in the heart. We must not specify to God the time, place, person, and measure, but leave all that to his own free will and cling only to asking.

May 16th - 1 John 5:6

It is the Spirit that bears witness, because the Spirit is truth.

John employs the word "witness" in connection with the thought of preaching; it is a word which he frequently uses. In the beginning of his gospel, where he speaks of John the Baptist, he says, "The same came for a witness, that he might bear witness of the light." So in the use of the words "witness" or "bearing witness," we are to understand simply the public preaching of God's Word. Christ says, that the

Holy Spirit shall bear witness of him; that is, it shall publicly fill the ministerial office. This is God's own witness to his Son.

This witness, Christ himself ordains, shall ever go forth, and remain in the Church. To this end Christ himself called and gave the Holy Spirit to the apostles and their successors, ministers, preachers, and teachers. For the sake of the uninstructed masses and the constantly rising young who, as yet in ignorance of the Word, need admonition—for the sake of these, the Spirit must bear public witness or administer the preaching office that they, too, may learn to know the grace of God manifest and given us through Christ, and that God's wondrous works may be publicly recognized and extolled by us in opposition to the devil and the world.

Wherever such witness is borne, there certainly will be some fruit; the witness never fails of effect. Some surely will be reached; some will accept and believe it. Since it is the witness of the Holy Spirit, he will be effective, producing in us that to which John refers when he says we are the children of God, and have the victory and eternal life. The Word and faith are vitally related. They are inseparable. Without faith, preaching will be fruitless; and faith has origin in the Word alone. Therefore, we should gladly handle and hear the Word. Where it is, there is also the Holy Spirit; and where the Spirit is, there must be at least some believers. If you have already heard the Word and obtained faith, it will always continue to strengthen you as you hear it. For the Spirit, as Christ says, breathes where he will, and touches hearts when and where he knows them to be receptive.

May 17th - Genesis 6:3

The Lord said, My spirit shall not always strive with man, for that he also is flesh: yet his days shall be an hundred and twenty years.

These are the words of a father who disinherits his son, for God simply fixes a hundred and twenty years as the time in which opportunity is granted for repentance. He threatens, should it not be improved, that his Spirit shall no longer reprove and strive, which means that henceforth he will not give his Word to men, since all teaching is in vain. This word pertains properly to the office of the ministry. For every preacher or servant of the Word is a man of strife and judgment, and is constrained, by reason of his office, to chide whatever is vicious, without considering the person or office of his hearer. When Jeremiah does this zealously, he incurs not only hate, but also the gravest dangers. For this reason Elijah is called by Ahab the godless king of Israel, the disturber of Israel.

When Noah, whom Peter calls a "preacher of righteousness," and his ancestors had preached nearly a thousand years, and yet the world continued to degenerate more and more, they announced God's decision to an ungrateful world and disclosed this as his thought: Why should I preach forever and permit my heralds to cry in vain? The more messengers I send, the longer I defer my wrath,—the worse they become. It is therefore necessary for preaching to cease, and for retribution to begin. I shall not permit my Spirit, that is, my Word, to bear witness forever. I am constrained to punish their sins. Man is flesh and is opposed to me. He continues in his carnal state, mocks at the Word, persecutes and hates my Spirit in the patriarchs, and the story is told to deaf ears.

This proclamation contains a public complaint, made by the Spirit through the patriarchs; but the flesh remained true to its nature. They despised faithful exhortation in their presumption and carnal security. God shows that he is displeased with the perversity of men, nevertheless, as a father would spare his son, but is compelled by his wickedness to be severe, so the Lord says, I do not gladly destroy the human race. I shall grant them one hundred and twenty years in which they may come to themselves, and during which I shall exercise mercy.

May 18th - James 1:21

Wherefore lay apart all filthiness and superfluity of naughtiness, and receive with meekness the grafted word, which is able to save your souls.

By filthiness, James means the impure life of the world—indulgence, voluptuousness, and knavery of every sort. These things, he says, should be far from you Christians who enjoy blessings so great and glorious. Could you rightly recognize and appreciate these blessings, you would regard all worldly pursuits and pleasures mere filth in comparison. Nor is this overdrawn; they are such when contrasted with the good and perfect heavenly gifts and treasures. You have the Word, says James, a Word which is yours, not by your own fancy or effort, but which God gave you and implanted in you by grace. It has free course, is preached, read and sung among you. It is of the utmost importance to receive it, to make profitable use of it, to handle it with meekness that we may hold it fast and not allow it to be effaced by anger under persecution or by the allurements of worldly lusts.

Meekness and patience are necessary to enable us to triumph over the devil and the world. Without them we shall not be able to hold fast the Word in our strife against those evil forces. We must fight and contend against sin, but if we essay to cool our wrath by grasping the devil and his followers by the hair and wreaking vengeance upon them, we will accomplish nothing and may thereby lose our treasure, the beloved Word. Therefore lay hold of the Word planted or grafted within you, that you may be able to retain it and have it bring forth its fruits in yourself. You have the Word; it is able to save you if you but steadfastly cling to it. Why then need you take any account of the world, and anything it may do? What injury can it render, what help even can it offer, as long as you hold the treasure of the Word?

The Word is implanted within you in a way to give you the certain comfort and sure hope of your salvation. Be careful not to permit yourselves to be wrested from it by the wrath or the filth of the world. Take heed to accept in purity and to maintain with patience the Word so graciously and richly given you by God without effort or merit on your part. Those, who are without the Word in their endeavor to attain heaven, accomplish nothing.

May 19th - John 16:20

Verily, verily, I say unto you, That you shall weep and lament, but the world shall rejoice: and you shall be sorrowful, but your sorrow shall be turned into joy.

This is said to all Christians, for every Christian must have temptations, trials, anxieties, adversities, sorrows, come what may. Therefore Christ mentions here no particular sorrow, nor trial, he simply says they shall weep, lament and be sorrowful, for the Christian has many persecutions. Some suffer loss of goods; there are others whose character suffers ignominy and scorn; some are drowned, others are burned; one perishes in this manner and another in that; it is the lot of the Christian constantly to suffer misfortune and adversity. This is the rod with which they are chastised. This is their court color by which the Christian is recognized, and if he wants to be a Christian, he dare not be ashamed of his livery.

No one need lay his cross upon himself, as some foolish persons have done and are still doing. They even court prison and death, saying: Since Christ of his own free will entered death, I will follow him in his example, as he commanded us to do. Such people do not understand divine things, they think they will suddenly enter death with Christ, whom they have never learned to know except in words. Thus was Peter also disposed, but he stood before Christ like a rabbit before one beating a drum. The old Adam lacks courage under the cross. The new man, however, can persevere through grace. Pious persons have no aim of their own in suffering, but if it be God's will they bear good fruit like a tree planted by the streams of water.

This is pleasing to God, since all presumption and show are condemned. He who battles heroically will receive joy for his suffering, the eternal in place of the temporal.

But why does God permit his own to be persecuted and hounded? In order to subdue the free will, that it may not seek an expedient in works; all serves to the end that we should accustom ourselves to build alone upon Christ, and to depend upon no other work, upon no other creature, whether in heaven or upon earth. But on this account we must suffer much. We must not only suffer shame and persecution, but the world rejoices at our great misfortunes. But this comfort we have that their joy shall not last long, and our sorrow shall be turned into eternal joy.

May 20th - John 16:3

These things will they do unto you, because they have not known the Father, nor me.

Christ tells what moves those who oppose the gospel to such hatred and persecution of Christians as to excommunicate them and even attempt to kill them. It is because they preach concerning Christ, whom they themselves do not know. That they do not know Christ is true without a doubt. Their own deeds prove it. They are blind and without the true knowledge of God and of Christ, opposing God and his Son with their acts of ban and murder under the very appearance and with the boast of thereby serving God. But Christ strengthens and comforts his own people that they fear not harsh judgment, nor are intimidated from preaching and confession, but say to their adversaries: "We must obey God rather than man."

Here Christ also fixes the standard of judgment and points out the difference between the true and the false Church. The Church is not to be judged by name and external appearance. Human reason cannot furnish the necessary qualifications for the true Church. The actual test is in ascertaining who have the real knowledge of Christ and who have not. What does it mean to know Christ and the Father? The papists boast of such a knowledge, as the Jews boasted of being able to recognize the Messiah. But an intellectual knowledge of God is not sufficient. He who wishes to know God truly must know him in the Word and promises which the Scriptures set forth about Christ, that Christ is the Son of God, sent by the Father as a sacrifice and ransom for the sins of the world; that he might appease the wrath of God and effect reconciliation for us, redeeming us from sin and death and securing for us righteousness and everlasting life.

Whenever, therefore, we have the knowledge of Christ, we must cease boasting and trusting in self-righteousness and in works. If Christ alone shall bear my sins I cannot at the same time atone for them by my own works and by my own pretended worthiness. This teaching points out the true Christ and the real knowledge of him. He who thus knows Christ, knows the Father also. This knowledge is the article of faith by which we become Christians, and is the foundation of our salvation.

May 21st - John 15:26

When the Comforter is come, whom I will send unto you from the Father, even the Spirit of truth, which proceedeth from the Father, he shall testify of me.

We have often heard that the gospel is the proclamation that no man can become just by means of the law; that God has sent his dear Son to shed his blood and die, since men cannot by their own power and works cancel their sins and get rid of them. But though I hear this preaching, I do not at once believe it. Therefore God adds his Holy Spirit, who impresses this preaching upon the heart, so that it abides there and lives. It is a faithful saying that Christ has accomplished everything, has removed sin and overcome every enemy, so that through him we are lords over all things. But the treasure lies in one pile; it is not yet distributed, nor invested. The Holy Spirit must come and teach our hearts to believe. When we feel that God has thus helped us and given us the treasure, everything goes well, and man's heart rejoices in God. When the Holy Spirit has impressed upon the heart that God is kind and gracious toward it, it believes that God can no more be angry, and it grows so happy and so bold that, for God's sake, it performs and suffers all things possible.

In this way you are to become acquainted with the Holy Spirit. You know to what purpose he is given and what his office is, namely, to invest the treasure—Christ and all he has; the Holy Spirit will enfold him in your heart so that he may be your own. But in all this we ought to exercise sense and understanding that a man receiving the Holy Spirit is not at once perfect, insensible to sin and pure in all respects. We do not preach that the Holy Spirit has completed and finished his work, but that he has only begun it and is now constantly engaged in it. Consequently you will not find a man who is without sin and sorrow, and full of righteousness and joy, and who serves everybody freely. The Scriptures indeed tell us that the office of the Holy Spirit is to redeem from sin and fear; but that does not say that this is altogether accomplished. The Christian at times feels his sin and the fear of death, but he has a helper, the Holy Spirit, who comforts and strengthens him.

May 22nd - John 14:18

I will not leave you comfortless: I will come to you.

We see many pious hearts that are always sad and downcast, tormenting and alarming themselves with their own thoughts, and being on the verge of despair because of the temptations of the devil. Where, say the world and our own flesh, do you find under these circumstances the Holy Spirit whom you Christians laud so much? A Christian should be wise here and not judge things according to his own thoughts and feelings; he should keep to the Word and the comfort of the preaching which the Holy Spirit gives to all poor and distressed hearts and consciences. God does not desire you to be sad or alarmed, but joyful and comforted with the certain promise of his grace, which the Holy Spirit offers you.

Of this promise and comfort to allay our feelings and fears, Christ assures us in the words, "I will not leave you comfortless." The word translated "comfortless" literally means "orphans." By the use of the word Christ would intimate the condition of the Church. In the eyes of the world, and even in our own estimation, she has not the appearance of a prosperous and well-ordered organization; rather she is a scattered group of poor, miserable orphans without leader, protection or help upon earth. Misery and fears grow upon one under the influence of the devil's power, when he pierces the heart with his bitter, poisonous, and murderous thrusts. Then the heart feels that it is not only forsaken by all men, but also by God himself. So it altogether loses Christ and sees no end to its misery. To be left thus, to feel that all things have conspired to leave us comfortless and helpless, is to be left orphans indeed.

As Christ has told his Christians beforehand of suffering, so also does he wish to give them this comfort and consolation beforehand, and desires to teach us not to despair because of suffering, but only to hold to his Word, even if it does seem that help is being too long delayed. He reminds us of the promise that he will not leave us in misery, but will come to us, and desires that we should accord him the highest honor due to God, by holding him to be true and faithful.

May 23rd - John 14:23

We will come unto him, and make our abode with him.

What mockery it must have been to the ears of the Jewish saints and priests and Pharisees when they heard the words that declare how God will make his habitation only with those who hear the words of this man! They were only a little handful of timid, poor, despised people. As if God did not have a better and more glorious habitation, becoming his majesty, in the saints and superior persons who were the bright lights and the eminent ones among God's people, in the holy city of Jerusalem! And the glorious temple and divine worship—did not the Scriptures call them the holy city and dwelling place of God, the chosen place where he would rest and that forever? Of this they boasted very haughtily, and claimed that their kingdom, their priesthood and divine worship, should never fail.

But here Christ ignores all these things as if he were totally indifferent to them, and utters the remarkable saying that the place of his own and his Father's abode—their habitation and their Church—is where a Christian is found, who keeps his Word. Thus he discards the old habitation of Judaism and the temple of Jerusalem and builds a new, holy, glorious Church and house of God, which is not Jerusalem or Judaism, but is spread abroad throughout the whole world, without distinction of person, place, or custom. Jews, Gentiles, priests or laymen—it matters not. This house of God is not of stone or wood, made by the hand of man, but newly created of God himself, namely a people that love Christ and keep his Word. Christ binds the Church to his Word and makes the distinguishing mark by which must be measured the teaching, the preaching, and rule of conduct. You have the warrant that God dwells therein and speaks and acts through that Church.

Observe now what a worthy being that man is who is a Christian, or who, as Christ says, keeps Christ's Word. A wonderful man is he upon earth, who is of more value in the eyes of God than heaven and earth; he is a light and saviour of the world, in whom God is all in all, and who in God is able to do all things. But to the world he is hidden and unknown.

May 24th - 1 Corinthians 3:16

Know you not that you are the temple of God, and that the Spirit of God dwells in you?

What a glorious, noble, loving, and precious guest and house companion man receives, God the Father and the Son and certainly with them also the Holy Spirit. This is certainly a sublime, beautiful promise, and one of the precious and exceeding great promises granted unto us poor, miserable sinners, that we through them should become partakers of the divine nature, and should be so highly honored as not only to be loved of God through Christ Jesus and to enjoy his favor and grace, but should even have the Lord himself dwelling completely in us.

Where else should God dwell? Those self-constituted saints, in their own estimation excellent, high and great, are much too proud, much too high, wise and holy. They have passed up through and far above heaven, so that they could not be his habitation upon earth, although they boast of being the only Church and people of God. Though they appear in all the pomp and glory and ornament of their self-made holiness, yet God does not do them the honor to look at them. He is found in the humble huts of the poor and despised, who fear and believe the Word of Christ and would gladly become Christians, but who feel that they are very unholy and unworthy sinners. "They are a temple of the living God."

These things are accomplished in this way: in addition to the grace by which a man begins to believe and to hold fast to the Word, God also rules in man through his divine power and agency, so that he constantly grows more and more enlightened, becomes richer and stronger in spiritual understanding and wisdom, and better fitted to understand all matters of doctrine and practice. He further makes daily progress in life and good works, becomes eventually a kind, gentle, patient man, ready to serve everyone with doctrine, advice, comfort, and gifts; is useful to God and man; through him and because of him men and countries are benefited; in short, he is a man through whom God speaks, in whom he lives and works. His tongue is God's tongue, his hand is God's hand, and his word is God's Word. His doctrine and confession as a Christian are not of men, but of Christ, whose Word he has and holds.

May 25th - John 14:26

The Comforter, which is the Holy Ghost, whom the Father will send in my name, he shall teach you all things, and bring all things to your remembrance, whatsoever I have said unto you.

Note well this text, how Christ here binds the Holy Spirit to his Word, and fixes his limit and measure, so that the Spirit may not go further than his Word. He shall remind you of everything which I have said, publishing it further through you. Thereby he shows that in the future nothing else shall be taught in all Christendom through the Holy Spirit than what the apostles had heard from Christ, but which they did not understand until the Holy Spirit had taught them. So the teaching may always proceed from the mouth of Christ, then be transmitted from one mouth to another, and yet always remain the Word of Christ. The Holy Spirit is thus the schoolmaster who teaches these things and brings them to remembrance.

It is shown here that this Word precedes, or must be spoken beforehand, and afterwards the Holy Spirit works through the Word. One must not reverse the order and dream of a Holy Spirit who works without the Word and before the Word, but one who comes with and through the Word and goes no further than the Word goes. The example of the apostles shows also how Christ rules his Church in her weakness; the Holy Spirit does not dwell in Christians at all times, nor so soon as they have heard the Word does he come with such power and effectiveness as to enable them to believe it all and rightly to understand and grasp it. Although the apostles are so far advanced as to hear Christ's Word willingly and to have begun to believe, yet even they cannot take these words of comfort to heart until the Holy Spirit teaches them after the departure of Christ.

So it is at present. We hear God's Word, which is in fact the preaching of the Holy Spirit, who is at all times present with it, but it does not always reach the heart at once and is accepted by faith; even in those who are moved by the Holy Spirit and gladly receive the Word, it does not at once bear fruit. Therefore it must come to this: in need and danger we look about and sigh for comfort; then the Holy Spirit can perform his office of teaching the heart and bringing to remembrance the Word preached.

May 26th - John 14:1

Let not your heart be troubled: you believe in God, believe also in me.

I notice, says Jesus, that my departure [spoken of in the preceding chapter] makes you sad and causes anxiety. But there is no need of fear, I shall come again; before that time, however, you will see many things happen to me, at which you will be grieved. They will crucify and miserably misuse me; but let it not disturb you, there will soon be a change for the better. So is the Father's will.

Here you can see how affectionately and faithfully the Lord Jesus deals with his dear disciples. He does not leave them comfortless, although he will be separated from them that very night and leave them in great danger, fear and terror. For the first misfortune experienced in tribulation is that not only is the body affected, but the heart is frightened and grieved. Since it is impossible to change flesh and blood, the Lord is especially eager that the heart be free and unmolested. He who in times of distress has a good conscience and a joyful heart is already more than half relieved of his troubles. Consequently Christ says: Be careful, that such suffering remain in the body, and by no means allow it to affect the heart.

As Christians, he would say, you are not like those who do not know God's Word and who do not believe. You are much affected on account of my death, but what you believe of God, you ought also believe of me. None of you fear that God will die, or that he will be cast down from his throne.

Why then should you fear on my account? Let death, the world, and the devil be as angry as they please, they will find nothing in me; for I am God. This believe and your hearts will be quieted and even find comfort in my death. For when death and I grapple with one another, death will be overcome; this shall be to your benefit. At present here on earth I am regarded as a poor, miserable, powerless man;

but after I shall be lifted up, I will draw all men unto me. But just as the disciples could not understand such comfort, so we do not understand it, when grief comes over us. We are immediately seized with fear, impatience, and despair, and no one can persuade us that our sadness shall be turned to joy.

May 27th - John 16:13

When he, the Spirit of truth, is come, he will guide you into all truth.

When the Holy Spirit comes he will enlighten your hearts, so that you will understand the truth, and will call to remembrance all things. But our doctors and highly learned men have made use of these words in a most frivolous manner and said that it was necessary to have something more than the Scriptures, that one ought also to hear what the councils and the pope decree. They endeavor to prove in this way that Christ says: Because he has not told them all things, it follows that he told them to the councils, popes, and bishops.

Now look at these fools, what they say. To whom does Christ speak? Without doubt to the apostles. Therefore, if Christ is not to lie, his Word must have been fulfilled at the time that the Holy Spirit came. The Holy Spirit must have said everything to the apostles and accomplished everything that the Lord here refers to, and, of course, led them into all the truth. Christ gives to understand that soon the Holy Spirit would tell and explain to them all things, and that afterwards the apostles should carry out everything, and through them should be made known to the world what they have learned from the Holy Spirit. But according to the councils and popes it depends upon what they say, teach, and command, even to the end of the world.

If what the councils teach be the truth, that one is to wear the tonsure, and the cap, and live a life of celibacy, then the apostles never came to the truth, since none of them ever entered a cloister, nor kept any of those foolish laws. Christ must have indeed betrayed us in this, when he said the Holy Spirit should guide us into all truth, when in reality he wished to teach us how we were to become priests and monks and not to eat meat on certain days, and like foolish things. To hear such things is exasperating and it should grieve our hearts to see how shamefully the people act against the precious Word of God, and that they make the Holy Spirit a liar. Should not this single passage be powerful enough against the pope and the councils, even if we had no other in the Scriptures?

May 28th - Acts 2:1

When the day of Pentecost was fully come, they were all with one accord in one place.

When God was about to lead the children of Israel out of Egypt, he permitted them to celebrate the Feast of the Passover on the night of their departure, and commanded them on every annual recurrence of the season to observe the same feast in commemoration of their liberation from bondage and their departure from Egypt. Fifty days later, in their journey through the wilderness, they arrived at Mount Sinai. There God gave them the law through Moses, and there they were commanded to observe annually, in commemoration of that giving of the law, the fiftieth day after the Feast of the Passover. Hence the name "Feast of Pentecost," the word "Pentecost" coming from the Greek "Pentecoste," or fiftieth day. So when the day of Pentecost was now "fully come"—when the Jews had properly commemorated the giving of the law of God on Mount Sinai—the Holy Spirit came, in accordance with Christ's promise, and gave them a new law. We now celebrate this feast, not because of the old historical event, but because of the new one—the sending of the Holy Spirit.

The occasion of the Jewish observance was the giving of the literal law; but it is ours to celebrate the giving of the spiritual law. There is the written law, commanded of God and composed of written words. It is called "written" or "literal" because it goes no farther and does not enter the heart. With dead hearts men could not sincerely observe the commandments of God. Were every individual left to do as he pleased, uninfluenced by fear, not one would be found choosing to be controlled by the law. As long as the law consists merely of written words, it can make no one righteous, can enter no heart.

The spiritual law is not written with pen and ink, nor uttered by lips as Moses read from the tables of stone. We learn that the Holy Spirit descended from heaven and filled all the assembled multitude, and there appeared on each of them parting, fiery tongues and they preached so unlike they were wont to do that all men were filled with amazement. The Spirit came pouring into their hearts, making them different beings, making them creatures who loved and willingly obeyed God. This change was simply the manifestation of the Spirit himself, his work in the heart.

May 29th - 1 Peter 5:8

Be sober, be vigilant; because your adversary the devil, as a roaring lion, walks about, seeking whom he may devour.

Since you are a people called to contend with this powerful spirit, which is more intent on seizing your souls than is the wolf of seizing the sheep, it is essential that you should take thought how to withstand him. Resistance is effected only through faith and prayer. But soberness and vigilance are necessary to enable one to pray. With gormandizers and drunkards reason is dethroned and they are rendered incapable of respecting anything, or of performing any good work. The ability to pray and call upon God has been taken from them, and the devil overcomes and devours them at his will.

The diligence in prayer which characterized Christians of the primitive Church, even while undergoing great persecution, is apparent to us. They were more than willing to assemble daily for prayer, not only morning and evening, but also at certain other appointed hours; and frequently they watched and prayed entire nights. Their habit of devotion morning, evening and at all times is commendable. With the cessation of this practice in the congregations, there succeeded the wretched order of monks, who pretended to do the praying for others. We still retain from the ancient custom the observance of morning and evening prayers in schools for children. But the same practice should obtain in every Christian family. Every father is under obligation to train up his children to pray at least at the beginning and the close of day, commending to God every exigency of this earthly life, that God's wrath may be averted, and deserved punishment withheld.

Under such conditions, we would be properly instructed and not have to be subjected to intolerable oppression and to prohibitions relative to eating, drinking, and dressing, being guided by nature's demands and our own honor and pleasure. Yet we would not be inordinate and brutish in these things, nor shamefully dethrone reason. Drunkenness is a sin and a shame to any man, and would be even were there neither God, nor commandment; much less can it be tolerated among Christians. There is more virtue in this respect among the heathen and Turks. Our characters ought to be so noble as to give no chance of offense at our conduct, that the name of God be not defamed, but glorified.

May 30th - Matthew 28:19

Baptizing them in the name of the Father, and of the Son, and of the Holy Ghost.

We have in the holy Scriptures and in the Creed sufficient information concerning the Holy Trinity, and all that is necessary for the instruction of ordinary Christians. That the simple Christian may recognize that there is but one divine essence and one God, who is tri-personal, a special work, peculiar to himself, is ascribed to each person. To the Father we ascribe the work of creation; to the Son the work of redemption; to the Holy Spirit the power to forgive sins, to gladden, to strengthen, to transport from death to life eternal.

The thought is not that the Father alone is Creator, the Son alone Redeemer, and the Holy Ghost alone Sanctifier. The creation and preservation of the universe, atonement for sin and its forgiveness, resurrection from the dead, and the gift of eternal life—all these are operations of the one Divine Majesty as such. Yet the Father is especially emphasized in the work of creation, which proceeds originally from him as the first person; the Son is emphasized in the redemption he has accomplished in his own person; and the Holy Spirit in the special work of sanctification, which is both his mission and revelation. Such distinction is made for the purpose of affording Christians the unqualified assurance that there is but one God and yet three persons in one divine essence—truths which the sainted fathers have faithfully gathered from the writings of Moses, the prophets, and the apostles, and which they have maintained against all heretics.

This faith has descended to us by inheritance, and by his power God has maintained it in the Church, against sects and adversaries, unto the present time. So we must abide by it in its simplicity and not attempt to be wise. Such articles of faith appear utterly foolish to reason. Paul aptly calls the gospel foolish preaching wherewith God saves such souls as do not depend on their own wisdom, but simply believe in the Word. Those who will follow reason in the things dealt with in these articles, and will reject the Word, shall be defeated and destroyed in their wisdom.

May 31st - 1 Peter 4:7

The end of all things is at hand: be you therefore sober, and watch unto prayer.

It is not becoming to Christians to lead heathenish lives, to indulge in gormandizing, guzzling, and carousing, by which they demoralize themselves. They have something nobler to do. They are to be occupied with the Word of God from which they derive their new birth and with which they preserve it. Being born anew they have enemies to fight. As long as they live on earth they must combat the devil and their own flesh. They must, therefore, not give way to drowsy indolence; much less may they become foolish, drunken sots, indifferent to all issues and heedless of their obligations. They need rather to be watchful and sober, ever ready with the Word and with prayer.

These are the two kinds of weapons with which the devil is vanquished and of which he is afraid. Whichever we wield is unendurable to him and he cannot abide it. Christians need both equipments that their hearts may ever turn to God, cling to his Word, and continually pray a perpetual Lord's Prayer. Christians should be diligent in hearing, learning, and practicing the Word of God, that they may receive instruction, comfort, and strength. They need to be sincere in their petitions upon the authority of that Word, cry and call to God for help when temptations and conflicts arise. One or the other of these weapons of defense should be continually in active exercise, effecting perpetual intercourse between God and man—God either speaking to us while we quietly listen, or hearing our utterances and petitions to him concerning our needs. The Christian should learn from the temptations and straits with which the devil, the world, and his own flesh constantly oppress him, to be ever on his guard, watching for the enemy's point of attack; for the enemy never sleeps, nor rests a single moment.

Peter therefore enjoins the Christian to keep within the bounds of physical temperance and sobriety. He is not to overload and injure his body by excessive eating and drinking. He who is not careful to discharge the obligations of his office or station with temperance and sobriety is incapable of praying or performing any Christian duty, and is unfit for any service.

June 1st - Romans 8:18

For I reckon that the sufferings of this present time are not worthy to be compared with the glory which shall be revealed in us.

Notice how Paul turns his back to the world and his face to the future revelation, as if seeing no suffering anywhere, but all joy. "Even if it does go ill with us," he would argue, "what indeed is our suffering in comparison with the unspeakable joy and glory to be revealed in us? It is too insignificant to be compared and unworthy to be called suffering." We fail to realize the truth of these words because we do not see with our bodily eyes the supreme glory awaiting us, because we fail to grasp fully the fact that we shall never die, but shall have a body that cannot suffer, nor be ill. If one could conceive the nature of this reward, he would be compelled to say: "Were it possible for me to suffer ten deaths, by fire or flood, that would be nothing in comparison with the future life of glory." What is temporal suffering, however protracted, contrasted with eternal life? It is not worthy to be called suffering or to be esteemed meritorious.

In this light Paul regards suffering, and he admonishes Christians to look upon it in a similar manner. Then shall they find the infinite beyond all comparison with the finite. The suffering of the world is always to be counted as nothing, measured by the glorious and eternal possessions yet to be ours. If you essay to be a joint heir with the Lord Jesus Christ and do not suffer with him, to be his brother and are not like unto him, Christ certainly will not at the last day acknowledge you as a brother and fellow-heir. Rather he will ask where are your crown of thorns, your cross, the nails and scourge; whether you have been, as he and his followers ever have from the beginning of time, an abomination to the world. If you cannot qualify in this respect, he cannot regard you as his brother. In short, we must all suffer with the Son of God and be made like unto him, or we shall not be exalted with him in glory.

June 2nd - 1 John 3:2

Beloved, now are we the sons of God, and it does not yet appear what we shall be: but we know that, when he shall appear, we shall be like him.

When our Lord Jesus Christ comes with his beloved angels and we are drawn up into the clouds to meet him in the air, he will bring to God's children a glory consistent with their name. They will be far more splendidly arrayed than were the children of the world in their lifetime, who went about in purple and velvet and ornaments of gold, as the rich man, in silk. Then shall they wear their own livery and shine as the sun in the kingdom of their Father. Such is the wonderful glory of the revelation, that the radiant beauty of poor Lazarus, who had lain in wretchedness at the rich man's gate, surpasses all expectation.

The hope of this wonderful glory is ours, and that of all creation with us, for creation is to be purified and renewed for our sakes. Then will we be impressed with the grandeur of the sun, the majesty of the trees, and the beauty of the flowers. Having so much in prospect, we should, in the buoyancy of our hope, attach little importance to the slight suffering that may be our earthly lot. What is it compared with the glory to be revealed in us? Doubtless in yonder life we shall reproach ourselves with the thought: "How foolish I was! I am unworthy to be called the child of God, for I esteemed myself all too highly on earth and placed too little value upon this surpassing glory and happiness. Were I still in the world and with the knowledge I now have of the heavenly glory, I would, were it possible, suffer a thousand years of imprisonment, or endure illness, persecution or other misfortunes. Now I am truly convinced that all the sufferings of the world are nothing, measured by the glory to be manifested in the children of God."

Here on earth men as a rule are dishonorable and wicked and obey not the will of the Lord God as it is done in heaven; but the day will come when only righteousness and holiness shall dwell on the earth—none but godly, righteous souls.

June 3rd - 1 Peter 3:10

He that will love life, and see good days, let him refrain his tongue from evil, and his lips that they speak no guile.

This injunction really applies to doctrine, meaning that we are to abide by the true Word of God and not to allow ourselves to be seduced by false teaching. On account of the faith and confession for which men are called Christians, they must suffer much; they are endangered, hated, persecuted, oppressed, and harassed by the whole world. Christians might easily believe that they have cause to return evil, and being mortals of flesh and blood, they are inevitably moved to be angry and to curse, or to deny their confession and doctrine and with unbelievers to join the false church with its idolatrous teaching. According to the nature of flesh and blood they fret because they are compelled to witness the prosperity of the world in its ungodly life and wickedness, how it despises and persecutes them with pride and indolence. But they are not to allow themselves to be easily provoked; they should strive to keep wrong, displeasure, vexations and worry outside their inner life.

When one is prompted to anger and to complain about injury and wrong, in his impatience and irritation he cannot speak fairly concerning the matter of offense, but invariably exaggerates. The individual that suffers a single adverse word immediately proceeds to abuse and slander his opponent. An angry heart knows no moderation, but makes of a splinter, or even a mote, a great beam, or fans a tiny spark into a volcano of flame, by retaliating with reviling and cursing. If possible, he would even murder the offender and commit a greater wrong than he has suffered.

Thus Peter admonishes you to restrain your tongues, to curb them, lest they suddenly get beyond your control and you sin in wicked words, doing twice as much injury as you have received. Guard your lips that you utter no guile or falsehood through your anger, and that it may not culminate, abuse and slander your neighbor in violation of the eighth commandment. Such conduct is, before God and man, unbecoming a Christian and leads to that most disgraceful vice of slander, which God supremely hates.

Therefore be all the more diligent to do good, that your heart may retain its honor and joy.

June 4th - Romans 12:16

Be of the same mind one toward another.

Harmony is the imperative virtue for the Christian Church. Before other virtues can be manifest, there must first be concord and unity of heart among all. It is impossible that outward circumstances of human life be always the same; much dissimilarity in person, station, and occupation is inevitable. To this very unlikeness and to the natural depravity of flesh and blood is due the discord and disagreement of men in this world. Let one become conscious of personal superiority in point of uprightness, learning, skill or natural ability, or let him become aware of his loftier station in life, and he immediately grows self-complacent, thinks himself better than his fellows, demands honor and recognition from all men, is unwilling to yield or to serve an inferior and thinks himself entitled to such right and privilege because of his superiority and virtue.

This matter of harmony is the first and most necessary commandment enjoined by the doctrine of faith; this virtue is the first fruit which faith is to effect among Christians, who are called in one faith and one baptism. It is to be the beginning of their Christian love. For true faith necessarily creates in all believers the spirit that reasons: "We are all called by one Word, one baptism and Holy Spirit, to the same salvation; we are alike heirs of the grace and blessings of God. Although one has more and greater gifts than another, he is not on that account better before God. By grace alone, without any merit of ours, we are pleasing to God. Before him none can boast of himself."

When one imagines himself better than his fellows, desiring to exalt and glorify himself above others, he is really no longer a Christian, because he is no longer in that unity of mind and faith essential to Christians. Christ with his grace is always the same, and cannot be divided or apportioned within himself. So long as unity of faith and oneness of mind survive, the true Church of God abides, notwithstanding there may be some weakness in other points. Of this fact the devil is well aware; hence his hostility to Christian unity. Christians should, therefore, be all the more careful to cherish the virtue of harmony, both in the Church and in secular government.

June 5th - Galatians 1:9

If any man preach any other gospel unto you than that you have received, let him be accursed.

God often in this life lays hold upon leaders of sects who blaspheme and slander him with their false doctrines. He inflicts upon them unusual punishments for the sake of warning others. All men must admit that God can have no pleasure in their doctrine, since he visits them with special marks of his displeasure, destroying them with a more severe punishment than ordinary befalls offenders.

History records that John the evangelist had as contemporary a heretic named Cerinthus, who first arose in opposition to the apostolic doctrine and in blasphemy against the Lord Jesus with the claim that Jesus is not God. This blasphemy spread to such an extent that John saw himself compelled to supplement the work of the other evangelists with this gospel, whose distinct purpose it is to defend and maintain the deity of Christ against Cerinthus and his rabble. Having on a certain occasion gone to a public bath with some of his disciples, John became aware that Cerinthus and his rabble were also there. Without hesitation he told his disciples to be up and away, and not abide among the blasphemers. The disciples followed his advice and departed. Immediately after their departure the building collapsed, and Cerinthus and his followers perished.

We also read concerning the heretic Arius, the chief foe of his time to the dogma of the deity of Christ. The injury done to the cause of Christ by this man occupied the Church for four centuries after his death; and to-day his heresy has not been entirely rooted out. With an oath Arius had impressed the emperor and his counsellors with the righteousness of his doctrine. The emperor commanded Alexander, the bishop, to restore him to the priestly office. The bishop resolved to seek help from God, where alone it is found in all things relating to God's honor. He prayed all night long that God should preserve his name and honor, and Christendom against the heretics. In a pompous procession the following day Arius suddenly became ill, withdrew, and died. Thus we see that God has preserved this doctrine against the devil and his blasphemers, and he shall preserve it in the future, that we may believe in God the Father, God the Son, and God the Holy Spirit.

June 6th - Luke 16:19

There was a certain rich man, which was clothed in purple and fine linen, and fared sumptuously every day.

We must not view the rich man according to his outward conduct; for he is in sheep's clothing, his life glitters and shines beautifully, while he tactfully conceals the wolf. The text does not accuse him of adultery, of murder or robbery, or of anything that the world would censure. He had been as honorable and respectful in his life as that Pharisee who fasted twice a week and was not as other men. Had he committed glaring sins, the gospel would have mentioned them, since it examines him so minutely as to describe even the purple robe he wore and the food he ate, which are only external matters, and God does not judge according to them. Hence he must have led an outwardly exemplary life.

But we must look into his heart and judge his spirit. The gospel has penetrating eyes and looks deep into the secret recesses of the soul, reproves the works which reason cannot reprove and looks not at the sheep's clothing, but at the true fruit of the tree to learn whether it is good or not. If we judge this rich man according to the fruits of faith, we will find a heart of unbelief. The gospel chastises him because he fares sumptuously every day and clothes himself so richly. He is not punished because he indulged in sumptuous fare and fine clothes; many saints, kings and queens in ancient times wore costly apparel; but because his heart was attached to them, sought them, trusted in them, and found in them all his joy and pleasure. He made them in fact his idols.

Where faith is, there is no anxiety for fine clothing and sumptuous living; there is no longing for riches, honor, pleasure and all that is not God himself. But there is a seeking and striving for God, the highest good. It is the same to the man of faith whether his food be dainty or plain, whether his clothing be fine or homespun. Though they even do wear costly clothes, possess great influence and honor, they esteem none of these things, but are forced to them, or come to them by accident, or they are compelled to use them in the service of others.

June 7th - Hebrews 11:6

Without faith it is impossible to please him: for he that cometh to God must believe that he is, and that he is a rewarder of them that diligently seek him.

It is the nature of faith to expect all good from God, and to rely only on him. From this faith man knows God, how good and gracious he is, and by reason of such knowledge his heart becomes so tender and merciful that he wishes cheerfully to do to everyone what he has experienced from God. Therefore he goes forth in acts of love and serves his neighbor with his whole heart, with his body and soul, with his means and honor, with his life and spirit, and makes him partake of all he has, just as God did to him. Therefore he does not look after the healthy, the high, the strong, the rich, the noble, the holy persons who do not need his care; but he looks after the sick, the weak, the poor, the despised, the sinful, to whom he can be of benefit, and among whom he can exercise his tender heart, and do to them as God has done to him.

But the nature of unbelief is that it does not expect any good from God. The heart is blinded so that it neither feels nor knows how good and gracious God is. Out of this blindness follows further that the heart becomes so hard, obdurate and unmerciful that the man has no desire to do any kindness to his fellow man. As he is insensible to the goodness of God, he takes no pleasure in doing good to his neighbor. Consequently it follows that he does not look after the sick, poor and despised, to whom he could and should be helpful and profitable; he sees only the high, rich and influential, from whom he himself may receive advantage, gain, pleasure and honor. Where unbelief reigns man is absorbed by vanities, seeks them and does not rest until he has acquired them, and after he possesses them he feeds and fattens on them as the swine, and finds his sole happiness in them. He never inquires how his heart stands with his God and what he possesses in God and may expect from him; his belly is his God; if he cannot get what he wants he thinks things are all going wrong. From this then follows the other sin, that he forgets to exercise love toward his neighbor. Thus we see that it is impossible to love, where no faith exists, and impossible to believe, where there is no love. Both must go together.

June 8th - Acts 10:44

While Peter yet spake these words, the Holy Ghost fell on all them which heard the word.

From this we should learn what is the office of the Holy Spirit in the Church, and how or by what means he is received in the heart and works there. It is through preaching Jesus Christ the Lord. The gospel is the message which God would have preached world-wide, declaring to every individual that since no man can be made righteous through the law, but must rather become more unrighteous, God sent his own beloved Son to shed his blood and die for our sins, from which we could not be released by our own effort. It is not enough simply that Christ be preached; the Word must be believed. Therefore, God sends the Holy Spirit to impress the preaching upon the heart, to make it inhere and live therein. Without doubt Christ accomplished all, enabling us to become, through him, lords over all things. But the treasure lies in a heap; it is not everywhere distributed and applied. Before we can enjoy it, the Holy Spirit comes and communicates it to the heart, enabling us to believe and say, "I too am one who shall have the blessing." Now, with the belief that God has come to our rescue and given us his priceless blessing, inevitably the human heart must be filled with joy and gratitude to God, and exultingly cry: "Dear Father, since it is your will to manifest inexpressible love and fidelity toward me, I will love you sincerely, and willingly do what is pleasing to you "

But in one sense know that all is not accomplished when the Holy Spirit is received. The possessor of the Spirit is not made entirely perfect and pure in all respects at once. We do not preach the doctrine that the Spirit's office is one of complete accomplishment, but rather that it is progressive. The Christian must, in some measure, still feel sin in his heart and experience the terrors of death; he is affected by whatever affects other sinners. But he is supported by the Holy Spirit, who consoles and strengthens him till the work is fully accomplished. As long as we live in the flesh, we cannot attain such a degree of perfection as to be wholly free from weakness and faults. The pious Christian is still flesh and blood, but he strives to resist evil lusts and all other sins.

June 9th - Jude 1:3, 4

It was needful for me to write unto you, and exhort you that you should earnestly contend for the faith which was once delivered unto the saints. For there are certain men crept in unawares ... turning the grace of God into lasciviousness, and denying the only Lord God, and our Lord Jesus Christ.

The reason I wish to write unto you, says Jude, is that you may continue in the faith which you have heard. There are already preachers at hand which advocate other doctrines than that faith; by these the people are gently and unsuspectingly led astray from the true way. Upon these false teachers the sentence of judgment, he says, has already been pronounced long ago, namely, that they are condemned.

We now understand this quite well, since we have learned that no one can become righteous or be justified (before God) by his own works, but through faith in Christ alone; that he must rely upon the work of Christ as the chief good and only support. Then after faith is present, whatever man does should be done for the benefit of his neighbor. The grace of God, which holds Christ before us, that is offered and given unto us through the gospel with all that he has, these men use only for leading impure lives. They call themselves Christians, praise the gospel, but live in wantonness, in eating and drinking. They boast that they are not in a secular, but in a spiritual state, and on that account claim all good, honor and luxury.

The denying of the Lord God is not with the mouth, for they confess that God is Lord; but they deny Christ in their deeds and works, considering him not as their Lord, but being their own lords unto themselves. For when they preach that fasts, pilgrimages, church institutions (ceremonies), chastity (celibacy), obedience (to the rules of ecclesiastical orders) poverty and the like are the way to salvation, they lead people astray. They say nothing about Christ, as though he were not needed and his work of redemption of no value. Thus they deny Christ, who has bought them with his own blood. They know not that our salvation is founded upon faith and love. They are offended when we reject their works and preach that Christ alone must help us with his works.

June 10th - 1 Peter 3:12

The eyes of the Lord are over the righteous, and his ears are open unto their prayers: but the face of the Lord is against them that do evil.

Inscribe this verse upon your heart in firm faith and see if it does not bring you peace and blessings. Try to believe that God sits above, sleepless and with his vigilant eye ever upon you. With watchful vision he beholds the righteous as they suffer violence and wrong. Why will you complain and become discouraged by reason of the harm and grief you experience, when the gracious eyes of God, the true Judge, are upon you with the intent to help you? All the wealth of the world would I give, if I could, to purchase that watchful care, or rather obtain the requisite faith; for surely the lack is not in God's regarding, but in our faith.

More than this, God's ears are open to the prayers of the righteous. As he looks upon you with gracious winning eyes, so also are his ears alert even to the faintest sound. He hears your complaint, your sighing and prayer, and hears them willingly and with pleasure; as soon as you open your mouth, your prayer is heard and answered.

But the face of the Lord is against them that do evil. God's eyes are upon the righteous, but he sees also the others. In this case he beholds not with a friendly look or gracious countenance, but with a displeased and wrathful face. When a man is angry the forehead frowns, the nostrils dilate and the eyes flash. Such a manifestation of anger we are to understand when the Scripture here refers to "the face of the Lord." On the contrary it illustrates the pleased and gracious aspect of God by "the eyes of the Lord."

What is the effect of "the face of the Lord" upon evildoers? According to the words of the Psalm, it is "to cut off the remembrance of them from the earth." This is a terrible sentence before which a heart may well be prostrate as from a thunderbolt. Ungodly hearts would be appalled were they not so hardened in despising God's Word. Verily it is no jest with God. In contrast, the righteous, because they have feared God and abode in their piety, shall, even here upon earth, live to see blessing and prosperity upon their children's children.

June 11th - Psalm 55:22

Cast your burden upon the Lord, and he shall sustain you: he shall never suffer the righteous to be moved.

Let not your burden rest upon yourselves; for you cannot bear it, and must finally perish beneath its weight. Confident and full of joy, cast it upon God, and say: Heavenly Father, you are my Lord and God, who created me and has redeemed me through your Son. Now, you have committed to me and laid upon me this office or work; things do not go as well as I would like. There is so much to oppress and worry, that I can find neither counsel nor help. Therefore I commend everything to you. Do you supply counsel and help, and be thou, thyself, everything in these things. Such prayer is pleasing to God, as he tells us to throw upon him all anxiety as to the issue and what we shall accomplish.

No heathen, philosopher or jurist, if he have not God's Word, can throw his care and complaint upon God. When trouble arises, he begins to murmur and argue against God and his government, as though God's rule merited criticism. But such men receive their deserts when God permits their calculations and hopes to fail and lets the reverse prevail. They spend their lives in many vain, useless cares and projects and in the course of their experience must learn and confess that many a time the very opposite of their judgment is the truth.

The Christian has the rare faculty, above all other people on earth, of knowing where to place his cares. He commits his troubles to God and proceeds with vigor against all that opposes. In time of danger and in the hour of death, when, with all his worrying, he cannot discover where he is or whither he is journeying, he must, with eyes, senses and thoughts closed to the world, surrender himself in faith and confidence to God and cast himself upon his hand and protection, and say: God has permitted me to live until this hour without my solicitude. He has given me his beloved Son as a treasure and sure pledge of eternal life. Therefore, my dear soul, journey on in joy. you have a faithful Father and Saviour, who has taken you into his own hand, and will preserve you.

June 12th - Philippians 1:9, 10

This I pray, that your love may abound yet more and more in knowledge and in all judgment; ... that you may be sincere and without offence till the day of Christ.

Paul says he thanks God for the fellowship of the Philippians in the gospel, and offers prayer in their behalf. It should be the joy of a Christian heart to see multitudes accept the offer of mercy, and praise and thank God with him. This desire for the participation of others in the gospel promotes the spirit of prayer. The Christian cannot be a misanthrope, wholly unconcerned whether his fellows believe or not. He should be interested in all men and unceasingly long and pray for their salvation; for the sanctification of God's name, the coming of his kingdom, the fulfilment of his will; and for the exposure everywhere of the devil's deceptions, the suppression of his murderous power over poor souls and the restraint of his authority.

This prayer should be the sincere, earnest outflow of the true Christian's heart. Paul's words indicate that his praise and prayer were inspired by a fervent spirit. He speaks in a way worthy of an apostle. He renders praise and prayer with keenest pleasure. He rejoices in his heart that he has somewhere a little band of Christians who love the gospel and with whom he may rejoice; that he may thank God for them and pray in their behalf. Was there not much more reason that all who had heard the gospel should rejoice and thank Paul in heart and expression for it, praying God in his behalf, should rejoice that they became worthy of the apostle's favor, were delivered from their blindness and had now received from him the light transferring them from sin and death into the grace of God and eternal life?

But Paul does not wait for them to take the initiative, as they ought to have done to declare their joy and their gratitude to him. In his first utterance he pours out the joy of his heart, fervently thanking God for them. Well might they have blushed, and reproached themselves, when they received the epistle beginning with these words. Well might they have said: "We should not have permitted him to speak in this way; it was our place first to show him gratitude and joy."

June 13th - Genesis 2:23

And Adam said, This is now bone of my bones, and flesh of my flesh.

As Adam was pure and holy the words of Adam may rightly be said to be divine words or the voice of God, for God spoke through him. All the words and the works of Adam in that state of innocency are divine, and therefore may truly be said to be the words and works of God. Eve is presented to Adam by God himself. And just in the same manner as the will of God is prepared to institute marriage, so Adam is prepared to receive Eve with all pleasure and holiness when brought unto him. So even now the affection of the intended husband toward his betrothed spouse is of a particular and elevated kind.

It is worthy of our greatest wonder and admiration that Adam, the moment he cast his eye on Eve, knew her to be a creature formed out of himself. He immediately said, "This is now bone of my bones, and flesh of my flesh." These are not the words of an ignorant one, nor of one who was a sinner; nor of one who was ignorant of the works and creation of God. They are the words of one righteous, wise and full of the Holy Spirit; of that Holy Spirit who reveals to the world, before ignorant of such high and holy wisdom, that God is the efficient cause of marriage and that the final cause of marriage is that the wife might be unto her husband a civil, moral and domestic habitation and cohabitation. This knowledge comes not from the five senses and reason merely. It is a revelation of the Holy Spirit.

That word "now" in this sentence most beautifully expresses the glad surprise and exulting joy of a noble spirit which had been seeking this delightful companion of life; a companionship full, not only of love, but of holiness. As if Adam had said, This woman is at length what and all I want. With her I desire to live, and with her to obey the will of God in the propagation of posterity.

Now, however, this true purity, innocence and holiness are lost. There still remains, indeed, a feeling of joy and affection in the intended husband toward his spouse; but it is impure and corrupt on account of sin. The affection of Adam, however, was most pure, most holy and grateful to God.

June 14th - 1 Peter 2:11, 12

I beseech you as strangers and pilgrims, abstain from fleshly lust, which war against the soul; ... that they (the Gentiles) may by your good works, which they shall behold, glorify God in the day of visitation.

Peter admonishes Christians to Christlike lives and works in view of the fact that they are called to great glory, having become through Christ a royal priesthood, a people of God and citizens of heaven. He would have them occupy this temporal world as guests, striving after another and eternal kingdom; that is, to abstain from all carnal lusts and maintain a blameless walk, a life of good works. The apostle assigns two reasons for such self-denial: first, that we may not, through carnal, lustful habits, lose the spiritual and eternal; second, that God's name and the glory we have in Christ may not be slandered among our heathen adversaries, but rather, because of our good works, be honored.

When Peter admonishes to "abstain from fleshly lusts, which war against the soul," he implies that if we do not resist carnal inclinations, we shall lose our priceless eternal inheritance. To be a stranger on earth, striving after another and better life, is inconsistent with living in fleshly lusts as if one's sole intent were to remain in the world forever. If you would have the things of one life, Peter says, you must forsake the things of the other. If you forget your fatherland and lie drunken in this carnal life, as does the heathen world in living in unbelief and without hope of eternal life, you will never reach yonder existence. It is necessary to strive if we are to withstand the lusts of the flesh; for these war against the soul—against faith and the good conscience of man. If lust triumphs, our hold on the Spirit and on faith is lost. If you would not be defeated, you must valiantly contend against carnal inclinations and maintain your spiritual, eternal good. Our own welfare demands the conquest.

But God's honor also calls for it. God's honor is affected by our manner of life here on earth. We are to avoid giving occasion for our enemies to open their mouths and malign God's name and his Word. Rather must we magnify the name of God by our confession and general conduct, and thus win others, who shall with us confess and honor him. "Let your light so shine before men, that they may see your good works, and glorify your Father which is in heaven."

June 15th - Psalm 4:2

How long will you love vanity, and seek after leasing?

To have vanity is not the greatest of evils, for every man is vain, and there is nothing new under the sun, and though it be an evil, it is bearable. For there is not one saint that does not hope, trust, desire, fear, love and hate, more or less, in a way and manner that he ought not. But this body of sin and death, these laws of sin, these vanities, he ought to hate, not to love, nor take pleasure in them. To use the comfort and help of a creature is not sin, nor wrong; but to love them and rest in them alone, and from a love of them, not to trust in God, is an ungodly sin.

Hence, nothing more pestilential and destructive can be taught a Christian than moral philosophy and the decrees of men, if they be so set before him as to make him believe that he can walk in and by them so as to please God. For by such instruction it will come to pass that, relying on this wisdom, he will judge, condemn, and persecute whatever he sees is against him, and will thereby reject the cross of Christ and utterly despise the way of God, which is in its best and most prosperous state when we are following, as through a desert and wilderness, Christ in a pillar of fire.

But all these things are better understood by experience in time of suffering and adversity than they can possibly be described in words, or imagined by the heart. If the affections and thoughts of men are without faith in God, they are without the Word of God; if they are without the Word of God, they are without truth. Thus all things which are without faith are vanities and lies; for faith is truth by the Word of truth in which it believes and to which it cleaves by believing. The true meaning of this verse then is, that all are ungodly idolaters and polluters of the glory of God who under any tribulation draw back from faith, hope and love, to a confidence and comfort in created things.

June 16th - Romans 8:19

For the earnest expectation of the creature waits for the manifestation of the sons of God.

Just as we Christians endure many kinds of injustice and consequently sigh for and implore help and deliverance in the Lord's prayer, so do the creatures sigh. Although they have not human utterance, yet they have speech intelligible to God and the Holy Spirit, who mark the creatures' sighs over their unjust abuse by the ungodly.

Nowhere else in the Holy Scriptures do we find anything like Paul's declaration here concerning the earnest expectation and waiting of the creatures for the revelation or manifestation of the children of God; which waiting the apostle characterizes as a sighing in eager desire for man's redemption. The sun, the moon, the stars, the heavens and earth, the bread we eat, the water or wine we drink, the cattle and sheep, in short, all things that minister to our comfort, cry out in accusation against the world, because they are subject to vanity and must suffer with Christ and his brethren. The accusing cry is beyond human power to express, for God's created things are innumerable. Rightly was it said from the pulpit in former times that on the last day all creatures will utter an accusing cry against the ungodly who have shown them abuse here on earth, and will call them tyrants to whom they were unjustly subjected.

Paul presents this example of the creatures for the comfort of Christians. You are not alone in your tribulation and your complaint of injustice; the whole creation suffers with you and cries out against its subjection to the wicked world. This is the explanation of Paul's wonderful declaration concerning the "earnest expectation of the creature." The creature continually regards the end of service, and freedom from slavery to the ungodly. This will not take place before the revealing of the sons of God. Therefore the whole creation cries: "Oh, for a speedy end of this calamity, and the dawning of glory for the children of God!"

June 17th - 1 Peter 3:9

You are there unto called, that you should inherit a blessing.

Wonderful and glorious fact, that God has decreed and appropriated to you this blessing whereby all the riches of his grace and everything good are yours! And that he will abundantly give you his Spirit to remain with you, blessing body and soul, if only you hold fast his grace and do not allow yourselves to be deprived of it. What price would you not gladly pay for this blessing, were it purchasable, instead of being freely given, without any merit, and were you privileged to buy the assurance of heart which would say, "I know I am a child of God, who has received me into his grace, and I live in the sure hope that I will be eternally blessed and saved." Think, what a vast difference God makes between you and others because you are a Christian. He has appointed you to be an heir of everlasting grace and blessing and of eternal life. But they who are not Christians—what have they but a terrible sentence like a weight about their necks? The sentence pronouncing them children of the curse and of eternal condemnation.

If men would take this to heart, it would be easy by teaching and persuasion to win them to friendship and kindness toward their fellow men; to induce them not to return evil or reviling from a motive of revenge, but when their own privileges and protection and the punishment of evil cannot be obtained, quietly and peaceably to suffer injury rather than lose their eternal comfort and joy. Christians have excellent reason and a powerful motive for being patient and not revengeful or bitter in the fact that they are so richly blessed of God and given that great glory whereof they cannot be deprived, nor suffer its loss, if only they abide in it. Only see that you keep a quiet conscience and a loving heart, not allowing yourself, on account of the devil and wicked men, to be disturbed and deprived of your good conscience, your peaceful heart and your God-given blessing.

June 18th - Genesis 2:23

She shall be called Woman, because she was taken out of Man.

This name which Adam gives to the woman contains in it a wonderful and sweet description of marriage, in which, as the lawyers express it, "The woman shines in the rays of her husband." For whatever the husband possesses, is possessed and held by the wife also. Not only is all their wealth possessed by them in common, but their children also, their food, their bed and their habitation. Their wishes are also equal. So that the husband differs from the wife in no other thing than in Exodus In every other respect, the woman is really a man. In a word the woman, as Paul remarks in his instructions to Timothy, is man-formed and man-made by her very origin; for Paul says to Timothy, Adam was first formed, then Eve from the man, and not the man from the woman.

Of this communion of all things in marriage we still possess some feeble remnants, though miserable indeed they be when compared with what they were in their original state. For even now the wife, if she be but an honorable, modest, and godly woman, participates in all the cares, wishes, desires, purposes, duties, and actions of her husband. And it was for this end indeed that she was created in the beginning, and for this end was called "woman," that she might differ in sex only from the father of the family, since she was taken from man.

Although this name can apply in its strictest and fullest sense only to Eve, who, alone of all women, was created thus out of man, yet our Lord applies the whole sentence of Adam to all wives when he says that man and wife are one flesh. Although, therefore, the wife be not made of your flesh and your bones, yet, because she is your wife, she is as much the mistress of the house, as you are the master thereof, except that by the law of God, which was brought in after the fall, the woman is made subject to the man. That is the woman's punishment, as are many other troubles also which come short of the glories of paradise. Had the innocency continued, the government of the man and the woman would have been equal and the same. Now the sweat of the brow rests upon the man; and the wife is commanded to be subject to her husband.

June 19th - Genesis 2:24

Therefore shall a man leave his father and his mother, and shall cleave unto his wife.

This sentence of Adam is prophetic. For as yet there was no father or mother; nor consequently were there any children. Through the Holy Spirit Adam prophecies of that married life, which should be in the world, and predictively describes the separate dwelling of man and wife, and the separate domestic authorities and governments of the several families in all ages; that each family should have its own habitation, authority, and rule. Even heathen nations have discovered that there is nothing more appropriate for man, nor beneficial for kingdoms, than this oneness of the life of married persons.

Christ applies these words of Adam as a common rule or law for our marriages since the loss of original innocence. If Adam had remained in his original innocency, the children born to him would have married and, leaving the table and dwelling-place of their parents, would have had their own trees under which they would have lived separate from their parents. They would have come from time to time to their father Adam, sung a hymn, spoken gloriously of God, called upon him, and then returned to their own homes.

Though all other things are now changed, yet this close bond between married persons still remains firm; so that a man would leave his father and mother much sooner than he would leave his wife. Where we find the contrary, for married persons are found to leave and forsake each other, all this is not only contrary to the present divine command by the mouth of Adam, but such things are awful signs of that horrible corruption, which has come upon man through sin.

This "leaving father and mother," however, is not to be understood as a command that the children of Adam, when married, should have nothing more to do with their parents. It only enjoins the children when married to have their own home. We often find that children are compelled to support their parents, when worn down with age. Had paradise and all its innocency continued, the state of life would have been inconceivably more exalted and blessed than our present fallen and sinful condition. Yet even then this same command would have been obeyed. The husband, through love of his wife, would have chosen his homestead with her, and would have left his father and mother for that purpose.

June 20th - John 14:15

If you love me, keep my commandments.

Keep his Word or commandment—that is what the soul must do who loves Christ, who understands and appreciates what he gets from Christ. No one is a Christian unless he keeps Christ's Word; and no one can keep it unless he first loves God. Where this love is not, all amounts to nothing, do as we will. If one were to take all the swords in the world in his hands, he would not bring a single heretic to the faith. The people may appear to accept the Word, but in their hearts there is no faith. Hence, he who wishes to be a true bishop arranges all his administrations to the end that he may win souls and develop a delight in God's Word and a love for it.

How does one acquire love? The human heart is so false that it cannot love unless it first sees the benefit of loving. No man can bring this love into the heart. Therefore God gave us his Son, graciously poured out his greatest treasures and sunk and drowned all our sins and filth in the great ocean of his love, so that this great love and blessing must draw man to love and be ready to fulfil the divine commandments with a willing heart. In no other way can the heart love or have any love; it must be assured that it was first loved. Now man cannot do this; therefore Christ comes and takes the heart captive and says: Learn to know me. I am Christ, who placed myself in your misery to drown your sins in my righteousness. This knowledge softens your heart, so that you must turn to him.

This loyalty to Christ's kingdom is now considered a simple thing by the presumptuous and inexperienced spirits who deem themselves so holy and so strong in the faith as to be able easily to do what they hear, and who think that the Word of God is something that is obeyed as soon as it is heard. But experience teaches how difficult it is to keep this Word, for the holy cross has been laid upon it. The Church upon earth must strive and contend with weakness, poverty, misery, fear, death, shame and disgrace, and our flesh and old nature prefer that which is easy and agreeable. But the Christian will love Christ, his Word and his kingdom more than all things of the earth.

June 21st - John 14:27

Peace I leave with you, my peace I give unto you: not as the world giveth, give I unto you.

This is bidding them a friendly good-night. Christ was willing and able to speak with his disciples in the most loving manner. I must away, he says, and cannot speak much more with you; let it be well with you. That is my last farewell.you shall suffer no hurt, nor want because of my departure. I will richly repay you, for you shall have from me the best that you can wish, namely, that in my Father you have a merciful God, whose thoughts toward you are those of a father's heart and love. In me you shall have a good, faithful Saviour, who will not forsake you in any need and will defend you against the devil, the world, and all wickedness, and will in addition send you the Holy Spirit, who shall so rule your hearts that you find in me true comfort, peace, and joy.

My peace is not given as the world gives peace. The world bases its peace only on transient things, as possessions, power, honor, friendship of men. When these are gone, then peace, confidence, and courage are gone. Though it were in the power of the world to give and preserve all these, yet it has not, nor can it have, true eternal peace, so that a heart enjoys God's favor and is certain of his grace and of everlasting life. But since this is not the world's peace, the holy cross is laid upon it; measured by reason and by our feelings, it means no peace, but dissensions, anguish, fear, and trembling. Christ says, "In the world you shall have tribulation: but be of good cheer; I have overcome the world;" this is to be your peace.

Thus Christ has assured and satisfied his Church with peace that abides in the midst of tribulation and temptation. Therefore, when the heart is oppressed, in anguish and terrified, as if a fugitive before God, this peace must be fixed by faith in the Word of Christ, that it may say: I know that I have God's pledge and the witness of the Holy Spirit that he wants to be my Father and is not angry with me, but assures me of peace and all good through Christ, his Son.

June 22nd - Romans 8:22

For we know that the whole creation groans and travaileth in pain together until now.

Paul uses forcible language here. Creation is aware, he says, not only of its future deliverance from the bondage of corruption, but of its future grandeur. It hopes for the speedy coming of its glory, and waits with the eagerness of a maiden for the dance. Seeing the splendor reserved for itself, it groans and travails unceasingly. Similarly, we Christians groan and intensely desire to have done at once with the Turks, the Pope and the tyrannical world. Who would not weary of witnessing the present knavery, ungodliness and blasphemy against Christ and his gospel, even as Lot wearied of the ungodliness he beheld in Sodom? Thus Paul says that creation groans and travaileth while waiting for the revelation and the glorious liberty of the children of God.

He declares creation to be weary of present conditions of servitude, and as eager for liberation as a mother for deliverance in the hour of anguish. Truly it is with spiritual sight, with apostolic vision, that Paul discerns this fact in regard to creation. He turns away from this world, oblivious to the joys and sufferings of earthly life, and boasts alone of the future, eternal life, unseen and inexperienced. Thus he administers real and effectual comfort to Christians, pointing them to a future life for themselves and all created things after this sinful life shall have an end.

Therefore, believers in Christ are to be confident of eternal glory, and with sighs and groans to implore the Lord God to hasten the blessed day of the realization of their hopes. For so Christ has taught us to pray in the Lord's Prayer, "Thy kingdom come." Our faith is not to be exercised for the attainment of earthly riches; we are not baptized unto the present life, nor do we receive the gospel as ministering to our temporal good; these things are to point us to yonder eternal life. God grant the speedy coming of the glad day of our redemption, when we shall realize all these blessings, of which we now hear and in which we believe through the Word.

June 23rd - John 3:16

God so loved the world, that he gave his only begotten Son, that whosoever believeth in him should not perish, but have everlasting life.

With these words Jesus leads us directly into the Father's heart, that we may see and know that it was the great and wonderful counsel of God, resolved from eternity, that we should receive help through his Son. All had to be fulfilled, that God's truth might stand, even as he had promised in the Scriptures. It is thus apparent that God does not intend to cast us out, and to condemn us on account of our sins, but that he wills that we should attain to eternal grace and life for the sake of the Saviour and Mediator, if we fear his wrath on account of our sins, and keep in mind this eternal divine life.

The Holy Spirit teaches everywhere that we do not possess the Father except through a mediator, and he will not allow us to approach the Father without one. Let us thank the Father for ordering it as he has and placing between us one who is God and equal with God, and also man, on a level with man; for we are human and he is God. Where God and man oppose each other, man meets with instant destruction, for he cannot stand against God. God has intervened by placing as mediator one who is alike true God and true man. Through him we are to come to the Father; with the price we can pay nothing is accomplished.

If there were another way to heaven, Jesus would doubtless have made it known to us. Therefore let us cling to the words, firmly pilot our hearts along this way and keep within it. If I had the merits of all the saints, the sanctity and purity of all virgins, and the piety of St. Peter besides, still I would not give a fig for all I call my own. I must have another foundation on which to build, namely, the words: God has given his Son, that whosoever believeth in him, whom the Father sent out of love, shall be saved. Let us fearlessly plant ourselves on these words, which neither Satan, hell, nor death can overthrow. Come what will, let us say: Here is God's Word; that is my rock and anchor; to that I cling and that abides; and where that abides, there I abide also. God cannot lie.

June 24th - John 1:8

He was not that Light, but was sent to bear witness of that Light.

O', what necessary repetition! First of all to show that this Light is not simply a man, but God himself; for the evangelist greatly desires to preach the divinity of Christ in all his words. If John, the great saint, be not that Light, but only a witness of it, then this Light must be something far different from everything that is holy, whether it be man or angel. If holiness could make such a light, it would have made one of John. In the second place, such a repetition is necessary to resist wicked preachers, who do not bear witness of Christ, the Light, but of themselves. All who preach the doctrines of men make man the light, lead men away from God to themselves, and set themselves up as the true Light, as the pope and his followers have done. He is, therefore, the Antichrist, that is, he is against Christ, the true Light.

This gospel text desires only to testify of Christ and lead men to him, who is the true Light, which lights every man coming into the world. Therefore these words, "He was not the Light," are truly worthy to be capitalized and to be well remembered against the men who set themselves up as the light and give to men doctrines and laws of their own fabrication. They pretend to enlighten men, but lead them with themselves into the depths of hell; for they do not teach faith and are not willing to teach it. Who does not preach the gospel to you, him reject and refuse to hear. But he preaches the gospel who teaches you to believe and trust in Christ, the eternal Light. Therefore beware of everything told you which does not agree with the gospel, as for example eating and drinking, which are necessary for your body, but by no means to your salvation. For this purpose nothing is necessary or of use to you except this Light.

O', these abominable doctrines of men, which are now so prevalent and which have almost banished this Light! They all wish to be this Light themselves, but not to be witnesses of it. They advocate their own fancies, but are silent about this Light, or teach it in a way so as to preach themselves along with it. This is worse than to be entirely silent.

June 25th - 1 John 3:11, 12

This is the message that you heard from the beginning, that we should love one another. Not as Cain, who was of that wicked one, and slew his brother. And wherefore slew he him? Because his own works were evil, and his brother's righteous.

What offense had godly Abel committed against his brother to be so hated? He had regarded that brother as the first-born, had done him all honor and loved him as became a brother. He was easily satisfied, desiring simply the grace of God. He prayed for the future seed, for the salvation and happiness of his parents, his brother and the entire human race. How could Cain be so unmerciful and inhuman to murder his own flesh and blood?

The answer is found in the fact that the devil had filled Cain's heart with pride and vanity over his birthright. He considered himself a man of distinction, whilst his brother was nothing. His heart is devoid of true brotherly love. He cannot endure God's manifest favor toward his brother, and will not be moved by the injunction to humble himself and seek God's grace. Anger and envy possess him so that he cannot tolerate his brother alive. He becomes a murderer, and then goes his way as if he had done right. This is what John means when he says that Cain had no other cause for his crime than that his works were evil and his brother's righteous.

Similarly that obedient daughter of Saint Cain, the world, hates the Christians; and for no other reason than the latter's love and goodness of heart. In this man Cain is pictured the world in its true characteristic colors; in him its true spirit stands reflected. On the other hand that poor, abject Abel well represents the obscure little brotherhood, the Church of Christ. She must yield to Cain, the lord, the distinction of being everything before God. He feels important in his imagined dignity and thinks that God cannot but favor and accept his offering rather than that of his brother.

Meanwhile pious Abel goes his way, meekly suffering his brother's contempt. He yields him the honor and beholds no consolation for himself aside from the pure mercy and goodness of God. He believes in God and in such faith he performs his sacrifice as a confession of his gratitude.

June 26th - Genesis 9:6

Whoever sheds man's blood, by man shall his blood be shed, for in the image of God made he man.

When God saw that the world was growing worse and worse, he finally enforced punishment against the wicked world by the flood. Here, however, God bestows a share of his authority upon man, giving him the power of life and death, that thus he may be the avenger of bloodshed. Whosoever takes life without due warrant, him God subjects not only to his own judgment, but also to the sword of man. But men have no authority to slay except where guilt is apparent and crime is proven. Hence courts have been established and a definite method of proceeding instituted for the purpose of investigating and proving the crime before the sentence of death is passed.

The importance of this text and its claim to attention consists in the fact that it records the establishment of civil authority by God with the sword as the sign of power, in order that licence may be curbed and anger and other sins prevented from growing beyond all bounds. God foresaw that wickedness would ever flourish, and established this external remedy to prevent the infinite spread of license. By this safeguard God protects life and property. We find here no less a proof of God's great love toward man than his promise that the flood shall never rage again.

Man is a noble creature, who, unlike other living beings, has been fashioned according to the image of God. While it is true that he has lost this image through sin, it is capable of being restored through the Word and the Holy Spirit. This image God desires us to revere in each other; he forbids us to shed blood by the exercise of sheer force. But the life of him who refuses to respect this image of God in man, and gives way to anger and provocation, is surrendered to civil authority by God, in that God commands that also his blood shall be shed.

Thus the passage under consideration teaches the establishment of civil authority in the world, which did not exist before the flood, by which they who have the sword are commanded to use it against those who have shed blood. Therefore it is for us to render obedience to the divine order and to endure it, so that we are not disobedient to the will of God at the very point where we derive benefit in so many ways.

June 27th - 1 Peter 5:6

Humble yourselves therefore under the mighty hand of God, that he may exalt you in due time.

The heart, through knowledge of its sin, becomes terrified in the presence of God's anger and anxiously seeks grace. Thus a humility is born, not merely external and before men, but of the heart and of God, from fear of God and knowledge of one's own unworthiness and weakness. He who fears God and trembles at his word will surely not boast against anyone. He will even manifest a gentle spirit toward his enemies. Therefore he finds favor with God and men.

The cause of this shall be "the mighty hand of God." God's hand is powerful and mighty in a twofold manner. It dashes down and overthrows the proud and self-secure, however hard and iron-like their heads and hearts may be. They must languish in dust and ashes; must lie despondent and desperate in the anguish and torments of hell, if he touch them but a little with the terrors of his anger. These are experiences through which the saints also pass, and concerning whose severity they lament.

In the second place God's hand is mighty to raise, to comfort and strengthen the humble and fearful, and to exalt them. Those who have been cast down in terror should not despair, or flee before God, but rise again and be comforted in God. God wishes to have it preached and published that he never lays his hand upon us in order that we may perish and be damned. But he must pursue this course to lead us to repentance, else we would never inquire about his Word and will. If we seek his grace, he is ready to help us up again, to grant us forgiveness of sins, the Holy Spirit and eternal life.

So God will also "exalt you in due time." Though his help be delayed, and the humble and suffering seem to lie oppressed all too long under his hand and to languish, let them hold to the promise Paul has given: God "will not suffer you to be tempted above that you are able," but will hear your cry, and will help at the proper time; and thus let us be comforted. God has already stretched forth his mighty hand, both to cast down the godless and to exalt the humble.

June 28th - John 3:17

God sent not his Son into the world to condemn the world; but that the world through him might be saved.

With these words one can apprehend God as he is to be apprehended. You do not seek him; he rather seeks you and pictures his Son before you as a Saviour and not as a judge. It is a common practice to represent the gracious Saviour as a judge, and from this practice has sprung a dependence upon the merits of saints, causing us to turn away from Christ and take refuge in the saints. We fancy that the saints are more gracious and more kindly disposed to us than even God himself. Therefore, one says, St. Peter is my apostle; another says, St. Paul is my patron; and so on. But God cannot permit this; the glory must belong to him. My conscience must rest upon the foundation, the eternal, all-knowing truth. God alone is the truth, and the conscience must rest upon him and nothing else.

If I picture Christ as a judge, I shall fear him. The result will be that soon I am constrained before him, grow afraid of him and then hate him, and my heart becomes corrupt and blasphemous. But when I know him as the gospel pictures him, and long for him as the best friend that my heart can choose, then love soon follows. No friend can do as much for us as he has done. I forget father and mother, I have a strong confidence in him. But if one simply fears him, one falls back on his good works and does not recognize Christ as Mediator, thinking to run into the presence of God without him. In this way he works his own ruin.

Learn then from this lesson to know Christ aright and to hold him between yourself and the Father; let him be the sacrifice alone, which shall secure heaven and salvation. When this passage comes to mind in the hour of death, when the test comes, what comfort to meditate on its message— how the Lord came not to condemn the world, but to save it. He who believes cannot be lost, but will be saved, since it is true that naught accomplishes our salvation except Christ alone, who came to be our Saviour. Thus it follows that where faith is, there sin does no harm; for faith makes us Christ's.

June 29th - John 10:3, 4

He calls his own sheep by name, and leads them out. And when he puts forth his own sheep, he goeth before them, and the sheep follow him.

This leading them out is Christian liberty. They are now free; no longer penned up and captive under anxious constraint and fear of the law and of divine judgment, but happily pastured and nourished in Christ's sweet kingdom of grace. This liberty does not mean that the sheep, now without a fold and without a keeper, may run from their shepherd unrestrained into error; or that Christians can do whatever the flesh lusts for. It means that now free from the terror of wolves, thieves, and murderers, they may live with their dear shepherd, in love and pleasure following where he leads and guides them; because they know that he defends and lovingly oversees them so that the law dare no longer accuse and condemn them, even though they are weak as to the flesh and have not perfectly fulfilled the law. For the Lord, God's Son, is the shepherd, who takes the sheep under his grace, his shelter and protection; he who will accuse or condemn the sheep must first accuse or condemn the Lord himself.

This is the Christian's life under their shepherd. Christ ever rules, leads and guides them. They remain with him in the liberty of faith, wherein they walk, following his example in obedience and good works. Christ's kingdom was not instituted that we might indulge the lusts of our flesh; but that we, released from the captivity of the law, under which we could not in sincerity do anything good, follow Christ cheerfully and with a good conscience in our lives and works. Each responds as Christ calls him, a special instrument for Christ's use.

To follow Christ means that our whole life and all our works be in the faith of Christ—a constant exercise of faith, wherein we are recognized and are assured that because of this dear shepherd we have favor with God. Thus our works and lives, weak and imperfect in obedience as they are, are also under the wings of the mother hen, and are pleasing to God because of the shepherd. In this confidence we now begin to be obedient, to call upon him in our temptations and needs, confess his Word, and serve our neighbors. To this end a Christian constantly needs the Word of Christ; he needs to learn from it and to exercise himself in it.

June 30th - Romans 8:20

For the creature was made subject to vanity, not willingly, but by reason of him who has subjected the same in hope.

Paul tells us the whole creation groans and travails with us, ungodly; "subject to vanity," he phrases it. The blessed sun, most glorious of created things, serves the small minority of the godly. Where it shines on one godly man it must shine on thousands of knaves, enemies of God, blasphemers, persecutors, murderers, robbers, thieves, adulterers, with whom the world is filled. To these it must minister in all their ungodliness and wickedness, permitting its pure and glorious rays to benefit the most unworthy, most shameful and abandoned profligates. This subjection is truly painful, and were the sun a rational creature, obeying its own volition rather than the decree of the Lord who has subjected it to vanity against its will, it might deny everyone of these wicked wretches even the least ray of light; that it is compelled to minister to them is its cross and pain, by reason of which it sighs and groans.

Paul tells us the whole creation groans and travails with us, as if desiring relief from anguish. The heavenly planets would gladly be free from serving; the earth would readily become unfruitful; all waters would voluntarily sink from sight and deny the wicked world a draught; the sheep would prefer to produce thorns for the ungodly instead of wool; the cow would rather yield them poison than milk. But they must perform their appointed work, Paul says, because of him who has subjected them in hope. God will finally answer the cry of creation; he has already determined that after the six thousand years of its existence now past, the world shall have its evening and end.

Since man has fallen in sin, we all—the whole creation—must suffer the consequence and be subject to vanity. All created things must be under the power of a condemned world, and compelled to serve with all their energies until

God shall overthrow the entire world and for the elects' sake purify again and renew the creature.

July 1st - Luke 10:23, 24

Blessed are the eyes which see the things that you see: for I tell you, that many prophets and kings have desired to see those things which you see, and have not seen them; and to hear those things which you hear and have not heard them.

This hearing and seeing must be understood as simply external, namely, that they saw Christ, heard his preaching, and witnessed the miracles which he performed. Certainly the Jews also witnessed these things with their natural eyes, and some of them indeed experienced them in part at least in their hearts; but in fact they did not recognize him as the Christ, like the apostles and like Peter, who, representing all the others, said, "You are Christ, the Son of the living God." Some of the Jews, indeed, like the apostles, recognized him as the Christ, but they were few.

In spirit, however, many prophets and kings saw Christ, as he himself says to the Jews concerning Abraham, "Your father Abraham rejoiced to see my day, and he saw it, and was glad." The Jews thought he spoke of natural seeing, but he spoke of spiritual sight, as all pious hearts saw him before he was born, and still see him. If Abraham saw him, doubtless many prophets in whom the Holy Ghost dwells saw him; and though this seeing made the holy fathers and prophets blessed, still they had a heartfelt desire to behold Christ the Lord in the flesh, as is intimated time and again in the prophets.

Therefore the Lord here says to his disciples, who saw both with their natural and spiritual eyes, "Blessed are the eyes which see the things that you see," as though we would say, This is a blessed time, an acceptable year, a special season of grace. That which is now at hand is so precious that the eyes which see it are truly called blessed. In the past ages the gospel was never preached so publicly and clearly unto all men as at present. The Holy Spirit was not yet publicly poured out, but Christ had begun the work of the Holy Spirit, and afterwards the apostles continued it in great earnestness. Therefore he calls all those blessed who hear and see this grace in Christ.

July 2nd - Romans 5:20

Where sin abounded, grace did much more abound.

When we preach that grace is bestowed upon us and the forgiveness of sins without any merit on our part, people are disposed to regard themselves as free from obligation and will do no works except those to which their own desires prompt them. This was Paul's experience when he so strongly commended the grace of Christ and its consolation. The rude crowd cried: Oh, is it true that great grace follows upon great sin? In that case we will cheerfully load ourselves with sin so that we may receive the greater grace.

Such argument Paul refutes. He says: It is not the intention of the gospel to teach sin or to allow it, but the very opposite—how we may escape from sin and from the awful wrath of God which it incurs. Paul does not teach that grace is acquired through sin, nor that sin brings grace, but on the contrary he says: "The wrath of God is revealed from heaven against all ungodliness and unrighteousness of men." Escape is not achieved by any doings of our own, but by the fact that God, out of pure grace, forgives us our sins for his Son's sake; for in us God finds nothing but sin and condemnation.

But because the sins of men which are taken away are so grievous and numerous, the grace which drowns and destroys them must be mighty and abundant also. Where there is great thirst, a great draft is needed to quench it. Where there is a mighty conflagration, powerful streams of water are necessary to extinguish it. In cases of severe illness, strong medicine is essential to a cure. But these facts do not give us authority to say: Let us cheerfully drink to satiety that we may become more thirsty for good wine; or, let us injure ourselves and make ourselves ill that medicine may do us more good. Still less does it follow that we may heap up and multiply sins for the purpose of receiving more abundant grace. Grace does not give license to sin, but where there are many and great sins, there also reigns great, abundant and rich grace.

July 3rd - Romans 6:3, 4

Know you not, that so many of us as were baptized into Jesus Christ were baptized into his death? Therefore we are buried with him by baptism into death.

The apostle speaks in his own Pauline style concerning the power of baptism, which derives its efficacy from the death of Christ. By his death he has paid for and taken away our sins; his death has been an actual strangling and putting to death of sin; it no longer has dominion over him. Through his death we have obtained forgiveness of sins; that sin may not condemn us, we die unto sin through that power which Christ—because we are baptized into him—imparts to and works in us.

He further declares that we are not only baptized into his death, but, by the same baptism, we are buried with him into death; for in his death he took our sins with him into the grave, burying them completely and leaving them there. To those who through baptism are in Christ, sin is completely destroyed and buried, and shall remain so; but we, through his resurrection—which, by faith, gives us the victory over sin and death and bestows upon us everlasting righteousness and life—should henceforth walk in newness of life.

Having these things through baptism, we dare no longer obey—live unto—the sin which still dwells in our flesh and blood in this life; we must daily strangle it so that it may have no power, nor life in us if we desire to be found in the estate and life of Christ. The fact that Christ himself had to die for sin is evidence of the severe wrath of God against sin. Sin had to be put to death and laid away in the grave in the body of Christ. Thereby God shows us that he will not countenance sin in us, but has given us Christ and baptism for the purpose of putting to death and burying sin in our bodies.

Thus Christ was buried that he might, through forgiveness, cover up and destroy our sin, whether actually committed or inherent in us. He was buried that he might, through the Holy Spirit, mortify this flesh and blood with its inherent sinful lusts; they must no longer have dominion over us, but must be subject to the Spirit until we are utterly free from them.

July 4th

Matthew 22:21

Render therefore unto Caesar the things which are Caesar's, and unto God the things that are God's.

We must keep this truth before our eyes; it is our rule of conduct toward the two kingdoms, God's and Caesar's, so as to give to each the honor due him. In both there are many who abuse the charge and position committed to them, especially toward Christians. We must suffer this, but at the same time we maintain our right to punish them by word of mouth, telling them the truth and hurling back the accusations heaped upon us. In so doing we satisfy justice and fulfil our duty; the rest we commit to God.

The teaching of Christ is the doctrine we insist on, that the two powers, God's and Caesar's, or spiritual and temporal kingdoms, must be kept apart, as Christ does here in clear and brief declaration, making not only a distinction, but also finely illustrating how each is to be considered and administered. It is ordained of God that subjects shall give to their rulers what they need; when he commands them to give, it is implied that these may take; and where we are to give what is due, there we infer that we owe them something, so that the language might be "return" rather than simply "render" or "give." This is something for subjects under civil authority.

On the other hand, there are restrictions placed upon rulers that they govern in the same spirit, and not take from their subjects what is not due them; that they remember to give and do also what they are in duty bound to do by virtue of their presiding over countries and nations, so that they may grow and prosper. That is why rulers are elevated by God to their respective positions of honor, not that they hold their positions as extortioners, doing what they like.

If this were emphasized it would be found that the world is full of real thieves and rogues, rulers as well as subjects, and the number would indeed be small, from the highest to the lowest, who obey and do what is right. Subjects are most generally disposed to cheat their ruler and appropriate to their own use what is his, to say nothing of giving cheerfully. Princes and officeholders wish to have the name of being Christians, yet they do only what suits them and would gladly usurp the places of their superiors.

July 5th - Ephesians 5:18

Be not drunk with wine, wherein is excess; but be filled with the Spirit.

God having in his infinite goodness so richly shed upon us in these latter times the gospel of light, we ought in honor and gratitude to him try to reform ourselves in the matter of intemperance. We should fear lest through this evil, besides committing other sins, we draw upon us the wrath and punishment of God. For naught else can result from the pernicious life of intemperance but false security and contempt of God. Individuals continually dead in drunkenness, buried in excesses, living like swine, cannot fear God, cannot be occupied with divine things. Such are the excesses now to be seen in the courts of princes—banqueting and drinking—that one would think they meant to devour the resources of the country in a single hour. Lords, princes, and noblemen—the entire country—are ruined, reduced to beggary, for the reason that God's gifts are so inhumanly wasted and destroyed.

The evil of drunkenness has, alas, gained such ascendancy as to be past restraint unless the Word of God may exert some controlling influence among the few, the individuals who are still human and who would be Christians. It is my opinion that if God does not sometime check the vice by a special judgment, even women and children will become inebriate, and when the last day arrives no Christian will be found, but all souls will descend drunken into the abyss of hell. Let all who desire to be Christians know that it is incumbent upon them to manifest the virtue of temperance; that drunken slobs have no place among Christians, and cannot be saved until they amend their ways, until they reform from their evil habits.

Just as idolatry and adultery are sins excluding from heaven, so drunkenness is a sin which bars from the blessings of baptism, from remission of sins, faith in Christ, and personal salvation. Hence, if you would be a Christian and be saved, you must lead a sober and temperate life.

O' God, how shameless and ungrateful we are, we so highly blessed of God in having his Word and in being liberated from the tyranny of the pope, who desired our sweat and blood—how ungrateful in the face of these things not to amend our lives in some measure in honor of the gospel, and in praise and gratitude to God.

July 6th - Genesis 4:8

And Cain talked with Abel his brother: and it came to pass, when they were in the field, that Cain rose up against Abel his brother, and slew him.

Cain is the image and picture of all hypocrites and murderers, who kill under the show of godliness. Cain, possessed by Satan, hides his wrath, waiting the opportunity to slay his brother Abel; meanwhile he converses with him, as a brother beloved, that he might the sooner lay his hands on him unawares. Let us learn to know a Cain and to beware when he speaks kindly as a brother to brother. It is in this way that our adversaries talk with us in our day, while they pretend a desire for concord, and seek to bring about doctrinal harmony.

Our ministry at the present day deserves no blame. We teach, we exhort, we entreat, we rebuke, we turn ourselves every way, that we may recall the multitude from their self-security to the fear of God. But the world, like an untamed beast, goes on and follows not the Word, but its own lusts, which it tries to smooth over with a show of uprightness. The prophets and apostles are before us as examples, and our own experience is also instructive.

Learn then what a hypocrite is, namely, one who lays claim to the worship of God and to charity, and at the same time destroys the worship of God and kills his brother. All this semblance of good will is only intended to bring about better opportunities of doing harm. Light is cast here upon the bondage of Satan by which our nature, entangled in sins, is oppressed. Hence Paul speaks of the "children of wrath" and declares that such are taken captive by Satan. For nature, destitute of the Holy Spirit, is impelled by the same evil spirit which impelled wicked Cain. If, however, there were in any one those ample powers, or that free will, by which a man might defend himself against the assaults of Satan, these gifts would most assuredly have existed in Cain, to whom belonged the birthright and the promise of the blessed seed. All men are in that very same condition; unless our nature be helped by the Spirit of God, it cannot maintain itself.

July 7th - John 6:44

No man can come to me, except the Father which has sent me draw him: and I will raise him up at the last day.

He must surely perish whom the Father does not draw. Thus it is decreed, that whoever does not come to this Son must be condemned forever. The Son is given us only to the end that he may save us; besides him, nothing saves us either in heaven or on earth. If he does not help us, nothing will. If the Father does not come first and draw men, they must forever perish. The Father must lay the first stone of the foundation in us, else we will never do anything. This is accomplished in the following way:

God sends his preachers, whom he has taught to preach to us his will. First he instructs us that our entire lives and characters, however holy and beautiful they may be, are nothing before him; this is called a preaching of the law. Then he offers us grace; he tells us that he will not utterly condemn and reject us, but makes us heirs of his kingdom, lords over all that is in heaven and upon earth. This is called preaching grace, or the gospel. But God is the origin of all; God first sends the preachers and constrains them to preach. Where the pure and plain Word of God goes, it breaks to pieces everything that is exalted of man, it makes valleys of all their mountains, and all their hills it makes low. Every heart that hears this Word must lose faith in itself, else it will not be able to come to Christ. God's works do nothing but destroy and make alive, condemn and administer salvation.

Hence, a person who is thus smitten in his heart by God to confess that he is one who must be condemned on account of his sins, is like the righteous man whom with the words of this gospel God first wounds, and because of that wound fixes upon him the band of his divine grace, by which he draws him, so that he must seek help and counsel for his soul. Before he could not obtain any help or counsel from God, nor did he ever desire it; but now he finds the first comfort and promise of God. From such promise he will ever continue to gain courage as long as he lives and will ever win greater and greater confidence in God.

July 8th - Matthew 23:27

How often would I have gathered your children together, even as a hen gathers her chickens under her wings, and you would not!

The Lord has given us here a lovely picture and parable of what he does for the sake of faith and believers, so that I do not know of a more beautiful passage in all the Scriptures. The Lord here emphasizes his good will and favor to the

Jews and says he would gladly be their mother hen, had they wished to be his little chickens. O man! In this picture you will see how you are to conduct yourself towards Christ, and to what end he is to benefit you, how you should make use of him and enjoy him.

It is certain that our souls are the chickens, and Satan and wicked spirits are the buzzards in the air, with only this exception that we are not as wise as the chickens which flee to the hen; while the spirits of Satan are more subtle to rob us of our souls than the buzzards are to steal the chickens. Faith, if it is true faith, is of such a nature that it does not rely upon itself, but holds to Christ, and takes refuge under his righteousness; he lets this righteousness be its shield and protection, just like the little chicken never trusts in its own efforts, but takes refuge under the body and wings of the hen.

It is not sufficient for one who is to stand before the judgment of God to say, I believe and have grace; for all that is within him is not able to protect him; but he proffers to this judgment Christ's righteousness which he permits to plead for him at the judgment seat of God. Under this righteousness he creeps, crouches and stoops, he confides in it and believes without doubt that he will be sustained by that same faith, not for his sake, nor for the sake of such faith, but for the sake of Christ and his righteousness under which he takes refuge. A faith that does not do this is not true faith. Thus also the Psalmist says, "He that dwells in the secret place of the Most High shall abide under the shadow of the Almighty. He is my refuge and my fortress. He shall cover you with his feathers, and under his wings shall you trust."

July 9th - Romans 6:15

Shall we sin, because we are not under the law, but under grace? God forbid.

When we preach the forgiveness of sins by pure grace without any merit of man, the perversity of the world claims that we either forbid good works, or else try to draw the conclusion that man may continue to live in sin and follow his own pleasure; the fact is, that people may be induced to do good works by our teaching to the praise, honor and glory of God. Our teaching, rightly apprehended, does not lead to pride and vice, but to humility and obedience.

In matters of temporal government, whether domestic or civil, it is understood that he who asks for pardon confesses himself guilty, acknowledges his error and promises to reform and transgress no more. When the judge extends mercy and pardon to the thief deserving the gallows, the law is canceled by grace. But though the law is indeed canceled for him and grace delivers him from the rope and the sword, life is not granted him that he may continue to steal and murder; he is rather supposed to become honest and virtuous. If he does not, the law will again overtake him and punish him as he deserves.

Everyone can readily comprehend this principle in temporal things; no one is so stupid as to tolerate the idea of grace being granted to extend opportunity to do wrong. It is only the gospel doctrine concerning God's grace and the forgiveness of sin that must suffer the slanderous misrepresentation that makes it abolish good works or give occasion for sin. We are told that God, in his unfathomable grace, has canceled the sentence of eternal death and hellfire which, according to the law and divine judgment, we deserved, and has given us instead the freedom of life eternal; thus our life is purely of grace. Certainly we are not pardoned that we may live as before when, under condemnation and wrath, we incurred death. We are to conduct ourselves as men made alive and saved, that we fall not from grace and pass again under judgment and the sentence of eternal death.

July 10th - John 6:48, 50

I am that bread of life ... This is the bread which cometh down from heaven, that a man may eat thereof and not die.

In these words the soul finds a well prepared table, at which it satisfies all hunger; for it knows of a certainty that he who speaks cannot lie. Therefore the soul falls upon the Word, clings to it, trusts in it, and builds its dwelling place in the strength of this well-prepared table. The living bread of which the Lord here speaks, is Christ himself. If in our hearts we lay hold of only a morsel of this bread, we shall have forever enough and can never be separated from God. The partaking of this bread is nothing but faith in Christ our Lord. He who eats of this food lives forever.

Notice that the Lord approaches us so lovingly and graciously, and offers himself to us in such gentle words that it should in all reason move the heart to believe on him; to believe that this bread, his flesh and blood, born of the Virgin Mary, was given because he had to pay the penalty of death and suffer in our stead the torments of hell, and besides suffer the guilt of sins he never committed, as if they were his own. This he did willingly and received us as brethren and sisters. If we believe this we do the will of the heavenly Father, which is nothing else than that we believe on the Son.

Therefore a Christian life is a life of bliss and joy. Christ's yoke is easy and sweet. If we rightly appropriated the words of Christ, they would be of much greater comfort to us. But these words are not to be misconstrued and made to refer to the sacrament of the altar. There is not a letter of it that refers to the Lord's Supper. The whole chapter from which the passage is taken speaks of nothing but the spiritual food, namely, faith. The sacrament of the altar is a testament and confirmation of this true supper, with which we should strengthen our faith and be assured that this body and this blood, which we receive in the sacrament, has rescued us from sin and death and all misery. It is now evident that whoever has faith in this bread of heaven, of which he here speaks, has already done the will of God and eaten of the heavenly manna.

July 11th - 1 Corinthians 12:2

You know that you were Gentiles, carried away unto these dumb idols, even as you were led.

Saint Augustine tells us that the city of Rome alone had more than four hundred gods, and that it erected a church for all the gods of the world—the Pantheon. Paul reminds the Corinthians of their manner of life before they became Christians, for he would have them pause to think that their gifts, past and present, are not of their own procuring, nor are any gifts bestowed upon them because of merit on their part. Recall, he would say, your manner of life before you came to Christ. What were you? Heathen in darkness, having no knowledge of God, but suffering yourselves blindly to be led by any one who would say anything to you of God. All your devotion was but a discordant worship. Each one—the child in the cradle, the infant at the mother's breast—must have his own idol. These superstitions you accepted as you were taught; you followed after them, praying and sacrificing to them, setting your hearts upon dumb idols which could not teach nor advise you, could not comfort, relieve nor help you.

But now you have turned from that manifold idolatry to the one true worship and have been enlightened by God's Word. More than that, great and glorious gifts have been bestowed upon you in Christ, as the discerning of the Scriptures, diversity of tongues, power to work miracles— things impossible to the world. It is unmistakably evident that you embrace the true God, who does not, like dumb idols, leave you to wander in the error of your speculations, uncounseled by the Word; a living God, who speaks to you that you may know what to expect from him, and works among you publicly and visibly. Therefore it is not for you to make divisions among yourselves after the manner of the heathen, where one runs to this idol and another to that, each claiming superiority for his own. Knowing that you all embrace the one true God and his Word, you are to hold together in one faith and one mind, not disagreeing as if you had a variety of gods, of faiths, of baptisms, spirits and salvations.

July 12th - John 3:5

Verily, verily, I say unto you, Except a man be born of water and of the Spirit, he cannot enter into the kingdom of God.

How a man is born again may easily be told in words. When, however, it is a matter of experience, as it was with Nicodemus, it is a hard matter to understand and it requires effort to attain the experience. To persevere in this, when it becomes a matter of experience and when we are really tested, requires pains and labor.

Now the beginning of this birth is in baptism. The water is baptism, the Spirit is that grace which is given to us in baptism. The result of this birth is clearly seen in the hour of death or in times of test by poverty and temptation. He who is born of the flesh fights to defend himself, looks hither and thither, employs his reason to make his living. But he who is born anew reasons thus: I am in God's hands who has preserved and nourished me before in a wonderful manner; he will also feed and preserve me in the future and save me from all sorrow and misfortune.

When we are about to die we feel that we must depart and we know not whither; the house of shelter is not ready and we know not whether it will be white or black. Where there is flesh and blood there is still the old Adam, who knows not whither he shall go, nor on what he shall rest his soul. There is anxiety and misery in the nature of a real hell; for the torments of hell are nothing but fear, terror and despair. But if I believe in God and am born anew, I close my eyes and do not grope about. I am willing that the condition of the soul be changed entirely. I think: O' God, my soul is in your hands; you have preserved it during my life and I have never known where you have put it, neither do I wish to know to which place you will assign it. I only know that it is in your hands and you will take care of it. Thus we must abandon the life of the flesh and enter into a new life, being dead to the old. There must be a real change and an entire transformation of nature; the state of nature and feeling must be completely overthrown.

July 13th - John 3:13

No man has ascended up to heaven, but he that came down from heaven, even the Son of man which is in heaven.

It is thus that Christ pictures his own person. He is the promised Saviour come from heaven; he is the true Son of God from eternity. If he is come from heaven he must have been with God from eternity. He descended from heaven again, but he has taken upon himself the nature of man and has dwelt among us on earth. For this reason he here calls himself the Son of man, that is, actual man, having flesh and blood like we have. He divested himself of the form of God, and went about in the form of a servant, enduring suffering and death, until such time as he was delivered from this state and was exalted again and seated at the right hand of God, having now been made Lord over death and hell and all elements of his human nature. All this he has manifested by his visible ascension when he was taken up in the clouds before the eyes of his disciples.

Of these things the Pharisees were in utter ignorance. They could not at all conceive that their Messiah had to be sent from heaven that he might redeem and reconcile all the world and particularly his own Jewish people. Much less did they understand that he had to die on the cross, that he must be crucified and become a sacrifice for their sins and the sins of the world. The reason was because they failed to recognize that the whole nature of man in the sight of God merited only damnation and perdition, and were so bold as to imagine that they could atone for their own sins by their good works and consequently would need no Messiah.

All ability of men, no matter how wise, learned and holy they are, is of no avail. No man can enter heaven as he descended from Adam. There never was a saint who in his own merit could go to heaven, whether Adam, Noah, Abraham, Moses, Elijah, John, or any other. Before man can enter the kingdom of heaven and receive eternal life, there must first come One who has eternal righteousness and life, who appeases God's anger and abolishes sin and death.

July 14th - Romans 6:5

If we have been planted together in the likeness of his death, we shall be also in the likeness of his resurrection.

Christ's death and resurrection and our baptism are intimately united with, and related to one another. Baptism is not to be regarded a mere empty sign, as the Anabaptists erroneously hold. In it is embodied the power of Christ's death and resurrection. Through baptism he dedicates us to himself and imparts to us the power of his death and resurrection, to the end that both death and life may follow in us. Hence our sins are crucified through his death and taken away, that they may finally die in us and live no longer.

Being subjected to the water in baptism signifies that we die in Christ. Coming forth from the water teaches and imparts to us a new life in him, as Christ remained not in death, but was raised again to life. Such life should not and cannot be a life of sin, because sin was crucified before in us and we had to die to it. It must be a new life of righteousness and holiness, as through his resurrection Christ finally destroyed sin, on account of which he had to die, and instead he brought to himself the true life of righteousness and imparts it to us. Hence we are said to be planted together with Christ or united with him and become one, so that we have in us the power of his death and resurrection.

The Christian's death and suffering on earth are not really death and harm, but a planting unto life; being redeemed from death and sin by the resurrection, we shall live eternally. For that which is planted is planted that it may sprout and grow. So Christ was planted through death unto life; for not until he was released from this mortal life and from the sin which rested on him and brought him into death on our account, did he come into his divine glory and power. Since this planting begins in baptism and by faith we possess life in Christ, it is evident that this life must strike root in us and bear fruit. For that which is planted is not planted without purpose; it is to grow and bear fruit. So we must prove by our new conversation and by our fruits that we are planted into Christ unto life.

July 15th - Luke 14:16

A certain man made a great supper, and bade many.

The man who prepared this supper is our Lord God himself. He is a great and rich Lord who once prepared a feast in accordance with his glorious majesty and honor. It was a supper called great and glorious not only on account of the host, who is God himself, but on account of the food, which is beyond all measure great and costly, namely, the holy gospel, yea, Christ our Lord himself. He is himself the food, offered unto us through the gospel, in that he made satisfaction by his death for our sins, and has redeemed us from the misery of eternal death, of hell, of the wrath of God, sin and eternal condemnation.

The preaching of Christ is the great and glorious supper, which feeds his guests, satisfies them through holy baptism, and comforts and strengthens them through the sacrament of his body and blood, that nothing may be wanting, a great plenty be on hand, and all become satisfied. Thus it is justly called a great and glorious supper on account of the food so richly prepared, that no tongue can describe it and no heart fully grasp it.

It is an eternal food and drink by partaking of which a man shall never more thirst nor hunger, but be forever satisfied and become joyful. Nor is it only for one man, but for the whole wide world, even if it were ten times wider. It is an inexhaustible food. To believe in Christ our Lord means to eat and drink, from which the people become satisfied, strong and joyful forever.

To this you have been invited, now is the time to come, now the supper is ready. Your Lord Jesus Christ is already born, has died and risen again, therefore do not remain away any longer, accept your promised treasure with joy, come to the table, eat and be happy.

July 16th - Romans 11:34

Who has known the mind of the Lord? Or who has been his counselor?

Paul writes these words against those impudent questions of wise reason, why God punished and rejected the Jews, and allowed the condemned heathen to come into gospel grace; why he so administers justice as to exalt the godless and allow the godly to suffer and be oppressed; why he elected Judas as an apostle and afterwards rejected him; why he accepted a murderer and malefactor. With these words he would command these would-be wise to cease their impertinent strivings after the things of the hidden Majesty, and to confine themselves to the revelation he has given them. All such prying into the secrets of God are in vain and are harmful. If you were to search forever you would nowhere attain the secret purposes of God, but you would only jeopardize the welfare of your own soul.

If you wish to proceed wisely you can do no better than to be interested in God's Word and works. In them he has revealed himself, and in them he may be comprehended. He presents you his Son on the cross—this is the work for your redemption. In it you may truly apprehend God, and learn that he will condemn you on account of your sins, but give you everlasting life, if you believe.

In Christ are hidden all the treasures of wisdom and knowledge. In this you will have enough to learn and ponder. You will marvel at the wonderful revelation of

God, and you will be delighted with him and love him. It is a mine which can never be exhausted in this life, no matter how much we study. Even the angels never tire in its contemplation, but find unceasing joy and pleasure in it.

I say this so that we may be prepared to instruct those we may meet who, assailed and tormented by such thoughts of the devil, are led to tempt God. Such individuals must be reminded of these things, and reproved by them.

July 17th - Romans 6:6

Knowing this, that our old man is crucified with him, that the body of sin might be destroyed, that henceforth we should not serve sin.

Man is here called old, not because of his years; for it is possible for a man to be young and strong and vigorous and yet to be without faith or a religious spirit, to despise God, to be greedy and vainglorious, or to live in pride or the conceit of wisdom and power. But he is called "the old man" because he is unconverted, unchanged from his original condition as a sinful descendant of Adam. The day-old child is included as well as the man of eighty years; we are all in the same condition from our mother's womb. The more sins a man commits, the older and more unfit he is before God. This old man, says Paul, must be crucified—utterly condemned, executed, put out of the way, even here in this life. For where he still remains in his strength, faith and spirit cannot be; man remains in his sins, drowned under the wrath of God, troubled with an evil conscience which condemns him and keeps him out of God's kingdom.

The "new man" is one who has turned to God in repentance, who has a new heart and understanding, and who, through the power of the Holy Spirit lives in accordance with the Word and will of God. It begins in baptism or in repentance and conversion. It resists and subdues the old man and its sinful lusts through the power of the Holy Spirit.

Although the "old man" is crucified in those who are new men, yet there remains in them in this life "the body of sin." By this we understand the remaining lusts of the "old man," which are still felt to be active in the flesh and blood, and which would fain resist the Spirit. But inasmuch as the head and life of sin are destroyed, these lusts cannot harm the Christian. Still he must take care not to become obedient to them, lest the "old man" come to power again. The new man must keep the upper hand; the remaining lusts must be weakened and subdued. And this body of ours must finally decay and turn to dust, thereby utterly annihilating sin in it.

July 18th - Luke 16:20, 21

There was a certain beggar named Lazarus, which was laid at his gate, full of sores, and desiring to be fed with the crumbs which fell from the rich man's table.

We must not judge poor Lazarus in his sores, poverty and anxiety according to his outward appearance. Many persons suffer from affliction and want, and gain nothing from it. Poverty and suffering make no one acceptable to God; but if he is already acceptable to God, his poverty and suffering are precious in God's eyes. Therefore we must look into the heart of Lazarus to seek the treasure, which make his sores so precious. This must surely have been his faith and love; for without faith it is impossible to please God. His heart must have confessed that even in the midst of poverty and misery he expected all good from God, and comfortably relied upon him, with whose blessings and grace he was so abundantly satisfied, and had such pleasure in them that he would have heartily and willingly suffered even more misery, if the will of his gracious God had so determined. A true and living faith softened his heart by the knowledge of the divine goodness, so that nothing was too heavy or too much to suffer or to do. Thus faith makes the heart clever and skillful, when it experiences the grace of God.

From this faith follows another virtue, namely, love to one's neighbor, so that he is willing and ready to serve everyone; but since Lazarus is poor and in misery himself, he had nothing with which he could serve others; therefore his good will is taken for the deed. But this lack of service in temporal things he abundantly makes good by his service in things spiritual. For even now, long after his death, he serves the whole world with his sores, hunger, and misery. His bodily hunger feeds our spiritual hunger; his bodily nakedness clothes our spiritual nakedness; his bodily sores heal our spiritual sores; by his example he comforts and teaches us how God is pleased with us, when we are not prosperous here on earth, if we believe; and warns us how God is angry with us, even if we are prosperous in our unbelief; just as God had pleasure in Lazarus in his misery, and was displeased with the rich man in his abundance.

July 19th - John 20:21

As my Father has sent me, even so send I you.

The first and highest work of love a Christian ought to do when he has become a believer is to bring others also to believe in the way he himself came to believe. Here you notice Christ begins and institutes the office of the ministry of the external Word in every Christian; for he himself came with this office and the external Word. Let us lay hold of this, for we must admit that it was spoken to us. In this way the Lord says: You have now received from me peace and joy and all you should have; you need nothing more for your person. Therefore labor now and follow my example, as I have done, so do you. My Father sent me into the world only for your sake, that I might serve you, not for my own benefit, but that I might serve you. I have finished the work, have died for you, and have given you all that I am and have; remember that you do likewise, and henceforth serve and help everybody. By faith you have enough of everything. Hence I send you into the world as my Father has sent me; namely, that every Christian should instruct and teach his neighbor, that he may also come to Christ. By this no power is delegated exclusively to popes and bishops, but all Christians are commanded to profess their faith publicly and also to lead others to believe.

By faith you will accomplish this. It will make you righteous before God and save you. But this faith you are to show in love; not that you are to seek to merit anything by your works; for all in heaven and earth is yours beforehand; but that you serve your neighbor thereby. So then I obey the civil government, for I know that Christ was obedient to it, and yet he had no need to be; he did it only for our sakes. Therefore I will also do it for Christ's sake and in behalf of my neighbor, and for the reason alone that I may prove my faith by my love. If you do not show such proofs of faith, it is certain that your faith is not right. In this manner the apostles also exhort us in their writings to do good works.

July 20th - 1 Corinthians 11:19

There must be also heresies (factions) among you, that they which are approved may be made manifest among you.

Discord is a deplorable offense among Christians, putting them in the worst possible light, and making it impossible for them to steer clear of factions. Divisions are an offense to the world's wisest and best, who cry out, "If the Christians' doctrine were true, they would preserve unity among themselves, but as it is, they envy and slander and devour one another." But we cannot altogether prevent discord in the Church. For wherever the Word of God has a foothold, there the devil will be. By the agency of his factions he will always build his taverns and kitchens by the side of God's house. So he did at first in Paradise. He entrenched himself in the family of Adam, establishing there his church. Such has been his practice ever since, and doubtless ever will be. He who takes offense at differences in the Church, who when he sees any discord at once concludes there is no Church there, will in the end miss both Church and Christ. You will never find any congregation of such purity that all its members are unanimous on every point of belief and teaching and all live in perfect harmony.

Paul had experience in this matter in the case of the beautiful and famed Church of Corinth, which he himself had planted and taught two years. Soon after his departure they began to disagree about their preachers and to attach themselves to certain ones—some to Paul, some to Peter, some to Apollos. Though they had been unanimous in their doctrine, yet men would cleave to a certain one because he was more gifted than the others, could speak better, or was more attractive in personal appearance. And among the ministers of the Church, if one had a special gift or office, he thought he ought to be a little better and a little greater than the others. Necessarily, from such division and inharmony grew hatred, strife and jealousy, resulting in great injury and disorder to the Church. We must, as far as possible, guard against this fatal evil, though we cannot altogether keep it out of the Church.

July 21st - Luke 14:16, 18

A certain man made a great supper, and bade many; ... and they all with one consent began to make excuse.

The many who are bidden are the Jews and all the people of Israel, who from Abraham on, and especially through the prophets, had been invited. To the patriarch Abraham as the father of this people was this supper first announced. After that the prophets carried it further and directed the attention of the people to it, so that nothing was wanting on the part of the Lord our God, but all were diligently invited. When the hour came to go to the table, that is, when the time came for our Lord Christ to be born, to suffer and rise again from the dead, then the servants went out, John the Baptist and the apostles, and said to the people of Israel: Hitherto you have been invited, now is the time to come, now the supper is ready. Your Messiah is already born, has died, and is risen again, do not remain away any longer, come to the table, eat and be happy, that is, accept your promised treasure with joy, who has according to promise delivered you from the curse of sin and condemnation and has saved you.

The Jews excused themselves thus: We cannot accept the doctrine, for it is opposed to the priesthood and to the law, which God himself has given us through Moses. Besides, it also creates divisions in our kingdom which God has confirmed. We must see how to maintain our own affairs. Thus the first one excuses himself with his land, the second with his oxen, and both think they do well; the third does not even excuse himself at all, but simply says he cannot come.

These are the excuses of the Jews as well as our own, which we prefer against the gospel, for we are no better than they were. In the same manner our Papists excuse themselves and say: The doctrine is right of course, but we must still adhere to the Church and her orderly government. We must above all things maintain obedience to the worldly power, so that there be no disturbance and insurrection. But how will it end with them? Just as it did with the Jews. They held so long to their law, priesthood, kingdom and treasures, until they went to destruction and they lost one after the other. They desired not this supper, but preferred their priesthood to the gospel.

July 22nd - John 20:25

He (Thomas) said unto them, Except I shall see in his hands the print of the nails, and put my finger into the print of the nails, and thrust my hand into his side, I will not believe.

Here we see what a poor thing the human heart is when it becomes faint, that we cannot strengthen and comfort it again. The other disciples and Thomas did not only hear during the time they were with the Lord that he taught the people with great authority, and later saw how he confirmed his doctrine by the great miracles performed on the blind, lame, lepers and dumb, whom he cured; but also that he raised three persons from the dead, one of whom had been in the grave four days. Such weak characters were the disciples of Christ, and especially Thomas, that they could not believe that the Lord arose from the dead and was alive.

We see in the apostles that we are truly nothing when Christ withdraws his hand and we are left to ourselves. The women had announced it, and now the disciples themselves proclaim that they had seen the risen Lord. Yet Thomas is stubborn and will not believe it; he will not be satisfied even if he see him, unless it be that he sees the print of the nails in his hands and puts his fingers into the print of the nails and his hand into his side. The beloved disciple will thus himself be lost and condemned, in that he will not believe. For there can be no forgiveness of sins, nor salvation, if one believes not. And Thomas would have perished and been condemned in his unbelief, had not Christ rescued him from it by this revelation.

Thus the Holy Spirit illustrates in this example that without faith we are simply blind and completely hardened, as we see everywhere in the Holy Scriptures that the human heart is the hardest thing in the world, harder than steel and adamant. On the other hand, if it be bashful, despondent and soft, there is not water, nor oil so soft as the human heart. So soon had the apostles forgotten all the signs and words they had seen and heard from him, that the Lord had enough to do during the forty days after his resurrection in various appearances and revelations, besides eating and drinking with them—all for the purpose that they might be assured that he is risen.

July 23rd - John 20:28

Thomas answered and said unto him, My Lord and my God.

This happened on the eighth day after the resurrection, when Thomas had maintained his unbelief in the face of the testimony of all the others, and no one had hoped that Christ would show himself in a special manner to Thomas. Just then Christ comes and shows him the same scars and wounds, as fresh as he had shown them to the other disciples eight days before, and tells him to reach hither his finger and hand and place them into the print of the nails and into his side.

Here you see that Christ is not satisfied to stop with the narrative; but he is concerned that Thomas becomes believing and is resurrected from his stubborn unbelief and sin. This is shown in a powerful way in that Thomas says, "My Lord and my God!" There is at once a different man, not the old Thomas as he was before, when he was so cold and stiff and dead in his unbelief. He commenced suddenly to deliver a glorious confession about Christ, the equal of which no apostle to that time had yet made, namely, that the person, the risen one, is true God and man. They are admirable words that he utters: "My Lord and my God!" He is not drunken, he is not jesting, nor mocking; he does not mean a false god; therefore he certainly does not tell a lie. Besides, he is not here chastised by Christ, but his faith is confirmed, and so it must be the truth and sincere.

It is by the power of the resurrection of Christ that Thomas, who was so deep and obdurate in unbelief, was so suddenly changed, became an entirely different man, who publicly and freely confesses that he not only believes that Christ is risen, but is also enlightened by the power of Christ's resurrection so that he firmly believes and confesses that he, his Lord, is the true God and man; so he will also arise from the dead on the judgment day and live forever with him in indescribable glory and blessedness.

The leading thought for us to learn and retain from this passage is, that we believe that Christ's resurrection is sure and that he works in us so that we be resurrected from sin and death. "Blessed are they that have not seen, and yet have believed."

July 24th - 1 John 3:14

We know that we have passed from death unto life, because we love the brethren. He that loves not his brother abide in death.

How do we know we have passed from death unto life? Because we love the brethren. When we fully believe in our Saviour's love, then our hearts respond with perfect love to God and our neighbor. The apostle directed this epistle especially against false Christians; many there are who extol Christ, and fail to bear the fruit of faith. It is not sufficient to boast of having passed from death into life; there must be evidence of the fact. Faith is not an inactive and lifeless thing. When there is faith in the heart, its power will be manifest. Where power is not in evidence, all boasting is false and vain. When the human heart is thrilled with spiritual comfort in its confidence of divine mercy and love, and also warmed into kindness, friendliness, humility, and patience toward the neighbor, envying and despising none, but cheerfully serving all and ministering unto necessity, even to hazarding body and life, then the fruits of faith are manifest. Such fruits are proof that the believer has truly passed from death into life.

Had he not true faith, but doubted God's grace and love, his heart would not prompt him to manifest love for his neighbor by reason of his love and gratitude to God. This interpretation of God's Word leaves in its integrity the foundation, justification, or deliverance from death through faith alone. Faith is the first element of Christian doctrine. The next question is whether the faith is real or simulated, being merely a deceptive show and unsupported claim. The clear information imparted by the apostles is that love does not deliver from death, but that deliverance from death and the presence of life become a matter of sight and knowledge in that love has been brought about. With true faith we must have come to the point where we no longer in our pride and conceit despise our neighbor; where we are not filled with envy, hatred, and bitterness; where we desire and promote the interest of our neighbor and do him good to the extent of our power. The reality of the inner life is known by the presence of love, which in turn attests the presence of faith in the heart.

July 25th - Romans 6:21, 22

What fruit had you then in those things whereof you are now ashamed? for the end of those things is death. But now being made free from sin, and become servants to God, you have your fruit unto holiness, and the end everlasting life.

Paul here contrasts the experience of the Romans in the two forms of service. He leaves it to them to determine which has been productive of benefit and which of injury, and to choose accordingly as to future service and obedience. Recall your manner of life when you were free from righteousness, he would say, and obeyed only the desires and enticements of sin. What pleasure or gain had you in it? None, except that for which you are now ashamed. Had you remained in it you would at last have found death. Only these two grand results—shame and death. Munificent reward indeed for him who, choosing freedom from righteousness, lives to his own pleasure. He is deceived into thinking he has chosen a highly desirable life, for it gratifies the fleshly desires, and he thinks to go unpunished.

But gratification is succeeded by two punishments: First, shame, confession of disgrace before God and the world. Thus Adam and Eve in Paradise, when they chose to violate God's command and, enticed by the devil, followed their desire for a forbidden thing, were made to feel the disgrace for sin; they were ashamed in their hearts to appear in the presence of God. The other punishment is death and the fires of hell.

Is it not better, then, to be free from the service of sin and to serve righteousness? So doing, you would never suffer shame or injury, but would receive a double blessing: First, a clear conscience before God and all creatures, proof in itself that you live a holy life and belong to God; second and chief, the rich and incorruptible reward of eternal life.

In these observations Paul is speaking after the manner of men, in a way comprehended and accepted by reason, even without knowledge of Christ. It is universally true in the world that evildoers, thieves, murderers and the like, are punished in addition to the public disgrace they feel. Similarly, they who do good receive, in addition to the honor of men, all manner of happy reward.

July 26th - Genesis 7:1

> *The Lord said unto Noah, Come you and all your house into the ark; for you have I seen righteous before me in this generation.*

As soon as that extraordinary structure, the ark, was built, the Lord commanded Noah to enter it, because the time of the deluge, which the Lord announced one hundred and twenty years before, was now at hand. All this convinced Noah that God was taking care of him; it gave him ample and abundant word to support and confirm his faith in such great straits. Noah, being holy and just, a kind and merciful man, often struggled with his own heart, hearing with greatest agitation of mind the voice of the Lord, threatening certain destruction to all flesh. It was needful, then, that repeated declaration should confirm his agitated faith, lest he might doubt.

Could words be more appalling than these, that Noah alone was righteous before the Lord? It is a fearful thing to live in such an evil and godless world. By the goodness of

God we are in the golden age, since we still have the light of God's Word. The sacraments are rightly administered in our churches, pious preachers proclaim the pure Word, and though magistrates be weak, wickedness is not desperately rampant. If there had been more godly teachers in the days of Noah, there might have been more righteous people. The fact that Noah alone was proclaimed a righteous man makes it evident that the godly teachers had been either destroyed or corrupted, leaving Noah the sole preacher of righteousness.

Noah's faith was truly great; he could rely upon God's utterance. I realize what weight the whole world's hostile and condemnatory judgment must carry. We are condemned in the judgment of the pope, the Sacramentarians, and the Anabaptists, but this is mere play and pleasure, compared to what the righteous Noah had to bear, who found not a single person in the whole world to approve of his religion or life, except his own sons and his pious grandfather. Therefore, Noah is a brilliant and admirable example of faith, who opposed the judgments of the world with an heroic steadfastness of mind in the assurance that he was righteous while all the rest of the world was wicked. It is helpful often to reflect upon such examples, since the prince of this world battles against us, endeavoring to kindle despair in us. It behooves us to be well armed.

July 27th - John 3:14, 15

As Moses lifted up the serpent in the wilderness, even so must the Son of man be lifted up: that whosoever believeth in him should not perish, but have eternal life.

Here Christ uses the Scriptures to point to himself. He means to say, that just as the Jews in the desert, who were bitten by fiery serpents, were saved by looking upon the serpent of brass, which Moses set upon a standard, so it is also with regard to me. No one who looks upon me will perish; all those who have an evil conscience, are tormented by sin and death, should believe that I have come down from heaven for their sakes and have ascended again. Then neither sin, nor death shall harm them. Whoever would enter heaven and be saved, must be saved by this serpent, which is Christ. Thus this gospel condemns free will and every human accomplishment, and points only to this serpent.

The spiritual significance of the narrative in Numbers is this: The serpent, which bit and poisoned the Jews, is sin, death and an evil conscience. I know that I must die and that I am under the power of death; I cannot free myself and must remain in this state until a dead serpent is set up for me, one which can harm no one, but rather benefit, as did the serpent of Moses. Now, this is Christ. I see him hanging on the cross, not beautiful, nor greatly honored; but I see him hanging in disgrace, like a murderer and malefactor; thus, reason must say that he is cursed before God. The Jews believed this to be true and they could only consider him the most cursed of all men before God and the world.

Moses had to set up a serpent of brass, which looked like the fiery serpents, but did not bite, nor harm anyone; it rather saved the people. Thus, Christ also has the form and the appearance of a sinner, but has become my salvation; his death is my life; he atones for my sins and takes away from me the wrath of the Father. If man believes that the death of

Christ has taken away his sin, he becomes a new man. The carnal, natural man cannot believe that God will gratuitously take away and forgive us all our sins. Reason argues: You have sinned, you must also atone for your sin. The gospel of Christ says: You have sinned, another must atone for you. Our works are nothing; but faith in Christ does it all.

July 28th - Psalm 46:1, 2

God is our refuge and strength, a very present help in trouble. Therefore will not we fear, though the earth be removed, and though the mountains be carried into the midst of the sea.

No power, might or protection which can comfort, or upon which one can rely, may be sought in the world. Wholly in God, and in God alone, must help be sought. By his divine power God must uphold the Church. He has always from the beginning wonderfully preserved it in the world, in the midst of great weakness, in disunion occasioned by schismatics and heretics, in persecution by tyrants. The government is wholly his, though he commits the office and service to men, whom he summons and uses to administer his Word and sacrament. Every Christian should be intent, in that whereunto God has called and appointed him, serving God faithfully and doing that which is commanded him. The anxiety respecting the Church's continued existence and her preservation against the devil and the world can be left to the Lord. He has taken this upon himself and so has removed the burden from our shoulders that we might be certain of the permanence of the Church. Christians have regard for God's Word and believe that God cares for them. They commend all things to him and at his word go on with courage. They have learned that they should not rely upon their own wisdom and reason and upon human help or comfort.

Let me illustrate from my own experience. What should I have done when I began to denounce the lies of the indulgence system, and later the errors of the papacy, if I had given heed to the terrible things all the world wrote and said would happen to me? How often I heard it said that if I wrote against such and such eminent persons I would provoke their displeasure, which would prove too severe for me and the whole German nation. But since I had not begun this work of myself, being driven and led thereto by reason of my office, I must continue. I commended the cause to God and let him bear the burden of care, both as to the result of the work and as to my own fate. Thus I advanced the cause more, despite tumultuous opposition, than I had ever before dared to think or hope. So let every Christian cast his heart and its anxieties upon God, who is strong and can easily carry the burden.

July 29th - Luke 14:23

Go out into the highways and hedges, and compel them to come in, that my house may be filled.

This refers to the heathen, who have dwelt in no city, who were without any worship of the true God, but were idolatrous, and did not know what God was. Go thither, he says, and compel them to come in. For the world arrays itself against the gospel in every way, and cannot tolerate this doctrine, and yet this leader of the house wants his house full of guests; he has made preparations, and now must have people to eat, drink and be joyful, even if he had to make them of stones.

But how shall we compel, as God does not want any forced worship? He desires that we should preach thus: Dear friend, do not despair because you are a sinner and have such a terrible sentence of condemnation passed upon you; but do this, go forth and be baptized and hear the gospel. Here you will learn that Jesus Christ has died for your sakes and has made satisfaction for your sins. If you will believe this you will be safe against the wrath of God and eternal death, and you shall eat here at this glorious supper and live well, become hearty and strong. When a man feels his wretchedness and misery, then is the time to say to him: Sit down at the table of this rich Lord and eat, that is, be baptized and believe in Jesus Christ, that he has made satisfaction for your sins. There are no means to aid you, except you be baptized and believe. Thus wrath will cease and heaven will shine with pure grace and mercy, forgiveness of sins and eternal life.

These words are, therefore, lovely and comfortable for the poor, miserable multitude of those who are constrained to come in, who before were lost and condemned heathen. By these words God desires forcibly to portray and show unto us his unfathomable grace. Thus God shows that he is immeasurably more anxious to give and help us than we are or ever can be to receive and pray; and that he requires nothing more difficult from us than that we open our hearts and accept his grace. This is the way we are to come to this supper, that from Jews and Gentiles there may be one Christian Church.

July 30th - Luke 15:1

Then drew near unto him all the publicans and sinners for to hear him.

Luke freely and plainly tells us what kind of people Christ had about him, namely, those who openly lived as they should not live. Thus it would appear that the Pharisees had sufficient reason to blame him, because he pretended to be a pious and holy man and kept company with such low characters. At that time men called publicans were scattered through the land, to whom the Romans gave charge of a city and required of them a certain amount of revenue. Those who collected such revenue or tax managed matters so as to have a profit from it. As the sum appointed for each city or office was large, these officers extorted without let or hindrance, so that they might enjoy more as their own. Their masters were so close with them that they could not gain much for themselves, if they would act justly and take advantage of no one. Hence they were reported in all lands as extortioners in whom little good or honesty could be found.

So other great crowds in general were called "sinners," who in other respects were worse people and publicly lived in a shameful and wild state, in covetousness, adultery and the like. Such drew near to Christ to hear him, since they had heard that in the light of his doctrine and his many miracles he was an excellent man. Now there was after all a spark or two of virtue and honesty in them, since they had a desire for Christ and gladly heard his doctrine and wished to see what he did. They had heard nothing but good of him, and they well knew that their doings did not harmonize with his life, yet they feel no enmity against him, but go to him, not to seek any evil in him, but to see and hear something good, and to hope that they might become better.

The scribes and Pharisees, who were held to be the most pious and holy, were such poisonous reptiles that they were not only enemies of Christ, but could not even suffer poor sinners to come to him and hear him that they might be made better. They called him a "drunk and a glutton" and a "friend of publicans and sinners." Such names he must bear from these holy people, not because he was given to gluttony and drunkenness, but because he permitted "publicans and sinners" to come to him.

July 31st - Genesis 6:9

Noah was a just man and perfect in his generations, and Noah walked with God.

Noah is called "just" because of his faith in God, because he first believed the general promise with respect to the seed of the woman and then also the particular one respecting the destruction of the world through the flood and the saving of his own offspring. On the other hand he is called "perfect" ("upright") because he walked in the fear of God and conscientiously avoided murder and other sins with which the wicked polluted themselves in defiance of conscience. Nor did he permit himself to be moved by the frequent offenses of men most illustrious, wise, and apparently holy.

Great was his courage. To-day it appears to us impossible that one man should oppose himself to all mankind, condemning them as evil, while they despise the Church and God's Word and worship, and maintain that he alone is a son of God and acceptable to him, therefore, is a marvelous man, and Moses commends this same greatness of mind when he plainly adds "in his generations," or "in his age," as if he desired to say that his age was, indeed, the most wicked and corrupt.

In the history of Enoch we explained what it means to "walk with God," namely, to advocate the cause of God in public. To be just and upright bespeaks private virtue, but to walk with God is something public—to advocate the cause of God before the world, to wield his Word, to teach his worship. Noah was not only just and holy for himself, but he was also a confessor; he taught others the promises and threats of God, and performed and suffered all that behooves a public personage in an age so exceedingly wicked and corrupt.

Peter beautifully sets forth what it means to walk with God when he calls Noah a preacher, not of the righteousness of man, but of God,—the righteousness which comes by faith in the promised seed. What reward Noah received from the ungodly for his message Moses does not indicate. The statement is sufficient that he preached righteousness, that he taught the true worship of God while the whole earth opposed him. What a noble example of patience and other virtues Noah is, who was just and irreproachable in that ungodly generation and walked with God.

August 1st - 1 Corinthians 4:1

Let a man so account of us, as of the ministers of Christ, and stewards of the mysteries of God.

To serve Christ, or God, is defined by Paul as fulfilling an office ordained of God, the office of preaching. This office is a service or ministry proceeding from Christ to us and not from us to Christ. To make himself clearly understood in this matter of service or ministry, Paul carefully adds to the word "ministers" the explanatory word "stewards," which cannot be understood otherwise than as referring to the office of the ministry.

He calls his office "service or ministry of Christ," and himself "minister of Christ," because he was ordained of God to the office of preaching. Thus all apostles and bishops are ministers of Christ; that is preachers, messengers, officers of Christ, sent to the people with his message. The meaning of the verse, then, is: Let every individual take heed not to institute another leader, to set up another Lord, to constitute another Christ. Rather be unanimously loyal to the one and only Christ. We apostles are not your lords, nor your masters; we do not preach our own interests, nor teach our own doctrines. We do not seek to have you obey us, or give us allegiance and accept our doctrine. We are messengers and ministers of him who is your Master, your Lord and Leader. We preach his word, enlist men to follow his commandments and lead only into his obedience.

He who so receives us, receives, not us, but Christ, whom we alone preach. But he who does not regard us, does us injustice, discards Christ, the one true Leader, sets up another in his stead and makes gods of us. Where more authority is assumed than God's command grants, idolatry results and the leader assumes a new character. The Church has no other doctrine than that of Christ, no other obedience than to obey him.

August 2nd - Psalm 33:5

The earth is full of the goodness of the Lord.

When a babe is born blind we see what a painful thing the lack of sight is, what a precious thing even one eye would be, and what a divine blessing a healthy, bright countenance is. The eye serves us our whole lifetime and without it one had rather be dead; and yet no one thanks God for it. The psalmist had pure eyes and could see far, that the whole world was full of the goodness and the lovingkindness of God. From whom does this goodness come? Have we deserved it? No, but it has pleased God to cast his gifts promiscuously into the world, which the unthankful receive almost as freely as the thankful. We are grieved when we are obliged to lose a few dollars, or to give them to the poor. How much of his goods does God daily cast into the world and no one thanks him for anything?

We may observe all God's creatures and become convinced of his goodness in them. "He makes his sun to rise on the evil and on the good, and sendeth rain on the just and unjust." He enlightens our eyes, but who acknowledges that it is God's blessing? If some morning the sun should not rise, what distress and anxiety it would cause, but since it rises and shines daily at the appointed time, no one considers it a blessing. So it is with the rain from heaven, with the grain in the field and with all that God has created. They exist in such abundance and are daily bestowed upon us so plenteously that we fail to see them.

At times God permits some man to fall into anxiety, into pain and distress; he becomes blind, lame, dropsical. The disciples asked the Lord concerning the man blind from his birth, whether he or his parents had sinned. The Lord answered, "Neither has this man sinned, nor his parents; but that the works of God should be made manifest in him." God sees that the treasures of this world do not move us. In his grace he presents to us a blind person, so that, when we do not recognize his grace and kindness in our good fortune, we may at least do so in our misfortune.

August 3rd - Romans 6:16

Know you not, that to whom you yield yourselves servants to obey, his servants you are to whom you obey; whether of sin unto death, or of obedience unto righteousness?

Necessarily your life must be obedient to some master. Either you obey sin, to continue in the service of which brings death and God's wrath, or you obey God in grace unto a new manner of life. Reason teaches, through the law, good works and forbids evil, but it is unable to comprehend why its teachings are not fulfilled. It perceives, from the results which follow disrespect for the law, that it is best to honor it, that it is right and praiseworthy not to steal and commit crime. But it fails to understand why, after its teachings are given, they are not naturally fulfilled. With sword, rack and gallows the judge may restrain public crime, but he cannot punish more than what is known and witnessed to before court. Whatever is done secretly and does not come before him, he cannot punish or restrain.

The Word of God, however, teaches how to crush the head of the serpent and to slay the evil, so that judge and executioner are no longer necessary. It tells us that a Christian has certain knowledge that through the grace of Christ his sins are forgiven, blotted out and deprived of condemning power. Because he has obtained and believes in such grace, he receives a heart abhorrent of sin. Although feeling within himself the presence of evil thoughts and lusts, yet his faith and the Holy Spirit are with him to remind him of his baptism. He says: Although time and opportunity permit me to do evil and I run no risk of being detected and punished, I will not do it, but will obey God and honor Christ my Lord, for I am baptized into Christ and as a Christian am dead unto sin, nor will I come again under its power.

So acted godly Joseph, who, when tempted by his master's wife, "left his garment in her hand, fled and got him out." He was but flesh and blood and naturally not insensible to her inducement, to the time and opportunity, to the friendship of the woman. But he restrained himself, not yielding even in thought to the temptation. Such obedience to God destroys, indeed, the source of sin and evil.

August 4th - 1 John 3:13

Marvel not, my brethren, if the world hate you.

Why this hostility? Because the apostles sought to deprive the world of its idolatry and damnable doings. Such good works the world could not tolerate. What it desires is nothing but praise and commendation for its own evil doings, expecting from God the impossible endorsement,

"Your deeds are good and well-pleasing to me. You are pious children. Just keep on cheerfully killing all who believe and preach my Word."

In the same way the world conducts itself to-day with reference to our gospel. For no other reason are we hated and persecuted than because we have, through God's grace, proclaimed his Word that has rescued us from the blindness and idolatry in which we had sunken as deeply as the world, and because we desire to rescue others. We preach no other doctrine than faith in Christ, which they themselves confess in words. We differ only in our claim that Christ having been crucified for us and having shed his blood to redeem us from sin and death, our salvation is not effected by our works, or holiness or devotion. The fact that we do not regard their faithless worship equal to Christ himself, but teach men to trust in the grace of God and not in their own worthiness, and to render him gratitude for his grace—this fact is intolerable to the world. No unity or harmony is to be hoped for; the world will not forsake its idolatry nor receive the faith.

So to understand the world as to know what we may expect from it is essential and valuable to the Christian. Thus armed he will not be dismayed and become impatient of suffering, nor permit its malice and ingratitude to mislead him to hate and desire for revenge. He will keep his faith and love, suffering the world to go its way if it refuse to hear his message. The Christian should expect nothing better from the world than its bitter persecution for his good works and love, Such knowledge is comforting to the godly little company of Christians. If they fare better, they thank

God for it. But they are ever to abide in love toward God, whose love they have received and felt, and likewise toward men, their enemies not excepted.

August 5th - Genesis 8:21

The imagination of man's heart is evil from his youth.

This is a powerful passage relating to original sin. Whoever weakens its force, goes groping like the blind man in the sunlight, failing to see his own acts and experiences. Look in how many ways sin manifests itself in our earlier years. What an amount of switching it requires until we are taught order and attention to duty! What then shall we say of the inward vices when unbelief, presumption, neglect of the Word, and wicked views grow up? Original sin is not a slight disorder or infirmity, but complete lawlessness, the like of which is not found in other creatures, except in evil spirits. Not even the saints are excepted. For we learn by experience that even holy men can scarcely stand firm; that even they are often entangled by gross sins, being overwhelmed by such natural corruptions.

The Hebrew *neurim* denotes the age when man begins to use his reason; this naturally occurs in the sixth year. Similarly the term *ne-arim* is used to denote boys and youths who need the guidance of parents and teachers up to the age of manhood. It will be profitable for each of us to glance backward to that period of life and consider how willingly we obeyed the commands of our parents and teachers, how diligent we were in studying, how persevering we were, how often our parents punished our sauciness. Who can say for himself that he was not much more pleased to go out for a walk, to play games and to gossip than to go to church in obedience to his parents.

Although these impulses can be corrected or bridled to a certain extent by discipline, they cannot be entirely rooted out of the heart, as their traces show when we are grown up. God, indeed, causes some persons to experience emotions which are naturally good; but they are induced by supernatural power. Thus Cyrus was impelled to restore the worship of God and to preserve the Church. But such is not the tendency of human nature. Where God is present with his Holy Spirit, there only the imagination of the human heart gives place to the thoughts of God. God dwells there through the Word and the Spirit. But Moses speaks here only of those who are without the Holy Spirit; they are wicked even at their best.

August 6th - Luke 24:39

Behold my hands and my feet, that it is I myself: handle me, and see; for a spirit has not flesh and bones, as you see me have.

As the text gives occasion, we may here speak of ghosts, or walking spirits, for we see here that the Jews and the apostles themselves held that spirits roam about and are seen by night and at other times. But the Scriptures do not say, nor give any example, that such are the souls of dead persons walking among the people and seeking help, as in our blindness and delusion by the devil we have heretofore believed.

We have good reason not to believe such apparitions of roaming, erring spirits that profess to be souls. First, because the Scriptures nowhere say that the souls of the deceased that have not yet risen should wander about among the people; whereas everything else we need to know is clearly revealed in the Scriptures. Not one word of this is given for our instruction, nor is it possible that we should grasp and understand the state of the spirits that have departed from the body before the resurrection and the day of judgment; for they are sundered and separated altogether from the world and from this generation. Furthermore, it is clearly forbidden in the Scriptures to consult the dead or to believe them who do. God will neither let one rise from the dead, nor preach, because we have Moses and the prophets, or the Scriptures.

Know therefore that all ghosts and visions, which cause themselves to be seen and heard, especially with din and noise, are not men's souls, but evidently devils that amuse themselves either to deceive the people with false claims and lies, or unnecessarily frighten and trouble them. A Christian should be well girded with God's Word and faith, that he may not be deceived nor afraid, but abide in the doctrine that he has learned and confessed from the gospel of Christ, and cheerfully despise the devil with his noise. Nor does he tarry long when he feels that a soul trusts in Christ and despises him.

That Christ shows his hands and his feet to his disciples signifies that they were weak. But he does not rebuke them; he lovingly comforts them that they might be strong and fearless. Hence they were also made cheerful and of good courage. Therefore we ought not to cast away the weak, but so deal with them that they may become strong and of good cheer.

August 7th - 1 Corinthians 12:3

No man speaking by the Spirit of God calls Jesus accursed.

No one can possibly possess the Holy Spirit, if he does not regard Christ as the Lord, much less if he call him accursed. Destroy the foundation and you destroy all; there will be no God, no Spirit, and all your claims, teaching and works are naught. You must recognize and be governed by the fact that either Christ must be received and believed in as the one true Lord, and praised and glorified as such, or else he will be cursed; between these alternatives is no medium. We are to make the doctrine of this verse the standard and authority as to what and how we preach concerning Christ. He who speaks by inspiration of the Holy Spirit certainly will not curse Christ; he will glorify and praise him. If his teaching is not to the glory of God, you may safely conclude that he is not true, not inspired by the Holy Spirit.

Thus Paul rejects the glorying and boasting of the sects over their offices and gifts—they who pretend to be filled with the Spirit and to teach the people correctly, and who make out that Paul and other teachers are of no consequence. Themselves the chief of apostles, the people must hear them and accept their baptism. More than that, they demand a higher attainment in the Spirit for gospel ministers, deeming faith, the sacrament and the outward office insufficient. All such teachers are in reality simply guilty of condemning, reproaching and cursing Christ, though themselves bearing and boasting that name. To slight Christ's Word and ministry, and exalt in their stead other things as mediums for obtaining the Holy Spirit and eternal life, or at least as being equally efficacious and essential—

what is this but scorning Christ and making him of no consequence? The tongue of a minister—the language he employs—must be of that simplicity which preaches naught but Christ. If he is to testify of the Saviour and glorify him, he cannot present other things whereby Christ would be ignored and robbed of his glory.

August 8th - Luke 15:2

The Pharisees and scribes murmured, saying, This man receiveth sinners, and eateth with them.

We have here the Pharisees and hypocrites, who are exceedingly pious

people and are over head and ears in holiness. We have also the open sinners and publicans, who were over head and ears in sin. These were despised by those shining saints, and were not considered worthy of their society. But Christ intervenes with his judgment and says that those saints are to stoop down and take the sinners upon their shoulders, and with their righteousness and piety they are to bear in mind to help the others out of their sins.

It is truly a Christian work to descend and get mixed up in the mire of the sinner, taking his sin upon ourselves and floundering out of it with him, not acting otherwise than if his sins were our own. We should rebuke and deal with the sinner in earnest; yet we are not to despise but sincerely to love him. There are great and good works in which we should exercise ourselves. But no man pays attention to them. Such works have entirely faded away, and it is to be feared that the holiest are in the deepest hell, and that sinners are mostly in heaven. Moses acted thus when the

Israelites worshiped the molten calf. He mingled freely with the people in their sins. He punished them severely, but afterward he went up and bowed down before God, and prayed that he would forgive the people their sin, or blot him out of the Book of Life. Here we have a man who knew that God loved him and had written his name in the book of the blessed. Thus Paul also at times severely rebuked the Jews, yet he writes to the Romans, "I could wish that myself were accursed from Christ for my brethren, my kinsmen according to the flesh." Thus we should act and serve our neighbor; but such a course is much too lofty for reason and passes beyond its conception. Our bearing toward sinners should be: inwardly, the heart in service; outwardly, the tongue in earnest. This is what Christ, our Captain, has manifested in himself. He could have justly condemned us as sinners, but de did not do so. He gave himself to be our Servant. His righteousness has served for our sins, his fullness for our feebleness, his life for our death.

August 9th - Luke 15:4

What man of you, having an hundred sheep, if he lose one of them, does not leave the ninety and nine in the wilderness, and go after that which is lost, until he find it?

Christ is the good shepherd. He has lighted the lamp, that is, the gospel, and he goes about in the desert, that is, the world. He seeks the lost sheep, when he comes with his Word and proclaims to us first our sins, and then his grace and mercy. Christ's declaration, that he is the Shepherd and has laid our sins upon his shoulders, makes us fully trust in him, and makes publicans and sinners run after him. These would not have come to him, had they regarded him as a hard and wrathful judge; they were drawn to him when they heard this loving doctrine.

Learn from this, that our neighbor is to be sought as a lost sheep, that his shame is to be covered with our honor, that our piety is to be a cover for his sins. When you come together, conceal the shame of others, and do not cause wounds which you cannot heal. Should you meet with anything like this in someone's house, throw your mantle over it and close the door. A very good reason for doing this is that you would have others do the same to you. Christ acts thus. He keeps silent and covers our sins. He could expose us to shame and tread us under foot, but he does not do so. All will be brought to light, however, at the final judgment. There is in God's judgment no greater sin on earth than when pious men and women despise those who lie in their sin.

Hence this gospel is very comforting to sinners. But while it is friendly to sinners, it is a source of great fear to Pharisees. It is spoken to those only who acknowledge their sins, and they acknowledge their sins when they repent of them. It is of no use to the Pharisees, for they do not acknowledge their sins. To those who acknowledge them and are about to despair, the gospel must be brought. When your sins are gnawing at you, and your heart is agitated, say: Oh, God! I have come to feel my sins, I need the one Shepherd who seeks me. I will freely venture on the gospel. When you thus come to God, you are already the sheep placed upon his shoulders. You have found the Shepherd.

August 10th - Romans 11:34

Who has known the mind of the Lord? or who has been his counselor?

The reason and wisdom of man go so far as to reach the conclusion, although feebly, that there must be one eternal being, who has created and who preserves and governs all things. Man sees such a beautiful and wonderful creation in the heavens and on the earth, one so wonderfully, regularly and securely preserved and ordered, that he must say: It is impossible that this came into existence by mere chance, or that it originated and controls itself; there must have been a Creator and Lord from whom all these things proceed and by whom they are governed.

But, even knowing this, we have not yet searched out or fathomed the exalted, eternal, divine essence of the Godhead. For even though I have learned that there is an only divine majesty, who governs all things, I do not thereby know the inner workings of this divine essence himself; this no one can tell me, except insofar as God himself reveals it in his Word. Now we Christians have the Scriptures which we know to be the Word of God. From these, and from no other source, we have obtained all that is known of God and divine works from the beginning of the world. And our knowledge is confirmed and proven by great miracles, even to the present day. These Scriptures declare that there is no God nor divine being save this one alone. They not only manifest him to us from without, but they lead us into his inner essence, and show us that in him there are three persons; not three Gods or three kinds of divinity, but the same undivided, divine essence.

Such a revelation is radiantly shed forth from the declaration of his divine counsel and will. In that counsel and will it was decreed from eternity and was proclaimed in his promises, that his Son should become man and die to reconcile man to God. This no angel nor any other creature could do; it must be done by God himself. It could not be done by the person of the Father, who was to be reconciled, but it must be done by a second person with whom this counsel was determined and through whom and for whose sake the reconciliation was to be brought about.

August 11th - Genesis 8:1

> *And God remembered Noah, and every living thing, and all the cattle that was with him in the ark.*

When that horrible wrath had exhausted itself, and all flesh and living things on the earth had been destroyed, the promise made by God to Noah and his sons, that they were to be the seed of the human race, began to be realized. No doubt this promise was to them an object of eager expectation. No life is so hedged about with difficulties as that of faith. This was the life lived by Noah and his sons, whom we see absolutely depending upon the heavens for support. The earth was covered with water. There was no bottom on which to stand. It was the word of promise that upheld them, as they drifted in this welter of waters.

The difficulty besetting Noah is hinted at in the words, "God remembered." Moses thus intimates that Noah had been tossed on the water so long that God seemed to have forgotten him entirely. They who pass through such mental strain, when the rays of divine grace are gone and they sit in darkness or are forgotten by God, find by experience that it is far more difficult to live in the Word or by faith alone than to be a hermit or a monk. Hence it is not a meaningless expression when the Holy Spirit says that "God remembered Noah." He means that from the day that Noah entered the ark, no word was spoken, nothing was revealed to him; that he saw no ray of divine grace shining, but merely clung to the promise which he had accepted, while the waters and waves raged as if God had certainly forgotten him.

The word "remembered" indicates that great sadness beset both man and beast during the entire time of the flood. It must have been by dint of great patience and extraordinary courage that Noah and the others bore this lapse from God's memory, which is simply unbearable to the flesh without the spirit, even in slight trials. True, God always remembers his own, even when he seems to have forgotten them; but Moses indicates that he remembered his people here in a visible way, by a sign, and by openly fulfilling what he had previously promised through the Word and the Spirit. This story sets before us an example of faith, of endurance and patience.

August 12th - Luke 15:6

When he cometh home, he calls together his friends and neighbours, saying unto them, Rejoice with me; for I have found my sheep which was lost.

This great and good Shepherd is not satisfied to seek his lost sheep so lovingly and carry it home so gently with joy; but when he brings it home he appoints a special feast and season of joy, and calls together his friends and neighbors to rejoice with him. Yea, he makes a great jubilee. Thus God in heaven together with all the heavenly hosts and all creatures rejoice over one sinner that repents. Here is shown who the lost sheep is, namely, the sinner who repents, that is, who feels his sins and is heartily sorry on account of them, and would gladly be free from them, come to Christ and amend his life. The character of Christ is such as to seek and carry no sheep except that which is lost and knows no refuge or help of its own.

How could Christ preach more effectively and comfortingly, or what more should he do to make the heart joyful and awaken a strong confidence in him? He is such a Shepherd as is not only unwilling to lose his sheep, but anxiously seeks it; and when he has found it, he carries it home with all joy, and instigates such a feast of joy that all the angels and saints in heaven and all creatures rejoice and smile so benignly that even the sun must shine more lovely. For when man is sorrowful, the sun and everything appears dark to him, but when the heart is joyful everything appears lighter and brighter to him.

He who will firmly believe Christ to be this kind Shepherd shall receive true consolation and joy in Christ the Lord; because he has here the promise, that if he cling unto Christ and permit himself to be carried on his shoulders, he is a dear guest in the kingdom of heaven and will be received with great joy. Therefore if you desire to possess true comfort and joy, learn to impress this lovely picture on your heart. In Christ you find all things, if you only remain under his protection and lie still upon his shoulders. You need not be troubled about sin, death or life, you have all things in Christ who carries and defends you.

August 13th - 1 Timothy 6:9

They that will be rich fall into temptation and a snare, and into many foolish and hurtful lusts, which drown men in destruction and perdition.

Those who plant themselves among the thorns of avarice, and seek after great possessions, must suffer the consequences of being stung and torn and must fall, not only into manifold temptations and dangers, but also into snares in which they are so thoroughly caught that they sink into a temporal destruction and eternal damnation from which they can never again escape. Of this we have daily examples even in those who boast of the gospel and Christianity. Everywhere we find robbery, oppression, assessment and usury, to such an extent that even God and conscience are set aside for the sake of a miserable penny. Then, as if such a fall were not deep enough, they harden themselves, and keep on their course defiantly and sacrilegiously, until they sink so far as to become enemies of the Word of God, become blind and deaf, so unblessed and accursed that they are of no service in any vocation of life, and can do nothing that is wholesome and good or useful to the pleasure and improvement of others.

All comes from this that men are bent on being rich. Such covetousness and cares do assuredly keep company with a pride that makes men aim at being something great and powerful. Covetousness would appropriate everything to itself. It would at first have this house, this field, this castle, this village. It grows greater and greater till it becomes a dragon's tail that draws everything after it. Where covetousness has once become rooted, it daily brings forth cares of a hundred different kinds; there the human heart boils and bubbles with countless insatiable lusts and desires that serve no other purpose than its own destruction, and springs from no other source than man's fall from faith, and thence from one temptation and snare to another. It is a dreadful plague that has taken such thorough possession of men that, on account of it, they can do nothing good or useful, and can no longer have any thought of serving God or man. The curse has already been pronounced that he shall never be satisfied and that he must endure all sorts of misfortune and heartaches through the very things he has coveted to his everlasting destruction.

August 14th - Luke 5:10

And Jesus said unto Simon, Fear not; from henceforth you shall catch men.

That Peter is not alarmed on account of his unworthiness and sins is an abundant comfort and grace. He is not only to have the forgiveness of sins, but is also to know that God intends to accomplish still greater things through him by making him a help and comfort to others. What Christ would say is, That which you have accomplished by the draught of fishes is much to little; really, it is nothing at all. you are henceforth to become a different kind of fisherman, in a different sea, with a different net and boat. I am going to engage you in a business which shall be called "catching men." This means that throughout the entire world, you are to draw away souls from the power of the devil into the kingdom of God. Then only will you become the sort of man that can help others, even as you yourself has been helped.

From this gospel let us rightly comprehend and grasp Christ and the power of his comfort, that we may comfort both ourselves and others, and may instruct and remind the consciences which are in distress and fear that may by no means run or flee away from Christ, but may much rather flee to him and wait for his comfort. Thus to fear and run away is nothing else than to drive your own salvation and happiness away from you. Christ has not come to make you afraid, but to remove your sins and distress from you. Nor does he draw nigh and follow after you to drive you away, but that he may kindly allure you to himself. "Fear not" speaks to your heart, and to the hearts of all troubled consciences, and pronounces absolution from all sins and removes all fear. He will grant you a still richer grace by making you such a holy, blessed and useful man in his kingdom that you can be of comfort to others and can bring those to him who like yourself are now full of fear and in need of comfort and grace. Here you see how a man is delivered from spiritual poverty and distress through Christ's Word. He obtains forgiveness of sins and peace of conscience with increase of spiritual gifts through the grace of Christ.

August 15th - Luke 5:4

When he had left speaking, he said unto Simon, Launch out into the deep, and let down your nets for a draught.

When Christ wished to bestow his gifts upon Peter and the others he did not cause the fish to leap into the boat without labor or nets, as he very well might have done. He commanded them to put out into the deep and let down their nets. They are to engage in the handicraft they understood and were accustomed to. Christ keeps aloof from the lazy, unfaithful idlers who will not do as they have been commanded, and will not keep their hands and feet from straying. Thus he teaches a twofold lesson, that he will not give us anything unless we work for it, and that the things that we obtain do not come from our work, but from God's help and blessing. You are to work, but you are not to depend upon that work, as if that which resulted from it were of your own accomplishment.

Our work produces and bestows nothing. Yet it is necessary as a means through which we may receive what God gives. The disciples must use their hands to let down the nets and draw them in, if they wish to secure anything, and must be willing to do so. Yet they must acknowledge that their labor did not bring about the result, otherwise they would have succeeded without Christ in the first place. He permits them to make a trial and discover by experience that the toil of this entire night has been in vain and to no purpose.

This he teaches us by daily experience in all kinds of affairs and doings on earth. Very often he permits us to labor long and arduously without results, till it becomes bitterly painful to us, and we are forced to complain with Peter: "We have toiled all night, and have taken nothing." This he does that we may not venture to depend upon our labor, but may know that he must grant it success, and that we have not secured this through our own efforts, skill, or diligence. All human life and nature are such that, until God gives the increase, we may often labor long and much to no purpose. But the work is not to cease on that account, nor should any man be found without work. God giveth the increase.

August 16th - 2 Corinthians 3:5

Our sufficiency is of God.

These words are blows and thrusts at the false apostles and preachers. We rely not upon ourselves or our wisdom and ability, Paul would say; we preach not what we ourselves have invented. But this is our boast and trust in Christ before God, that we have made of you a divine epistle; have written upon your hearts, not our thoughts, but the Word of God. We are not glorifying our own power, but the works and power of him who has called and equipped us for such an office; from whom proceeds all you have heard and believed.

It is a glory which every preacher may claim, to be able to say with full confidence of heart: This trust have I toward God in Christ, that what I teach and preach is truly the Word of God. Likewise when he performs other official duties in the Church—baptizes a child, absolves and comforts a sinner—it must be done in the same firm conviction that such is the command of Christ. Who would teach and exercise authority in the Church without this glory, "it were better for him that a millstone were hanged about his neck, and that he were drowned in the depths of the sea." For the devil's lies is what he preaches, and death is what he effects.

God puts into our heart and mouth what we should say, and impresses it upon your heart through the Holy Spirit. We cannot ascribe to ourselves any honor, cannot seek our own glory as the self-instructed, proud spirits do; me must give to God the honor, and must glory in the fact that by his grace and power he works in you unto salvation through the office committed unto us. Nothing should be taught and practiced in the Church but what is unquestionably God's Word. Man's achievements, man's reasoning and power, are of no avail in spiritual matters save in so far as they come from God. For it is of no moment that men observe our greatness and ability; the important thing is that poor souls may rest assured of being presented with God's Word and works, whereby they may be saved.

August 17th - Romans 8:13

If you through the Spirit do mortify the deeds of the body, you shall live.

Here the apostle confesses that even in the Christian there is a remnant of the flesh, that must be put to death—all manner of temptation and lusts in opposition to God's commandments. These are active in the flesh and prompt to sin. They are here called the "deeds of the body." Of this nature are thoughts of unbelief and distrust, coldness and indolence with respect to God's Word and prayer, carnal security and presumption instead of the fear of God, impatience and murmurings under suffering, anger and vindictiveness, or envy and hatred against our neighbor, avarice, unchastity and the like. Such inclinations as these dwell in flesh and blood and cease not to move and tempt man. Because of human infirmity they at times overtake him when he is not careful enough about transgression. They will surely overpower him unless he resolutely opposes them, and puts to death these "deeds of the body." To do this means a severe struggle, a battle, which never abates, nor ceases as long as we live. The Christian dare never become slothful or negligent in this matter. He must constantly put to death the flesh lest he himself be put to death by it.

This constitutes the difference between those who are Christians and sanctified and those who are without faith and the Holy Spirit, or who grieve and lose the Spirit. For although believers, as well as unbelievers, are not wholly free from the sinful lusts of the flesh, they yet remain in repentance and the fear of God; they hold fast to the belief that their sins are forgiven for Christ's sake, because they do not yield to them, but resist them. Therefore they continue under forgiveness, and their remaining infirmity is not fatal, nor damning to them as it is to those who, without repentance and faith, go on in carnal security and purposely follow their evil lusts against their own conscience, casting away from themselves both faith and the Holy Spirit. Having received the Holy Spirit, Christians are to comfort themselves with the fact that they have help and strength to resist and mortify sin.

August 18th - Genesis 6:21

Take you unto you of all food that is eaten, and you shall gather it to you; and it shall be for food for you, and for them.

As the flood was to last a whole year, it was necessary to remind Noah of the food to be collected from the herbs and the fruits of the trees in order to preserve the life of man and of animals. Though the wrath of God was terrible to the destruction of everything born on earth, yet the goodness of the Lord shines forth in this awful calamity. He looks to the preservation of man and the animals, and through their preservation to that of the species. The animals chosen for preservation received food suitable to their nature. As for man he did not yet use flesh for food. He ate only of the vegetation of the earth, which was far more desirable before the flood than at present, after the remarkable corruption of the earth through the brackish waters.

It would have been an easy matter for God to preserve Noah and the animals for the space of a full year without food, as he preserved Moses, Elijah and Christ without food. But God in the government of the things created allows them to perform their functions. In other words, God performs his miracles along the lines of natural law. God also requires that we do not discard the provisions of nature, which would mean to tempt God, but that we use the things God has prepared for us with thanksgiving. A hungry man, who looks for bread from heaven, rather than tries to obtain it by human means, commits sin. Christ commands the apostles to eat what is set before them. Noah is here enjoined to employ the ordinary methods of gathering food. God did not command him to expect in the ark a miraculous supply of food from heaven.

The life of the monks is all a temptation of God. They abstain from certain meats, though God has created them to be received with thanksgiving by them that believe, and by those who know the truth, that every creature of God is good and nothing to be rejected, if it be received with thanksgiving.

We observe here the providence of God, by whose counsel the evil are punished and the good saved. By a miracle God preserves a portion of his creatures, when he punishes the wicked, and graciously makes provision for their posterity.

August 19th - Genesis 6:22

Thus did Noah; according to all that God commanded him, so did he.

This is the first passage in which praise for obedience to God is clothed in such a form of words. Later we find it stated repeatedly that Moses and the people did according to all that God commanded them. But Noah received commendation as an example for us. His was not a dead faith, which is no faith at all, but a living and active faith. He renders obedience to God's commands, because he believes both God's promises and threats; and he carefully carries out what God commanded with reference to the ark, the gathering of the animals and the food. This is unique praise for Noah's faith, that he remains on the royal road—adds nothing, changes nothing and takes nothing from the divine command, but abides absolutely in the precept he has heard.

It is the most common and the most noxious sin in the Church, that people either altogether change God's commands, or render something else paramount to them. They sin who swerve too much to the left by failing to perform the divine commands. Those who swerve to the right and do more than God has commanded, like Saul when he spared the Amalekites, sin even more grievously. They add a sham piety. While those who err on the left cannot excuse their error, these do not hesitate to ascribe to themselves remarkable merit, and such error is exceedingly common. God is wont sometimes to command common, ridiculous and even offensive things; but reason delights in splendid things. From the common ones it shrinks or undertakes them under protest. Thus the monks shrank from home duties and chose for themselves others, apparently of greater glamor. To-day the great throng, hearing that common tasks are preached in the gospel, despise it as a common thing and lacking in elegance. Such is the madness of man's wisdom.

Hence Moses rightly commends Noah's obedience when he says that he did everything the Lord had enjoined. That means to give God credit for wisdom and goodness. Noah kept his eye on the majesty of him who gave the command. That was enough for him, even though the command be absurd and apparently impossible. All such objections he passes by and takes his stand upon the one thing commanded by God.

August 20th - Philippians 4:7

The peace of God, which passes all understanding, shall keep your hearts and minds through Christ Jesus.

This is the true peace that satisfies and quiets the heart; not in times when no adversity is at hand, but in the midst of it, when outwardly there is nothing but strife. This is the difference between worldly and spiritual peace. Worldly peace consists in removing the outward evil that disturbs the peace; when enemies besiege a city there is no peace; but when they depart peace returns. Such is the case in poverty and sickness. While they afflict you, you are discontented; but when they are removed and there is health and plenty, there is peace and rest again. He who experiences this peace is not changed, being just as faint-hearted whether the evil be present or not; only he feels it and is frightened when it is present.

Christian or spiritual peace, however, just turns the thing about, so that outwardly the evil remains, as enemies, sickness, poverty, sin, death and the devil. These are there and never desist, encompassing us on every side; nevertheless, within there is peace, strength and comfort in the heart, so that the heart cares for no evil, is really bolder and more joyful in its presence than in its absence. Therefore it is peace which passes and transcends all understanding and all the senses. Reason cannot grasp any peace except worldly or external peace; it knows not how to comfort or satisfy a person in times of affliction. But when the Spirit comes, he lets the outward adversity remain, but strengthens the person, making the timid fearless, changing the troubled into a quiet, peaceful conscience.

Whence does he receive this? From his faith in Christ. For if I truly believe in the Lord from the depth of my heart, so that it can truly say: My Lord Christ has by his resurrection conquered my need, my sin, death and all evil, and will be with and in me; it is impossible for me to be faint-hearted and timid, no matter how much sin and death oppress me. If you look to Christ and believe on him, no evil that may befall you is so great that it can harm you and cause you to despair. Therefore it is impossible for the fruit of peace to be absent where faith is.

August 21st - Luke 6:36

Be you therefore merciful, as your Father also is merciful.

How is God our heavenly Father merciful? In this that he gives us all things, natural and spiritual, temporal and eternal, gratuitously and out of pure goodness. For should he give unto us according to our merits, he would have to give us only eternal condemnation. Therefore what he gives us in our possessions and honor is given out of pure mercy. He sees that we are captives of death; he is merciful and gives us life. He sees that we are the children of hell; but he is merciful and gives us heaven. He sees that we are poor, naked and exposed, hungry and thirsty; but he is merciful and clothes, feeds and gives us drink, and satisfies us with all good things. Thus, whatever we have, for the body or spirit, he gives us out of mercy, and pours his blessings over us and into us. Therefore Christ says: Imitate your Father and be also merciful as he is merciful.

This is not a common mercy, nor one that reason teaches. For that is selfish; it gives to the great and learned; it loves those who are beautiful; it gives to those from whom it has some benefit or advantage. It is a politic, beggarly, piece-meal mercy. Christians must not seek their own, but look at all alike, whether friend or foe, as our heavenly Father does. Where this mercy is not, there is also no true faith. For if your heart is not in the state of faith so that you know your God has revealed himself to you as good and merciful, without any merit on your part, while you were still an enemy and a child of wrath; if you believe this, you cannot refrain from showing yourself in like manner to your neighbor, and do all, out of the love of God, for your neighbor's welfare. Therefore see to it that you make no distinction between friend and foe, the worthy and the unworthy. This has been said of faith and works, namely, that the motion of faith is inwards and upwards, of works, outward and downward. For thus we are righteous before God and men, in that we honor God and look direct to him and believe according to his Word, and in love do what we can for our neighbor.

August 22nd - Luke 5:8

When Simon Peter saw it, he fell down at Jesus' knees, saying, Depart from me; for I am a sinful man, O' Lord.

A sinful conscience is apt to do just as Peter does here, flee from its Saviour, and think: O' God, I am not worthy to be saved and sit among the saints and angels! That treasure is far too high for me! But this is foolish; for should you establish yourself upon your own holiness, you would build on the sand. Not until Peter considered himself unworthy did he become really worthy. Just because you are a sinful person you must the more trust in God. In this matter you must open wide and greatly expand your heart that grace may freely flow into it.

It is proper that you know yourself, and the more thoroughly you do this, the better it is; but you must not on that account reject grace because of your sins. If you find that your conscience troubles you and would drive you to despair, you are most fortunate; then you will find consolation in the words of Micah and say: "Who is a God like unto you, that pardons iniquity and casteth our sins into the depths of the sea?" All gods that do not take away sin are idols. These wish to discover righteousness, but the Lord God brings it. Therefore when your God comes to you and your conscience feels its sins, you must not despair. The more you feel your disgrace, the quicker God imparts grace.

The Scriptures praise God because he takes away sins and casts them into the depths of the sea. Gods says: "I, even I, am he that blotteth out your transgressions for mine own sake; I will not remember your sins." We cannot become rid of our sins by our works, nor become righteous by means of any power within ourselves. God will do that without merit and without works, out of pure grace. Therefore the more you feel that you are a sinful man and the more you wish to flee from God, the more you should press toward him. Do not desist, but approach God with renewed confidence and hold fast to him.

August 23rd - James 1:20

The wrath of man works not the righteousness of God.

To God alone belong honor, judgment, and vengeance, hence also wrath. But I fear this will not be done as long as we are in this life, and yet it would be grace, if we only became so pious as to make a beginning; for as soon as we suffer an injury, flesh and blood at once act as flesh and blood; we begin to rage and rave in anger and impatience. It is natural for us to feel hurt when suffering, injustice and violence attack us, hence it becomes necessary to check and restrain the feelings of anger and to resist them.

The feeling that you are injured will pass away, but that desire to avenge yourself in any way is prohibited. If you cannot secure your rights without doing greater harm, let it go. It is not good to check or punish one wrong with another, nor is God willing to have universal justice perish because of your petty claims.

We know that God has committed the judiciary to the civil government and to that end established princes and lords, who bear the sword in God's stead. Aside from this they are personally exactly like the other people are, having no more right to be angry than anyone else. The judge or executioner, in condemning and executing a man that never personally did them an injury, does so in God's stead, officiating in God's place, inasmuch as the malefactor has become liable to God's sentence and penalty. There should be no anger, nor bitterness in man's heart, while God's wrath and sword accomplish their work.

The same holds good in war, when you must defend yourself, thrust, beat and burn, then wrath and revenge are likely to reign supreme, and yet it should not proceed from the heart of man, but emanate from divine authority and command, so that the wicked be punished and peace be maintained. Hence where such wrath exists it is not to be called man's wrath, but God's. When unhappily you commingle God's and man's wrath, it is the miserable doings of the devil. Thus the wrath of man is at all times full of envy to his neighbor, but God's wrath is administered according to his command and springs from a good heart, that deplores the fact that man should suffer any ill, and yet God must punish and abolish wickedness.

August 24th - Romans 8:14

For as many as are led by the Spirit of God, they are the sons of God.

Like ourselves, Paul had to deal with two classes of people, the true and the false Christians. There is not so much danger from the adversaries of the doctrine; their opposition is so open that we can readily beware of them. But since the devil sows his seed among us who are called Christians and boast of the gospel, it behooves us to take heed of those who claim to be Christians. It is easy enough to boast of God and of Christ and of the Spirit. But whether such boasting has any foundation depends on whether or not the Spirit so works and rules in us as to subdue and mortify sin. For where the Spirit is, there assuredly he is not idle, nor powerless. He proves his presence by ruling and directing man and prevailing on him to obey and follow his promptings.

To be "led by the Spirit of God" means to be given a heart which gladly hears God's Word and believes that in Christ it has grace and the forgiveness of sins; a heart which confesses and proves its faith before the world; a heart which seeks, above all things, the glory of God, and endeavors to live without giving offense, to serve others and to be obedient, patient, pure and chaste, mild and gentle; a heart which, though at times overtaken in a fault, and may stumble, soon rises again by repentance and ceases to sin. All these things the Holy Spirit teaches one if he hears and receives the Word, and does not willfully resist the Spirit.

The devil, who is also a spirit, persuades the hearts of the worldlings; but it soon becomes evident that his work is not that of a good or divine spirit. For he leads men to do the reverse of that which the Spirit of God leads them to do; they find no pleasure in hearing and obeying God's Word, but despise God, and become proud and haughty, avaricious, unmerciful. Let everyone therefore take heed that he deceive not himself. For there are many who claim to be Christians and are not. We perceive this from the fact that not all are led by the Spirit of God.

August 25th - Ephesians 4:1

I therefore, the prisoner of the Lord, beseech you that you walk worthy of the vocation wherewith you are called.

The chief thing that should influence a Christian's outward walk is the remembrance of his calling and appointment by God. He should be mindful why he is called a Christian, and live consistently. He must shine before the world; that is, through his life and God's work, the Word and the name of Christ the Lord must be exalted. Paul would say: "You have received God's grace and his Word and are a blessed people. In Christ all your needs are happily supplied. Be mindful of this and remember you are called to a far different and vastly higher life than others know. Show by your manner of living that you seek a higher good than the world seeks, that you have, indeed, received far greater blessings. Let your lives honor and glorify the Lord who has given you such blessings.

The so-called Christian life that does not honor Christ makes its sin the more heinous for the name it bears. Every sin the people of God commit is a provocation of Jehovah; not only in the act of disobedience itself, but also in the transgression of the second commandment. The enormity of the sin is magnified by the conditions that make it a blasphemy of God's name and an occasion of offense to others. Paul says, "The name of God is blasphemed among the Gentiles because of you." So a Christian should by all means guard the honor of God in his life. He must take heed that he be not guilty of blaspheming that name and of doing wickedness. The devil, aided by the world, construes every act, when possible, to reflect upon God's honor and glory. His purpose is to injure the Church by charging offenses, thus deterring unbelievers from embracing the gospel and causing the weak to fall away.

To guard against such disaster, Christians should be particularly careful to give no occasion for offense in their conduct, and to value the name and honor of their God too highly to permit blasphemy of them. Let them remember that upon keeping sacred the name and honor of God depends their own standing before God and men. God promises, "Them that honor me will I honor."

August 26th - Genesis 8:22

While the earth remains, seedtime and harvest, and cold and heat, and summer and winter, and day and night shall not cease.

Following this text, the Jews divide the year into six parts, each comprising two months. But it seems to me that Moses simply speaks of the promise that we need not fear another general flood. During the time of the flood such confusion reigned that there was no season, either of seedtime or harvest, and by reason of the great darkness caused by the clouds and the rain, day could not readily be distinguished from night. The meaning is simply that God here promises Noah the imminent restoration of the earth, so that the fields might again be sowed; that the desolation caused by the flood should be no more; that the seasons would run their course in accordance with regular law, harvest following seedtime, winter following summer, cold following heat in due order.

This text should be carefully remembered in view of the common notions concerning the signs before the last day. Some declare there will be eclipses of ever so many days' duration. They say foolishly that for seven years not a single child will be born. But this text declares that neither day, nor night, neither summer, nor winter, shall cease; therefore these natural changes will go on, and there will never be an eclipse which will rob human eyes of an entire day.

Nor is it a phrase devoid of meaning when he says, "While the earth remains," for he gives us to understand that the days of this earth shall sometime be numbered, and other days, days of heaven, shall follow. As long as the days of the earth endure, so long shall the earth abide and with it the rotation of seasons. But when these days of the earth shall pass, then all these things shall cease, and then shall follow days of heaven, that is eternal days. Then shall be one Sabbath after the other, when we shall not be engrossed with bodily labor for the purpose of gaining a livelihood; for we shall be as the angels of God. Our life will be to know God, to delight in God's wisdom and to enjoy the presence of God. This life we attain through faith in Christ, in which may the eternal Father mercifully keep us, through the merit of his Son, our Saviour, Jesus Christ, by the ruling and guidance of the Holy Spirit.

August 27th - Mark 8:2

I have compassion on the multitude, because they have now been with me three days, and have nothing to eat.

Behold, what a sympathetic Christ we have, who even provides food for us. Here new hope is awakened and man is comforted through the words of Christ, when he says: Here they are and listen to me until the third day. I must now give them also what they need. Here you see that all who faithfully cling to the Word of God will be fed by God; for that is the nature and power of faith, which flows alone out of the Word of God.

Therefore let us make a beginning to believe; for unbelief is the cause of all sin and vice, which now abounds in all stations of life. How does it come to pass that everywhere there are so many foolish women and rogues, so many rank impostors, thieves, robbers, usurers, murderers, and sellers of indulgences? It all comes from unbelief. For such men judge alone according to human reason, and the reason judges only according to that which it sees; what it does not see it does not wish to accept.

But Christ wishes to set before us a twofold picture, namely, one of faith, that we should not be overanxious; and also a picture of love, that as he does to us, is anxious about our welfare, feeds and clothes us out of free love, not for the sake of his own advantage or because of our worthiness; so we should also do to our neighbor, freely and gratuitously, out of pure love. This is beautifully portrayed in the visible picture of the four thousand men who cling to God by a faith which says: God will indeed feed us. They commend themselves to God and freely lay all their need upon him. Then Christ comes, before they have any care and before they ask him to come, takes all more to heart than they do themselves, and says to his disciples, "I have compassion on the multitude." In this confidence and hope let your faith run its course, acknowledge that God is your friend, flee to him in greatest need; believe and expect it and he will help you; this you should not doubt. In harmony with this you should serve your neighbor freely and gratuitously.

August 28th - Mark 8:8

They did eat, and were filled: and they took up of the broken meat that was left seven baskets.

It is God's will that we do not squander his gifts uselessly; but be economical and prudent with them, and use the abundance which he gives faithfully for our benefits and needs, and preserve them for the future, when we may have further use for them. That is honoring the precious food and not permitting the crumbs to lie under the table; just as our fathers taught their children from this example and added the proverb: "He who saves when he has will find when he needs." It is a malignant, shameless vice and great contempt of the gifts of God, that the world is now flooded with cloisters, pomp and expenditure of money for everything far beyond its ability to pay. From this then must follow such robbing, stealing, usury, hoarding and pinching by which the country and the people, rulers and subjects, are ruined as a punishment.

We should not shamefully expend and destroy that which we have in abundance and cannot enjoy either in our need or in our pleasure. If such is expended and destroyed in an unchristian manner, the poor have not only their little torn from their teeth by our greed, but we even merit that God does not permit us to enjoy that which we have raked together, extorted and saved by pinching. The jaws of avarice can devour the property of a prince faster than a whole city can give it to him, and yet no person is happy or better because of it. A prince must have more for banking, for sports, for display in dress than his people and country can afford. Consequently there is lack everywhere in those things we need for the Church and the school, for government and the common advantage of all, for our nourishment and necessities.

It can no more be called enjoying the gifts of God, which he gives so richly and abundantly to the end for us to enjoy; for man will not use them in the praise of God and enjoy them for himself, but only for the dishonor of God and for the destruction of the blessings given. No one has any thought of saving anything for posterity, but all live as if they rejoiced in destroying everything at once. But in all this destruction God will nevertheless help us, since we have no other desire.

August 29th - Matthew 7:15

Beware of false prophets, which come to you in sheep's clothing, but inwardly they are ravening wolves.

We should well consider this passage, for Christ our Lord here commands and gives all Christians the power to be judges of all doctrine, and he gives them power to judge what is right and what is not. It is now well on a thousand years that this passage has been perverted by false Christians, that we have had no power to judge, but had to accept what the pope and the councils determined without any judgment of our own. Either the gospel lies or the pope and the councils do. Christ says, we have the right to judge all doctrines, and whatever is proposed for us to keep or reject. The Lord does not speak to the pope here, but to all Christians. As the doctrine, "Whatsoever you would that men should do to you, do you even so to them," is proclaimed to all; so likewise the words, "Beware of false prophets," exclude no one.

Hence I say, Pope, you and the councils have resolved, and now I have to decide whether I may accept it or not, because you will not stand and answer for me when I die, but I must see to it myself how I stand before God, so that I may be certain of my fate. You must be certain in regard to this matter, that it is God's Word, as certain and more so than you are that you are living, for on this alone your conscience must rest. God commands his Word to be told you through men, and especially has he permitted it to be proclaimed and written for you by the apostles, who did not preach their own word, but God's Word. Surely a person can preach the Word to me, but no one is able to put it into my heart except God alone, who must speak to the heart, or all is in vain; when he is silent the Word is not spoken. Hence no one shall draw me from the Word which God teaches me.

All this you must now believe, not as a word that Peter preached, but the Word that God has commanded you to believe. You must return to the gospel and observe where the foundation has its source; you must be judges and have the power to judge over all things that are offered you. But no one can judge false doctrine, except the man who is spiritual.

August 30th - Matthew 7:20

Wherefore by their fruits you shall know them.

No one knows others by their fruits, except he who is born again. Therefore he who has not the Spirit cannot have this knowledge. The fruit by which we are to know them is unbelief. One can know them to some extent by open sins, yet this judgment is deceptive, for Christians also fall. Hence the fruit by which they are known is an inner fruit, and I must have the Holy Spirit and judge according to his guidance. The fleshly eye and reason are not sufficient. You may see two persons go to the Lord's Supper, the one is a believer, the other not, and yet their external work is the same. What then makes the difference? Faith in the heart and unbelief, because the one regards it as a good work, the other not. Tauler said that believers and unbelievers were often so similar in external appearance that no one could distinguish them, nor is reasonable to judge unless we have the Spirit of God. For this reason the decision and judgment of spiritual things should not be based on external things, as on the work and person, but on the inner condition of the heart. The fruits and the good works do not make any one pious or good; but he must first be good and pious at heart. The apples do not make the tree, but the tree must be there before the fruit.

If I understand this, then I notice that there is no work so bad as necessarily to condemn a man, nor none so good as to save him. Faith alone saves us, and unbelief alone condemns us. The deed of the adulterer does not condemn him; the adultery only shows that he has fallen from the faith, and this condemns him. Nothing makes any one good but faith, and nothing makes one wicked but unbelief. The tree shall be cut down; he does not say, the fruit shall be cut down. Thus the works of love do not make me good, but faith, in which I do these works and bear this fruit. We must begin with faith, but the pope begins with works, just as though I could bear apples before I was an apple tree. Thus unbelief is the foundation of all sin.

August 31st - 2 Corinthians 3:6

Who (God) has made us able ministers of the new testament; not of the letter, but of the spirit: for the letter kills, but the spirit gives life.

The "letter" is the whole law of Moses, or the doctrine of the ten commandments, which teach how we should obey God, honor parents, love our neighbors, and the like—the very best doctrine to be found in all books, sermons and schools. There is another message, which Paul terms the "ministration of a new covenant or of the Spirit." This doctrine does not teach what works are required of man; but it makes known to him what God would do for him and bestow upon him, indeed what he has already done; he has given his Son Christ for us; because, for our disobedience to the law, which no man fulfils, we were under God's wrath and condemnation. Christ made satisfaction for our sins, effected a reconciliation with God and gave to us his own righteousness. This doctrine is revealed through the Holy Spirit. The Holy Spirit works in the hearts of them who hear and accept the doctrine. Therefore this ministration is termed the ministration "of the Spirit."

It is of design that the apostle does not term the two dispensations "law" and "gospel," but names them according to the respective effects produced. For it is impossible to keep the law without Christ, though man may, for the sake of honor or property, or from fear of punishment, feign outward holiness. The heart which does not discern God's grace in Christ cannot turn to God, nor trust in him; it cannot love his commandments and delight in them, but rather resists them. Therefore, God would have his gospel message unceasingly urged as the means of awakening man's heart to discern his state and recall the grace and lovingkindness of God, with the result that the power of the Holy Spirit is increased constantly. No influence of the law, no work of man is present here. The force is a new and heavenly one—the power of the Holy Spirit. He impresses upon the heart Christ and his works, making it a true book which does not consist in tracing mere letters and words, but in true life and action.

September 1st - Mark 7:33, 34

He took him aside from the multitude, and put his fingers into his ears, and he spit, and touched his tongue; and looking up to heaven, he sighed, and said unto him, Ephiphas a, that is, Be opened.

The people bring the poor man to the Lord, who takes him aside, lays his fingers into his ears, spits and touches his tongue with spittle, looks up toward heaven, and sighing says, Ephiphas a, that is, be opened. This is a lovely picture. Those who bring the deaf-mute to the Lord signify the office of the ministry. Apostles and ministers lead the poor consciences of men to God.

This is done in three ways, by preaching, by a godly life and by intercession. With the preaching of the Word, though it be by a sinner, men are brought to God; a godly life serves to show the Word so much the mightier in its power; to pray for the people leads them on the road to faith and works.

If the Word thus goes on its way in a threefold manner, it cannot fail to bring forth fruit. God says, "My Word, that goes forth out of my mouth, shall not return unto me void." This is indicated by the bringing of the deaf-mute into Christ's presence. The ministers bring the sinners before God, who opens their eyes, ears and mouth. When persons are thus brought to God, he gives them grace to believe. By laying his fingers into the man's ears Jesus signifies that through the Word he breathes the Holy Spirit into him, and makes the heart believing, chaste and holy. The spittle laid on the man's tongue typifies the Word of God which is put into his mouth that he may be able to speak it. For wherever there is true faith, the Spirit will give you no peace. "I believe," says David, "therefore have I spoken."

That Christ takes the man aside and looks up to heaven teaches us that such power must come from heaven, working in the heart of man by divine power. Thus we must first hear the Word of God and, through the intercession of Christ, obtain faith. Then we will publicly confess and praise God forever.

September 2nd - 1 John 3:17

Whoever has this world's good, and sees his brother have need, and shuts up his bowels of compassion from him, how the love of God dwells in him?

John uses an illustration plain enough for anyone to understand, and from which we may judge that the soul wanting in small duties will be deficient in great ones. According to the apostle, if one possesses this world's goods and sees his neighbor in want, being able to render assistance without injury to himself, and closes his heart against him, not assisting him even with the slightest work of love, how can the love of God dwell in him, since he appreciates it so little that he will not spare his needy brother a penny? How can he be expected to render a greater service—to lay down his life for his brother? What right has such a soul to boast that Christ has laid down his life for him and delivered him from death?

Frequently people are found who have this world's goods and are able to help the needy, yet close their hearts against the unfortunate. Where shall we find in imperial courts, among kings, princes and lords, any who extend a helping hand to the needy Church in the maintenance of the poor, of the ministry, and of schools? How would they measure up in the greater duty of laying down their lives for the brethren, and especially for the Christian Church?

But the merely selfish may well escape our censure in comparison to those who not only close their purses to the poor, but shamelessly and forcibly deprive and rob their needy neighbor of his own by overreaching, by fraud, oppression and extortion; who take from the Church the property rightfully hers and especially reserved for her. Not only is the papistical rabble of to-day guilty of such sin, but many who would be known as evangelical practice the same fraud with reference to the parochial estates and general property of the Church, and tyrannically harass and torment the poor ministers. But oh, how heavy and terrible the impending judgment for those who have denied to Christ the Lord in his thirst even the cup of cold water. Therefore let him who would prove himself a Christian show himself such by his deeds and works.

September 3rd - Exodus 20:3

You shall have no other gods before me.

The Jews abstained outwardly from idolatry, but their hearts were far from God, full of mistrust and unbelief. Outwardly they appeared beautiful, as though they meant it in all sincerity, but within they were full of idolatry. They understood this law to mean no more than that they should not set up idols and images to worship, and when they could confess with their lips that they have only one God and honor no other gods, they thought they had kept this commandment.

Now we must have high regard for the law. Thou, thou, it says, thou, and everything you are; especially does it mean the heart, the soul, and all the powers. It does not speak of the tongue, or the hands, or the knees; but it speaks of the whole body and of all you have and art. If I am to have no other God, then I must surely possess the only true God with my heart, I must in my heart be affectionate to him, evermore cleave to him, depend upon him, trust him, have my desire, love and joy in him, and always think of him. You shall love God with all your heart, so that your whole body from the crown of the head to the soles of the feet, inwardly and outwardly, goes forth in love, rejoices in God and honors him.

Now find me a man who is chaste and otherwise pious with a burning passion and love; there is none such on the earth. We find ourselves much more inclined to anger, hatred, envy, worldly pleasures. You see, you poor condemned creature, you should have delighted in God's law, and you have no pleasure in it. Had we now remained in this condemnation, we would have had to perish forever. Therefore Christ comes and offers his mercy, and says: You are to love God with all your heart, but you have not done it; now believe in me. Then when we come before God the Father, Christ will say: Father! Although they have not wholly fulfilled your law, yet I have done so, let this be to their benefit because they believe in me.

September 4th - Matthew 13:16

Blessed are your eyes, for they see: and your ears, for they hear.

Christ spoke these words especially to his disciples at the time when he was greatly moved with spiritual delight and praised his heavenly Father for the revelation of the gospel. He was especially anxious to speak with them because their own salvation also depended upon that revelation. They are nothing more than words of thanksgiving that the disciples lived in the time of the revelation of the gospel, which brings deliverance and salvation from sin and misery to the world. The beloved prophets had prophesied of this time in a glorious manner, they longed for it beyond measure. Therefore, he would say, you are blessed and more than blessed; for you now enjoy the truly golden year, the pure kingdom of grace and the blessed time; only be careful that you retain it and make good use of it.

On the one hand he exhorts to thanksgiving for such grace; and on the other he laments over the great ingratitude of the world, because there are so few people who know and receive this grace, and many even despise it. Therefore Christ especially turned to his disciples and praised them, as though he wished to say: Your eyes and ears are indeed blessed, which see and hear this gospel grace; alas, there are many eyes and ears that do not wish to see and hear it, although they have it right before them. This is a great and superabundant treasure, but the great mass of the people only despise it, and even persecute it.

But the blessed treasure really depends upon a right seeing and hearing; for it is plainly revealed and stands in the clear light before their eyes. But the great mass cannot see nor understand it. What did it help the Pharisees that Christ himself preached the gospel to them? What would it help all the fanatics and critics if forgiveness of sins were preached twice as clearly as it is? They are so completely chilled and choked with thoughts of their own conceits and pleasures dear to them that they can neither see nor hear anything else. But these are indeed blessed eyes and ears that can make a right use of the blessed time or dispensation of the gospel, and know what God has given them in it.

September 5th - Mark 8:6

He commanded the people to sit down on the ground: and he took the seven loaves, and gave thanks, and brake, and gave to his disciples to set before them; and they did set them before the people.

Christ commands the disciples to set the loaves before the multitude, by which he shows that he will administer his work and gifts through the instrumentality of human agencies. He thus teaches those who have an office or commission and those who stand before others faithfully and conscientiously to serve the people in obedience to Christ by cheerfully and meekly giving of their own and imparting to others what God entrusted and gave to them. Especially would he teach them to be useful and bring comfort to the poor flock of Christians by their good example of faith and love in order to strengthen their faith and love. He here shows how he gives and will give rich blessings to the end that such office and service may accomplish much good, and bring forth much fruit.

Let us also learn that the gifts and good things which God gives, are not profaned, if they are used in helping the poor in acts of charity, as Christ promises when he says: "Give, and it shall be given unto you; good measure, pressed down, and shaken together, and running over, shall men give into your bosom." This has been experienced by many pious people everywhere who have liberally given before our time for the support of the ministerial office, schools, the poor and the like. God gave to them for so doing good times, peace and quiet. Hence arise the proverbs among the people which have been confirmed: One loses no time by going to church; giving alms does not impoverish; possessions unjustly gotten bring no blessing.

But the world will not believe this. It goes on with its raking and scraping together of riches and will let no one be satisfied with what he has; every man desires more than his fellow and seeks riches by robbing, stealing and oppressing the poor. It is evident from this that there is no blessing in such riches; but only the curse of God, misery, misfortune and agony of heart. Therefore a Christian should think much more of a dollar that God gives him than of all the great treasures of the rich misers upon the earth. He has this beautiful treasure in his home which is called godliness, a peaceful quiet heart in God.

September 6th - Matthew 7:21

Not everyone that said unto me, Lord, Lord, shall enter into the kingdom of heaven; but he that does the will of my Father which is in heaven.

If we are to do God's will, we must first know for a certainty what it is, and how to do it. This our own wisdom and thoughts do not teach, or all men, heathen and Turks, could do it as well, and every fanatic would come and pretend that whatever pleases him was God's will. Therefore we must hear God's Word alone, which reveals plainly unto us what the will of God, the Father, is. First that he has sent his only begotten Son into the world to reconcile us sinners unto God by his death, to purify and sanctify us through his blood without our merits; this he has proclaimed to everyone by the gospel, and requires you to believe and accept it. Then, when we have received such grace and salvation, have been baptized into Christ and believe, his will is that we should afterwards live accordingly, obey God and do what is commanded in the ten commandments, everyone in his calling confess God's Word, honor and support it, avoid and flee from sin, be good, patient, chaste, modest, kind, faithful and true.

This God will have preached not only with the mouth, but in the heart and in the deed. Whoever neglects this or teaches, believes and acts contrary, should know that he has not done God's will and is already judged, that he does not belong to the kingdom of heaven, because he is without faith and love. It will do him no good to boast of Christ as though he were serving him faithfully, preached much and did great wonders. On the other hand, if you earnestly do this will of God, cheerfully hear and believe God's Word, honor him and do good to your neighbor, you can bravely and joyfully say before God: Lord, Lord, and comfort yourself with the kingdom of heaven which God has given you. Whether on this account the world reviles and condemns you need not trouble you. For now you hear that God does not wish you to seek praise and honor when you say: Lord, Lord! But you are to do the deed and bear fruit of him, who does the will of God. Then measure all doctrine and life with this rule to the praise of God and you will not be deceived.

September 7th - Luke 17:5

The apostles said unto the Lord, Increase our faith.

There are those who hear and read the gospel and what is said by faith, and immediately conclude that they have a correct conception of what faith is. They think that faith is something which is altogether in their own power to have or not to have, as any other natural human work. When in their hearts they begin to think that the doctrine is right, and believe it is true, they immediately conclude that faith is present. But as soon as they see and feel in themselves and others that no change has taken place, that they remain in their old ways, they conclude that faith is not sufficient, that they must have something more and greater than faith. Then they cry: "Faith alone does not do it." Why? Because there are so many who believe, and are no better than before. Such people are those whom Jude in his epistle calls dreamers, who deceive themselves with their own dreams.

The true faith, of which we speak, cannot be manufactured by our own thoughts, for it is solely a work of God in us without any assistance on our part. It is God's gift and grace. Faith is something very powerful, active, restless, effective, which at once renews a person and regenerates him and leads him altogether into a new manner and character of life, so that it is impossible not to do good without ceasing. Just as natural as it is for the tree to produce fruit, so natural it is for faith to produce good works.

Whoever has not this faith talks but vainly about faith and works, and does not know what he says. For he has not received it; he juggles with lies and applies the Scriptures where they speak of faith and works to his own dreams and false thoughts, which is purely a human work. Whereas the Scriptures attribute both faith and good works not to ourselves, but to God alone. We should therefore despair of ourselves and pray to God for faith as the apostles did. When we have faith we need nothing more, for it brings with it the Holy Spirit, who not only teaches us all things, but also firmly establishes us in them, and leads us through death and hell to heaven.

September 8th - Luke 19:41, 42

When he was come near, he beheld the city, and wept over it, saying, If you had known ... the things which belong to your peace! but now are they hid from thine eyes.

If you only knew what belongs to your peace, you would yet this day consider, and redeem the time. But you are blind and will neglect the opportunity until there shall be neither help, nor counsel. The Jews were stubborn and depended on God's promises. They vainly thought they owned the temple, and that God dwelt there; besides, they thought they had mighty men, money and treasures enough to defy all their enemies. They trusted in their own glory and built their own confidence on a false delusion, which finally deceived and destroyed them.

The Lord, however, saw deeper into the future than they when he said: O Jerusalem! if you had known what I know, you would seek your peace. Peace in the Scriptures means that all things go well with us. You now think you have pleasant days, but if you knew how your enemies will encamp round about you, compass you about and hedge you in on every side, crush you to the ground and demolish all your beautiful buildings, and leave not one stone upon another, you would eagerly accept the Word, which brings solid peace and every blessing to you.

God caused his threat to be executed; the city was besieged at the time of the Easter festival, when the Jews from every land were assembled within the walls of Jerusalem. There were together at that time about three million people. One hundred thousand would have been enough to crowd the city. But all this great multitude God in his wrath intended to bake, melt and weld together into one mass of ruin. The apostles and Christians were all out of the city. They had withdrawn and were scattered in Samaria, Galilee and among the heathen. Thus God separated and saved the good grain and heaped the chaff into one place.

Here let us learn a lesson, for this concerns also us. God has now opened the precious treasures of his holy gospel unto us, by which we can learn God's will. Yet no one will earnestly believe it; we rather despise it and make light of it. God has great patience; he waits to see how we will deal with his gospel; but when we once let the opportunity slip, he will take his Word from us, and then the wrath which consumed the Jews will also consume us.

September 9th - 1 Peter 5:9

Knowing that the same afflictions are accomplished in your brethren that are in the world.

This is a precious and comforting passage, the truth of which Peter learned, not only by inspiration of the Holy Spirit, but from his own experience. One instance of his experience was when, in the high priest's house, he thrice denied his Lord, and soon thereafter fell into such anxiety and despair that he would have followed the traitor Judas had not Christ turned and looked on him. It was for this reason that Christ, so soon after his resurrection, first of all commanded that the glad tidings be announced to Peter.

Weak Christians suffer beyond measure because they are plagued and beset so constantly by the devil. Their afflictions oppress them so sorely that they imagine no one suffers as severely as they do. Especially does this seem the case in the great spiritual temptations which come to those endowed with peculiar gifts and called to positions of prominence in the Church. Thus Paul often laments his great temptations, which the common people do not understand and cannot endure. These sufferings are often such that even the great and strong would languish and wither beneath them, were it not for the comfort God bestows. These troubles grip the heart and consume the very marrow. It is true that temptations differ and come from different sources, and so everyone may imagine his own a peculiar kind, yet the sufferings and temptations of all Christians are alike in this, that the devil tries to drive them all from the fear of and confidence in God into unbelief, contempt, hatred, and blasphemy against God.

Amid such temptations Peter comforts suffering Christians by telling them that they are not the first, nor the only ones, to be thus assailed. They are not to feel as if it were a wonderful and unheard of cross which they bear and were bearing it alone. They are to know that their brethren, Christians of all times, and scattered through all the world, must suffer the same things at the hands of Satan and his minions. It assuages and comforts the sufferer beyond measure to know that he does not suffer alone, but with a great multitude.

September 10th - Mark 7:32

They bring unto him one that was deaf, and had an impediment in his speech; and they beseech him to put his hand upon him.

In this text both faith and love are presented to us. Faith, in that these people had before heard how kind and compassionate Jesus was and how he had helped those who had come to him. Although the text does not state this, yet we must so conclude, and the facts prove that they must have previously heard the good tidings of Christ the Lord, on account of which they believed. This was the beginning of their faith. For the Word must first have been heard, and must have entered the human heart, showing the mercy of God in such a way as to create faith. Then they clung to these tidings, trusted them, went thither, and hoped to receive of him what they had heard. In this way faith grows out of the Word of God. We must, therefore, earnestly search the gospel in order thus to lay the first stone. The Word first informs us of the mercy and goodness of God; faith then lays hold on the Word with firm confidence, and we obey it. We now become conscious of it in our hearts and are satisfied. For as soon as we believe we are already justified and are with Christ in his inheritance.

This text also sets forth the works of love in this, that these people go and take care of this poor man, just as Christ sent forth the tidings to them, showing his goodness and mercy, without any merit in them or their efforts to obtain it. As soon as they lay hold on that mercy and drink from its fountain, they again send it forth freely and impart it to their neighbor. These people do not need this work themselves, they are not looking for a reward, nor do they even think of themselves, but are only thinking of the poor man and how they may help him. So Christians should carefully consider how love works and how it cares for others. "Love seeks not its own." "Look not every man on his own things, but every man also on the things of others."

September 11th - Romans 8:15

Ye have not received the spirit of bondage again to fear; but you have received the Spirit of adoption, whereby we cry, Abba, Father.

This is a noble and comforting text, worthy of being written in letters of gold. Because you now through faith, he means to say, have the Holy Spirit and are led by him, you are no longer in bondage as you were when under the law; you need no longer be afraid of its terrors and its demands, as if God would condemn and reject you on account of your unworthiness and the remaining infirmity of your flesh. But you have the consolation that, through faith, you have the assurance of God's grace, and may consider God your Father and call upon him as his children.

Paul speaks of the "spirit of bondage" and the "spirit of adoption" according to the customs of his times. In those days manservants and maidservants were the property of the master of the house in the same sense that a cow was his property. He bought them with his money; he did with them as he pleased, just as with his cattle. They were afraid of their master and had to expect stripes, imprisonment and punishment even unto death. They could only say: Here I serve for my bread only; I have nothing to expect but stripes, and must be content to have my master cast me out or sell me to someone else whenever he chooses. They could never have a well-grounded hope of release from such fear and bondage and coercion.

Such a slavish, captive, fearful and uncertain spirit you do not have, says the apostle. You are not compelled to live continually in fear of wrath and condemnation as are the followers of Moses and all who are under the law. On the contrary, you have a delightful, free spirit, one confident and contented, such as a child entertains toward its father, and you need not fear that God is angry with you or will cast you off and condemn you. For you have the Spirit of his Son in your hearts and know that you shall remain in his house and receive the inheritance, and that you may comfort yourselves with it and boast of it as being your own.

September 12th - Luke 17:12, 13

As he entered into a certain village, there met him ten men that were lepers, which stood afar off: and they lifted up their voices and said, Jesus, Master, have mercy on us.

This is a plain, simple history or transaction, which requires little explanation. Yet as plain as it is, great is the example it presents to us. In the leper it teaches us faith, in Christ it teaches us love. Now, faith and love constitute the whole character of the Christian. Faith receives, love gives. Faith brings man to God, love brings man to his fellow man. Through faith he permits God to do him good, through love he does good to his brother. For whoever believes has everything from God, and is happy and rich. He needs nothing more and does and orders all things for the good and benefit of his neighbor. Through love he does to his neighbor as God did to him through faith. He reaps good from above through faith, he gives good below through love.

It is characteristic of faith boldly to trust God's grace, and to form a bright vision and refuge in God, doubting nothing. Where there is no true faith there is no true prayer, nor any seeking after God. But where it exists it makes man bold and anxious freely to bring his troubles unto God, and earnestly to pray for help. It is not enough to believe there is a God, and pray many words as the wretched custom is now. But observe in the leper how faith is constituted, how without any teacher at all it teaches us how our prayers may be truly fruitful. You here observe how they had a good opinion of and a comforting assurance in Christ, and firmly thought he would be gracious to them. This thought made them bold and anxious to bring their troubles to him, and to cry for help with great earnestness and a loud voice.

Luke does not relate three things of the lepers in vain: first, that they went to meet him; second, they stood; third, they lifted up their voices. By these three things their strong faith is commended to us as an example. The going forth to meet him is the boldness excited by comforting assurance. The standing is the firmness and sincerity against doubt. The lifting up of the voice is the great earnestness in prayer, growing out of such confidence.

September 13th - 1 Timothy 6:10

The love of money is the root of all evil: which while some coveted after, they have erred from the faith, and pierced themselves through with many sorrows.

We see from daily experience what a shameful and accursed vice covetousness is, and what harm it does, especially in high places, whether clerical or lay. If the money fiend has taken possession of a pastor's or preacher's heart, so that like the rest of the world he aims at securing for himself great riches, then, like Judas, the traitor, he has already fallen into the jaws of the devil and is prepared to betray Christ, his Word and his Church for a few pieces of silver. Thus the pope has introduced all sorts of idolatries and abominations in the name of God and the Church in order to secure and maintain his riches and dominion; he has led multitudes of souls to the devil, so filling them with false terrors of his ban that no one dares to say a word against it.

How harmful it is in civil government when lords and princes are dominated by this shameful vice, aiming to appropriate everything to themselves! On this account they forget to exercise their princely office so as to be of help to the land and people over whom they have been placed as lords for this purpose, and thus they have forfeited the commendation and love, which they should receive with all honor and praise as the fathers of their people and their country. They do not concern themselves about the spread of God's Word, the administration and support of churches and schools, or the maintenance of law and order among their subjects. They permit destitute pastors with their wives and children, the widows and orphans, to suffer injustice, violence and want. In the meantime they go about with their tax lists, and consider only how they may collect money enough for their extravagant expenditures and pomp.

Nowadays everyone who has the power by means of his money impoverishes his neighbors and thus sets God and conscience aside. Upon such unchristian doings must come the fearful wrath and punishment of God. The time will come when he will turn us out of doors; since we do not heed his Word and admonition, he himself may put a forcible end to this godless business. This the believer escapes who with godly fear quietly occupies his station in life, satisfied with the things that God gives him.

September 14th - Luke 19:45, 46

He went into the temple, and began to cast out them that sold therein, and them that bought; saying unto them, It is written, My house is the house of prayer: but you have made it a den of thieves.

Here the Lord tells us what the temple of God is: "My house shall be called a house of prayer for all people." This is a strong passage. The words, "for all people," "for all Gentiles," is against the Jews, who trusted in the temple of God at Jerusalem, and thought that it was impossible for God to demolish this temple or destroy this city. They stoned Stephen, because he said, "Jesus shall destroy this place, and shall change the customs which Moses delivered to us." But we must rightly understand this expression, that the city of Jerusalem, the temple and the people, should remain until the time of Christ. With this agree all the prophets, who have given all things into the hands of Christ; as he would then dispose of them, so it would be and remain.

It is true that God himself had established the temple at Jerusalem and had himself consecrated and sanctified it with his Word, when he said: This house is my house! for his Word was preached in it. Wherever God's Word is preached, there is God's own true house, there God most certainly dwells with his grace. Wherever his gospel is, there is a house of prayer, there men shall and may truly pray and God will also hear their prayer. But where the Word of God is not found, there the devil has full sway.

That we have imitated the Jews and have built so many churches would be well enough, if we had done it in order that the Word of God might be preached there; for where the Word goes there God is present and pours out his grace. But Jesus says to the Jews: You have made my house a den of thieves. Truly he gives it a scandalous name. But he does it because they no longer respect the house of God, but make it a market house. The priests did not inquire whether the Word of God was preached in it, although they sang and babbled and read the prophets and Moses. But God cares nothing for such babbling of psalms, and Christ is therefore justly angry at such a desecration of his temple by these bloated misers, who not only forsake the true worship of God, but trample it under their feet.

September 15th - John 1:29

John sees Jesus coming unto him, and said, Behold the Lamb of God, which takes away the sin of the world.

With reference to the forgiveness of sins let me say that you will not find anything in your heart with which you can pay them off, nor raise any funds for which God might recognize you and cancel the debt in the ledger. But if you seize Christ as the one who has become your substitute, who has taken your sin upon himself, and who has given himself with all his merit and worthiness for you, no sin can avail anything against you. If I am a sinner, he is holy and Lord over sin, death, Satan and hell, so that no sin can harm me, because he has been given me as my righteousness and salvation.

Through grace we have, indeed, the forgiveness of all sins, but in no way except in and through Christ alone, and in him only it must be sought and can be obtained. Whoever will come before God with any kind of work, which God is to recognize as meritorious for obtaining grace, will be disappointed and deceived, yea, instead of grace he will heap wrath upon himself. All other ways and means are condemned as the doctrines of devils, as when men are led and directed to their own works, or to the holiness and merits of others, as of the saints who have led ascetic lives or have suffered and expiated a great deal; or as those have done who have comforted people in the throes of death by admonishing them to suffer death willingly for their sins. Whoever dares to offer anything else for sin or to atone for it himself does nothing less than deny the Lord Jesus Christ, disgrace and slander him, as if the blood of Christ were of no more consequence than our repentance and satisfaction, or were not sufficient to take away all the sins of the world.

Would you, then, be freed from your sins, you need not chastise yourself with them, nor have anything to do with them, but simply creep under the wings and into the bosom of Christ, as he is the one who has taken them away and has laid them upon himself.

September 16th - Luke 10:27

You shall love the Lord your God with all your heart, and with all your soul, and with all your strength, and with all your mind.

God is a jealous God and cannot suffer us to love anything above himself. God allows us indeed to love his creatures; they were created for this purpose and are good. All things that are attractive and beautiful by nature cause us to love them. This God permits us to do. But that I should cling to the creature and love it with the same love with which I love God, the Creator, this he cannot and will not allow. The love of the creature should stand far, far below our love to him; and as he is the chief good, his will is also to be loved in the highest degree above all other good.

To love God with all the heart is to love him above all creatures. I must be affectionate towards him, evermore cleave to him, depend upon him, trust him, have my desire, love and joy in him, and always think of him. To love God with all the soul is to devote your entire bodily life to him. The soul in the Scriptures signifies the life of the body, which acts through the five senses, seeing, hearing, feeling, smelling, and tasting, and everything that the soul does through the body, as eating, drinking, sleeping. All this I will give up before I forsake my God, you must be able to say. To love God with all our strength is to devote all our members and whatever we may be able to do through our bodies to the love of God, and sacrifice all rather than do anything contrary to his will. To love God with all the mind is to take to nothing except what is pleasing to God.

But there is not a man on earth who thus fulfils the law. Thus this law makes us all sinners in that not the least letter of this commandment is fulfilled even by the most holy person in the world. No one clings so firmly to God with all the heart, that he would forsake all things for God's sake. What would we do if we had to give our lives for God's and Christ's sake? Still the law requires it. Therefore it is safer to confess that we are sinners, than to have respect to our works and beautiful, glittering lives.

September 17th - Ephesians 4:26

Be you angry, and sin not: let not the sun go down upon your wrath.

This passage sounds as though permission were given to be angry. But Paul is taking into consideration the way of the world. Men are tempted and moved to anger. There are no clean records. Under sudden provocation the heart swells with ire, while the devil lustily fans the flame; he is ever alert to stamp us with his seal and image and make us like unto himself, either through error and false doctrine, or through wrath and murder in conflict with love and patience. These two forms of evil you will encounter, especially if you make an effort to be a godly Christian, to defend the truth and to live uprightly in the sight of all. You will meet with all manner of malice aforethought and deceit, and with faithlessness and malignity on the part of those you have benefited. This will hurt you and move you to wrath. In your own house and among your dear Christian brethren you will often meet with that which vexes you; a word of yours may hurt their feelings. It will not be otherwise. This life of ours is so constituted that such conditions will exist. Flesh and blood cannot but be stirred at times by wrath and impatience, especially when it receives evil for good; the devil is ever at hand kindling your anger and endeavoring to fan into a blaze the wrath and ill humor between yourself and your neighbor.

But right here, says the apostle, you should beware and not sin; not give rein, nor yield to the impulse and promptings of wrath. That you may indeed be moved, the apostle would say, I well know, and you may fancy you have the best of reasons for exhibiting anger and vengeance; but beware of doing what your wrath would have you do; if overcome by wrath and led to rashness, do not continue in it, do not harbor it, but subdue and restrain it, the sooner the better. Do not suffer it to take root or to remain with you overnight. If followed, wrath will cause you to fall and sin against God and your neighbor. When wrath attacks you, go into your chamber, pray the Lord's Prayer and confide in God; he will uphold your right.

September 18th - Luke 18:13

The publican, standing afar off, would not lift up so much as his eyes unto heaven, but smote upon his breast, saying, God be merciful to me a sinner.

Surely this is the art of a great master, which is entirely foreign to, high and far above human understanding. Reason cannot harmonize what this publican has here put together to construct a prayer from words entirely opposed to each other. It does not at all seem proper that such a sinner and condemned person should dare come before God and pray. Sin and mercy are opposed to each other, like fire and water. Mercy does not belong where sin abounds, but wrath and punishment. How then does this man discover the art to harmonize and unite them, and how dare he desire and call for grace to cover his sins? To this belongs more than to know the law and the ten commandments, an art, of which the Pharisee knew nothing at all.

This is preaching the precious gospel of God's grace and mercy in Christ, which is published and offered to condemned sinners without any merit of their own. The publican must have heard of this, and the Holy Spirit must have touched and moved his heart with it, as he feels his sins through the law, that he comes before God and offers his prayer, that he certainly believes as he has heard from the Word of God, that God will be merciful and forgive sins, will turn away his wrath and eternal death for the sake of his Son, the promised Messiah. Such faith united and bound together these two opposing elements in this prayer.

This preaching of the gospel is heard by many, and it appears an easy matter to say it; but it is not as common as men think. No one better understands how difficult it is than the few who study and exercise themselves to believe and pray like the publican. The reason of this is, that the pious Pharisee is still within us and hinders us from thus uniting them. Thus you have in this publican a beautiful example of true Christian repentance and faith. He gives honor and praise to God alone for his divine grace; he prays to him from the heart and in true confidence in his Word and promise. You see here an excellent masterpiece of spiritual wisdom and the proper fruits that follow faith.

September 19th - Matthew 6:33

Seek you first the kingdom of God, and his righteousness, and all these things shall be added unto you.

This is the chief passage in this sermon, and states the manner in which we are to proceed to obtain the divine or eternal gift, and what we need for this life. Would you rightly look to that of which it behooves you to take care, then let this be the first, aye, your only care, that you strive according to God's Word to do your duty, to serve him in his kingdom as his Word teaches you—for in this consists the righteousness belonging to this kingdom—and to prize his Word more highly than all pertaining to this temporal life.

If you have done this you have done well and provided well, and you need not take any further burdens upon you, nor cherish any cares in your heart; indeed, it should be much too small a thing for you to care for so slight a matter as the wants of your daily bread, and thus to aggrieve yourselves. Rather do this for the honor of God and for your own benefit, that you strive after the great and eternal good; if you attain and keep this, the rest will surely take care of itself. Neither can you obtain it from God in any better way than by first seeking and asking of him great things.

It is to his liking that we ask great things of him, and he is pleased to give them. Since he gladly gives great things, he will not stint the small things, but will throw them into the bargain. God has often caused many pious people, who have helped in building up God's kingdom, have served the Church and furthered God's Word, to experience this. God has richly blessed them with goods and honor. This is evidenced not only by the examples of the Scriptures, but also by the history of some of our pious kings and princes, who, having liberally given for the ministry and for schools, have not become poorer, but were more richly blessed of God and have reigned in peace, in victory and good fortune. God would gladly do this still, if the world would happily follow the well-meant advice which is given here, and not with unbelief, greed and unchristian scheming rage against his Word to its own harm and ruin.

September 20th - Matthew 6:34

Take therefore no thought for the morrow: for the morrow shall take thought for the things of itself. Sufficient unto the day is the evil thereof.

The world is always anxious about the future, and thinks thereby to be removed from danger and to protect and support itself. It sees not its own vanity, and that its projects may be wrong; that it is true and experience testifies, as Christ here says, that each day brings its own misfortune and evil. Thus it happens with such plottings and prudence of its own, with which it means to insure itself and to forestall all coming danger, the world only causes more woe and harm. Whenever worldlings see that things do not go as they expected, or that an accident happens, they begin to despond, think of one remedy and another, and imagine they must look for help, protection and safety, wherever they can and as best they can. They begin to patch and think to help matters by all sorts of strange craftiness and practices against God and their consciences to which they are driven by unbelief. Hence comes so much misfortune, misery, murder, war, and all misdoings of the wicked world. Each one means to carry out his affairs without God, to oppress and choke everyone who would hinder them, and to throw all things higgledy-piggledy in a heap, rather than desist from his intent. From this all order is destroyed and naught but evil grows in governments and all other affairs.

Against this Christ would caution his believers that they may not waver, nor stake their affairs on that which is uncertain, vainly caring for the future, but at all times do that which is right; that they may not worry at the outcome of things, nor allow themselves to be swerved by future and uncertain good or evil. He would rather commend care to God, and then take everything that happens to them in good part and overcome it with faith and patience. On earth it cannot be otherwise than that each one in his daily calling meets with things other than he welcomes, which cause him trouble and labor. Hence Christ calls this life daily evil or misfortune. He would have us know it and be prepared for it, and not hanker after the world and become partakers in its unrighteousness and evil affairs, which lead us and others into ruin and damnation.

September 21st - Romans 8:16, 17

The Spirit itself bears witness with our spirit, that we are the children of God: and if children, then heirs; heirs of God, and joint heirs with Christ; if so be that we suffer with him, that we may be also glorified together.

Here you have the great boast, the honor and glory of the Christian. Leave to the world its splendor, its pride and its honors, which mean nothing else—when it comes to the point—than that they are the children of the devil. But consider the marvel of this, that a poor, miserable sinner should obtain such honor with God as to be called, not a servant of God, but a son and an heir of God. Any man might well consider it a privilege to be called one of God's lowest creatures; but the apostle declares that we who believe in Christ shall be his heirs, his sons and daughters. Who can sufficiently magnify God's grace? But the apostle adds the words, "if so be that we suffer with him," to teach us that while we are on earth we must so live as to approve ourselves good, obedient children, who do not obey the flesh, but who for the sake of this dominion endure whatever befalls them or causes pain to the flesh.

O' how noble it is in a man not to obey his lusts, but to resist them with a strong faith, even though he suffer for it! To be the child of a mighty and renowned king or emperor means to possess nobility, honor and glory on earth. How much more glorious it would be, could a man truthfully boast that he is the son of one of the highest angels! Yet what would all that be compared with one who is named and chosen by God himself, and called his son, the heir of exalted divine majesty? Such sonship and heritage must assuredly imply great and unspeakable glory and riches, and power and honor, above all else that is in heaven or on earth. This very honor, even though we had nothing but the name and fame of it, ought to move us to become the enemies of this sinful life on earth and to strive against it with all our power, notwithstanding we should have to surrender all for his sake and suffer all things possible for a human being to suffer. But the human heart cannot grasp the greatness of the honor and glory to which we shall be exalted with Christ. It is altogether above our comprehension or imagination.

September 22nd - Luke 7:14, 15

(Jesus said,) Young man, I say unto you, Arise. And he that was dead sat up, and began to speak. And he delivered him to his mother.

These words are instantly followed by such power and efficacy that the dead man did not lie as before, but sat up, bound and covered as he was, began to speak and showed that he was no longer dead, but alive. This was a wonderful and quick change from death to life. Where the spark of life had long been extinguished and there was no sign of life, there are fully and instantly restored breath, blood, sensibility, movement, thought, speech and everything else that belongs to life. Christ, with one word, turned the sad and sorrowing procession into a joyous, lovely and beautiful procession of life, in which both the youth, carried by four or more to be buried under ground, and his mother, joyously follow the Lord Jesus into the city, accompanied by the whole crowd, forgetting death, the bier and the grave, and speaking joyously and thankfully only of life.

But the glory and honor of this work belong to the Lord Jesus, through whose power and authority alone death can be removed and life brought forth from it. Hence the fame and report concerning Christ, of which the gospel speaks, saying that it went forth throughout the whole country, is recorded for our consolation and joy over against the fear and dread of death, that we may know what kind of a Saviour we have in Christ. He so manifested himself on earth in his ministry and form of a servant, that he can be known as the Lord both of death and life, to destroy the former and bring the latter to light. He met death and fought with it, as in the case of Jairus' daughter and again that of Lazarus, and at last in his own person, when he finally overcame and destroyed it.

We should learn to believe this and comfort ourselves in the hour of death and in all other times of distress. We should be firmly assured that in Christ we have obtained victory over death and life. Yea, the more misery and death are in us, the more richly we shall find comfort and life in him, provided we hold fast to him by faith, to which he spurs us on and admonishes us both through his Word and by such examples as the one mentioned above.

September 23rd - Matthew 22:37

Jesus said unto him, you shall love the Lord your God with all your heart, and with all your soul, and with all your mind.

Consider it an established fact that reason can never understand and fulfil the law, even though it knows the meaning of the law. Human nature alone will never be able to accomplish what God requires in this commandment, namely, that we surrender our will to the will of God, so that we renounce our reason, our will, our might and power, and say from the heart: your will be done. You will nowhere find a person who loves God with his whole heart and his neighbor as himself. It may indeed happen that two companions live together in a very friendly manner, but even there hypocrisy is hidden, which continues until you are offended by him; then you will see how you love him, and whether you are flesh or spirit. But this commandment requires me to be friendly with all my heart to him who has offended me.

Take to yourself this commandment: you shall love the Lord your God with all your heart, and think upon it; how far you are from fulfilling it, that you have not yet made a beginning to suffer and to do from the heart what God demands of you. When God does our pleasure, then we can easily say: How I do love God, he is my Father! How gracious he is to me! But when he sends misfortune and adversity, we no longer regard him as our God, nor as our Father. True love to God does not act in this way, but thinks in the heart and says with the lips: Lord God, I am your creature; do with me as you will; if you desire, I will suffer any misfortune or die this very hour; I will cheerfully do so. But you will never find a person who will always regulate himself according to this commandment.

Therefore there is no human being who is not condemned, for no one has kept this commandment, and God requires everyone to keep it. We stand in the midst of fear and distress, unable to help ourselves. Our human nature is unable to keep the law, which wants the heart, and unless done from the heart, it avails nothing before God. This is never done except man is born anew through the Holy Spirit. When you realize this, the law has accomplished its work.

September 24th - Romans 3:20–24

By the law is the knowledge of sin ... For all have sinned, and come short of the glory of God; being justified freely by his grace, through the redemption that is in Christ Jesus.

The law is known when I learn from it that I am a sinner and am condemned, and see that there is no hope nor comfort anywhere for me, and I cannot help myself, but must have another one to deliver me. Then is the time I look around for him who can help, and he is Christ Jesus, who for this purpose became man, like unto us, in order that he might help us out of the mire into which we have fallen. He loved God with all his heart and his neighbor as himself, and submitted his will to the will of his Father, fulfilled the law in every respect; this I could not do and yet I was required to do it. God accepts him; and that which he fulfilled in the law, he offers me. He freely gives me his life with all his works, so that I can appropriate them to myself as a possession that is my own and is bestowed upon me as a free gift.

Christ has through his death secured for us the Holy Spirit; he fulfils the law in us and not we. For that Spirit, whom God sends into your heart for the sake of his Son, makes an entirely new man out of you, who does with joy and love from the heart everything the law requires, which before would have been impossible for you to do. This new man submits himself wholly and entirely to the will of God. Whatever God does with him, is well pleasing to him. This Spirit you cannot merit yourself, but Christ has secured it. When I believe from the heart that Christ did this for me, I receive also the same Holy Spirit that makes me an entirely new man. Then everything God commands is sweet, lovely and agreeable, and I do what he desires of me; not by my own strength, but by the the strength of him that is in me, as Paul says, "I can do all things through Christ that strengtheneth me."

But take heed that you do not undertake to secure this faith in Jesus Christ by your own works or power. The Holy Ghost must do it, and faith alone is sufficient to this end. Our good works are for another purpose, namely, to prove our faith.

September 25th - Luke 7:12

When he (Jesus) came nigh to the gate of the city, behold, there was a dead man carried out, the only son of his mother, and she was a widow.

This was indeed a sad condition in the life of the widow. She had lost her husband, and now her only son, whom she loved, had died. Among those people it was regarded a great misfortune, if parents could not leave their name, or children. They regarded this a great disfavor of God. Hence the widow, who, after the death of her husband, had placed all her hope and comfort in her only son, must have had great sorrow when her son was torn from her and she had nothing left on earth. She undoubtedly thought: You are also one of the accursed women to whom God is such an enemy as to compel you to pass from the earth without leaving an offspring.

Therefore this woman had great sorrow, not only because she had been robbed of her husband and afterwards of her son, the family being thereby destroyed before her eyes; but, what seemed far more serious, she was forced to think: Now I see that God is unfavorable to me and I am cursed; for this punishment has been executed upon me, because God in the Psalms and the Prophets has threatened the ungodly to destroy them root and branch. This has happened to me. If someone had then said to her: your son shall live again before thine eyes, she would undoubtedly have replied: Alas! do not mock me in my deep sorrow. Grant me at least so much that I may bewail my great misery, and do not add to it by mockery.

But all this is portrayed here that we might learn that with God nothing is impossible, whether it be misfortune, calamity, anger, or whatever it may be, and that he sometimes allows misfortune to come upon the good as well as upon the wicked. Yea, God even permits at times the ungodly to sit at ease, and meet with success in all their undertakings, while he appears to the pious as if he were angry with them and unfavorable to them. So it happened to the godly Job, all whose children were sadly destroyed in one day, who was robbed of his cattle and land, and his body terribly tormented. He was an innocent man and yet he was compelled to endure a punishment such as no ungodly person had suffered.

September 26th - Ephesians 3:13

Wherefore I desire that you faint not at my tribulations for you, which is your glory.

Having been imprisoned at Rome by order of the emperor, Paul thus consoles his beloved converts at Ephesus, admonishing them to cleave to the doctrine learned from him, and not to be frightened from it by his fate. He reminds them of that whereunto God has called them, and of that they have received through his preaching.

Such admonition is still, and will ever be, necessary in the Christian community. The weak must endure severe conflicts in the tribulations which the gospel inevitably entails. The trial is especially hard when they must lose their leaders and teachers, and in addition hear the shameful, bitter taunts of the calumniators. We in this day have to expect that some will be offended when teachers are assailed. We should therefore be prepared, and when any of our number fall away from our faith to flatter tyrants and the pope, and become liars and knaves, we must individually lay hold of the gospel in such a way as to enable us to stand and to say: "Not because a certain one has taught thus, do I believe. It matters not what becomes of him or what he may be, the doctrine itself is right. This I know, whatever God may permit to befall myself or others because of it."

How could I comfort myself and stand firm unless I were able to say: "Though ten other worlds and everything great, lofty, wise and prudent, and all my friends and brethren as well, should turn from me, the doctrine still remains true. I will adhere to the Word of God, stand or fall what may." When the trying hour arrives, we are able to accomplish as little against the enemy as Paul when he lay in chains, powerless to succor a soul. He was obliged to commit his cause to the Lord. At the same time, as a faithful apostle, he ceased not to admonish and warn to the full extent of his power. Well he knew that many false apostles were ready, as soon as he said a word, to pervert it. For the sake of affording his converts comfort and strength, Paul proceeds to make his sufferings and tribulations pleasing to them by speaking of these afflictions in unusual and beautiful terms.

September 27th - Luke 10:30

A certain man went down from Jerusalem to Jericho, and fell among thieves, which stripped him of his raiment, and wounded him, and departed, leaving him half dead.

The man who lies here half dead, wounded and stripped of his clothing, is Adam and all mankind. The murderers are the devils who robbed and wounded us and left us lying prostrate and half dead. We still struggle a little for life; but there lies horse and man, we cannot help ourselves to our feet, and if we were left thus lying we would have to die by reason of our great anguish and lack of nourishment. If the poor wounded man had desired to help himself he would only have done harm to himself and irritated his wounds. Had he remained lying quiet, he would have suffered all the same. This parable pictures us perfectly.

Thus we are when left to ourselves. We are always lost, we may lay hold where we will. Hitherto man has thought out many ways and methods how he might reform his life and get to heaven. One invented this way, another that; therefore there arose the many kinds of orders, the letters of indulgence, and the crusades; but they have only made evil worse. The world is thus finely portrayed in this wounded man; it lies in sins over head and ears and cannot help itself.

But the Samaritan, who is our Lord Jesus Christ, has fulfilled the law and is perfectly healthy and sound. He comes and does more than both priest and Levite. They saw the wounded man lying helpless and half dead, but they could not help that. He who lay there half dead saw it too, but could not improve matters. The dear sainted fathers saw very well that the people lay in their sins over their ears, and felt the anguish of sin, but what could they do to remedy it? But Christ, the true Samaritan, goes to him and does not require the helpless one to come to him; for here is no merit, but pure grace and mercy; he binds up his wounds and pours in oil and wine. This is the whole gospel from beginning to end. Cling firmly to this Samaritan, Christ the Saviour, he will help you, and nothing else in heaven or on earth will.

September 28th - 1 Corinthians 10:9

Neither let us tempt Christ, as some of them also tempted, and were destroyed of serpents.

In Numbers, chapter 21st, we read that after the people had journeyed forty years in the wilderness and God had brought them through all their difficulties and given them victory over their enemies, as they drew near to the promised land, they became dissatisfied and impatient. They were setting out to go around the land of the Edomites, who refused them a passage through their country, when they began to murmur against God and Moses for leading them out of Egypt. Thereupon God sent among them fiery serpents and they were bitten, a multitude of the people perishing.

Complaining against God is here called tempting him. Men set themselves against the Word of God and blaspheme, as if God and his Word were utterly insignificant, because his disposing is not as they desire. Properly speaking it is tempting God when we not only disbelieve him, but oppose him, refusing to accept what he says as true and desiring that our own wisdom rule. Such was the conduct of the Jews, notwithstanding God's promise to remain with them and to preserve them in trouble; and notwithstanding that he proved his care by daily providences in special blessings and strange wonders.

Paul, in speaking of how they tempted God, says, "They tempted Christ," pointing to the fact that the eternal Son of God was from the beginning with his Church and with the people who received the promise of his coming in the form of man. They believed as we do that Christ was the Rock that followed them. That sin and blasphemy was the real meaning of their murmurings is indicated by the fact that Moses afterward, in the terrible punishment of the fiery serpents by which the people were bitten and died, erected at God's command a brazen serpent and whoever looked upon it lived. It was a sign to them of Christ who was to be offered for the salvation of sinners. It taught the people that they had blasphemed against God, incurred his wrath and deserved punishment, and therefore in order to be saved from wrath and condemnation, they had no possible alternative but to believe again in Christ.

September 29th - Matthew 6:24

You cannot serve God and mammon.

Mammon means goods or riches, and such goods as one does not need, but holds as a treasure, and it is gold and possessions that one deposits as stock and storage provisions. This Christians do not do, they gather no treasures; but they ask God for their daily bread. Others, however, are not satisfied with this, they gather a great store upon which they think they can depend; in case our God should die to-day or to-morrow, they would be able to keep themselves.

To have money and possessions is not forbidden, as we cannot get along without them. Abraham, Lot, David, Solomon and others had great possessions and much gold; and at present there are many wealthy persons who are pious, in spite of their riches. But it is one thing to have possessions and another to serve them; to have mammon and to make a god of it. Job also was wealthy, he had great possessions and was more powerful than all who lived in the East; yet he says: "If I have made gold my hope, and said to the fine gold, you are my confidence; have I rejoiced because my wealth was great, and because my hand had gotten much?"

Whoever possesses riches is lord of the riches. Whoever serves them, is their slave and does not possess them, but they possess him; for he dare not make use of them when he desires, and cannot serve others with them; yea, he is not bold enough to dare to touch them. But if he is lord over his riches, they serve him, and he does not serve them; then he dare use them and casts his care only upon God; he aids the poor with his wealth and gives to those who have nothing. We see here and there many pious poor people existing only for the purpose that the wealthy may help and serve them with their riches.

The sum of it all is, that God cannot allow us to have another Lord besides himself. He is a jealous God and cannot suffer us to serve him and his enemy. It is his will that we serve not gold and riches, and that we be not over anxious for our life; but that we labor and commend our anxiety to him.

September 30th - John 20:23

Whoever's sins you remit, they are remitted unto them; and whose soever sins you retain, they are retained.

This is a great and mighty power which no one can sufficiently extol, given to mortal men of flesh and blood over sin, death, hell and all things. The pope, too, boasts in the canon law, that Christ has given him power over all earthly things; which indeed is correct if the people rightly understood it. They apply it to the civil government; this is not Christ's thought; he wishes to say that when you speak a word concerning a sinner it shall be spoken in heaven and shall avail as much as if God himself had spoken it. This is not civil, but spiritual power.

If Christ speaks a word, it must be so, since he is Lord over sin and death. When he says to you: your sins are forgiven, they must be forgiven and nothing can prevent it. If he says: your sins shall not be forgiven you, they remain unforgiven, so that neither you, nor an angel, nor a saint, nor any creature, can forgive your sin, even if you tortured yourself to death. But in this matter one must not do like the popes. They have reached the point to claim the power that whatever they say, so it must be. If the pope says: your sins are forgiven you, they are blotted out, even though you do not repent, nor believe. They mean by this that they have the power to open or shut heaven. From this it would follow that our salvation depended upon the authority and power of man. Since this is in conflict with all the Scriptures, it cannot be true. These words do not establish the power of him who speaks, but of him who believes. God has given us the Word and authority to speak. This power belongs to every Christian, since Christ has made us all partakers of his power and dominion. Here is not a civil but a spiritual rule, and Christ's followers rule spiritually. Christ's meaning is: you shall have the power to speak the Word, and to preach the gospel, and whosoever believeth has the remission of his sins; but whosoever believeth not has no remission of sin. Therefore if you believe the Word, you gain this power; but if you believe not, then what I speak or preach will avail nothing even though it be God's Word.

October 1st - Romans 8:16

The Spirit itself bears witness with our spirit, that we are the children of God.

Paul describes here the power of the kingdom of Christ, the real work and the true exalted worship which the Holy Spirit effects in believers, the comfort by which the heart is freed from the fear and terror of sin and given peace, and the heartfelt supplication which in faith expects of God an answer and brings his help. These blessings cannot be secured through the law or through our own holiness. That we are children of God and may confidently regard ourselves as such, we learn from the witness of the Spirit, who, in spite of the law and our unworthiness, testifies to it in our weakness and assures us of it. Where there is faith in Christ, there the Holy Spirit brings comfort and childlike trust, which doubts not that God is gracious and will answer prayer as he has promised, not for the sake of our worthiness, but for the sake of the name and merit of Christ, his Son. This witness is the experience within ourselves of the power of the Holy Spirit working through the Word and the knowledge that our experience accords with the Word and the preaching of the gospel. For you are surely aware whether or no, when you are in fear and distress, you obtain comfort from the gospel, whether your heart is assured of God's graciousness, and you no longer flee from him, but can't cheerfully call upon him in faith, expecting help.

This is the true inward witness by which you may perceive that the Holy Spirit is at work in you In addition to this you have also external witnesses. It is a witness of the Holy Spirit in you that he gives the special gifts, spiritual understanding, grace and success in your calling; that you have pleasure and delight in God's Word, confessing it before the world at the peril of life and limb; that you hate and resist ungodliness and sin. Those who have not the Holy Spirit are neither willing nor able to do these things. Even in the Christian these things are accomplished in great weakness; but the Holy Spirit governs them in this weakness, and strengthens them in this witness, as Paul says: "The Spirit also helpeth our infirmities."

October 2nd - Luke 17:16

(He) fell down on his face at his feet, giving him thanks; and he was a Samaritan.

Why was it necessary for the evangelist to write that this one leper was a Samaritan? By this he opens our eyes and warns us that God has two kinds of people who serve him. The one kind has the appearance and name of having a great, spiritual, holy life, wholly wrapped up in it, but all in vain. They are nothing more than ravenous wolves in sheep's clothing. Yet they have the honor and are regarded as the true worshipers of God; therefore goods, friendship and everything the world has comes to them. The others are of the opposite appearance, and are without show or name, as though no one were less God's people than they.

The Jews alone had the name of being God's people, and they alone had God and his worship in preference to all other people on the earth. They hated the Samaritans above all nations, for they too claimed to be God's people along with the Jews; therefore a Samaritan was to them as an apostate Christian is to us. It is true that the Samaritans did not have the right belief and that the Jews had the true law of God. But as God loves the truth and is an enemy to hypocrisy with all its boasting, he turns it round and accepts the Samaritans and lets the Jews go. Thus it happens that they are not his people who still have the name, the appearance and honor of his people. Again, they who are his people, and have the name and appearance, are regarded as heretics, apostates and the devil's children.

So it is even at the present time. The clergy, priests and monks call themselves and are regarded the servants of God. No one is a Christian who does not believe as they do, although no one is less a Christian. Those whom they regarded as heretics, many of whom they have burned and exiled, dare not be called Christians, although they alone are the true Christians. No one falls on his face at the feet of Christ, except the Samaritans, the despised, the condemned, the accursed. Therefore let us guard against everything that makes only a show, it certainly is deceiving; and let us not reject what does not make a display, so that we do not reject Christ and God, as the Jews did.

October 3rd - Ephesians 3:14

For this cause I bow my knees unto the Father of our Lord Jesus Christ.

The apostle alludes to his prayer by naming its outward expression —bending the knees. But the external posture, if accompanied by nothing else, is sheer hypocrisy. When prayer is genuine, possessing the fire by which it is kindled, prompted by a sincere heart which recognizes its need and likewise the blessings that are ours as proclaimed in the Word, and when faith in God's Word—in his promise— revives, then the individual will be possessed with a fervor prompting him to fall upon his knees and pray for strength and for the power of the Spirit. When the Spirit of prayer is kindled and burns within the heart, the body will responsively assume the proper attitude; involuntarily, eyes and hands will be upraised and knees bended. Recall the examples of Moses, David and even Christ himself.

Paul here establishes the doctrine that no one should presume to speak to God, to entreat him for any favor, unless approaching, as Paul does here, in the name of "the Father of our Lord Jesus Christ." For Christ is our sole Mediator, and no one need expect to be heard unless he approach the Father in the name of that Mediator and confess him Lord given of God as intercessor for us and ruler of our bodies and souls. Prayer according to these conditions is approved. Strong faith, however, is necessary to lay hold of the comforting Word, picturing God in our hearts as the Father of our Lord Jesus Christ.

The statement that Christ is our Lord is very comforting, though we have made it terrifying by regarding Christ as a stern and angry judge. But the fact is that he is our Lord for the sole purpose of securing us against harsh lords, tyrants, the devil, the world, death, sin and every sort of misfortune. We are his inheritance, and therefore he will espouse our cause, deliver us from violence and oppression of all kinds and better our condition. The name "Lord" is altogether lovable and comforting to us who believe, and gives us confidence of heart. Naught is here for me but real help and pure grace. God designs to have me his child in Christ, placed above all things temporal and eternal.

October 4th - Philippians 3:17

Brethren, be followers together of me, and mark them which walk so as you have us for an example.

Paul, contemplating with special interest and pleasure his Church of the Philippians, is moved by parental care to admonish them to hold steadily to what they have received, not seeking anything else and not imagining themselves perfect with complete understanding in all things. He particularly admonishes them to follow him and to mark those ministers who walk as he does; also to shape their belief and conduct by the pattern they have received from him. He not only makes an example of himself, but introduces those who similarly walk, several of whom he mentions in this letter to the Philippians. The individuals whom he bids them observe and follow must have been persons of special eminence. But it is particularly the doctrine which the apostle would have the Philippians pattern after. Therefore we should be chiefly concerned about preserving the purity of the office of the ministry and the genuineness of faith. When these are kept unsullied, doctrine will be right, and good works spontaneous.

Apparently Paul is a rash man to dare boast himself a pattern for all. Other ministers might well accuse him of wishing to exalt his individual self above others. "Think you," our wise ones would say to him, "that you alone have the Holy Spirit, or that no one else is as eager for honor as yourself?" Just so did Miriam and Aaron murmur against Moses, their brother, saying: "has the Lord indeed only spoken by Moses? has he not spoken also by us?" Paul, however, does not say, "I, Paul, alone;" but, "as you have *us* for an example." That does not exclude other true apostles and teachers. He admonishes his church, as he everywhere does, to hold fast to the one true doctrine received from him in the beginning. They are not to be too confident of their own wisdom in the matter; but rather to guard against pretenders to a superior doctrine, for so had some been misled. At that time many Jews went about with the intent of perverting Paul's converts, pretending that they taught something far better, drawing the people away from Christ and back to the law in order to establish and extend their Jewish doctrines.

October 5th - Hebrews 11:1

Now faith is the substance of things hoped for, the evidence of things not seen.

This means as much as to say, faith is the means by which one trusts in possessions he does not see, namely, that I should expect temporal things which I can neither see nor hear, but must only hope for. If I were a man who had a wife and children, had nothing for them and no one gave me anything; then I should believe and hope that God would sustain me. But if I see that it amounts to nothing and I am not helped with food and clothing, what takes place? As an unbelieving fool I begin to doubt and take whatever is at hand, steal, deceive, cheat the people and make my way as best I can. This is what shameless unbelief does. But if I am a believer, I close my eyes and say: O God, I am your creature and your handiwork. I will depend entirely upon you who cares more for my sustenance than I do myself; you will indeed nourish, feed, clothe and help me when and where you know best.

Thus faith is a sure foundation through which I expect that which I see not. Therefore faith must always have sufficient; before it should fail the angels would have to come from heaven and dig bread out of the earth in order that believing persons should be fed. The heavens and the earth would have to pass away before God would let his believers lack clothing and the other necessaries of life. The comforting and powerful Word of the divine promise demands this. But when one inquires of reason for counsel it soon says: It is not possible. You must wait a long time until roasted ducks fly into your mouth, for reason sees nothing, grasps nothing, and nothing is present. Concerning spiritual blessings I wish to say that when we come to die we will see before our eyes very death, when we would eagerly wish to live; we will see very hell, and yet we would fondly wish to possess heaven. In brief, we will not see a single thing we would like to have. But faith is the principle by which I secure what I do not see. I fully trust that God, by virtue of his promise, will give me life and salvation.

October 6th - James 2:26

As the body without the spirit is dead, so faith without works is dead also.

Faith is an active, living thing. But in order that men may not deceive themselves and think they have faith when they have not, they are to examine their works, whether they also love their neighbors and do good to them. If they do this, it is a sign that they have the true faith. If they do not do this they only have the sound of faith and they are as one who sees himself in a glass; when he leaves it, he sees himself no more, but sees other things, forgetting the face in the glass. From this passage deceivers and blind masters have demolished faith and established only good works as though righteousness and salvation did not rest on faith, but on our works.

But James means that a Christian life is nothing but faith and love. Love is being kind and useful to all men, to friends and enemies. Where faith is right it certainly loves, and does to others in love as Christ did to him in faith. Thus everyone is to beware lest he has in his heart simply a dream and fancy instead of faith, and thus deceives himself. This he will not learn as well anywhere as in doing the works of love. Beware, if your life is not in the service of others, and you live only for yourself, and care nothing for your neighbor; then your faith is certainly nothing, for it does not do what Christ has done for you. Paul also says: "If I have faith enough to remove mountains, and have not charity (love), I am nothing." This explains the whole matter, not that faith is insufficient to make us pious, but that a Christian life must embrace and never separate these two, faith and love. But the presumptuous undertake to separate them, they want only to believe and not to love, they despise their neighbor, and yet pretend to have Christ. This is false and must fail. Thus we say, then, that faith is everything and saves us, that a man needs no more for his salvation. But he is on this account not idle, but labors much for the benefit of his neighbor and not for himself; for he does not need it, he has enough in Christ.

October 7th - Luke 17:14

When he saw them, he said unto them, Go shew yourselves unto the priests. And it came to pass, that, as they went, they were cleansed.

How very friendly and lovingly the Lord invites all hearts to himself in this example and stirs them to believe in him! There is no doubt that he desires to do for all what he does here for these lepers, if we only freely surrender ourselves to him for all his favor and grace. The Lord desires that we should joyfully and freely venture to build on his favor before we feel or experience it. He has here sufficiently testified that he hears them willingly without any hesitation. He does not first say he will do it, but as though it were already done, he did as they wished. He does not say: I will have mercy on you, and cleanse you; but merely: "Go show yourselves unto the priests." As though he would say: There is no use of asking, your faith has already acquired and obtained it, before you begin to ask; you were already cleansed in my sight when you began to expect such things of me; only go and show yourselves to the priests; as I consider you and as you believe, so you are and shall be.

Behold, so powerful is faith to obtain all it wants of God, that God considers it done before the asking. Of this the prophet Isaiah has already said, "It shall come to pass, that before they call, I will answer; and while they are yet speaking, I will hear." Not as though faith or we were worthy of it, but in order that he might show his unspeakable goodness and willing grace, that he might stir us to believe in him, and with joyful and unwavering consciences to look to him for every good thing. For thus Christ hears these lepers before they call, and before they cry out he is prepared to do all their hearts desire. Are not these strong incentives that make the heart joyful and eager? His grace permits itself to be felt and grasped, yea, it grasps and satisfies us.

The lepers have taught us how to believe; Christ teaches us to love. Love does to its neighbor as it sees Christ has done to us. This is a Christian life; it does not need much doctrine, nor many books, it is wholly contained in faith and love.

October 8th - Hebrews 11:17, 18

By faith Abraham, when he was tried, offered up Isaac: and he that had received the promises offered up his only begotten son, of whom it was said, That in Isaac shall your seed be called.

To reason it was a foolish command God gave to Abraham to slay his son. If reason should be the judge all mankind would come to no other conclusion than that it was an unfriendly and hostile command. How could it be from God, since he himself had said to Abraham that he would multiply his seed through this son, and that it should become as innumerable as the stars of the firmament and as the sand by the sea. Therefore to reason it was a foolish, a grievous and hard commandment. But what did Abraham do? He closes his senses, takes his reason captive, and, obeying the voice of God, goes and does as God commanded him.

By this Abraham proved that he obeyed from the heart; otherwise, even if he had put his son to death a hundred times, God would not have cared for it; but God was pleased that the deed came from the heart and was done from true love to God. It came from a heart that must have thought: Even if my son dies, God is almighty and faithful, he will keep his word, he will find ways and means beyond that which I am able to devise; only obey, there is no danger. Had he not had this boldness and faith, how could he have had it in his fatherly heart to proceed to kill his only and well beloved son?

Later the Jews wanted to follow this example and offered their children to God, hoping thereby to perform a service well-pleasing to God; but it was far from it. O, how many healthy, noble and beautiful children perished! The prophets protested against this service, they preached, warned and wrote against it, telling the people that it was a deception, but all in vain. Many a prophet lost his life because of this, as the history of the Books of the Kings shows.

But why was this service of the Jews displeasing to God? Because it did not come from the heart, and was not done out of love to God; but they simply looked upon the service without the command and word of God. There must be first love in the heart, then follows the service that will be pleasing to God. Abraham proved by his act that he loved God with his whole heart.

October 9th - Romans 13:10

Love works no ill to his neighbour; therefore love is the fulfilling of the law.

All the works of the law tend in the end to prove our love to God. This love the law requires and will have above everything else. We are to observe that all the works of the law are not commanded merely for the purpose of being performed. If God had even given us more commandments, he would not want us to keep them to the injury and destruction of love. If these commandments oppose the love of our neighbor, God wants us to annul them. Moses brought the children of Israel out of Egypt, leading them for forty years through the wilderness, and not one of them was circumcised, although it was commanded them. Was God angry with them, because they did not obey his commandment? No, there was a higher commandment in force at that time, namely, that they were to obey God who commanded them to come out of Egypt in haste to the promised land. By their marching they daily obeyed God, otherwise God would have been angered by disobedience. Both the need and the love were at hand, for it would have been unbearable to endure the pain of circumcision and at the same time the burden of the journey. Thus love took the place of the commandment.

In like manner Christ excused his disciples, when they plucked the ears of corn and ate them on the Sabbath day, and the Jews accused them of transgressing the law by doing on the Sabbath day that which was not lawful to do. The Lord gave them to understand that here is no Sabbath day; the body needs food, necessity demands it; we must eat even though it be on the Sabbath day. Thus David went into the house of God and ate the show bread, which it was not lawful for him, nor for those with him, to eat, but only for the priests. David ate the bread, though he was not a priest, because hunger pressed him to do it. Neither did Ahimelech, the priest, violate the law in giving the bread to David, for love was present and urged him to do it. Therefore we have need of the law, that love may be manifested; but if it cannot be kept without injury to our neighbor, God wants us to suspend it.

October 10th - Matthew 9:2

Jesus seeing their faith said unto the sick of the palsy, Son, be of good cheer; your sins be forgiven you

These words contain in brief what the kingdom of Christ is, namely, this sweet voice penetrating our inmost soul, "Thy sins are forgiven." In no other sense are we to view the kingdom of Christ than to know how we stand before God. From it follows that the kingdom of Christ is realized where comfort and the forgiveness of sins reign, not only in proclaiming the words, which is also necessary, but where they reign in reality. Christ did not only speak these words into the ear of this sick man; but he also forgave his sins and comforted him. It is well for us Christians to know this. These words are indeed easily and quickly said and heard; but when it comes to the test the light is soon extinguished and Satan begins to lead us astray. We must beware and properly learn the character and nature of the kingdom of Christ. You know how reason is inclined to fall from faith to works. But here you see no works at all, no merit, no command; there is only the offering of Christ's assistance, his comfort and grace.

If the kingdom of Christ is to grow, we must keep the law out of it, and not be busy with works. For it is not in harmony with Christ's kingdom to say: Run hither and thither and atone for your sins; you must observe and do this and that, if you will be free from sin. Your sins are forgiven out of pure grace without any work or law. The fanatics profess to have a nobler spirit; they urge and insist upon our doing something first of all, and allow faith and love to be overlooked.

This of course is not of the Holy Spirit. Christ first takes possession of the conscience, and when it is right in faith toward God, then he also directs us to do works toward our neighbor. He first highly extols faith and keeps works in the background. This the fanatics cannot understand. Yet so it must be, Christ will prove his Word, and examine who has received it and who not. Let us therefore remain on the right road to the kingdom of Christ with the words of the gospel which comfort the conscience: Be of good cheer, your sins are forgiven.

October 11th - John 20:23

Whoever's sins you remit, they are remitted unto them; and whoever's sins you retain, they are retained.

The forgiveness of sins is of two kinds: the first is to drive sin from the heart and infuse grace into it; this is the work of God alone. The second is the declaration of the forgiveness of sin; this man can do to his fellow man. Christ did both. He instills the Spirit into the heart and externally he declared forgiveness through the word, which is a declaration and public preaching of the internal forgiveness.

All men who have been baptized and are Christians have this latter power. With this power they praise Christ, and the word is put into their mouth, so that they may and are able to say, if they wish, and as often as it is necessary: Behold, O man! God offers you this grace, forgives you all your sin; be comforted, your sins are forgiven; only believe, and you will surely have forgiveness. This word of consolation shall not cease among Christians until the last day. Such language a Christian may always use and in this manner has power to forgive sins. Therefore if I say to you: your sins are forgiven, then believe it as surely as though God himself had said it to you.

Now if there were no man on earth to forgive sins, and there were only law and works, what a weak and miserable thing a poor troubled conscience would be. But now when God adequately instructs everyone so that he is able to say to others: your sins are forgiven you, wherever you are, the golden age has arrived. On this account we are to be defiant and boastful against sin, so that we can say to our brother, who is in anxiety and distress on account of his sins: Be of good cheer, your sins are forgiven; although I cannot give the Holy Ghost and faith, I can yet declare them unto you; if you believe, you have them. They who thus believe these words, praise and glorify God. He has given man power to forgive sins, and thus the kingdom of Christ is spread, the conscience is strengthened and comforted. This we do now through the Word. God grant that we may also thus understand it. But who could do this if Christ had not descended and instructed us.

October 12th - John 17:24

Father, I will that they also, whom you have given me, be with me where I am; that they may behold my glory, which you have given me.

These words are the last petition of this prayer, but the most comforting one for all those who cling to Christ. We are here assured of what we are finally to receive, where we shall find rest and abide, because in this world we are wretched, despised and have no sure abiding place.

Therefore, as a kind, faithful Saviour, Christ encourages us, by saying that he will prepare mansions for us, that we are to be with him, and are to be as happy as he is with his Father. He would say: Do not worry as to your abiding place; let the world and the devil rave and rage, you shall be taken care of and come to the place you desire, where you may rest and remain in spite of the world and the devil. These words should be a pillow and a downy bed for our souls; and when the last hour shall arrive and we are to be freed from sin, from the world, from the power of the devil and from every evil, and are to be brought to our eternal rest and joy, we should go thitherward with cheerful hearts.

We are not only to be with him, but we are also to come to a clear, bright view of his glory. Here upon earth we have it and recognize it only by faith. We do not really see it, but only through the Word as through a dark glass. Our knowledge is still obscure, as when a dark cloud overshadows the bright sun. No human heart can understand the greatness of Christ's glory, since he appeared so very obscure while on earth. But in the world beyond another light will shine most brilliantly in our very presence, which we shall behold with unspeakable joy. What injury can the world do us, though it deprive us of property, honor, and life, if thereby we are brought to Christ and may behold his glory. But we are too cold and sluggish to believe this. It is beyond human understanding to comprehend that our poor, decaying bodies should ever reach such a position of honor as to be able to see this excellent, divine glory forever; yea, our bodies shall become more brilliant and brighter than the sun and the stars.

October 13th - 1 John 1:9

If we confess our sins, he is faithful and just to forgive us our sins, and to cleanse us from all unrighteousness.

All hear the gospel, but it does not enter the hearts of all, for they do not all feel their sins. But the gospel teaches that everything we have in us is sin. Therefore it also offers comfort, forgiveness of sin. But if I am to receive forgiveness of sins. I must have knowledge of sin. Forgiveness of sins consists in nothing more than two words, in which the whole kingdom of Christ consists. There must be sins, and if we are conscious of them, we must confess them; when we have confessed them, forgiveness and grace are immediately present. Before there is forgiveness, there is nothing but sin. This sin must be confessed that I may feel and know that all that is in me is blindness; forgiveness of sins cannot exist where there is no sin. There is, however, no lack of sins to confess, but the lack is in not feeling and knowing our sins.

When God forgives sins it is quite a different thing from man's forgiving. When one man forgives another his sins, he thinks of them again, or perhaps even lays them up to him. But God condemns no more, he banishes all wrath from him, he thinks no more of sin. Now when this wrath is gone, then hell, death, the devil and all misfortune that the devil may bring with him, must also disappear; and instead of wrath God gives grace, comfort, salvation and everything good that he himself is. Sin is all unhappiness, forgiveness is true happiness. The divine majesty is great, great is also that which it forgives. But you must know in your heart how great these words are in which you must trust and for which you can cheerfully die. Only a few rightly receive these words, therefore there are but few true Christians.

This then is the kingdom of Christ. Here there is no work, but only the acknowledgment of all our misfortune, and the reception of all the gifts of God. Therefore it is not by merit; it is a simple gift. This is the gospel upon which faith depends. I need no works before God, and need only be careful rightly to confess my sins. Then I have forgiveness of sins and am one with God, all of which the Holy Spirit works in me.

October 14th - 1 Corinthians 12:3

No man can say that Jesus is the Lord, but by the Holy Ghost.

To call Jesus "Lord" is to confess oneself his servant and to seek his honor alone; to act as his messenger or the bearer of his Word and command. Paul refers here chiefly to the office which represents Christ and bears his Word. Where the office answers these conditions and points to Christ as the Lord, it is truly the message of the Holy Spirit, even though the occupant of the office does not in his own person possess the Spirit; the office itself is essentially of the Holy Spirit. Hypocrisy and invention have no place here. One must proceed in sincerity if he would be certain he is Christ's minister, or apostle, and really handles his Word. Only the inspiration of the Holy Spirit can give one this assurance.

All Christians—each in his own sphere—may equally call Christ "Lord." One may be assured he serves Christ if he can call him "Lord," for only by the Holy Spirit is he enabled to do that. Let him try for a single day—from morning until evening—whether or no he can truly say at all times that he is the servant of God and of Christ in what he does. When delivering a sermon or listening to one, when baptizing a child or bringing one to baptism, when pursuing your daily duties, ask yourself if the act is attended by such faith that you can, without misgiving and not hypocritically, nor mechanically, boast—if necessary, die by your boast—that you serve and please Christ therein. This is calling Christ "Lord." Unquestionably you will often feel your heart doubting and trembling over the matter. Flesh and blood is too weak to obtain this glorious confidence; the Holy Spirit is essential.

I often used to wonder that St. Ambrose was so bold as to call himself a servant of Jesus Christ. I supposed we all ought to be terrified at thoughts of this kind, and that none but the apostles might boast of such honor. But the fact is, we must all say to Christ: you are my Lord and I am your servant; for I believe in you and aspire to be with you and all the faithful and to possess your Word and Sacrament. Otherwise Christ will not acknowledge us.

October 15th - Luke 17:17, 18

Were there not ten cleansed? but where are the nine? There are not found that returned to give glory to God, save this stranger.

The stranger sincerely gives God all the glory. O', what a terrible example is this! Among ten only one, and he among the least and most worthless. How entirely does God overlook that which is great, wise, spiritual and honorable! Yet such people have no fear, but become hardened and petrified in their nature. It is also terrible that the Lord knows that ten were cleansed, of this they did not think. He inquires after and seeks them: Where are the nine? O, what a frightful thing it will be when they at some future time will feel this inquiry and must answer whither they went, that they did not give God the glory. Then they will say: Well, we have nevertheless praised and thanked God, and thus our priests have taught us! Then it will appear whether it will help us to follow the doctrines of men in the name of God, and to forsake the doctrine and will of God. We are sufficiently warned in the gospel, so that no excuse will help us if we allow ourselves to be deceived. In Baptism we have all vowed to follow Christ and his doctrine; no one has vowed to follow the pope, the bishops and clergy. Thus Christ has thoroughly rejected and forbidden the doctrines of men.

Christ comforts his poor Samaritans, who for his name's sake must risk their lives with the priests and Jews, and strengthens their hope with the sentence and judgment that he demands the nine and judges them as God's thieves, who steal God's glory, but he justifies the Samaritan. This hope gives them strong courage, that their cause before God will be rightly maintained and will stand, and that that of the others will be condemned, it matters not how great they were and what power they had on earth.

Before Christ justifies the Samaritan, he judges the nine, that we should be sure not to hasten or desire revenge, but leave it only to him, and go our way. For he himself is so careful to defend the right and punish the wrong. Nor does he wait long to have them accused before him, but of his own free will summons them, so that without doubt the cause of unbelievers affects him more and sooner than it strikes or harms us.

October 16th - Ephesians 4:22

That you put off concerning the former conversation the old man, which is corrupt according to the deceitful lusts.

What Paul calls "the old man" is well known to us, namely, the whole nature of man as descended from Adam after his fall in paradise, being blinded by the devil, depraved in soul, not keeping God before the eyes, nor trusting him, yea, utterly regardless of God and the judgment day. He portrays the old man as given to error, coming short of the truth, knowing naught of the true knowledge of Christ and faith in him, indifferent alike to God's wrath and God's grace, deceiving himself in his own conceit that darkness is light.

Out of this error proceeds the other corruption, the lusts of the body, which are the fruits of unbelief. Unbelief causes men to walk in sinful security and yield to all the appetites of their flesh. Such have no inclination for what is good, nor do they aim to promote order, honor or virtue. They take desperate chances on their lives, wanting to live according to the lusts of their flesh and yet not be reprimanded.

This, says the apostle, is the old man's course and nature. He will do naught but ruin himself. The longer continued, the greater his debasement. He draws down upon himself his own condemnation and penalty of body and soul; in proportion as he becomes unbelieving and hard-hearted, does he become haughty, hateful and faithless, and eventually a perfect scoundrel and villain. This was your former manner of life, when as yet you were heathen and non-Christian. Therefore you must by all means put off the old man and cast him far from you; otherwise you cannot remain a Christian, for glorying in the grace of God and the forgiveness of sin is inconsistent with following sin, remaining in the former unchristian life and walking in error and deceitful lusts. A life and walk of this nature is not becoming a Christian, who is regarded, and truly is, a different order of being from his former self. A Christian must take care that he deceive not himself; he differs from the hypocrite, who may honor God's Word and the gospel, yet in reality he is unchanged. True Christians so live that it is apparent from their lives that they keep God before their eyes and truly believe the gospel.

October 17th - Ephesians 4:23, 24

And be renewed in the spirit of your mind; and that you put on the new man, which after God is created in righteousness and true holiness.

The new man has the Spirit and the truth, by which the heart is illuminated unto righteousness and holiness wherein man follows the guidance of God's Word and feels a desire for a godly walk and a good life. This new man is created after God, as an image of God, and must of necessity differ from such as live in error and in lusts, without the knowledge of God and disobedient to him. For if God's image is in man, man must consequently have the right knowledge of God and right conceptions and ideas, and lead a godly life consistent with holiness and righteousness as found in God himself.

Such an image of God Adam was when first created. He was, as to the soul, truthful, free from error, possessed of true faith and knowledge of God; and as to the body, holy and pure, that is, without the impure, unclean desires of avarice, lasciviousness, envy, hatred and the like. Thus the whole life of the man was a beautiful portrait of God, a mirror wherein God himself was reflected; even as the lives and natures of the holy spirits and angels are wrapped up in God and represent true knowledge of him, assurance, and joy in him and utterly pure and holy thoughts and works according to the will of God.

All Adam's children—all men—would have so remained from their birth, if Adam had not suffered himself to be led astray by the devil and to be thus ruined. But since Christians, by the grace and Spirit of God, are now renewed in this image of God, they are so to live that soul and spirit are righteous and pleasing to God through faith in Christ; and that also the body—meaning the whole external life—be pure and holy. They thus enter again into their former relation and into the true paradise of perfect harmony with God and of justification; they are comforted by his grace. They are disposed to lead a godly life and resist ungodly lusts and ways. They begin to taste God's goodness and lovingkindness and to realize what they lost in paradise. He, therefore, that would be a Christian should strive to be found in this new man created after God,—in the very essence of righteousness and holiness before God.

October 18th - 1 Corinthians 1:5

That in everything you are enriched by him, in all utterance, and in all knowledge.

What Paul terms being enriched "in all utterance"—which, in the exalted spiritual meaning of the words, bears on life everlasting—is having the comfort of faith in Christ and of invocation and prayer. "Enriched in all knowledge" means having true conception and right judgment in all things of our physical life and in all our earthly relations. All things that a Christian should know and should possess are comprehended in these two terms. These blessings are gifts and treasures indescribably great. He who will contrast them with the destitution of our former condition cannot but be joyful and thankful.

The Christian has indeed inestimable treasures. In the first place he has the testimony of the Word of God, which is the word of eternal grace and comfort, that he has a right and true conception of Baptism, the Lord's Supper, the Commandments and the Creed. In addition he has the sure refuge of God's promise to deliver us from every trouble in which we shall call upon him, and to give us, as he promised by the prophet Zechariah, the Spirit of grace and of prayer. And the Christian, by virtue of his enlightened understanding, can wisely discern what are good works and what callings are pleasing to God; on the other hand, his judgments are equally true as to unprofitable and vain works and false services. Formerly we had not this wholesome knowledge. We knew not what we believed, or how we prayed and lived. We sought comfort and salvation in self-devised trivialities, in penances, confessions and satisfactions, in self-righteous works of the monks and in obedience to the commands of the Pope. We believed such works to be fully satisfactory and, indeed, the only things that were holy; the pursuits of common Christians we considered worldly and dangerous. In contrast to this darkness, consider the priceless and to-be-cherished blessing of knowing with certainty wherein the heart is to take comfort, how to seek help in distress and how to conduct oneself in one's own station. Truly we should now render to God heartfelt thanks for the great favor and blessing of restored light and understanding in Scripture and the right conception of doctrinal matters.

October 19th - Psalm 34:19

Many are the afflictions of the righteous: but the Lord delivers him out of them all.

God kindly sends upon his Christians temptation, sorrow and affliction. These preserve them from carnal satiety and teach them to seek comfort and help. God did thus also in former ages, in the time of the martyrs, when he daily suffered them to be violently seized in person and put to death by sword, fire, blood and wild beasts. In this way he truly led his people to school, where they were obliged to learn to know his will. Faith taught them and confirmed to them that such suffering was God's purpose and immutable will concerning themselves, which, whatever attitude towards them he might assume, he could not alter, even as he could not in the case of Christ himself. This discipline and experience of faith strengthened the martyrs and soon accustomed them to suffering, enabling them to go to their death with joy and pleasure.

What noble and enlightened, what strong and courageous people God produced by the discipline of cross and affliction! We, in contrast, because unwilling to experience such suffering, are weak and enervated. If but a little smoke gets into our eyes, our joy and courage are gone, likewise our perception of God's will, and we can only raise a loud lamentation and cry of woe. Just so Christ's disciples in the ship, when they saw the tempest approach and the waves beat over the vessel, quite forgot, in their trembling and terror, the divine will, although Christ was present with them. So also in the time of the martyrs, many Christians became timid and at first denied Christ from fear of torture or of long confinement in prison.

It is God's will that we, too, should learn to accustom ourselves to these things through temptation and affliction, though these be hard to bear and the heart is prone to become agitated and utter its cry of woe. We can quiet our disturbed hearts, saying: I know what is God's thought, his counsel and will in Christ, which he will not alter: he has promised me through his Son, and confirmed it through my baptism, that he who hears and sees the Son shall be delivered from sin and death, and live eternally. The heart possessing such knowledge is kindled by the Holy Spirit and armed against the flesh, the world and the devil.

October 20th - Ephesians 6:11

Put on the whole armour of God, that you may be able to stand against the wiles of the devil.

The devil neither sleeps nor rests, and consequently it is not safe for a Christian to fold his hands and be idle. He is to consider how he may fortify himself against the power of the devil; for he is not called the prince of this world in vain. He rules the world, howls and rages, and cannot bear that a

Christian makes progress. For thereby a rupture is made in his kingdom and his net broken. Hence, wherever possible, he hinders the growth and development of the Christian life. When the fire of faith is kindled and burns, and the devil feels it and becomes aware of it, he immediately attacks it with all his cunning, for he knows how his kingdom is endangered by it. Therefore he endeavors to protect his kingdom with great zeal and exerts himself to retain all under his obedience. For that rogue has a sharp vision and easily becomes conscious of the presence of a true Christian. Therefore he tries to entrap him, surrounds and attacks him on all sides; for he cannot bear that any one should desert his kingdom.

On this account it is dangerous to live heedlessly, for the devil is likely to take us by surprise. This happens even to the great ones among the saints, who rightly apprehend the Word of God. When they think they stand securely, this rogue is behind them, strikes them down and wrestles with them until they are vanquished. This is what happened to the great men of God, to Moses, to Aaron and to the princes of Judah. They had an excellent faith, when they led the people out of Egypt, and all the people went in faith through the Red Sea, through the wilderness and through many wonderful experiences, in which they manifested their faith. At last they came to a point where they feared that they would have to die of hunger and thirst in the parched wilderness. Is it not a pity that after manifesting their faith in so many great trials, wrestling with them and overcoming them, they should allow themselves to be overcome by their belly and murmur against God, and be so fiercely attacked that they succumbed and allowed themselves to be overthrown by Satan. Hence no one is secure, unless his faith continues to grow stronger and stronger.

October 21st - Matthew 18:26

The servant therefore fell down and worshipped him, saying, Lord, have patience with me, and I will pay you all.

What does the servant do? He foolishly thinks he will pay the debt, falls down and asks the Lord to have patience with him. This is the torment of all consciences, when sin comes and smarts deeply until they feel in what a sad state they are before God; then there is no rest; they run hither and thither, seek help here and there to be freed from sin, and in their presumption think they can do enough to pay God in full. Thus we were taught hitherto. From this also have come so many pilgrimages, cloisters, masses and other nonsense. So we fasted and scourged ourselves, and became monks and nuns. All this came because we undertook to begin a life and to do many works of which God should take account and allow himself to be paid by them. Thus we thought to quiet the conscience and put it at peace with God. We acted just like this foolish servant.

Now a heart that is thus smitten with the law, feels its blows and distress, is truly humiliated. Therefore it falls before the Lord and asks for grace, except that it still makes the mistake of intending to help itself, for this we cannot root out of our nature. When the conscience feels such misery, it dare promise more than all the angels in heaven are able to fulfil. When our consciences were forced in the confessional, we did everything that was imposed upon us and gave more than was demanded of us. What should the poor people do? They were glad to be helped even in this manner; they ran and martyred themselves to be rid of their sins. Yet it did no good whatever, for the conscience remained in doubt as before, and did not know on what terms it stood with God.

But the Lord comes and sympathizes with this distress, because the servant is captive and bound in his sins, and yet is such a fool as to want to help himself; he looks for no mercy, knows nothing to say of grace, and feels nothing but sins, which press him heavily, and knows of no one to help him. Then his lord has mercy on him and sets him free. Thus God deals with us. He forgives our debt, because he hears our cries and sees our humiliation.

October 22nd - Psalm 1:1, 2

Blessed is the man that walks not in the counsel of the ungodly, nor stands in the way of sinners, nor sits in the scat of the scornful. But his delight is in the law of the Lord; and in his law does he meditate day and night.

There is a common inquiry among men concerning blessedness; there is no one who does not wish that it may be well with him, and does not dread the thought that it should be ill with him. Yet all who have ever inquired into the matter have wandered from the knowledge of true blessedness, and those have wandered the most widely who have inquired with greatest diligence, such as the philosophers, the greatest of whom have placed true blessedness in the works of virtue, having rendered themselves more unhappy than the rest; they have deprived themselves of the blessings both of this life and of that which is to come. The common people, although their ideas were the more grossly mad by making blessedness to consist in carnal pleasure, enjoyed at least the good of this life. This teacher, however, deriving his doctrine from heaven and detesting all the devoted endeavors of men, gives this only true definition of blessedness which is wholly unknown to men—that he is the blessed man who loves the law of God. It is a short definition, but it contains a savor that is contrary to all human ideas, and especially to human wisdom.

Is he not a blessed man and one strong in the faith who does not walk in the broad way in the midst of the multitudes; who suffers reproaches and many evils from the same, and yet does not consent unto them so as to walk with them? Who is not deceived by the most specious counsel of the ungodly, which might deceive the very elect? It is a great thing not to be overcome by riches, pleasures and honors; but to overcome the specious righteousness and wisdom of the ungodly, who direct their attacks most of all against pure faith, is the greatest of all victories. But you are to notice that these words are the words of faith and that they do not speak of men according to what they appear to be. For no one would imagine such to be the ungodly. The prophet here speaks in the spirit; and spiritually that is ungodly which the world considers most godly, because it is devoid of faith. The ungodly are secure and confident in their lives, and there is no fear of God before their eyes.

October 23rd - Philippians 1:3, 5

I thank God upon every remembrance of you, ... for your fellowship in the gospel from the first day until now.

Paul rejoices in the gospel with his inmost soul. He thanks God that others have come into its fellowship. His confidence is firm regarding certain beginners in the faith, and he is so interested in their salvation as to rejoice in it as much as in his own, apparently unable to thank God sufficiently for it. He prays unceasingly that he may live to see many come with him into such fellowship and be preserved therein until the day of the Lord Jesus Christ, who shall perfect and complete all the defects of this earthly life. He prays these beginners may go forth faultlessly in faith and hope until that joyful day.

Thus the apostle pours out the depths of his heart, filled with the real fruits of the Spirit and of faith. He burns with love and joy whenever he sees the gospel recognized, accepted and honored, and the Church flourishing. For the converts he can conceive of no loftier desire—can offer no greater petition for them than to implore God that they may increase and persevere in the gospel faith. Such is the inestimable value he places upon possessing and holding fast God's Word.

Paul is here an example of gratitude for us. It behooves the Christian who recognizes the grace and goodness of God, expressed in the gospel, first of all to manifest his thankfulness toward God and then toward men. As Christians who have abandoned the false services and sacrifices that in our past heathenish blindness we zealously practiced, let us remember our obligation henceforth to be the more fervent in offering true service and right sacrifices to God. We can render him no better service than the thank-offering, as the Scriptures call it. That is, receiving and honoring the grace of God and the preaching and hearing of his Word, and furthering their operation, not only in word, but sincerely in our hearts and with all our physical and spiritual powers. This is the truest gratitude.

These words therefore give us an exact delineation of the Christian that believes in the holy gospel. Such hearts are rare in the world and especially difficult to find, unless it be among the beloved apostles or those who approach them in the likeness of Christ. Let us not be found unthankful, and forgetful of God's infinite goodness.

October 24th - Matthew 5:16

Let your light shine before men, that they may see your good works, and glorify your Father which is in heaven.

Let the Christian know that his earthly life is not unto himself, nor for his own sake; his life and work belong to Christ, his Lord. Hence his walk must be such as shall contribute to the honor and glory of his Master, whom he should so serve that he may be able to say with Paul, not only with respect to the spiritual life—the life of faith and righteousness by grace—but also with respect to its fruits—the outward conduct: "It is no longer I that live, but Christ lives in me." The world is to recognize Christ by his shining in us.

It is an astonishing fact that the world is merged into so great darkness that it utterly disregards the Word of God and the conditions he designed for our daily living. If we preach faith in God's Word the world receives it as heresy. If we speak of works instituted of God himself and conditions of his own appointing, the world regards it as idle talk. Living a simple Christian life in one's own family, or performing faithfully the duties of a servant, is of no value, but it says: "Oh, that is merely the following of worldly pursuits. To do good works you must set about in a different way. You must creep into a corner, don a cap, make pilgrimages to some saint; then you may be able to help yourself and others to gain heaven."

The Scriptures teach no other good works than God enjoins upon all men in the ten commandments and which pertain to the common conditions of life. True, these do not make such a brilliant show in the eyes of the world as do the self-appointed ceremonials constituting the divine service of the hypocrites; but they are true, worthy, good and profitable works in the sight of God and man. What can be more acceptable to God and advantageous to man than a life lived, in its own calling, in the way that contributes to the honor of God, and that by its example influences others to love God's Word and to praise his name? Therefore, influence men by your godly walk and good works to believe in Christ and to glorify him.

October 25th - Ephesians 4:3

Endeavouring to keep the unity of the Spirit in the bond of peace.

Christians should feel bound to maintain the unity of the Spirit, since they are all members of one body and partakers of the same spiritual blessings. They have the same priceless treasures—one God and Father in heaven, one Lord and Saviour, one Word, baptism and faith; in short, one and the same salvation, a blessing common to all, whereof one has as much as another, and cannot obtain more.

The unity of the Church does not consist in similarity of outward form of government, likeness of law, tradition and ecclesiastical customs. The Church is called "one holy, Christian Church," because it represents one plain, pure gospel doctrine, and an outward confession thereof, always and everywhere, regardless of dissimilarity of physical life, or outward ordinances, customs and ceremonies. But they are not members of the true Church of Christ who, instead of preserving unity of doctrine and oneness of Christian faith, cause divisions and offenses by human doctrines and self-appointed works for which they contend, imposing them upon all Christians as necessary.

One of the wickedest offenses possible to commit against the Church is the stirring up of doctrinal discord and division, a thing the devil encourages to the utmost. This sin usually arises in certain haughty, conceited, self-seeking leaders who desire peculiar distinction for themselves and strive for personal honor and glory. They will give honor to no one, even when they recognize the superiority of his gifts over their own. In their envy and vengefulness they seek occasion to create factions and to draw people to themselves. Many are deceived and immediately respond to the new doctrine presented in specious words by presumptuous leaders thirsting for fame. Many weak but well-meaning ones fall to doubting; many become reckless pleasure lovers, disregarding all religion and ignoring the Word of God. Even they who are called Christians come to have hard feelings against one another, their love grows cold and faith is extinguished. Christians, then, should be careful to give no occasion for division or discord. They must strive against them, submitting to all suffering and performing all demands to prevent, so far as possible, any disturbance of the unity of doctrine, of faith and of Spirit.

October 26th - 1 Corinthians 1:4

I thank my God always on your behalf, for the grace of God which is given you by Jesus Christ.

We have before us the opening words of the first Epistle to the Corinthians, which Paul was moved to write because of unpleasant conditions in the church at Corinth after his departure. Divisions had arisen and sad confusion prevailed in doctrine and life. Hence the apostle was constrained to rebuke their wickedness and correct their infirmities. Because of these wholesome admonitions, the reading and heeding of this epistle is not only profitable but essential, for the devil takes no respite, but whenever the gospel is preached in its purity he mixes with the children of God and sows his tares.

Paul begins very leniently, showing them what they have received through the gospel. His purpose is to arouse their gratitude to God, and to induce them, for his honor and glory, to be harmonious in doctrine and life, avoiding divisions and other offenses. Paul would say: What abundant grace and gifts have been given you of God! They are bestowed, not because of your righteousness, merits and works; nay, all these blessings have been freely given you in Christ and for his sake, through the preaching of the gospel. The gospel is a grace which brings to you all manner of gifts, by him enriching you in everything.

He gives them an example of his own gratitude, thanking God on their behalf, for the purpose of calling forth their especial gratitude when they should consider what they formerly were and what they now had received through the gospel. He would have them beware lest, forgetful of their former misery and present grace, they relapse into their old blindness. We are aware of the great benefits bestowed upon us, but at the same time we see and realize that the devil instigates divisions and scandals. The cause of these evils may be traced to our ingratitude. Where God's mercies are lightly dismissed from the mind and disregarded, gratitude and regard for God's Word cannot be the result; satiated, listless Christians go their way fancying that their spiritual conditions always were and always will be as now. The people, therefore, must be awakened to consider their former destitution, the wretchedness in which they were, that they may return thanks to God and recount the superior and wonderful gifts which have enriched them in all things.

October 27th - Proverbs 17:13

Whoever rewards evil for good, evil shall not depart from his house.

The heathen everywhere, despite their ignorance of God and his grace, condemned even to the utmost the evil of ingratitude. They regarded it the mother of evils, than which was none more malevolent and shameful. Among many examples in this respect is one left us by a people in Arabia called Nabathians, who had an excellent form of government. So strict were they in regard to this evil that any one found guilty of ingratitude to his fellows was looked upon as a murderer and punished with death.

No sin is more abominable to human nature, and of none is human nature less tolerant. It is easier to forgive and forget the act of an enemy who commits a bodily injury, or even murders one's parents, than it is to forget the sin of him who repays simple kindness and fidelity with ingratitude and faithlessness; who for love and friendship returns hatred. In the sentiment of the Latin proverb, to be so rewarded is like rearing a serpent in one's bosom. God likewise regards this sin with extreme enmity and punishes it.

Thus we have the teaching of nature and of reason regarding the sin of men's ingratitude toward one another. How much greater the evil, how much more shameful and accursed, when manifested toward God, who, in his infinite and ineffable goodness, conferred upon us while yet enemies of him and deserving of the fires of hell, not ten dollars, not a hundred thousand dollars even, but redemption from divine wrath and eternal death, and abundantly comforted us, granting safety, a good conscience, peace and salvation! These are inexpressible blessings, incomprehensible in this life. And they will continue to occupy our minds in yonder eternal life. How much more awful the sin of ingratitude for these blessings as exemplified in the servant mentioned in the gospel to whom was forgiven the debt of ten thousand talents and who yet would not forgive the debt of his fellow-servant who owed him a hundred pence!

October 28th - Romans 15:5

Now the God of patience and consolation grant you to be like minded one toward another according to Christ Jesus.

God gives patience and consolation. As he is the God of heaven and earth, so he is the God of patience and consolation. All are his gifts. If they are given, they are not of nature, but of grace. If God does not direct his Word to the heart to fit the needs of the individual, the heart will never discover this patience and consolation. But when he gives grace to search the Scriptures, he likewise gives these gifts. There is no more marked manifestation of God's wrath than the fact that he permits the decline of his spoken and written Word. On the other hand, God gives no greater blessing than when he exalts his Word among us and permits it to be read.

The apostle enjoins the Romans to be of one mind and tolerant of one another. The weak in conscience should accept as right what they of strong faith and sound conscience observe. The effort should be for a oneness of faith and conscience, and a sameness of opinion to avoid the wrangling occasioned by conflicting personal ideas of what is right. It is not necessary that we should all follow the same occupation. One may be a smith and another a tailor without impairing unity of faith and purpose, only let one tolerate the outward calling of the other. As privilege of occupation is right, so in external things of meats, apparel and place, we are at liberty to follow our own pleasure. It is not wrong to fast in honor of the name of an apostle, or to confess during Lent. But neither does he who omits these things commit any evil by this omission. Let not one censure, judge, condemn and quarrel with his fellow over the matter. But I refer to toleration only in things wherein we are at liberty to be lenient. We are to permit the weak in faith to continue in their practices for a time until we are finally able to extricate them from error. They must not be too hastily and rashly rejected with disastrous results to their consciences.

The apostle enjoins us to be likeminded according to Christ Jesus; that is, from a Christian point of view. For unbelievers, too, are like minded, but according to the flesh, the world and the devil, and not according to Christ. The Jews were of one mind against Christ and against his Church. Christian unity resists sin and everything opposed to the religion of Christ.

October 29th - Matthew 22:44

The Lord said unto my Lord, Sit on my right hand, till I make thine enemies your footstool.

Here Christ does not explain, but only says that David in his Psalm called Christ his Lord. "How then does David in the Spirit call him Lord?" It does not sound right and it is contrary to nature for a father to call his son lord, be subject to him and serve him. Now David calls Christ his Lord, and to whom the Lord himself says: "Sit you on my right hand until I make thine enemies your footstool," that is, be like me, acknowledged and worshiped as the right and true God; for it is right for none other to sit at his right hand; he is indeed so jealous that he allows no one to sit equal to him, as he says: "My glory will I not give to another."

Since the Lord now makes Christ equal to himself, he must be above all creatures. Therefore he proposes to the Jews a great question, without solving it; for they did not understand it and the time had not yet come to make this publicly known. But the meaning is as our articles of faith teach us to believe, that Christ was both David's true natural son, of his blood and flesh, and also David's Lord, whom David himself must worship and hold as God. However, it was impossible to make these statements harmonize, as it is still impossible for human reason, where the Holy Spirit does not reveal it, to comprehend how the two should be at the same time in the one Christ, that he was truly David's seed and God's Son by nature.

Now Christ propounded this question to teach that it is not enough to have the law, which only shows from what state we have fallen; but that Christ must be born, not in sin as David and all men are born, but had to be born without man of the virgin, sanctified by the Holy Spirit, born a real, true man, yet without sin. He is the only man that has been able to keep and fulfil the law. This one must intercede in our behalf before God and be our right hand and protection, in whom we have forgiveness of sins and deliverance from God's anger and hell. He also gives us the Holy Spirit to follow him until we come to him and be like him without any sin and in perfect righteousness.

October 30th - Psalm 1:6

The Lord knoweth the way of the righteous: but the way of the ungodly shall perish.

The way of the ungodly is so specious that unto men they may seem to rise in the judgment and to stand in the congregation. But he who cannot be deceived understands their ways and knows that they are ungodly; in his eyes they are not at all among the members of his Church. He knows the righteous only and not the sinners, that is, he approves the one and not the other. Therefore, their way shall perish, a thing they least of all expect or believe, though it continues with such success as to seem to be eternal. God knoweth only the way of the righteous, although it is hidden even to the righteous themselves. God's right hand leads them on in a wonderful way, seeing that it is a way, not of sense, nor of reason, but of faith only; even of that faith that sees in darkness and beholds things that are invisible.

When, therefore, we are subject to ungodly shepherds, we do not obey the ungodly, but men; for we do not follow their ungodliness, but we endure the presence of their persons. When men cast out and put down such, is it the ungodly that are put down? No, the persons are put down; for the ungodly who are put down remain ungodly still. The ungodly man is only then put down when he is led from ungodliness to godliness. This is not done by external violence but by love, internally praying and externally admonishing, while God condescends to work at the same time.

When you hearest that all things "prosper" for the righteous man, you are to desire it for yourself and to sigh for all those who are placed in any adversity, of whatsoever kind it may be; when you hearest that their leaf does not wither and that the pure Word of God flourishes in the Church of Christ, all fables and dreams of men are cast out; when you see any of these things thus take place anywhere you are to congratulate thyself, to rejoice and give thanks unto the divine goodness. And do not think that you are thus exhorted to impossibilities; only make the attempt and you will be compelled to rejoice and be thankful.

October 31st—Reformation Day - Psalm 2:1, 2

Why do the heathen rage, and the people imagine a vain thing? The kings of the earth set themselves, and the rulers take counsel together, against the Lord and against his anointed.

It is evident that by "kings" is signified Herod and Pilate, even though Pilate was not a king; for these two operated together to fulfil that which the counsel of God had foreordained to be done, namely, to destroy Christ. By "rulers" are to be understood the leaders among the priests; by "heathen" the Roman soldiers under Pilate, who seized Jesus, scourged and crucified him; and by "people" we are clearly to understand the common people of the Jews.

Observe here the tenderness and modesty of the prophet, how feelingly and sympathetically he speaks of the fury of these men, when he might with justice have mentioned those enraged expressions of the Jews, "Away with him, crucify him," and all those other infuriated clamors with which they accused Christ, frenzied and maddened, but he calls them only "meditations." Meditation is a continual prating or talking and is here used in a bad sense. For as a lover is always spontaneously saying many things about the object loved, so the hater is assiduously prating the worst of things about the object hated. There is the same modesty also in the words "rage" and "take counsel together;" the act itself was far more atrocious than the purport of these words would seem to indicate. We are thereby taught not to exaggerate the evil conduct of men, but as much as possible lessen it, and thus show that we do not feel so much indignation on our own account as pity on theirs.

"Against the Lord and against his anointed," is also a word of faith. God orders his words thus, that we may learn for our consolation and exhortation that we never suffer any injury, but what it offends God first, more than it does us; and such is the care of God our Father over us, that he feels every injury done to us before we do, and aims a greater indignation against it. This David holds forth to us, that we may keep ourselves from all feeling of revenge; that we may rather pity those whom we see rushing upon such majesty unto their own perdition. They do not in the least injure us, but horribly destroy themselves.

November 1st - Matthew 22:2

The kingdom of heaven is like unto a certain king, which made a marriage for his son.

The great love Christ has for us is presented to us in this picture of the marriage feast. There are many kinds of love, but none is so fervent as a bride's love for her bridegroom and that of the bridegroom for his bride. True love has no regard for pleasures or presents, or riches or gold rings, but cares only for the bridegroom. Even if he gave her all he had, she would regard none of his presents, but would say: I will have only you And on the other hand if he has nothing at all, it makes no difference to her, she will in spite of all that desire him. This is the true nature of the love of a bride. But where she has regard to pleasure, she does not care for him, but for the money; such love does not last long.

This true bride-love God presents to us in Christ, in that he allowed him to become man for us and be united with our human nature that we might thus perceive and appreciate his good will toward us. As the bride loves her betrothed, so also does Christ love us; and we on our part will love him, if we believe and are the true bride. Although he gave us the wisdom of all the prophets, the glory of all the saints and angels, and even heaven, yet would we not esteem them unless he gave us himself. The bride can be satisfied with nothing; the only one thing she wants is the bridegroom himself. "My beloved is mine and I am his."

So is Christ also disposed toward me; he will have me only and nothing besides. If I gave him all I could, it would be of no use to him; he would not regard it, if I wore all the hoods of all the monks. He wants my whole heart; the outward things, as the outward virtues, are only maid-servants, he wants the wife herself. He demands my heart. This marriage union is accomplished by faith, so that I rely fully and freely upon him, that he is mine. If I really have him, what more can I desire? If I am his and he is mine, I have eternal life, righteousness and all that belongs to him, so that neither death, sin, hell nor Satan can harm me.

November 2nd - Acts 22:16

Arise, and be baptized, and wash away your sins, calling on the name of the Lord.

The benefit of the Sacrament of Baptism is this, that therein God unites himself with you and becomes one with you in a gracious, comforting covenant. You desire, in accordance with the purpose and meaning of Baptism, to die from your sins and to be renewed on the last day, a hope inspired by the sacrament. On the strength of such desire on your part, God admits you to Baptism. The renewing work begins from that hour; he imparts to you his grace and Holy Spirit, and the Holy Spirit begins to kill the sin in your nature and to prepare the latter for death and for the resurrection on the last day.

You pledge yourself to remain in this state, and throughout your life, to the moment of death, to destroy sin more and more. God, accepting your pledge, exercises you during your whole life by imposing many good works, and not a few sufferings. Since such is your pledge to God, God in turn shows you grace and covenants with you that he will not impute to you the sins remaining in your nature after Baptism and will not regard them, nor condemn you on account of them. He is pleased with your effort to destroy sins and your desire to be rid of them. Though evil thoughts and desires may stir, though at times you sin and fall, yet if you arise and renew your covenant, your sins are forgiven by virtue of the covenant based upon the Sacrament of Baptism. If it were not for this covenant, every sin, however small, would condemn us. Hence there is no greater comfort on earth than Baptism, in which we pass under the jurisdiction of God's grace and mercy.

Therefore one should not be terrified when he feels evil lust; when one's thoughts and desires burn with passion; even when one falls from grace, still there is no ground for despair. But he should call to mind his baptism and joyfully comfort himself with the fact that God there covenanted to slay his sins and not to impute them unto condemnation, provided he refuses to consent to them and remain in them; provided he calls upon God for grace in order to make self-discipline possible; to battle against sin until released by death.

November 3rd - Romans 15:6

That you may with one mind and one mouth glorify God, even the Father of our Lord Jesus Christ.

All the good we can do to God is to praise and to thank him. This is the only true service we can render him. We receive all blessings from him, in return for which we should make the offering of praise. If anything else purporting to be service to God is presented for your consideration, rest assured it is erroneous and delusive. The distracted world attempts to serve God by setting apart houses, churches, cloisters, vestures, images, bells, organs and candles; the money for this expense should have been appropriated for the poor, if the object was to make an offering to God. Service to God is praise to him. It must be free and voluntary at table, in the chamber, in house or field, in all places, with all persons, at all times.

But how shall there be honor and praise of God, when we do not love him? How shall we love him when we do not know him and his blessings? How shall we know him and his blessings when no word is preached concerning them and when the gospel is left to lie under the table? Where the gospel is not in evidence, knowledge of God is an impossibility. Then to love and praise him is likewise impossible. True divine service of praise cannot be established with revenues, nor be circumscribed by laws and statutes. It emanates from the gospel, and certainly is as often rendered by a poor, rustic servant as by a great bishop.

Divine service must be rendered with "one mind" and with "one mouth." One needs Christ as much as another. We render divine service when we are harmonious, and when we recognize our common equality and our common blessings in Christ; when none exalts himself above another, nor assumes special advantages. We all receive the same baptism and sacrament, the same faith, the same Christ and Spirit, the same gospel—in a word, the same God. Here in this wilderness the heavenly bread is impartially distributed. Then how can it possibly be right for one to exalt himself over his fellow? Since there is one common blessing for the weak and the firm in faith, for the strong in Christian conduct and for the weak, one should not esteem another more lightly than himself, nor reject him.

November 4th - Matthew 22:12

He said unto him, Friend, how camest you in hither not having a wedding garment? And he was speechless.

Among the company sitting at table, there was also found a rogue, whom the king, in looking over the guests, speedily recognized to have on no wedding garment, and to have come, not in honor of the wedding, but disgracing the bridegroom and the lord who had invited him. These are such as permit themselves to be numbered among the Christians, hear the gospel, are in the outward communion of the right Church and act before the people as if they might also be of the gospel, but are not in earnest about it.

Such people the Christians must suffer in their gatherings and cannot prevent them from being amongst them; nor can they remove them, nor turn them out of their gatherings. They cannot judge and recognize them all, but must bear them and suffer their company until God himself comes with his judgment, so that they become manifest and betray themselves by their wicked life or false belief and spirit of heresy as not being true and honest Christians. So Paul says: "There must be also heresies among you, that they who are approved may be made manifest among you." Thus the king comes in himself and makes manifest him who has not on the wedding garment.

It is easy to understand what is meant by this man's being without a wedding garment, namely, without the new adornment in which we please God, which is faith in Christ, and therefore also without truly good works. He remains in the old rags and tatters of his own fleshly conceit, unbelief and security, without penitence and without understanding his own misery. He does not from the heart seek comfort in the grace of Christ, nor better his life by it, and looks for nothing more in the gospel than what his flesh covets. This wedding garment is the new light of the heart, kindled in it by the knowledge of the graciousness of this bridegroom and his wedding feast, which takes place especially through faith, by which the heart is renewed and purified. Where there is no faith, there the Holy Ghost is not, nor such fruits as please God. Whosoever does not know Christ through faith will also care little for God's Word, nor think of living in accordance with it. He remains proud and insolent, but weeping and gnashing of teeth come soon enough.

November 5th - Psalm 51:3

I acknowledge my transgressions: and my sin is ever before me.

Every Christian who wishes to make confession of his sins should place his confidence without reserve in the merciful promises and invitations of God, firmly believing that Almighty God will graciously forgive him his sins. Before he confesses his sins to a confessor, let him with due diligence make confession to the Lord God himself. Let him enumerate to the divine Majesty all his sins and infirmities, his conversation, deeds and manner of life without extenuating or concealing anything, just as if he dealt with a very familiar friend. His sinful and wicked thoughts also, so far as can be recalled, should be confessed.

Every Christian who would confess his sins should possess the honest intention and determination to amend his life and to forsake every manner of open, mortal sin. A confession without this purpose would be a dangerous and unpromising undertaking. When one discovers that he lacks the steady purpose to amend his life, he should fall upon his knees and pray to God for it. One must consider that it is impossible to call to mind and confess all his mortal sins; he should remember that after applying all diligence he confesses only the smallest part of his sins. The sins to be confessed, therefore, are the manifestly mortal sins and such as press upon a man's conscience at the time of confession. It is quite impossible to confess all mortal sins in view of the fact that when God sits in judgment and passes sentence upon them, not according to his gracious mercy, but his stern justice, even our good works render us guilty of death and condemnation.

The sum of the matter is this, that those persons are saved who place their trust solely in God, not in their works, nor in any creature.

Consequently man should learn to have greater confidence in God's mercy than in the zeal with which he makes confession. One cannot be too active, determined and guarded against the accursed evil of confiding in one's own works. Therefore we should accustom our consciences to trust in God, and let it be done with the understanding that to believe and trust in God is pleasing to him, and that unreserved trust in God is his highest glory.

November 6th - Psalm 2:4

He that sits in the heavens shall laugh: the Lord shall have them in derision.

These things are written for our sake, "that through patience and through comfort of the Scriptures we might have hope." What is written in this psalm with reference to Christ is applicable to all Christians, for whoever sincerely desires to be a Christian, will bear with his Herods, his Pilates, his rulers, his kings, his people and his heathen who rage against him, meditate vain things, rise up and take counsel together against him. For if these things are not done by men, they will be done by devils, or at least by men's own conscience, and certainly in the hour of death; then there is need of remembering this and like consolations, "He that sits in the heavens shall laugh at them; the Lord shall have them in derision," and of standing firmly in this hope and being moved by no circumstances whatever.

But this derision is divine. God made the Christ-murdering Jews and Gentiles a derision to the whole world by raising Christ from the dead and making, out of his despairing kingdom among that one people, a kingdom that shall flourish eternally over all creatures, thus turning all their endeavors into an event the very contrary of what they expected. Therefore as in the preceding verses the passion and death of Christ are prophesied, so in this verse his resurrection is predicted, though by a somewhat obscure allusion. Who would have thought, while Christ was suffering and the Jews triumphing, that God was laughing at them all the while! So also while we are oppressed, how shall we believe that God is holding our adversaries in derision, when it seems to us as though we were held in derision both by God and men? What a power of faith is required in all these words!

But his sitting in heaven is so secret and hidden that unless you are in heaven you cannot not know and understand it. you are suffering upon earth and the hope of help is denied you in all things by all, until, rising by faith and hope above all things, you mountest up to reach unto him who sits in the heavens. Here it is that the anchor of our heart is to be cast in all tribulation, and all the evils of the world will not only be made easy to bear, but will become a derision.

November 7th - Luke 22:19

This do in remembrance of me.

If you desire to render a precious noble service to God, and duly to honor the passion of Christ, bethink yourself of the Sacrament and partake of it. His praise and honor are bound up with it. This is his memorial. There is no show of garment or ceremony filling the eye. The only agent at work is the spoken Word. On earth the Word may be lowly esteemed; but no eye can see, no ear can hear, no heart can comprehend its worth and sublimity in the eyes of God and his angels. God's Word and work at first but feebly impress. Hence they require application and meditation. This art is effectively taught in the words, "This do in remembrance of me." Receive, proclaim, praise and laud the tidings of the grace manifested in Christ and thank him for it. Thus you will confess with heart and mouth, with body and soul, that you have given God nothing, that you can give him nothing, but everything you have has been received from him, especially eternal life and infinite righteousness in Christ.

He who remembers Christ and honors his passion is safeguarded against error and devilish delusions of every kind. He serves and honors God. He does not despise God's institution and order, but observes it with humility and joy. God certainly receives such honor gladly, since he has instituted the Holy Supper to be appropriated, and not to be neglected. Surely he cannot be delighted when man does not approach and receive it. Such neglect means to charge God with the folly of instituting unnecessary ordinances and with uncertainty as to what we need. But he who partakes, honors God by celebrating and aiding in the perpetuation of this memorial of Christ by proclaiming, praising and blessing the grace manifested by Christ, through his suffering, to us poor sinners. With the Lord's Supper God has bound up his own honor, for in Christ alone he desires to be acknowledged and worshiped as our God. So far as the Holy Supper is a confession before men, the communicant proclaims Christ and teaches faith in him. He helps to spread and preserve the kingdom of Christ, strengthens the influence of gospel and sacrament, aids in the conversion of sinners and in storming the devil's kingdom.

November 8th - John 4:50

Jesus said unto him, Go your way; your son lives. And the man believed the word that Jesus had spoken unto him, and he went his way.

The nobleman must have had faith, else he would not have asked the Lord to come to his son. He believed that if Christ would come to his house, he could heal his son; but unless he were present, he could not effect the cure. His faith was not strong enough to realize that Christ could heal without being present. Hence, his faith had to attain a higher stage. When Christ said, "Except you see signs and wonders, you will not believe," his faith drooped and he feared lest Christ would refuse to help him. The earthen vessel was shattered and he thought his son had to die. But Christ approached, raised him up, and placed him on a higher plane of faith. "Go your way; your son lives." Thus the man advanced from his first faith, when he believed that Christ could heal if he were present, to a higher stage of faith, by reason of which he now believed the mere Word of Christ. For if he had not believed the Word, he would not have ceased until the Lord had accompanied him to his house; but he accepted the Word, believed Christ and clung to his Word.

This is a pure and strong faith, that requires the individual to cast away all sense, understanding and reason, and sink himself into one little word, be satisfied with it and feel secure in it. Reason would have led him to say: When I left my son, he was ill. As I left him so shall I find him. But faith says the contrary, abides firmly by the Word and is immersed in it; it does not at all doubt that it shall be as the Word declares. The father accepted the word of Christ, "Go your way; your son lives," and so he said in his heart: My son is ill, but I shall find him well. This was faith over against reason and experience. Thus faith does not remain idle or quiet, but progresses and rises higher.

So Christ also deals with us and permits us to be tried to strengthen our faith. If at the close of our lives we shall have a spark of such faith, it will be well with us. It matters not how insignificant faith may be, the power lies in seeing that it be not overthrown.

November 9th - Romans 15:4

Whatsoever things were written before were written for our learning, that we through patience and comfort of the scriptures might have hope.

The apostle gives us a general admonition from the Scriptures, saying that not only this passage, but the entire Scriptures were written for our learning. The Bible contains much about Christ, and also about numerous saints—Adam, Abel, Noah, Abraham, Isaac, Jacob—which was not recorded for their sakes. The Bible was written long after their time; they never saw it. Thus, however much is written about Christ, it is not for his sake; he had no need of it. It is recorded for our instruction. The record of Christ's words and deeds is for our edification, the model for us to follow. Although the words are about Christ, they are directed to us, for our learning; we are to conduct ourselves as the Scriptures tell us Christ and his saints conducted themselves.

Mark the book the apostle here presents for the perusal and study of Christians—none other than the holy Scriptures. He tells us it contains doctrine for us. Now if our doctrine is to be found in the Bible, we certainly should not seek it elsewhere; all Christians should make daily use of this book. No other bears the title here given by Paul—book of comfort—one that can support the soul in all tribulations, helping it not to despair, but to maintain hope. For thereby the soul apprehends God's Word and, learning his gracious will, cleaves to it and continues steadfast in life and death. He who knows not God's will must doubt, for he does not know what relation he sustains to God.

Since the life to come is not evident to mortal sense, it is necessary for the soul to have something to which it may cling in patience, something to help it to a partial comprehension of that future life, and upon which it can rest. That something is God's Word. Paul mentions "patience" before "comfort" to indicate that he who is unwilling to endure suffering and seeks consolation elsewhere cannot taste the comfort of the Word. It is the province of the Word alone to comfort. It must therefore meet with patience first. To maintain Christian patience under trials, the afflicted must comfort themselves with those portions of Scripture that show Christ's example. Thus the hope of the soul continues steadfast.

November 10th - John 5:39

Search the scriptures; for in them you think you have eternal life; and they are they which testify of me.

The external word or preaching belongs to Christianity as a channel or means through which we attain unto the forgiveness of sins, or the righteousness of Christ, with which Christ reveals and offers us his grace or lays it in our bosom, and without which no one would ever come to a knowledge of this treasure. Whence would any man know, or in what man's heart would it ever come, that Christ, the Son of God, came from heaven for our sake, died for us, and rose from the dead, acquired the forgiveness of sins and eternal life, and offers the same to us, without publicly having it announced and preached? Although he acquired this treasure for us through his suffering and death, no one could obtain or receive it, if Christ did not have it offered, presented, and applied. All that he had done and suffered would be to no purpose, but would be like some great and precious treasure buried in the earth, which no one could find or use.

Therefore I have always taught that the oral word must precede everything else, must be comprehended with the ears, if the Holy Ghost is to enter the heart, who through the Word enlightens it and works faith. Faith does not come except through the hearing and oral preaching of the gospel, in which it has its beginning, growth and strength. Therefore the Word must not be despised, but held in honor. We must familiarize ourselves with it and constantly practice it, so that it ever bears fruit. It can never be understood and learned too well.

Here then you have all that belongs to the article of the righteousness of Christ. It consists in the forgiveness of sins, offered to us through Christ, and received by faith in and through the Word, purely and simply without any works on our part. Yet I do not mean that Christians should not do good works, but that these are not to be mingled in the doctrine of faith and decorated with the shameless delusion that they avail before God as righteousness. After we have this righteousness of faith, works are to follow and continue here on earth. Both faith and works are to be maintained, each in its proper place, the former before God above all works, the latter in works of love to our neighbor.

November 11th - Psalm 2:9

> *You shall break them with a rod of iron; you shall dash them in pieces like a potter's vessel.*

Here the vain dreams of the flesh are to be removed, and no one is to imagine that the kingdom of Christ is either founded on or preserved by iron or arms; because it is written that he delighted not in chariots, nor in horses, nor in the legs of a man. The apostle says: "The weapons of our warfare are not carnal." The Turks, whom at this day we never seek to conquer by any other means than the sword, we ought to conquer by increasing the number of Christians among them.

Why do we not attack with the sword also the wicked among ourselves? But God forbid. The kingdom of Christ consists in righteousness, truth and peace. By these it was obtained and by them it will be preserved. Hence, when he said above that he was appointed king, he recommended no other office whatever than that of the Word, saying, "I will declare the decree of God," not, I will ride fine horses, I will lay waste cities, I will seek the treasures of the world; but I will do this one thing—declare those things which God has commanded, that is, that Christ is God and man, which Paul calls the gospel, saying, "Separated unto the gospel of God, which he had promised afore, concerning his Son Jesus Christ."

You see that this whole verse is an allegory which really takes place in fact and life. As the word "Christ" is the word of salvation and peace, not in the flesh, but in the spirit, it follows of necessity that it subdues and drives out the safety, peace and easy life of the flesh. Where it does this, it appears unto the flesh harder and more unfeeling than iron itself. Wherever the carnal man is savingly touched by the Word of God, one thing is felt, another is wrought, namely, "The Lord kills and makes alive." Though God is the God of life and salvation and these are his proper works, yet, in order to accomplish these, he kills and destroys, that he may come unto his proper work. He kills our will, that he may establish his own in us. He mortifies the flesh and its desires, that he may implant the Spirit and his desires; and thus "the man of God is made perfect, thoroughly furnished unto all good works."

November 12th - Matthew 22:14

Many are called, but few are chosen.

God deals with us in a way to put down arrogance, that we may not become haughty and wanton, but may always remain in fear. For when temptation comes we are liable to fall into error. Peter on the water retained his pure faith as long as he unhesitatingly ventured on the water according to the word of Christ. Had he remained in this faith, he might have walked hundreds of miles on the water; but as soon as he wavered he began to sink. So Moses also had a strong faith, but at times fell from it. Thus it happens that one may have a strong faith, but doubts and falls. By faith Moses led the people of Israel through the midst of the sea and through death, and Peter boldly ventured on the sea; but they both fell, although God raised them up again. The thief on the cross laid hold on faith once for all and clung to it.

We have a beautiful parable of this in the tree which begins to blossom in the spring and is soon covered with white blossoms. But as soon as the rain falls on them, many of the blossoms are ruined and the frost utterly destroys many more of them. When the fruit begins to appear and the winds arise, much of the young fruit falls to the ground; later the caterpillars and worms make their appearance and they prick and destroy the fruit to such an extent, that scarcely the twentieth, yea, hardly a hundredth part ripens.

The same thing happens to the gospel. At first everybody wants to become a Christian, and the gospel promises to do well, but as soon as the rain and wind of temptation come, large numbers fall away. Afterwards come the sects and factions, like worms and beetles, which prick and pollute the fruit of the gospel, and so much false doctrine is taught, that only a few remain faithful to the gospel.

The first thing that faith requires is that we be not secure and presumptuous, but remain in fear. We need to cling to God and pray: Merciful God, you have permitted me to become a Christian, help me to continue to be one and to increase daily in faith.

November 13th - Psalm 5:11

Let all those that put their trust in you rejoice ... let them also that love your name be joyful in you

Here we are told when and what joy is, namely, confidence and a good conscience resting in the mercy of God. They that have had experience in these things say that there is no joy above that of a pure conscience, nor any sorrow greater than that of a guilty and troubled one. A pure and joyful conscience comes in no other way than by looking steadfastly to the mercy of God. In the former part of this verse he describes the joy in tribulation; in the latter part the joy of prosperity, which cannot be true and sincere unless it be a rejoicing in God only. This verse briefly makes a distinction between prosperity and adversity. It is impossible that he who does not trust in the Lord should not be filled with sorrow when tribulation comes upon him. He who is in sorrow cannot but continually murmur, because there is no praising of God without joy of heart, and this sorrowful and impatient murmurer must displease God and be more and more forsaken of him.

On the other hand it is impossible that he should not rejoice who trusts in God. If the whole world should burst upon the head of such a one he would stand unmoved amid the falling ruins. He who is joyful in such hope cannot but think well of God, exult in his praise, and encourage himself in him. The man who thus rejoices is patient, happy and in a state to be protected of God. Nor will such a one rejoice, hope and exult in vain, for God will preserve him. If then your soul be sad and cast down, begin some joyful song or psalm or something that brings your God to your memory and you will find relief and will prove that the counsel of the wise man it good: "In the day of evil be not unmindful of good things."

By the name of the Lord we may understand Jesus Christ, or Father, Son and Holy Spirit. All these are names of God. They who love the name of Jesus love the salvation of God, the truth, the mercy and the wisdom of God; all these are included in the name of the Lord. If a man love these he must of necessity love the name of the Lord.

November 14th - Luke 22:19, 20

This is my body, which is given for you: ... This cup is the new testament in my blood, which is shed for you.

The words "my" and "you" are words of unmistakable significance. Who is it that says "my body," "my blood"? The Lord Jesus Christ, the Son of God, who shed his blood and died for you. When he says, "my body," "my blood," he merely asks "you" to acknowledge and believe it, to rest in such faith and render him thanks for what cost him so bitterly. He would not have you shamefully despise his Sacrament or lightly neglect it because it is to be had without price or effort.

But you may argue that the statement of Paul is too awful, when he says, whosoever eats the bread and drinks the cup of the Lord unworthily, eats and drinks judgment unto himself, and is guilty of the body and the blood of the Lord. Dear friend, you must not consider yourself so much from the standpoint of worthiness or unworthiness of your person as from that of your need, which makes the grace of Christ necessary. If you recognize and feel your need, you have the requisite worthiness and preparation. The Holy Supper has been instituted by Christ, not as a poison for us and as a sign of Christ's wrath, but as a means of comfort and salvation. Above all, you must realize that however great your unworthiness, the merit of your Lord Jesus Christ cannot be doubted. It is your duty to praise, honor and thank him, and to be one of the observers of his ordinance and institution, as he has a right to expect and as you have vowed in your baptism.

There is a twofold reason for you to receive the Lord's Supper. It means gratitude and praise for Christ, and grace and solace for yourself. To occupy the standpoint of this twofold reason does not argue wickedness and a misuse of the Sacrament; it is the right standpoint and pleasing to God. Our relation to God is right only when we occupy the standpoint of gratitude and supplication. In rendering thanks we honor him for the blessings and grace already received, in supplication for those we crave for the future. When one goes to the Holy Supper with this disposition, what is his act but the declaration: Lord, I thank you for all the grace I have received at your hands, and I pray you to supply still further my need? You cannot more highly honor God.

November 15th - Philippians 3:9

Not having mine own righteousness, which is of the law, but that which is through the faith of Christ, the righteousness which is of God by faith.

As far as the righteousness of the law is concerned, Paul dares to say that he regards it as filth and refuse; notwithstanding in its beautiful and blameless form it is unsurpassed by anything in the world. Only the righteousness of faith teaches us how to apprehend God— how confidently to console ourselves with his grace and await a future life, expecting to approach Christ in the resurrection. By "approaching" him we mean to meet him in death and at the judgment day without terror, not fleeing, but gladly drawing near and hailing him with joy as the one awaited with intense longing.

Now, the righteousness of the law cannot effect such confidence of mind. Hence, for me it avails nothing before God. What does avail is God's imputation of righteousness for Christ's sake through faith. God declares to us in his Word that the believer in his Son shall, for Christ's sake, have God's grace and eternal life. He who knows this is able to wait in hope for the last day, having no fear, no disposition to flee.

But is it not treating the righteousness of the law with irreverence and contempt to regard it as something not only useless, but loathsome and abominable? Should we not condemn as a heretic this preacher who goes beyond his prerogative and dares find fault with the law of God? Paul would say: I, too, was such a one. In my most perfect righteousness of the law I was an enemy and persecutor of the Church of Christ. It was the legitimate fruit of my righteousness that I thought I must be a party to the most horrible persecution of Christ and his Christians. Thus my holiness made me an actual enemy of Christ and a murderer of his followers.

Whence such a disposition? It naturally springs from human righteousness. Every individual who professes human righteousness, and knows nothing of Christ, holds that righteousness efficacious before God. He relies upon it and gratifies himself with it, presuming thereby to present a flattering appearance in God's sight and to render himself especially acceptable to him. His enmity is greater and his hatred more bitter toward the preaching that dares to censure such righteousness and assert its futility to merit God's grace and eternal life.

November 16th - Ezekiel 16:49, 50

This was the iniquity of your sister Sodom, pride, fulness of bread, and abundance of idleness was in her and in her daughters, neither did she strengthen the hand of the poor and needy. And they were haughty, and committed abomination before me: therefore I took them away as I saw good.

These same conditions now exist everywhere. Every peasant, burgher, nobleman is simply gathering dollars, waits and saves, eats and drinks, is insolent and mischievous as though God were nothing at all. No one cares for the despised Jesus in his poverty; nay, he is even trod under foot, until all obedience, discipline and honor are destroyed among us, as they were in Sodom and Gomorrah, and matters become so bad as to become unbearable, because all admonition and preaching seem to be of no avail. The world will not recognize that it must die and stand before God in judgment, but rages against known truth. Let us give heed and take it to heart, that the wrath of God may not also sweep us away. What else would God need to do to that end than let loose both the Turks and Satan against us. The Turk would be compelled to cease doing what he has done and is still doing, were we not so hardened in blindness and impenitence and so completely ripe for judgment. The reason is that we rage so blasphemously against God's Word and his proffered help.

I hold that if we Lutherans, as they call us, were only dead, the whole world would immediately cry, *"Victory,"* as though they had already devoured every single Turk. But it shall happen to them also that a hundred shall be slain by one Turk. The leaders at Jerusalem thought, if they could only put the prophet Jeremiah out of the way they would surely be safe from the king of Babylon. What happened? After they had cast Jeremiah into the dungeon, the king came and led them all into captivity.

I can also see that God has spun a web over Germany as it is determined to be guilty of willful blindness, wickedness and ungratefulness in opposing the precious gospel. It is determined to be guilty of foolishness before God for which it will have to pay dearly. May God preserve us and grant us and our little flock that we may escape this terrible wrath, and be found among those who honor and serve our dear Christ, and await the judgment at his right hand joyously and blissfully. Amen.

November 17th - Romans 15:7

Receive you one another, as Christ also received us to the glory of God.

There are two reasons why we should receive one another. The first is because of Christ's example. The Scriptures present Christ to us as one upon whom fell the infamy of our sins—for us he was ignominious in God's sight—and who did not despise, reject nor revile us, but received us, that he might redeem us from our sins. We are, then, under particular obligation to receive one another. The other reason the apostle presents for our receiving one another is that thus we contribute to the praise and honor of God. This we learn from Christ. He everywhere testifies that all he does is in obedience to his Father's will, and that he came for no other purpose than to do the will of God. It is certain, then, that he bore the ignominy of our sins simply because it was his Father's will.

Mark the exceeding mercy of the Father's controlling will in placing upon his beloved Son our sins, and permitting him to bear the shame of them, merely that we might escape condemnation. A true recognition of this, God's gracious will, must evoke sincere love and praise to him and gratitude for his mercy. Christ has in himself upheld the honor of God by receiving us and bearing our sins. So should we likewise take upon ourselves the burdens, the sins and imperfections of our neighbors, and bear with them and help reform them.

When such Christian conduct is manifest before sinners and the spiritually weak, their hearts are attracted to God and forced to exclaim: Truly, he must be a great and gracious God, a righteous Father, whose people these are; for he desires them not to judge, condemn nor reject us poor, sinful and imperfect ones, but rather to receive us, to give us aid and to treat us as if our sins and imperfections were their own. Should we not love and exalt such a God? Should we not praise and honor him and give him the implicit confidence of our hearts in all things? This is the praise God would have from us, that we receive and regard our neighbor's condition as our own. Such conduct on our part will encourage others to believe and will strengthen the faith of believers.

November 18th - Genesis 6:18

With you will I establish my covenant; and you shall come into the ark, thou, and your sons, and your wife, and your sons' wives with you.

Interpreters discuss what that covenant was. Lyra explains it as the promise to defend him against evil men who had threatened to murder him..Burgensis claims this covenant refers to the perils amid the waters, which were to be warded off. Still others believe it was the covenant of the rainbow, which the Lord made with Noah. In my opinion he speaks of a spiritual covenant, or of the promise of the seed which was to bruise the serpent's head. The giants had this covenant, but when its abuse resulted in pride and wickedness, they fell from it. So it was afterward with the Jews, whose carnal presumption in reference to God, the law, worship and temple led to their loss of these gifts, and they perished. To Noah, however, God confirms this covenant by certainly declaring that Christ was to be born from his posterity and that God would leave, amid such great wrath, a nursery for the Church. This covenant not only includes protection of Noah's body, the view advocated by Lyra and Burgensis, but also eternal life.

He plainly states "with you" He mentions not the sons, nor the wives, whom he was also to save, but he mentions Noah alone, from whom the promise was transmitted to his son Shem. This is the second promise of Christ, which is taken from all other descendants of Adam and committed to Noah alone. Afterward this promise is made clearer from time to time. It proceeded from the race to the family, and from the family to the individual. From the race of Abraham it was carried forward to David alone; from David to Nathan; from Nathan down to one virgin, Mary, who was the dead branch or root of Jesse, and in whom this covenant finds its termination and fulfilment. The establishment of such a covenant was most necessary in view of the imminence of the incredible and incalculable wrath of God.

It was no easy matter to believe that the whole human race was to perish. The world consequently judged Noah to be a dolt for believing such things and ridiculed him. In order to strengthen his mind amid such offenses God speaks with him often, and now even reminds him of his covenant.

November 19th - Ephesians 5:16

Redeeming the time, because the days are evil.

The time is unquestionably good as long as the gospel is faithfully preached and received. At the same time, even today the world is filled with evils, factions, false theories and bad examples of every sort; much of this wickedness is inherent in ourselves. With these things the Christian must always contend; the devil pursues, and our own flesh discourages and allures us from recognition and observance of the divine will. If we strive not against it, we shall soon lose sight of God's will, to our own injury, even while listening to the gospel. For the devil's strongest fury is exerted to befoul the world with fanaticism, and to draw from the pure doctrine of faith into that evil even those who possess the gospel. Being flesh and blood we are always self-secure, unwilling to be led by the Spirit, indolent and unresponsive in relation to the Word of God and to prayer. In the outward walks of life, obstacles and evils meet us everywhere, impeding our spiritual progress and impelling us to suppress the gospel and to rend the Church.

Let no one, then, expect to enjoy an era of peace and pleasure here on earth. Although the present time is in itself good, and God bestows upon us the golden year of his Word and his grace, yet the devil is here with his factions and followers, and our own flesh supports him. He corrupts the blessed days of grace at every possible opportunity, and so oppresses Christians that they must contend against him with their utmost strength and vigilance if they would not, through the influence of evils and obstacles, be wrested from the gospel they have received and would persevere therein to the end.

Wherefore we have the best reasons to adapt ourselves to the present time in the best possible way; to walk wisely and circumspectly, showing all faithfulness to the will of God; obeying it while we have opportunity—while still in possession of God's Word, his grace and his Spirit. Being opposed and obstructed by the devil and our own flesh, we must be wise and careful and guard against following them. So, then, we are to understand by "evil days" the allurements that lead us away from God's Word and his will.

November 20th - Psalm 119:11

Thy word have I hid in mine heart, that I might not sin against you

A man may be familiar with God's Word, yet if he walks in self-security, concerned about other matters, or perhaps, being tempted, he loses sight of God's Word, it may easily happen that he is seduced and deceived by the secret craft and cunning of the devil; or of himself become bewildered, losing his wisdom and being unable to find counsel or help even in the most trivial temptations. For the devil and reason, or human wisdom, can dispute and syllogize with extraordinary subtlety in these things until one imagines that to be true wisdom which is not. A wise man soon becomes a fool; men readily err and make false steps; a Christian likewise is prone to stumble; and even a teacher and prophet can easily be deceived by reason's brilliant logic. So there is need of understanding, of careful, keen discernment, that wisdom be not perverted and falsified, and man be deceived with its counterfeit.

Man is prone to stumble and to fail in understanding when not watchful of his purposes and motives, to see how they accord with the wisdom of God's Word. Particularly is his understanding unreliable when the devil moves him to wrath, impatience, dejection, melancholy, or when he is otherwise tempted. Often they who have been well exercised with trials become bewildered in small temptations and uncertain what course to take. In this one needs to be watchful and not go by his reason or his feelings, but remember God's Word, or ascertain if he does not know what it is, and be guided thereby. Man cannot judge aright by the dictates of reason when he is tempted. Therefore he ought not to follow his own natural intelligence, nor to act from hasty conclusions. Let him be suspicious of all his reasoning and beware of the cunning of the devil, who seeks either to allure or to intimidate us by his specious arguments. Let him call upon the understanding born of his wisdom in the gospel, what his faith, love, hope and patience counsel, what God's will eloquently teaches everyone and under all circumstances, and let him strive and pray to be filled with such knowledge.

November 21st - Luke 24:47

That repentance and remission of sins should be preached in his name among all nations.

The gospel is the preaching of repentance and remission of sins. It should not be preached in a corner, but before all men, whether it be received or not, for it is to spread even farther that it may be heard and bear fruit. We are not to be offended though few receive it, nor say it has been given in vain. We should be content that Christ has commanded us to preach it in all the world, that he who will may receive it.

By repentance Christ means a change for the better; not what we have called repentance, when one scourges and chastises himself and does penance to atone for his sin, or when the priest imposes this or that upon any one for penance. Scripture does not speak of it in this sense. Repentance signifies a change and reformation of the whole life; so that when one knows that he is a sinner and feels the iniquity of life, he desists from it and enters upon a better course of life in word and deed, and does it from the heart.

But we should preach also forgiveness of sins. This signifies that the gospel should be preached, which declares unto all the world that in Christ the sins of all the world are swallowed up, that he suffered death to put away sin from us, and arose to blot it out. All this he did, that whoever believeth should have the comfort and assurance that it is reckoned unto him even as if he himself had done it. This continues as long as we live until the day of judgment. Forgiveness is so great and powerful that God not only forgives your past sins, but forgives also the sins you will yet commit. He will not condemn us for our daily infirmities, but forgives all, in view of our faith in him, if we only strive to press onward and get rid of sin. Repentance in his name is done when in those who believe in Christ God through that faith works a change for the better, not for a moment, nor for an hour, but for their whole life. A Christian is not perfectly nor instantaneously cleansed, but the reformation and change continues as long as he lives. Nothing will be accomplished except in Christ's name. That alone has power to save.

November 22nd - 1 John 2:1, 2

If any man sin, we have an advocate with the Father, Jesus Christ the righteous: and he is the propitiation for our sins: and not for ours only, but also for the sins of the whole world.

Since we are unable to keep the law, Christ came and stepped between the Father and us, and prays for us: Beloved Father, be gracious unto them and forgive them their sins. I will take upon me their transgressions and bear them; I love you with my whole heart, and in addition the entire human race, and this I will prove by shedding my blood for mankind. I have fulfilled the law and I did it for their welfare in order that they may partake of my fulfilling the law and thereby come to grace.

Thus there is first given us through Christ the sense that we do not fulfil the law and that sin is fully and completely forgiven; however, this is not bestowed in a way or to the end that we need not keep the law in the future, and may forever continue to sin, or that we should teach, if we have faith we need no longer to love God and our neighbor. But the meaning is that the fulfilling of the law may now for the first time be successfully attempted and perfectly realized, and this is the eternal, fixed and unchangeable will of God. To this end it is necessary to preach grace that man may find counsel and help to come to a perfect life.

But the help offered us is that Christ prays the Father to forgive us our sins against the law, and not impute what we are still owing. He promises also to give the Holy Spirit, by whose aid the heart begins to love God and to keep his commandments. God is not gracious and merciful to sinners to the end that they might not keep his law, nor that they should remain as they were before they received grace and mercy; but he condones and forgives both sin and death for Christ's sake, who has fulfilled the whole law to make the heart glad and through the Holy Spirit to kindle and move the heart to begin again to love from day to day more and more. Thus begins in us not only love, but also truth, a true character, as the law requires. Christ is full of grace and truth, and through him grace and truth grow in us.

November 23rd - Matthew 25:31, 32

When the Son of man shall come in his glory, and all the holy angels with him, then shall he sit upon the throne of his glory: and before him shall be gathered all nations: and he shall separate them one from another, as a shepherd divides his sheep from the goats.

Had it not been told us we should be inquisitive beyond measure to know what would happen on the last day, and what Jesus would say and do on that day. Here we are now told of and have set before us, first of all, death, which no one can escape; but after that the day of judgment. Then it will come to pass that Christ will bring together by means of the resurrection all who have ever lived upon earth; and at the same time he will descend in inexpressible majesty, sitting upon the throne of judgment, with all the heavenly host hovering around him; and all the good and bad will appear, so that we shall all stand exposed before him and no one will be able to conceal himself.

The appearance of this glory and majesty will immediately become a great terror and pain to the condemned, lest they shall suffer punishment, even eternal destruction from the face of the Lord and from the glory of his might. Even if there were no more than a single angel present, there would not remain in his presence one fickle, wicked conscience, were it possible to escape, any more than a thief and a rascal can bear to come before a human judge. If he could escape he would much prefer it, if only for the purpose of escaping public disgrace, to say nothing of his being compelled to hear the judgment passed upon him.

What a terrible sight it will be, when the ungodly shall see not only all of God's angels and creatures, but also the Judge in his divine majesty, and shall hear the verdict of eternal destruction and hell-fire pronounced upon them forever. This should surely be a powerful admonition for us to live as Christians, so that we may stand in honor and without fear at the right hand of this majestic Lord, where there will be no fear, nor terror, but pure comfort and everlasting joy. Whoever is not moved and aroused by these words can certainly never be moved by anything.

November 24th - Matthew 25:34

Then shall the King say unto them on his right hand, Come, you blessed of my Father, inherit the kingdom prepared for you from the foundation of the world.

This will take place publicly in the presence of all angels, men and creatures, and before the whole rabble of an ungodly world, that it may be seen who have been pious, honest Christians, as well as who have been hypocrites. Such a separation cannot take place in the world until that day, not even in the assembly which constitutes the Christian Church. The good and the bad must remain together in this world, as we learn from the parable of the wedding guests, or as Christ himself had to tolerate Judas among his apostles. Christians are much grieved that they must remain in the midst of a crooked, perverse, ungodly people, which is the kingdom of Satan.

While Christians have their sufferings here upon earth, they will also have their comfort on the coming day of judgment, when Christ will separate them from the other flock, so that after that day no false, ungodly men, nor death, nor devil can ever touch them or offend them. Christ will pronounce the verdict in the very words in which he has already prepared it and set it forth and will certainly not change it. Therefore see to it that you are among those who are kind and merciful here upon earth for Christ's sake, or who even suffer for his sake, then you may joyfully await the last day, and need not be afraid of the judgment; for he has already selected you and placed you among those who shall stand at his right hand.

We who are Christians should hope for the coming of this judgment and desire it with our whole heart, as we pray in the words: your kingdom come; your will be done; deliver us from evil; so that we may also hear the glad and welcome words: Come, you blessed, into the kingdom of my Father. This is the verdict we await; for this we are Christians. For we must constantly see and hear the maliciousness which

Satan and the world practice against the gospel. There is so much misery upon earth that we ought to be tired of this life and cry aloud: Come, dear Lord, and deliver us. For there are certainly souls who are joyfully awaiting the judgment of Christ with a good conscience.

November 25th - 1 Peter 5:8, 9

Be sober, be vigilant; because your adversary the devil, as a roaring lion, walks about, seeking whom he may devour; whom resist steadfast in the faith.

The devil does not sleep; he looks around and exerts himself to exterminate the pure doctrine in the Church and will finally, it is feared, bring it to this, that should one pass through all Germany he would find no pulpit where the pure Word of God is preached as in former days. He tries with all his might to prevent the pure doctrine from being taught, for he cannot endure it. To escape from the enemy is most difficult. He lurks and watches everywhere, and pushes his affairs so hard that even the learned fall and the elect stumble, as did Moses, Peter and the other apostles. We think we are safe and permit matters to drift. We should pray and call on God to maintain the gospel and cause his holy name to be proclaimed more and more widely; but no one cares, no one prays for the advancement of the gospel. The consequence must be that God will overthrow both us and Satan. The end will be that our rashness and indifference shall bring us into great misery.

The heart must thoroughly grasp this idea, that although we may feel secure concerning a matter and have Scripture for it, and be prepared and fortified in the best possible manner with clear proofs, it is after all the will and power of God that protect us and defend us against the devil, our adversary and most bitter foe. But this occurs only when God awakens us and keeps us in his fear, so that we may always be concerned and cry: "Lord, increase our faith." Our hearts should always be in a condition as if we had only begun to believe to-day, and always be so disposed toward the gospel as if we had never before heard it. We should make a fresh beginning each day. Our faith must constantly grow and become stronger. Man is a poor, weak creature. Paul says, "We have this treasure in earthen vessels." This treasure is the gospel. An earthen vessel is easily broken and its contents spilled. When the devil notices what a treasure faith is and in what a poor vessel it is kept he rages and storms in his wrath to shatter the vessel and spill the treasure. Man is a poor, weak earthen vessel; if God would permit, Satan would soon utterly destroy the whole vessel.

November 26th - John 21:22

Jesus said unto him, If I will that he tarry till I come, what is that to you? follow you me.

Christ teaches us a beautiful and touching lesson. Notwithstanding the examples and lives of all the saints every person should attend to the work entrusted to him and guard the honor of his calling. This is truly a needed and wholesome teaching. Many persons are found like Peter, looking around to the saints Christ loved, and turning their backs to the commission and calling to follow Christ. As no one now is without some commission and calling, so no one is without some kind of work, if he desires to do what is right. everyone therefore is to take heed to continue in his calling, look to himself, faithfully do what is commanded him, and serve God and keep his commandments; then he will have so much to do that all time will be too short, all places too cramped, all resources of help too weak.

Moreover it is a common plague that no one is satisfied with his own lot, so that the heathen say: How does it happen that there is always better fruit in another field, and that the neighbor's cow gives more milk than our own? How does it come that no one is content with his own state and thinks that of another is better than his own? If God allowed one to change his lot with all his will, even then he would be like everyone else, would become more tired and at last stay with his own. Hence one ought not to think of changing his lot, but of changing his spirit of discontent. Cast aside and change that restless spirit, then the lot of one will be like that of another and all will be prized alike.

To overcome such unrest, discontent and disgust in one's self, faith is helpful and necessary—a faith which is of the firm conviction that God governs all alike, places each one in the lot that is the most suitable for him. This faith brings rest, contentment and peace; it banishes the tired spirit. Hence we see how faith is needed in everything and how it makes everything easy, good and sweet, even if you were in prison or in death, as the martyrs prove. Without faith all things are difficult and bitter, though you possessed the pleasures of the whole world, as all the great lords and wealthy prove, who at all times lead the most wretched lives.

November 27th - Colossians 1:9

For this cause we ... do not cease to pray for you, and to desire that you might be filled with the knowledge of his will in all wisdom and spiritual understanding.

The apostle's words are "be filled," that is, not only hear and understand God's will, but become rich in the knowledge of it, with ever increasing fullness. You have begun well; you are promising shoots. But something more than a good beginning is required, and the knowledge of God's will cannot be exhaustively learned at once on hearing the Word. "Knowing the will of God" means more than simply knowing about God, that he created heaven and earth and gave the law, a knowledge which even the Jews and Turks possess. When this point has been reached further enlightenment is necessary if man is to be saved. He must know the meaning of Christ's words: "This is the will of my Father, that everyone which sees the Son, and believeth on him, may have everlasting life."

This spiritual knowledge, or confidence, is not so easily learned as other things. It is not so readily apprehended as the knowledge of the law written in nature. Indeed, that more than anything else hinders the Christians and saints from obtaining the knowledge of God's will in Christ, for it compels the heart and conscience to plead guilty in every respect and to confess having merited the wrath of God; therefore the soul naturally fears and flees from God. Then, too, the devil fans the flame of fear and sends his fiery arrows of dismay into the heart. The wicked world eagerly contributes its share of hindrance against Christians as a people of the worst type, condemned enemies of God. Our flesh and blood is a drawback, making much of its own wisdom and holiness and seeking thereby to gain honor and glory or to live in security of life and wealth, pleasure and covetousness. Hence on every side a Christian must be in severe conflict, if he is to succeed in preserving the knowledge of God's will. Verily, there is need of earnest and diligent use of the Word of God and prayer, that Christians may not only learn to know the will of God, but also to be filled with it. Only so can the individual walk always according to God's will, and gain strength to enable him to face fears and terrors against the devil, the world, flesh and blood.

November 28th - Luke 21:25, 26

There shall be signs in the sun, and in the moon, and in the stars; and upon the earth distress of nations, with perplexity; the sea and the waves roaring; men's hearts failing them for fear.

The signs preceding the judgment day are many and great. They will all be fulfilled, even though none or very few men take note of or esteem them as such. Two things must take place according to the Word and prophecy of Christ and the apostles: first, many and great signs will be made manifest; second, the last day will come unawares; the world will not expect it, even though that day be at the door. Though men see those signs and be told that they are signs of the last day, still they will not believe. Some, indeed, will see it and it will be those who least expect it. That there will be such security and indifference among men we prove from the words of Christ and the apostles. Christ says: "Take heed to yourselves, lest haply your hearts be overcharged with surfeiting, and drunkenness, and cares of this life, and that day come on you suddenly as a snare, for so shall it come upon all them that dwell on the face of the earth."

From these words it is clear that men in great measure will give themselves over to surfeiting and drunkenness and the cares of this life, and that, drowned as it were in these things, they will rest secure and continue to dwell on the earth as if the dreadful day were far away. For were there no such security and heedlessness, that day would not break in unawares. But he says it will come as a snare by which birds and beasts are caught at a time when most concerned about their food and least expecting to be entrapped. In this figure he gives us clearly to understand that the world will continue its carousing, eating and drinking, building and planting, and diligently seeking after earthly things, and will look upon the day of judgment as yet a thousand and more years off, when, in the twinkling of an eye, they may stand before the terrible judgment bar of God. Whatever other signs may appear before Christ's coming, I know that, according to Christ's words, surfeiting and drunkenness, building and planting, buying and selling, marrying and giving in marriage and other cares of this life will be in evidence.

November 29th - 2 Thessalonians 1:6

It is a righteous thing with God to recompense tribulation to them that trouble you.

Whatever the Christian suffers here on earth at the hands of the devil and the world befalls him simply for the sake of the name of God and for his Word. True, as a baptized child of God the Christian should justly enjoy unalloyed goodness, comfort and peace on earth; but since he must still dwell in the kingdom of the devil, who infuses sin and death into human flesh, he must endure the devil. Yet all Satan's afflictions and the world's plagues, persecutions, terrors, tortures, even the taking of the Christian's life, and all its abuse, is wrought in violence and injustice. But to offset this, the Christian has the comforting assurance of God's Word that because he suffers for the sake of the kingdom of Christ and of God he shall surely be eternally partaker of that kingdom. Certain it is, no one will be worthy of it unless he suffers for it.

Christians should certainly expect this and comfort themselves in the confidence that God will not permit the wrongs of his people to continue unpunished and unavenged. We might think he had forgotten, were we to judge from the facts that godly Abel was shamefully murdered by his brother, that God's prophets and martyrs—John the Baptist, Jeremiah, Paul and others—suffered death at the hands of bloodhounds like the Herods, Neros and other shameless, sanguinary tyrants of that sort, and this when God had, even in this life, given glorious testimony of their being his beloved children. A judgment must be forthcoming that tyrants may suffer pains and punishments, and that the godly, delivered from sufferings, may have eternal rest and joy. Let all the world know that God does not forget even after death.

This is the consolation which the future judgment at the resurrection of the dead holds, that, as God's righteousness requires, the saints shall receive for their sufferings a supremely rich and glorious recompense. Paul seems to present, as the principal reason why God must punish the world with everlasting pain, the fact that the world has inflicted tribulation on Christians. This is indicated where we read that Christ shall say on the last day: "Depart from me, you cursed ... inasmuch as you did it not unto one of these least, you did it not unto me."

November 30th - Philippians 3:21

Who shall change our vile body, that it may be fashioned like unto his glorious body, according to the working whereby he is able even to subdue all things unto himself.

We Christians are expectantly to await the coming of the Saviour. His coming will not be to our injury or shame as it may be in the case of others. He comes for the salvation of our unprofitable, impotent bodies. Wretchedly worthless as they are in this life, they are much more unprofitable when lifeless and perishing in the earth. But, however miserable, powerless and contemptible in life and death, Christ will at his coming render our bodies beautiful, pure, shining and worthy of honor, until they correspond to his own immortal, glorious body. Not like it as it hung on the cross or lay in the grave, blood-stained, livid and disgraced, but as it is now, glorified at the Father's right hand. We need not then be alarmed at the necessity of laying aside our earthly bodies; at being despoiled of the honor, righteousness and life adhering in them, to deliver it to the devouring power of death and the grave—something well calculated to terrify the enemies of Christ; but we may joyfully hope for and await his speedy coming to deliver us from this miserable, filthy pollution.

Think of the honor and glory Christ's righteousness brings even to our bodies! How can this poor, sinful, miserable, polluted body become like unto that of the Son of God, the Lord of glory? What are you—your powers and abilities, or those of all men, to effect this glorious thing? But Paul says human righteousness, merit, glory and power have nothing to do with it. Another force intervenes, the power of Christ the Lord, who is able to bring all things into subjection to himself. Now, if he has power to subject all things unto himself at will, he is able also to glorify the pollution and filth of this wretched body, even when it has become worms and dust. In his hands it is as clay in the hands of the potter, and from the polluted lump of clay he can make a vessel that shall be a beautiful, new, pure, glorious body, surpassing the sun in its brilliancy and beauty. The righteousness of Christ inspires with power, making evident that we worship the true and living God, who delivers from sin, death and condemnation, and exalts this perishable body to eternal honor and glory.

December 1st - Matthew 7:12

Whatsoever you would that men should do to you, do you even so to them: for this is the law and the prophets.

Faith brings and gives Christ to you with all his possessions. Love gives you to your neighbor with all your possessions. These two things constitute a true and complete Christian life; then follow suffering and persecution for such faith and life, and out of these grows hope in patience. Where, then, are the good works which you are to do to your neighbor? They have no name. As the good works which Christ does to you have no name, so your good works are to have no name.

They have no name so that there may be no distinction made and they be not divided, else you might do some and leave others undone. You shall give yourself entirely to him with all you have, the same as Christ gave himself wholly to you, with praying, fasting, all works and suffering, so that there is nothing in him that is not yours and was not done for you. Thus it is not your good work that you give alms and pray, but that you offer yourself to your neighbor and serve him, whenever he needs you and in every way you can, be it with alms, prayer, work, counsel, comfort, apologizing, clothing, food, and if need be, with suffering and death.

If you have ears to hear, listen and learn what good works are. A work is good for the reason that it is useful and benefits or helps the one for whom it is done; why else should it be called good? A tree bears fruit, not for itself, but for the good of man and beast, and these fruits are its good works. You are not to do good to God and to his dead saints, they are not in need of it; still less to wood and stone, to which it is of no use, but to men. To men you should do everything that you would they should do to you. A man is to live, suffer and die for his wife and child, the wife for the husband, children for parents, servants for masters, masters for servants, the government for subjects and subjects for governments, each one for his fellow man, even for his enemies. Such are truly Christian and good works, and should be done at all times, in all places, and toward all people.

December 2nd - Zechariah 9:9

Rejoice greatly, O daughter of Zion; ... behold, your King cometh unto you: he is just and having salvation.

Learn from these words what takes place when God begins to make us godly, and what is the first step in becoming so. There is no other beginning until your King comes to you and begins to work in you. It is done in this way: the gospel comes first and must be preached and heard. In it you hear and learn how all your works count for nothing before God and that everything that you work and do is sinful. Your King must first be in you and rule you. Here is the beginning of your salvation; you relinquish your works and despair of yourself, because you see and hear that all you do is sin and amounts to nothing, as the gospel tells you. You receive your King in faith, cling to him, implore his grace and find consolation in his mercy alone.

But when you hear and accept this it is not your power, but God's grace, that renders the gospel fruitful in you, so that you believe that you and your works are nothing. For you see how few there are who accept it, so that Christ weeps over Jerusalem. Nor is it by virtue of your power and your merit that the gospel is preached and your King comes. God must send him out of pure grace. Hence, no greater wrath of God exists than where he does not send the gospel; there is only sin, error and darkness, there man may do what he will. Again, there is no greater grace than where he sends his gospel, for there must be grace and mercy in its train, even if not all, perhaps only a few, receive it.

This is what is meant by "Thy King cometh unto you " You do not seek nor find him; he seeks and finds you. The preachers and their sermons come from him, not from you; your faith and everything that your faith works in you comes from him, not from you; when he does not come, you remain outside; where there is no gospel, there is no God, but only sin and damnation. Therefore you should not ask where to begin to be godly; there is no beginning, except where the King is proclaimed and enters.

December 3rd - Matthew 21:5

Behold, your King cometh unto you, meek, and sitting upon an ass, and a colt the foal of an ass.

"Behold." With this word the evangelist at once rouses us from sleep and unbelief as though he had something great or remarkable to offer, something we have long wished for and now receive with joy. Such waking up is necessary, because everything that concerns faith is against reason; for example, how can reason comprehend that an individual should be king of Jerusalem who enters in such poverty and humility as to ride upon a borrowed ass? But the nature of faith is that it does not judge nor reason by what it sees, but by what it hears. It depends upon the Word alone and not on vision or sight. Christ is received as King only by the followers of the word of the prophet, by the believers in Christ. These are the true daughters of Zion.

This King is distinguished from all other kings. It is "thy" King who was promised to you, whose own you are. For him you have yearned from the beginning, him the fathers have desired to see, he will deliver you from all that has hitherto burdened, troubled and held you captive. This is a comforting word to a believing heart, for without Christ man is subject to many raging tyrants who are not kings, but murderers, at whose hands he suffers great misery and fear.

But where the heart receives the King in firm faith, it is secure and does not fear sin, death, hell, nor any other evil; for it well knows and in no wise doubts that this King is the Lord of life and death, of sin and grace, of hell and heaven, and that all things are in his hands. Thus he became our King and came down to us that he might deliver us from these tyrants and rule over us himself alone. He who is under this King cannot be harmed either by sin, death, hell, Satan, man nor any other creature. Such boundless gifts are brought by this poor, despised King. All this reason does not understand, nor nature comprehend; it can be comprehended by faith alone.

December 4th - John 12:15

Fear not, daughter of Zion: behold, your King cometh, sitting on an ass's colt.

We will direct our attention to the reason why the evangelist quotes the words of the prophet, in which was described long ago and in clear, beautiful and wonderful words, the bodily public entrance and advent of our Lord Jesus Christ to the people of Zion or Jerusalem. The prophet wanted to show to his people and to all the world, who the Messiah is and in what manner he would come and manifest himself. He thereby anticipates the mistaken idea of the Jews, who thought that, because there were such glorious things said and written of Christ and his kingdom, he would manifest himself in great worldly pomp and glory, as a king against their enemies, especially the Roman empire, to the power of which they were subject, and that he would overthrow its power and might, and in its place set up the Jews as lords and princes. Thus they expected nothing in the promised Christ but a worldly kingdom and deliverance from bodily captivity. They were led to this notion, and strengthened in it, by their false priests, preachers and doctors, who perverted the Scriptures concerning Christ and interpreted them according to their own worldly understanding as referring to bodily, worldly things, because they would fain be great earthly lords.

But the dear prophets plainly foretold that we should not think of such an earthly kingdom, nor of bodily salvation, but give attention to the promise of a spiritual kingdom and of a redemption from the pernicious fall of mankind in paradise. This is a different salvation from that of bodily freedom, power and glory, the end of which is death.

The evangelist therefore quotes this saying of the prophet to punish the blindness and false notions of those who seek bodily and temporal blessings in Christ and his gospel, and to convince them by the testimony of the prophet, who shows clearly what kind of a king Christ was and what they should seek in him, in that he calls him just and having salvation and adds this sign of his coming by which they are to know him: "He cometh to you, meek, and riding upon a colt, the foal of an ass." This verse takes away all support for excuse, if they do not receive Christ, and it cuts off all hope and expectation for another. It distinctly announces that he would come on this wise and he has fulfilled everything.

December 5th - Galatians 4:4, 5

But when the fullness of the time was come, God sent forth his Son, made of a woman, made under the law, to redeem them that were under the law.

In the article of faith, in which we say that the Son of God became man and that he was of the same nature as we ourselves are, in order that he might redeem us from sin and death and give us eternal life without any merit or worthiness of our own, we give Jews and Turks no less occasion for laughter and mockery than when we speak of the three persons in the Godhead. For this is a more absurd assertion by far, in the estimation of human reason, which speculates in its Jewish and Turkish, yea, heathenish teachings, on this wise: God is an only, almighty Lord of all, who has created all men and given them the law according to which they are to live; accordingly it follows that he will be merciful to the good and obedient, but will condemn and punish the disobedient. Therefore he who does good works and guards himself against sin, God will reward. These are nothing but heathenish conclusions drawn from earthly, worldly experience and observation.

Such heathen ideas of wisdom, holiness and service of God are taught and practiced by the pope. So we believed, myself and others, while we were under him, not knowing any better; otherwise we would have done and taught differently. In fact, he who has not this revelation and Word of God, can neither believe nor teach other than pagan doctrine. For human reason knows no better; and how can it know better without the revelation? Even when the revelation was proclaimed, human wisdom would not heed it, but despised it and followed its own fancies.

But to us this counsel and mind of God, in giving his Son to take upon himself our flesh, is revealed and declared. From the Word of God we have the knowledge that no man of himself can be righteous before God; that our whole life and all our deeds are under wrath and condemnation, because we are wholly born in sin and by nature are disobedient to God; but if we would be delivered from sin and be saved, we must believe on this mediator, the Son of God, who has taken our sin and death upon himself, by his own blood and death rendering satisfaction, and has by his resurrection delivered us.

December 6th - Luke 21:25

There shall be signs in the sun, and in the moon, and in the stars; and upon the earth distress of nations.

"The sun shall be darkened" (Matthew 24:29). Some think that the sun is to be darkened never to shine again; but this cannot be the meaning, for day and night must continue to the end. "While the earth remains day and night shall not cease." This sign therefore dare not interfere with day and night and still be fulfilled before the judgment day. "The moon shall not give her light." The same is to be said of this as of the signs of the sun. Is it not true that scarcely a year has passed in which sun and moon have not been eclipsed? Astronomers have told us, and rightly so, that these eclipses are but natural phenomena. As a result the tokens are the more despised and carnal security is increased. "The stars shall fall from heaven." This is seen almost daily. Aristotle again talks about the nature of the thing; but the gospel, which is the Word and wisdom of God, pronounces the falling of the stars a sign. Wherefore if the stars fall or the sun and moon fail to give their light, be assured that these are signs of the last day; for the gospel cannot utter falsehood. While in these years there have been so many showers of stars, they are all harbingers of the last day, as Christ says; they must appear often that the great day may be abundantly proclaimed. These signs appear and pass, but no one heeds them; they are waiting for other signs, just as the Jews are waiting for another Christ.

"Distress of nations" does not, indeed, mean that all nations and all people among these nations will so suffer; for you must note that these are to be signs. Stars do not fall from heaven at all times; the sun does not lose its brightness for a whole year; all these may be tokens without changing the order of things. "Distress of nations" does not refer to the body. For there will be peace and joy in abundance. People will eat and drink, buy and sell, marry and be given in marriage and wrap themselves up in this present life as if they expected to abide here forever. I take it that it is the condition of agonized conscience. Sin and conscience oppress. By these the sinner becomes so distressed that he knows not what to do, nor whither to flee.

December 7th - Luke 21:26

The powers of heaven shall be shaken.

By the powers of heaven some understand the angels of heaven. But since Christ speaks of signs and says we shall see them and recognize in them the coming of the last day, they must surely be visible tokens and be perceived with the bodily senses. For those people whose consciences are in distress and whose hearts are failing from fear, though this be an affection of the soul, yet manifest it by word and countenance. Therefore these powers of heaven must be such as can be really shaken and so perceived.

The Scriptures speak in a twofold way concerning the powers of heaven. At one time they are spoken of as the heavens which are the most powerful among all creatures, "and God called the firmament—expanse or fortress—heaven." Every creature under heaven is ruled and strengthened by the light, heat and movements of the heavens. What would the earth be without the heavens but a dark and desert waste? At another time the powers of heaven signify the hosts of heaven: "and the heavens and the earth were finished and all the hosts of them." It is common in the Scriptures to speak in this way of the powers of heaven. And it is clear from this and other passages that the hosts or powers of heaven include all that is in them; in the heavens, the sun, moon, stars and other heavenly bodies; on earth, man and beast, birds and fish, trees, herbs and whatsoever lives upon it. The passage before us may therefore mean the powers of heaven in both senses, probably chiefly the hosts of heaven. Christ could say that all creatures shall be shaken and shall serve as tokens of that day; sun and moon with darkening, the stars with falling, the nations with wars, men with hearts failing from fear, the earth with earthquakes, the waters with winds and roaring, the air with infection and pestilence, and the heavens with their hosts.

Christ calls these signs and desires us to take special notice of them, appearing, as they do, not alone, but with a multitude of other tokens. Let the unbeliever doubt and despise God's tokens and speak of them as simply natural; but let us hold fast to the gospel.

December 8th - Luke 21:28

When these things begin to come to pass, then look up, and lift up your heads; for your redemption draweth nigh.

How shall we look up and lift up our heads, which evidently means, how shall we manifest any joy in and longing for these signs? In answer I would say that all this is spoken only to those who are really Christians and not to heathen and Jew. True Christians are so afflicted with all manner of temptations and persecutions that in this life they are miserable. Therefore they wait and long and pray for redemption from sin and evil; as we also pray in the Lord's Prayer, "Thy kingdom come," and, "Deliver us from evil." If we are true Christians we will earnestly and heartily join in this prayer. If we do not so pray, we are not yet true Christians.

If we pray aright, our condition must truly be such as to look up to them with joy and earnest desire, however terrible these signs may be, as Christ admonishes: "When these things come to pass, look up." He does not say, Be filled with fear or drop your heads; for there is coming that for which we have been earnestly praying. If we really wish to be freed from sin and death and hell, we must look forward to this coming of the Lord with joy and pleasure.

But what do those do who are filled with fear and do not desire to have him come, when they pray, "Thy kingdom come," "Thy will be done"? Do they not stand in the presence of God and lie to their own hurt? Do they not strive against the will of God who will have this day for the redemption of the saints. It is necessary that we exercise great care lest we be found to hate and to dread that day. Such dread is a bad omen and belongs to the damned, whose cold minds and hard hearts must be terrified and broken, if perchance they might reform.

To believers that day will be comforting and sweet. To them that day will be the highest joy and safety; just as in this life the truths of the gospel are exceedingly sweet to the godly and exceedingly hateful to the wicked. Why should the believer fear and not rather exceedingly rejoice, since he trusts in Christ who comes as judge to redeem him and to be his everlasting portion?

December 9th - Romans 8:23

We ourselves groan within ourselves, waiting for the adoption, to wit, the redemption of our body.

You say, I would indeed await his coming with joy, if I were holy and without sin. I answer, What relief do you find in fear and flight? It would not redeem you from sin if you were to be filled with terror for a thousand years. The damned are eternally filled with fear of that day, but this does not take away their sin; this fear rather increases sin and renders man unfit to appear without sin on that day when it comes.

There is no one so well prepared for the judgment day as he who longs to be without sin. If you have such desire, what do you fear? You are then in perfect accord with the purpose of that day. It comes to set free from sin all who desire it, and you belong to that number. Return thanks to God and abide in that desire. Christ says his coming is for our redemption. But do not deceive yourself and be satisfied, perhaps, with the simple desire to be free from sin and to await the coming of the day without fear. Perhaps your heart is false and you are filled with fear, not because you would be free from sin, but because in the face of that day you cannot sin free and untrammeled. See to it that the light within you be not darkness. For a heart that would be truly free from sin will certainly rejoice in the day that fulfils its desire. If the heart does not so rejoice there is no true desire to be loosed from its sin.

From this we learn how few there are who pray the Lord's Prayer acceptably. There are few who would not rather that the day would never come. This is nothing else than to desire that the kingdom of God may not come. Yet, he who feels such fear must not despair, but rather use it wisely. He does so who permits such fear to urge him to pray for grace that his fear might be taken away and he be given joy and delight in that day. Therefore those who fear are nearer their salvation than the hard-hearted, who neither fear nor find comfort in that day.

December 10th - Romans 13:11

Knowing the time, that now it is high time to awake out of sleep.

For the sake of effect and emphasis the apostle in his admonition employs a pleasing figure and makes an eloquent appeal. The word "sleep" is used as a simile to help us grasp the spiritual thought. Since for the sake of temporal gain men rise from sleep, put aside the things of darkness and take up the day's work when night has given place to morning, how much greater the necessity for us to awake from our spiritual sleep, to cast off the things of darkness and enter upon the works of light, since our night has passed and our day breaks. "Sleep" here stands for the works of wickedness and unbelief. For sleep is properly incident to the night time. Then, too, the explanation is given in the added words: "Let us cast off the works of darkness." Similarly in the thought of awakening and rising are suggested the works of faith and piety. They that sleep, sleep in the night; and they that be drunken are drunken in the night. But let us, who are of the day, be sober, putting on the breastplate of faith and love; and for an helmet the hope of salvation.

Paul, of course, does not enjoin against physical sleep. His contrasting figures of sleep and wakefulness are used as illustrations of spiritual lethargy and activity—the godly and the ungodly life. Note the analogy between natural and spiritual sleep. The sleeper sees nothing about him; he is not sensitive to any earthly realities. In the midst of them he lies as one dead and useless, without power or purpose. Though having life in himself he is practically dead to all outside. His mind is occupied, not with realities, but with dreams, in which he beholds mere images, vain forms of the real; and he is foolish enough to think them true. But when he wakes, these illusions or dreams vanish. Then he begins to occupy himself with realities.

So it is in the spiritual life. The ungodly person slee Psalm He is in a sense dead in the sight of God. He does not recognize the real spiritual blessings extended him through the gospel; he regards them as valueless. For these blessings are only to be recognized by the believing heart; they are concealed from the natural man.

December 11th - Genesis 22:18

In your seed shall all the nations of the earth be blessed.

The blessing here promised to the patriarch in his seed is simply the grace and salvation in Christ which the gospel presents to the whole world. For Christ is the seed of Abraham, his own flesh and blood, and in Christ all believing inquirers will be blessed. This promise to the patriarch was later more minutely set forth and more widely circulated by the prophets. All of them wrote of the advent of Christ, his grace and gospel. The divine promise was believed by the saints prior to the birth of Christ; thus, through the coming Messiah they were preserved and saved by faith.

But faith is not abolished in the fulfilment of the promise; rather it is established. As they in former time believed in the future fulfilment, we now believe in the completed fulfilment. Faith in the two instances is essentially the same; but one belief succeeds the other as fulfilment succeeds promise. In both cases faith is based on the seed of Abraham, that is, on Christ. In one instance it precedes his advent and in the other it follows. He who would now, like the Jews, believe in Christ yet to come, as if the promise were still unfulfilled, would be condemned. For he would make God a liar in holding that the word is unredeemed, contrary to fact. Were the promise not fulfilled, our salvation would be still far off; we would have to wait its future accomplishment.

Having in mind faith under these two conditions, we must now believe not only in the promise but in its past fulfilment. For though the faith of the fathers is one with our faith, they trusting in Christ to come and we in a Christ revealed, yet the gospel leads from the former faith to the latter. It is now necessary to believe the promise, and also its fulfilment. Abraham and the ancients were not called on to believe in the accomplished fulfilment, though they had the same Christ as we have. There is one faith, one spirit, one Christ, one community of saints; but they preceded, while we come after, Christ. Thus we—the fathers and ourselves—have had and still have a common faith in the one Christ, but under different conditions. Because of this common faith believers unite in Christ as one body.

December 12th - Matthew 11:2, 3

When John had heard in the prison the works of Christ, he sent two of his disciples, and said unto him, are you he that should come, or do we look for another?

The disciples of John had learned from him many excellent testimonies concerning Christ, that he was the Lamb of God and the Son of God, that Christ must increase while he must decrease. All this his disciples and the people did not believe, nor could they understand it, as they and all the people thought more of John than of Christ. Consequently they clung so closely to John, that for his sake they became jealous of Christ and were dissatisfied with him, when they saw that he also baptized and drew the people to himself.

To this error they are led for two reasons. First, Christ was not yet known to the people, but only to John; neither had he yet performed any miracle. The second reason was that Christ appeared so humble, being the son of a carpenter and of a poor woman. He did not belong to the priesthood, nor to the learned, nor had he ever studied, but was only a layman and a common apprentice. Hence it seemed that the excellent testimony of John concerning Jesus of Nazareth did not at all seem true. They were looking for one who might appear in an imposing manner among them, or like a highly learned leader among the priests or like a mighty king. From this delusion John could not dissuade them.

But when Jesus began to perform miracles and became famous, John thought that he would direct his disciples from himself to Christ, that they might not establish a new sect and become Johnites, but might cling to Christ and become Christians. They must learn that the works and coming of Christ would not be attended by drums and bugles and the like worldly pomp, but by spiritual power and grace; that by virtue of such power and grace the dead would be raised up, the blind receive their sight, the deaf hear, and all kinds of bodily and spiritual evil be removed. This would be the coming and glory of this King, the least of whose works could not be performed by all the kings, all the learned and all the rich of the world.

December 13th - Luke 21:33

Heaven and earth shall pass away: but my words shall not pass away.

Some men have wondered how heaven and earth shall pass away and call Aristotle to their aid. He must interpret the words of Christ for them, and he says, heaven and earth will not pass away as to their essence, but only as to their form. But let us suffer the blind to go, and know that just as our bodies will be changed as to their essence, so at the last day heaven and earth with all the elements will be melted with fervent heat and turned to dust, together with the bodies of men, so that there will be nothing but fire everywhere. Then will everything be newly created in greatest beauty; our bodies will shine in brilliancy, and the sun be much more glorious than now. Peter says, "The day of the Lord will come as a thief in the night; in the which the heavens shall pass away with a great noise, and the elements shall melt with fervent heat, and the earth also and the works that are therein shall be burned up. Nevertheless we, according to his promise, look for new heavens and a new earth, wherein dwells righteousness."

But where do our souls dwell when the abode of every creature is afire and there is no earthly dwelling place? Answer: My dear hearer, where is the soul now? Or where is it when we sleep and are not conscious of what is taking place in our bodies and in the world around us? Do you think that God cannot so preserve or hold the souls of men in his hand that they will never know how heaven and earth passed away? Or do you think that he must have a bodily home for the soul, just as a shepherd has a stable for his sheep? It is enough for you to know that they are in God's hands and not in the care of any creature. Though you do not understand how it happens, do not be led astray. Since you have not yet learned what happens to you when you fall asleep or awaken, and can never know how near you are to waking or sleeping, though you daily do both, how do you expect to understand all about this question? The Scripture says, "Father, into your hands I command my spirit," and so let it be.

December 14th - Matthew 11:6

Blessed is he, whosoever shall not be offended in me.

There are two kinds of offenses, one of doctrine, and the other of life. The offense of doctrine comes when one believes, teaches or thinks of Christ in a different way than he should, as did the Jews, teaching that Christ was other than he really was, expecting him to be a temporal king. Christ and Paul always dwell upon this offense, scarcely mentioning any other. It is not without reason that men are admonished to remember this. Under the reign of the pope this offense has been hushed entirely, so that neither monk nor priest knows of any other offense than that caused by open sin and wicked living, which the Scriptures do not call an offense. They teach the people to believe that the mass is an offering and a good work, that by works men may become pious, may atone for sin and be saved, all of which is nothing less than rejecting Christ and destroying faith.

The offense of life is, when one sees and teaches an openly wicked work of another. It is impossible to avoid this offense, inasmuch as we must live among the wicked, but it is not so dangerous, since everybody knows that such offense is sinful, and no one is deceived by it. There is no disguise nor deception. But in the offense of doctrine there may be the most beautiful religious ceremonies, the noblest works, the most honorable life, so that it is impossible for common reason to censure or discern it. Only faith through the Spirit recognizes that it is all wrong. Against this offense Christ warns us, saying: "Whoever shall offend one of these little ones, which believe in me, it were better for him that a millstone were hanged about his neck, and that he were drowned in the depth of the sea."

Whoever does not preach Christ, or who preaches him otherwise than the gospel teaches, namely, as one caring for the blind, the lame and the poor, teaches us how to become unhappy and stumble in Christ. It is truly a great blessing not to be offended in Christ, and there is no other help or remedy than to look at his works and compare them with the Scriptures. Otherwise it is impossible to keep from being offended at Christ.

December 15th - James 2:17

Faith, if it has not works, is dead, being alone.

Faith receives the good works of Christ, love bestows good works on our neighbor. Our faith is strengthened and increased when Christ is held forth to us in his own natural works, namely, that he associates with the blind, the deaf, the lame, the lepers, the dead and the poor; that is, in pure love and kindness toward all who are in need and in misery, so that finally Christ is nothing else than consolation and a refuge for all the distressed and troubled in conscience. Here is necessary faith that trusts in the gospel and relies upon it, never doubting that Christ is just as he is presented to us in this gospel, and does not think of him otherwise, nor lets anyone persuade us to believe otherwise. That gospel which suffers Christ to be seen and to be doing good only among the needy will not belie you.

If you desire to believe rightly and to possess Christ truly, then you must reject all works that you intend to place before God. They are only stumbling blocks, leading you away from Christ and from God. Before God no works are acceptable but Christ's own works. Let these plead for you before God, and do no other work before him than to believe that Christ is doing his works for you and is placing them before God in your behalf. God demands of us no other work that we should do for him than to exercise faith in Christ. With that he is satisfied, and with that we give honor to him, as to one who is merciful, patient, wise, kind and truthful. After this think of nothing else than to do to your neighbor as Christ has done to you, and let all your works together with all your life be applied to your neighbor. Look for the poor, sick and all kinds of needy, help them and let your life's energy appear in this, so that they may enjoy your kindness, helping wherever your help is needed, as much as you possibly can with your life, property and honor. Know that to serve God is nothing else than to serve your neighbor in love, whether he be enemy or friend, or whether you can help in temporal or spiritual matters. This is serving God and doing good works.

December 16th - Philippians 4:6

Be careful for nothing; but in everything by prayer and supplication with thanksgiving let your requests be made known unto God.

Here Paul teaches us to cast our care upon God. Should anything transpire to give you care or anxiety, turn to God with prayer, with supplication, entreating him to accomplish for you all you would seek to effect by care. Do so in thankfulness; you have a God solicitous for you, to whom you may freely come with all your anxieties. Whoever does not so when misfortune befalls him, but endeavors to measure it by his reason and to overrule it by his counsel, and thus falls into anxiety—this man plunges himself into deep wretchedness, loses his joy and peace in God, and all to accomplish nothing. Of this fact we have daily testimony in our experience and in that of others. But let no one conclude that he will be utterly careless and rest upon God, making no effort, no exertion, not even resorting to prayer. Whoever adopts this course must soon fail and fall into anxiety. We must ever strive. Many care-engendering things befall us for the very purpose of driving us to prayer. Many things transpire which tend to create in us anxiety, but we must not let them make us overanxious. We must commit ourselves to God and implore his aid for our needs.

Prayer is made vigorous by petitioning; urgent by supplication; pleasing and acceptable by thanksgiving. Strength and acceptability combine to prevail and secure the petition. This, we see, is the manner of prayer practiced by the Church; the holy fathers in the Old Testament always offered supplication and thanks in their prayers. The Lord's Prayer opens with praise and thanksgiving and the acknowledgment of God as Father. It earnestly presses toward him through filial love and a recognition of fatherly tenderness. For supplication this prayer is unequaled. Hence it is the sublimest and noblest prayer ever uttered.

These words of Paul beautifully spiritualize and explain the mystery of the golden censer of which Moses has written much in the Old Testament, detailing how the priests should burn incense in the temple. We are all priests and our prayers are censers. The golden vessel signifies the precious words of prayer; the live coals stand for thanksgiving for benefits in prayer; the ascending smoke is our faith, when we believe our appeal reaches God and is heard. We must not doubt that God hears us.

December 17th - Philippians 4:7

The peace of God, which passes all understanding, shall keep your hearts and minds through Christ Jesus.

By "peace of God" we must understand, not that calm and satisfied peace in which God himself dwells, but the peace and contentment he produces in our hearts. This peace is the gift of God and is called the "peace of God," because, having it, we are at peace with him even if we are displeased with men. This peace is beyond the power of mind and reason to comprehend. They who know nothing of fleeing to God in prayer, when overtaken by tribulation and adversity and when filled with care and anxiety, proceed to seek that peace alone which reason apprehends and which reason can secure. But reason apprehends no peace apart from the removal of the evil. But they who find their peace in God, rejoice in him and are contented. They calmly endure tribulation; standing firm, they await the inner strength wrought by faith. It is not theirs to inquire whether the evil will be long or short in duration; they ever leave it to God's regulation. They are not anxious to know when, where or by whom termination of the evil is to come. God affords them grace and removes their evils, bestowing blessings beyond their expectation.

This is the peace of the cross, the peace of God, the peace of conscience, Christian peace, which gives us eternal calm and makes us satisfied with all men and unwilling to disturb any. Reason cannot understand how there can be pleasure in crosses and peace in disquietude. Such peace is the work of God, and none can understand it until he has experienced it. "Heart" and "mind" here must not be supposed to mean human will and understanding; but faith and love are meant in all their operations, in all their inclinations toward God and men. The reference is simply to a disposition to trust and love God, a willingness of heart and mind to serve God and man to the utmost. Briefly, this text is a lesson in Christian living, in the attitude of the Christian toward God and man. It teaches us to let God be everything to us, and to treat all men alike, to conduct ourselves toward men as does God toward us, receiving from him and giving to them. It may be summed up in the words "faith" and "love."

December 18th - Romans 13:12

The night is far spent, the day is at hand.

This is equivalent to saying, "salvation is near us." By the word "day" Paul means the gospel; the gospel is like day in that it enlightens the heart or soul. Christ and his grace, promised to Abraham, are now revealed; they are preached in all the world, enlightening mankind, awaking us from sleep and making manifest the true, eternal blessings, that we may enjoy ourselves with the gospel of Christ and walk honorably in the day. By the word "night" we are to understand all doctrines apart from the gospel. For there is no other saving doctrine; all else is night and darkness.

Paul designates the most beautiful and vivifying time of the day—the delightful, joyous dawn, the hour of sunrise. In response to the morning dawn, birds sing, beasts arouse themselves and all humanity arises. At daybreak, when the sky is red in the east, the world is apparently new and all things reanimated. In many places in the Scriptures, the comforting, vivifying preaching of the gospel is compared to the morning dawn, to the rising of the sun. The gospel day is produced by the glorious Sun, Jesus Christ. Malachi calls him the Sun of Righteousness with healing in his wings. The natural sun makes the natural day, but the Lord himself is the author of the spiritual day. Christ is the Sun, the source of the gospel day. From him the gospel brightness shines throughout the world. As the natural heavens bring the sun and the day, so the apostles in their preaching bring us the real Sun, Christ.

The Scriptures sublimely exalt the gospel day, for it is the source of life, joy, pleasure and energy, and brings all good. Hence the name "gospel," joyful news. Who can enumerate the things revealed to us by this, the gospel day? It teaches us everything—the nature of God, of ourselves, and what has been and is to be in regard to heaven, hell and earth, to angels and devils. It enables us to know how to conduct ourselves in relation to these, whence we are and whither we go. In permitting ourselves to be blinded by human doctrines, we return to the night. Whatsoever is not the gospel day surely cannot be light. The gospel declares him the Light and Sun of the world.

December 19th - Matthew 11:5

The poor have the gospel preached to them.

Among the works of Christ none is greater than the preaching of the gospel to the poor. This means that to the poor the divine promise of grace and consolation in and through Christ is preached, offered and presented, so that to him who believes all his sins forgiven the law is fulfilled, conscience is appeased and at last life eternal is bestowed upon him. What more joyful tidings could a poor, sorrowful heart and troubled conscience hear than this? How could the heart become more bold and courageous than by such consoling, blissful words of promise. Sin, death, hell, the world, the devil and every evil are scorned when a poor heart receives and believes this consolation of the divine promise. To give sight to the blind and to raise up the dead are but insignificant deeds, compared with the preaching of the gospel to the poor.

Surely these poor are not the beggars and the bodily poor, but the spiritually poor, namely, those who do not covet and love earthly goods; those poor broken-hearted ones who in the agony of their conscience seek and desire help and consolation so ardently as to covet neither riches nor honor. Nothing but a merciful God will help them. These are the ones for whom such a message is intended, and they are delighted in their hearts with it.

Though the gospel is heard by all the world, yet it is not accepted but by the poor only. It is to be preached and proclaimed to all the world as a message only for the poor, as the rich cannot receive it. Whosoever would receive it must first become poor, just as Christ says, he came not to call the righteous, but sinners only, although he called all the world. In like manner all should become poor who hear the gospel, that they might be worthy of the gospel. Hence you see who are the greatest enemies of the gospel, namely, the work-righteous saints, who are self-conceited. The gospel has not the least in common with them. They want to become rich in works, but the gospel wills that they are to become poor. So they clash with the gospel.

December 20th - Romans 13:12

Let us therefore cast off the works of darkness, and let us put on the armour of light.

We are not profited by the shining of the sun, and the day it produces, if our eyes fail to perceive its light. Similarly, though the gospel is revealed and Christ is proclaimed to the world, none are enlightened but those who receive it, who have risen from sleep through the agency of the light of faith. They who sleep are not affected by the sun and the day; they receive no light and receive as little as if there were neither sun nor day. It is to our day that Paul refers when he says: "Knowing the season, that already it is time for you to wake out of sleep." In the light of our spiritual knowledge we are to rise from sleep and lay aside the works of darkness. Paul is not addressing unbelievers. He tells the Romans they know the time is at hand, that the night is past and the dawn appears.

But why this passage to believers? Because no one ever gets to the point of knowledge where it is not necessary to admonish him, continually to urge him to new reflections upon what he already knows; for there is danger of his untiring enemies—the devil, the world and the flesh—wearying him and causing him to become negligent, and ultimately lulling him to sleep. There should, therefore, be continuous exhorting to vigilance and activity. Hence the

Holy Spirit is called the Comforter or Helper, who incites and urges to good.

Not the works of darkness Paul calls "armor," but the works of light. Why "armor" rather than "works?" Doubtless to teach that only at the cost of conflicts, pain, labor and danger will the truly watchful and godly life be maintained. But it is no easy thing to stand always in battle array during the whole life. Good trumpets and bugles are necessary, preaching and exhortation of a sort to enable us valiantly to maintain our position in battle. Good works are armor. Let not the works of darkness get such control of you as to render your members weapons of unrighteousness. The word "light" here carries the thought of faith. The "armor of light" is simply the works of faith. "Darkness" is unbelief; it reigns in the absence of the gospel and of Christ through the instrumentality of the doctrines of men, instigated by the devil.

December 21st - Philippians 4:4

Rejoice in the Lord always: and again I say, Rejoice.

Joy is the natural fruit of faith. Until the heart believes in God, it is impossible for it to rejoice in him. When faith is lacking man is filled with fear and gloom and is disposed to flee at the very mention, the mere thought of God. The unbelieving heart is filled with enmity and hatred against God. Conscious of its own guilt, it has no confidence in his gracious mercy; it knows God as an enemy to sin who will terribly punish the same. One may as well try to persuade water to burn as to talk to such a heart of joy in God. All words will be without effect, for the sinner feels upon his conscience the pressure of God's hand. The psalmist says, "Rejoice, you righteous; and shout for joy, all you that are upright in heart." It must be the just and the righteous, then, who are to rejoice in the Lord. This text, therefore, is not written for the sinner, but for the saint. We must first tell the sinners how they can be liberated from their sins and perceive a merciful God. When they have been released from the power of an evil conscience, joy will naturally result.

But how shall we be liberated from an accusing conscience and receive the assurance of God's mercy? He who would have a quiet conscience and would be sensitive of God's mercy must place no hope whatever in works, but must comprehend God in Christ, comprehend the gospel and believe its promises. But what does the gospel promise other than that Christ is given for us, bears our sins and is our Bishop, Mediator and Advocate before God, and that only through him and his works is God reconciled, our sins forgiven and our consciences set free and made glad? When this sort of faith in the gospel really exists, the heart confidently feels his favor and grace. It is secure and in good spirits because God has conferred upon it, through Christ, superabundant goodness and grace. It will enjoy sincere pleasure in God as its beloved and gracious Father. Such is the rejoicing of which Paul here speaks—a rejoicing where is no sin, no fear of death and hell, but rather a glad and all-powerful confidence in God and his kindness.

December 22nd - Matthew 11:10

Behold, I send my messenger before your face, which shall prepare your way before you.

We must accustom ourselves to the Scriptures, in which angel means a messenger; not a bearer of messages or one who carries letters, but one who is sent to solicit orally for the message. Hence in the Scripture this name is common to all messengers of God in heaven and on earth, be they holy angels in heaven, or the prophets and apostles on earth. Thus they who proclaim God's Word are called his angels or messengers and solicitors. But the heavenly spirits are called angels chiefly because they are the highest and most exalted messengers of God. Thus John the Baptist is also an angel or word-messenger, and not only that, but one who also prepares the way before the face of the Master in such manner that the Master himself immediately follows him, which no prophet ever did. For this reason John "is more than a prophet," namely an angel or messenger, and a forerunner, so that in his day the Lord of all the prophets himself comes with his messenger.

The preparing here means to make ready the way, to put out of the way all that interferes with the course of the Lord, just as the servant clears the way before the face of his master by removing wood, stones, people and all that is in the way. But what was it that blocked the way of Christ and that John was to remove? Sin, without doubt, especially the good works of the haughty saints; that is, he should make known to everybody that the works and deeds of all men are sin and iniquity and that all need the grace of Christ. He who knows and acknowledges this thoroughly is himself humble and has well prepared the way for Christ.

Thus John is not a prophet, but a messenger. And not a messenger who stays at home, but one that goes before the face of his master and brings the master along with him, so that there is but one time for the messenger and for the master. Thus Christ pleads with the Jews to take John as a messenger, and not as a prophet. To this day it is the delusion of the Jews that they look for another time. They, therefore, remain shaken reeds and soft raiment seekers.

December 23rd - John 1:21

They asked him, What then? are you Elias? And he said, I am not. are you that prophet? And he answered, No.

The question arises, Did John really confess the truth when he denied that he was Elijah or a prophet, when Christ himself called him Elijah and more than a prophet. He himself knew that he had come in the spirit and power of Elijah, and the Scriptures called him such. The truth of the matter is that he simply confessed the truth in a straightforward manner, namely, that he was not that Elijah about whom they asked, nor a prophet. The prophets commonly led and taught the people, who sought advice and help from them. Such a one John was not and would not be, for the Lord was present, whom they were to adhere to and follow. He did not desire to draw the people to himself, but to lead them to Christ, which was needful before Christ himself came. A prophet foretells the coming of Christ. John, however, shows him present, which is not a prophet's task. John directs the people to Christ, and this is a higher and greater office than that of a prophet, yet it is not on account of his merit, but on account of the presence of his Master. In praising John for being more than a prophet, not his worthiness but that of his Master, who is present, is extolled. For it is customary for a servant to receive greater honor and reverence in the absence of his master than in his presence.

The rank of a prophet is higher than that of John, although his office is greater and more immediate. A prophet rules and leads the people, and they adhere to him; but John does no more than direct them away from himself to Christ, the present Master. Therefore, in the simplest and most straightforward manner, he denied being a prophet, although abounding in all the qualities of a prophet. This he did for the sake of the people, in order that they might not accept his testimony as the foretelling of a prophet and expect Christ in other future times, but that they might recognize him as a forerunner and guide, and follow his guidance to the Lord, who was present. The gospel through which Christ has come into the world is the last message before the day of judgment.

December 24th - John 1:29

Behold the Lamb of God, which takes away the sin of the world.

By this John means to say: I have, by my teaching, made you all sinners, having condemned your works and told you to despair of yourselves. But in order that you may not also despair of God, I will show you how to get rid of your sins and obtain salvation. Not that you can strip off your sins or make yourselves pious through your works; another man is needed for this; nor can I do it, I can point him out, however. It is Jesus Christ, the Lamb of God. He, he, and no one else in heaven or on earth, takes our sins upon himself. You yourselves could not pay for the very smallest of your sins. He alone must take upon himself not alone your sins, but the sins of the world, and not some sins, but all the sins of the world, be they great or small, many or few.

Now if you are able to believe that this voice of John speaks the truth, and if you are able to follow his finger and recognize the Lamb of God carrying your sins, then you have gained the victory, then you are a Christian, a master of sin, death, hell and all things. Then your conscience will rejoice and become heartily fond of this gentle Lamb of God. Then you will love, praise and give thanks to our heavenly Father for his infinite wealth of mercy, preached by John and given in Christ. Finally you will become cheerful and willing to do his divine will, as best you can, with all your strength. What lovelier and more comforting message can be heard than that our sins are not ours anymore, that they no more lie on us, but on the Lamb of God. Lying on him, sin must be vanquished and made to nothing, and likewise death and hell, being the reward of sin, must be vanquished also. Behold what God our Father has given us in Christ.

Take heed lest you presume to get rid of the smallest of your sins through your own merit before God, and lest you rob Christ, the Lamb of God, of his credit. John indeed demands that each one should know himself, repent and grow better, yet not in himself, but in Jesus Christ alone.

December 25th—Christmas Day - Luke 2:11

Unto you is born this day in the city of David a Saviour, which is Christ the Lord.

Faith comes first, and it is proper that we recognize it as the most important in every word of God. The right and gracious faith which God demands is, that you firmly believe that Christ is born for you, and that his birth took place for your welfare. The gospel teaches that Christ was born, and that he did and suffered everything in our behalf. It is not simply said, Christ is born, but to *you* he is born. The right ground of salvation which unites Christ and the believing heart is that they have all things in common. But what have they?

Christ has a pure, innocent and holy birth. Man has an unclean, sinful and condemned birth. David says: "Behold, I was shapen in iniquity; and in sin did my mother conceive me." Nothing can help this unholy birth except the pure birth of Christ. But Christ's birth cannot be distributed in a material sense, neither would that avail anything; it is imparted spiritually through the Word; it is given to all who firmly believe, so that no harm will come to them because of their impure birth. In this way we are cleansed from the miserable birth we have from Adam. For this purpose Christ willed to be born, that through him we might be born again. Christ takes our birth from us and absorbs it in his birth, and grants us his, that in it we might become pure and holy, so that every Christian may rejoice and glory in Christ's birth. Whoever does not believe this, or doubts, is no Christian.

O, this is the great joy of which the angel speaks. This is the comfort and exceeding goodness of God that, if a man believes this, he can boast of the treasure that Mary is his rightful mother, Christ his brother, and God his father. But this cannot occur except through the faith that teaches us rightly to understand the gospel and properly to lay hold of it. This is the only way that Christ can be rightly known so that the conscience is satisfied and made to rejoice. Out of this grow love and praise to God who in Christ has bestowed upon us such unspeakable gifts. This gives courage to suffer everything that is well pleasing to God.

December 26th - Luke 2:7

And she brought forth her firstborn son, and wrapped him in swaddling clothes, and laid him in a manger; because there was no room for them in the inn.

He was born of the virgin Mary. There is no deception here, for the Word clearly states that it was an actual birth. Mary's experience was not different from that of other women, so that the birth of Christ was a real natural birth, Mary being his natural mother and he being her natural son. But she brought forth without sin, without shame, without pain and without injury, just as she had conceived without sin. The curse of Eve did not come upon her, where God said: "In sorrow shall you bring forth children."

Grace does not interfere with nature and her work, but rather improves and promotes it. I mention this that we may be grounded in the faith and know that Jesus was a natural man in every respect just as we are, the only difference being in his relation to sin and grace, he being without a sinful nature. It is a great comfort to us that Jesus took upon himself our nature and flesh. Therefore we are not to take away from him or his mother anything that is not in conflict with grace, for the text clearly says that she brought him forth, and the angels said, Unto you he is born.

How could God have shown his goodness in a more sublime manner than by humbling himself to partake of flesh and blood, so that henceforth even that can be regarded godly, honest and pure, which in all men is ungodly, shameful and impure? These are real miracles of God, for in no way could he have given us stronger, more forcible and purer pictures of chastity than in this birth. When we look upon this birth, and reflect how the sublime Majesty moves with great earnestness and inexpressible love and goodness upon the flesh and blood of this virgin, we see how all evil lust and every evil thought is banished. No woman can inspire such pure thoughts in a man as this virgin; nor can any man inspire such pure thought in a woman as this child. If in reflecting on this birth we recognize the work of God that is embodied in it, only chastity and purity spring from it.

December 27th - Luke 2:8

There were in the same country shepherds abiding in the field, keeping watch over their flock by night.

The shepherds were in the field, under the canopy of heaven, and not in houses, showing that they do not cling to temporal things. They are in the fields by night, unknown to the world which sleeps in the night, and by day delights to walk that it may be noticed. They represent all the lowly who live on earth, often despised and unnoticed but dwell only under the protection of heaven; they eagerly desire the gospel.

That they were "shepherds," means that no one is to hear the gospel alone for himself, but everyone is to tell it to others who are not acquainted with it. For he who believes for himself has enough and should endeavor to bring others to such faith and knowledge, so that one may be a shepherd of the other to lead him into the pasture of the gospel in this world, during the night time of this earthly life. At first the shepherds were sore afraid because of the angel; for human nature is shocked when it first hears the gospel that all our own works are nothing and are condemned before God, for it does not easily give up its prejudices and presumptions.

Now let everyone examine himself in the light of the gospel to see how far he is from Christ, what is the character of his faith and love. Many are kindled with dreamy devotion, when they hear of the poverty of Christ, are almost angry with the citizens of Bethlehem, denounce their blindness and ingratitude, and think, if they had been there, they would have shown the Lord and his mother a more becoming service, and would not have permitted them to be treated so miserably. But they do not look by their side to see how many of their fellow men need their aid, whom they let go on in their misery unaided. It is altogether wrong for you to think that you have done much for Christ, when you have done nothing for those needy ones. Had you been in Bethlehem you would have paid as little attention to Christ as they did; but since it is now made known who

Christ is, you profess to serve him, but you would hardly have done it before.

December 28th - Luke 2:15

As the angels were gone away from them into heaven, the shepherds said one to another, Let us now go even unto Bethlehem, and see this thing which is come to pass, which the Lord has made known unto us.

Had not these shepherds believed the angel they would never have gone to Bethlehem, they would have done none of those things related of them in this gospel. One might say, I would gladly believe if an angel from heaven were to preach to me. But whoever does not receive the Word for its own sake will never receive it for the sake of the preacher, even if all the angels preached it to him. He who receives it because of the preacher does not believe in the Word, neither in God through the Word, but he believes the preacher and in the preacher. Hence the faith of such persons does not last long. But whoever believes the Word, does not care who the person is that speaks the Word, and neither will he honor the Word for the sake of the person; but on the contrary, he honors the person because of the Word, and always subordinates the person to the Word. If the preacher perishes, or even falls from the faith and preaches differently, he will forsake the person of the preacher rather than the Word of God.

All who believed Christ because of his person and his miracles fell from their faith when he was crucified. So it is in our day and so it has always been. The Word itself, without any regard to persons, must be enough for the heart; it must lay hold of man as if taken captive, so that he feels how true and right it is, even if the world, all the angels, all the princes of hell said differently, even if God himself spake otherwise; as he at times tempts his own elect and appears as if different from what he had before declared. So it was with Abraham when commanded to offer his son Isaac; with Jacob, while wrestling with the angel; with David, when persecuted by his son Absalom. This faith triumphs in life and death, and nothing is able to overthrow it; because it rests upon nothing but the Word without any regard whatever to persons. Such faith these shepherds possess; they cleave to the Word so strongly that they forget the angels who declared it to them. They do not say, Let us go and see what the angels made known to us, but what the Lord has made known to us.

December 29th - 2 Thessalonians 1:4

We ourselves glory in you in the churches of God for your patience and faith in all your persecutions and tribulations that you endure.

One of the chief reasons why God permits Christians to suffer on earth is to make plain the distinction between their reward and that of the ungodly. In the sufferings of believing Christians, and in the wickedness, tyranny, rage and persecution directed by the unrighteous against the godly, is a certain indication of a future life unlike this and a final judgment of God in which all men, godly and wicked, shall be forever recompensed. When Paul speaks of the tribulations and sufferings of Christians, he means to say that these afflictions are the indication of God's righteous judgment, and a sign that you are worthy of the kingdom of God for which you suffer. In other words: "O beloved

Christians, regard your sufferings as dear and precious. Think not God is angry with you, or has forgotten you, because he allows you to endure these things. They are your great help and comfort, for they show that God will be a righteous judge, will richly bless you and avenge you upon your persecutors. In this you have unfailing assurance. You may rejoice and console yourselves, believing without the shadow of a doubt that you belong to the kingdom of God, and have been made worthy of it, because you suffer for its sake."

But it is impossible that it should continue to be, as now, well with the world and evil with you. God's righteousness will not admit of it. Just because he is a righteous judge, things must be eventually different: the godly must have eternal good, and the wicked, on the other hand, must be punished forever. Otherwise God's judgment would not be righteous; in other words, he would not be God. This is an impossible proposition, since God's righteousness and truth are immutable, in his capacity as judge he must perforce in due time come from heaven, when he shall have assembled his Christians, and avenge them of their enemies, recompense the latter according to their merits, and confer eternal rest and peace upon his followers for the temporal sufferings they have endured here. Necessarily, then, he has planned a future state for Christians and for non-Christians, in either instance unlike what they know on earth.

December 30th - John 1:1

In the beginning was the Word, and the Word was with God, and the Word was God.

That this gospel may be more easily understood, we must go back to the passages of the Old Testament upon which it is founded, namely, the beginning of the first chapter of Genesis. "In the beginning God created the heavens and the earth; and God said, Let there be light; and God said, Let there be a firmament; and God said, Let there be sun, moon and stars." From these words of Moses it is clearly proved that God has a Word, through which or by means of which he spoke, before anything was created; and this Word cannot be anything that was created, since all things were created through this divine utterance. The Word must therefore have preceded the light, since light came by the Word; consequently it was also before all creatures, which also came by the Word, as Moses writes.

If the Word preceded all creatures, and all creatures came by the Word and were created by it, the Word must be a different being than a creature, and was not made or created like a creature. When all things began it was already there, and cannot be confined to time nor to creation; rather time and creation are made and have their beginning through it. Thus whatever is not temporal must be eternal; that which has no beginning cannot be temporal; that which is not a creature must be God. Besides God and his creatures there is nothing. Hence the Word of God, which was in the beginning and through which all things were made and spoken, must be God eternal and not a creature.

Again, the Word and he that speaks it are not one person; for it is not possible that the speaker is himself the Word. What sort of speaker would he be who is himself the Word? But Scripture here speaks in strong, lucid words:

"God said." Thus God and his Word must be two distinct things. Thus the words of Moses show conclusively that there are two persons in the Godhead from eternity, before all creatures, that the one has his existence from the other, and the first has his existence from nothing but himself. Yet the Scriptures firmly maintain that there is only one God. Thus there must be two persons in the Godhead and yet be one God.

December 31st - Romans 14:8

Whether we live therefore, or die, we are the Lord's.

In the past much has been written and ingeniously devised on the topic of preparing for death and the final judgment. But it has only served to further confuse timid consciences. For these comforters were not able to show anything of the comfort to be found in the riches of grace and bliss in Christ. They directed the people to oppose with their own works and good life, death and God's judgment. In place of this delusion is now evident the precious truth; he who knows the gospel doctrines, goes on and performs his own work and duty in his respective calling. He takes comfort in the fact that through baptism he is grafted into Christ; he receives absolution and partakes of the Holy Supper for the strengthening of his faith, commending his soul and body to Christ. Why should such a one fear death? Though it came at any time, in form of pestilence or accident, it will always find the Christian ready and well prepared, be he awake or asleep; for he is in Christ Jesus.

For all these things the Christian may well thank and bless God, realizing that he has no further need, nor can he gain anything better than he already has in the remission of sins, the gift of the Holy Spirit and the faithful prosecution of his calling; however, he should remain and daily grow in faith and supplication. But we cannot hope to attain to another and better doctrine, faith, Spirit, prayer, sacrament and reward than had all the saints, John the Baptist, Peter, Paul, or in fact than has now every Christian that is baptized. Therefore I need not idly spend time in trying to prepare people for death and inspire them with courage by such commonplaces as recalling and relating the innumerable daily accidents, ills and dangers of this life. This method will not answer; death will not thereby be frightened away, nor will the fear of death be removed. The gospel teaching is: Believe in Christ, pray and live in accordance with God's Word, and then, when death overtakes or attacks you, you will know that you are Christ the Lord's. We Christians live upon this earth to the very end that we may have assured comfort, salvation and victory over death and hell.

Printed in Great Britain
by Amazon